Quiet Enjoyment

Protection from rogue landlords

Andrew Arden QC founded Arden Chambers in 1993 to provide a centre for specialist practice, primarily in the area of housing law, together with local government and property. The set has been described in Chambers and Partners as 'a trailblazer ... extremely well-regarded and strong in its niche areas of local government, property and housing' and in Legal 500 as 'a pre-eminent set for housing law'.

Andrew Arden QC has appeared in many of the leading cases in housing law over the past 30 years. He is author or editor of the principal practitioner texts on housing law, including the *Encyclopaedia of Housing Law, Housing Law Reports, Journal of Housing Law, Arden & Partington's Housing Law, Local Government Constitutional and Administrative Law* (all Sweet & Maxwell), *Manual of Housing Law* and *Homelessness and Allocations* (LAG).

Robert Brown is a barrister and member of Arden Chambers. He specialises in housing and public law. Robert is an editor of the *Housing Law Reports* and a co-author of *Judicial Review Proceedings* (3rd edn, 2013, LAG) and *Arden & Partington's Housing Law* (Sweet & Maxwell).

Sam Madge-Wyld is a barrister and member of Arden Chambers. He specialises in housing and local government law. Sam is co-author of *Housing Law Casebook* (7th edn, 2017) and *Defending Possession Proceedings* (8th edn, 2016) (both LAG) and a contributor to the *Local Government Encyclopaedia* (Sweet and Maxwell). Sam has written articles that have appeared in the *Journal of Housing Law, New Law Journal, Local Government Lawyer* and *Judicial Review*.

Available as an ebook at www.lag.org.uk/ebooks

Quiet Enjoyment

Protection from rogue landlords

EIGHTH EDITION

Andrew Arden QC, Robert Brown and
Sam Madge-Wyld

 Legal Action Group
2017

This edition published in Great Britain 2017
by LAG Education and Service Trust Limited
National Pro Bono Centre, 48 Chancery Lane, London WC2A 1JF
www.lag.org.uk

First published 1980
Second edition 1985
Third edition by Sylvester Carrott and Caroline Hunter 1990
Fourth edition by Caroline Hunter and Siobhan McGrath 1994
Fifth edition by David Carter and Andrew Dymond 1998
Sixth edition by Andrew Arden QC, David Carter and Andrew Dymond 2002
Seventh edition by Andrew Arden QC, Rebecca Chan and Sam Madge-Wyld 2012

British Library Cataloguing in Publication Data
a CIP catalogue record for this book is available from the British Library.

Crown copyright material is produced with the permission of the Controller of
HMSO and the Queen's Printer for Scotland.

This book has been produced using Forest Stewardship Council
(FSC) certified paper. The wood used to produce FSC certified
products with a 'Mixed Sources' label comes from FSC certified
well-managed forests, controlled sources and/or recycled
material.

Print ISBN   978 1 908407 96 2
ebook ISBN   978 1 908407 97 9

Typeset by Regent Typesetting, London
Printed in Great Britain by Hobbs the Printers, Totton, Hampshire

Preface

Quiet Enjoyment: protection from rogue landlords, 8th edn;
Manual of Housing Law, 10th edn and *Homelessness and
Allocations*, 10th edn

Background

For the first time, these three books are being published contemporaneously and by the same publisher.

Historically, the first of these books started life as *Housing: security and rent control*, in 1978, originally paired with *Housing: repairs and improvements*, by Tom Hadden (1979). Both were published by Sweet & Maxwell, as have been all subsequent editions of the *Manual of Housing Law* (as it became from the second edition in 1983, expanded to include the material in *Repairs and Improvements*). The first edition of *Quiet Enjoyment, remedies for harassment and illegal eviction*, co-authored with Martin Partington, was published by LAG, also in 1978, a booklet rather than a full-length book. The first edition of *Homelessness and Allocations*, under the title *The Homeless Persons Act*, followed from LAG in 1982. Over the years, I have been joined by a number of co-authors; there was a small number of editions of the LAG books which I did not write. Here I find myself, still writing them just shy of 40 years after they were first published, the books still in use.

Until the mid-1970s, the term 'housing law' was in scant use: it was a term applied to a sub-division of planning law and on occasion merited a mention in landlord and tenant or local government. The subject covered the powers and duties of local authorities, mainly in relation to slum clearance (by area or individual unit), the provision of public housing and related matters such as improvement grants. Reflecting the growth of legal aid, the introduction of law centres and the underlying social demand for rights, housing law began to develop in the early 1970s – largely through the pages of the *LAG Bulletin* (as *Legal Action* was then called) – bringing together all the law as it affected the use of a property as a home, whether derived from private rights or from the public powers and duties conferred or imposed on local authorities, whether formally identified as housing or because it impacted on housing in practice.

At that time, LAG did not publish many full-length books; hence the observation that *Quiet Enjoyment* was initially no more than a booklet. This was one reason why the *Manual* was published by Sweet & Maxwell, one of the two leading legal publishers. Sweet & Maxwell had, however, given the subject a further boost when, in the same year as the first edition of what became the *Manual* was published, it decided to expand the coverage of the *Encyclopaedia of Housing Law and Practice* to reflect the new vision of housing law.

The topics taken into the subject through the efforts of these two publishers included the Rent Acts (governing private sector security and harassment/illegal eviction), leasehold enfranchisement and extension, matrimonial law so far as it affected the family home on domestic breakdown, environmental health (statutory nuisance and other provisions affecting housing), social security, mobile homes, judicial review (enjoying its own period of unprecedented growth, itself in part a reflection of the same rise in rights awareness), as well as some planning law, compulsory purchase, conveyancing, landlord and tenant, contract and tort. Subsequent significant developments include the mass of law directly or indirectly reflecting policies on anti-social behaviour, much of it focused on housing, enhanced long leaseholder rights, human rights and the divergence of housing law as between England and Wales.

Sweet & Maxwell continues to publish the *Encyclopaedia*, along with the *Housing Law Reports*, the *Journal of Housing Law* and *Arden & Partington's Housing Law*, but for a change of direction in relation to titles such as the *Manual*, it would have remained in its list – regardless of legalities, it would not have been right to seek to move it after the publisher had done so much for the subject, as it continues to do through these other titles; and, while I am delighted both to bring the *Manual* 'home' to LAG and to be able to publish it as part of a discrete set, it would be wrong not to mark the departure by expressing my own gratitude for its support for the title over so many years.

Books

The three books have had different aims. Since the 1970s, the *Manual of Housing Law* has sought to provide a guide to housing law as described above, for a fairly wide array of interested individuals: the practitioner starting out in housing law; the non-specialist practitioner who needs occasional but ready access to the subject; lay advisers; students both of housing and of law; housing officers in local authorities and other social housing providers; environmental health officers working in housing; and, local councillors with a remit or interest in the subject.

Without claiming to describe all the detail of the subject, the intention has remained the same: to enable the reader to understand housing law as a whole, to know where to find it and to know how to apply it, whether to the problems of individuals or to the policies and practices of landlords and local authorities. This has been the essential approach to housing law as a subject: it exists not for its theory but to be applied.

While the focus of *Quiet Enjoyment* and *Homelessness and Allocations* has been on particular – and particularly important – aspects of the subject, that approach is also at their core, although their target audiences have been somewhat different, aimed primarily at actual and emerging specialist practitioners, specialist lay advisers and specialist officers in local authorities rather than students and others: the emphasis has nonetheless throughout been on practical application of the law. Hence, each of them contains specimen documentation to help the adviser bring cases into court as quickly as they usually need (although this did not arrive in *Homelessness and Allocations* until the seventh edition, the second one following the introduction of the right of appeal on a point of law to the county court by Housing Act 1996, before which it was uncommon for judicial review applications to be prepared by anyone other than relatively experienced public law counsel).

Status

It is this central approach of practical application which generated the proposition that the fundamental starting-point in relation to any housing law problem or discussion requires identification of the *status* of the occupier, which is to say the class of occupational right both at common law and under statute which determines the body of rights, duties and remedies to which the occupation is subject, without which the occupier's entitlements are unknown and, of as much importance, without which the implications are uncertain as to how a problem or other matter should be addressed so as to achieve the greatest gain in living conditions for the occupier while averting the worst consequences, in particular eviction and rent increases.

The number of statuses has long been a problem. Even during the 1970s, there were Rent Act protected and statutory tenancies subject to full and partial exceptions, furnished tenants, tenants with resident landlords, restricted contracts, tenants and licensees exempt from any protection, Rent (Agriculture) Act 1976 tenancies and licences for tied workers in agriculture and forestry, as well as residual controlled tenancies dating from before repeal of the previous security and rent regime in 1957. Moreover, there were housing association tenancies within rent regulation but outside security and other lettings wholly outside both, primarily local authority tenancies but also those from other bodies, such as New Town Development Corporations and the Crown.

The Housing Act 1980 introduced the secure tenancy for most public sector tenants – and licensees – as well as for those in the remainder of the social rented sector, ie housing associations and trusts, together with its own schedule of exceptions, full and qualified; at the same time, it sought to revivify the private rented sector by means, first, of new protected shorthold tenancies and, secondly, a class of new-build letting called assured tenancy, modelled on the security available to business tenants under the Landlord and Tenant Act 1954 Part 2, the latter of which attracted negligible interest. In addition, the 1980 Act brought tenants of the Crown into Rent Act security and rent control if the property was under the management of the Crown Estate Commissioners.

In 1988, the modern assured tenancy was introduced for the fully private sector as well as for housing association and trust tenants, together with assured shorthold tenancies and assured agricultural occupancies, again subject to their own exceptions; the regime also replaced the short-lived new-build 1980 Act predecessor of the same name. In 1996, introductory tenancies were added to the secure tenancy regime. Subsequent developments include demoted tenancies (from both secure and assured status) and family intervention tenancies. In 2011, the dawn of putative localism brought with it the flexible tenancy – in effect, a shorthold secure tenancy albeit for somewhat longer periods than usual in the private sector. The year 2016 brought the distinction between old (existing) secure tenancies and new secure tenancies (which are not secure at all), which is, as it were, still waiting at the platform for the government to set in motion.

I should add that, obviously, this reflects wholesale disregard in England for the Law Commission's *Renting Homes: The Final Report* (2006), the proposals by Martin Partington and his team, *inter alia* to reduce the number of available forms of rental occupation of residential property to two (standard contract and secure contract) and for model contract terms. These were, however, taken up by the Welsh Government, which accepted the recommendations (revisited in *Renting Homes: a better way for Wales*, May 2013) and enacted them in the Renting Homes (Wales) Act 2016, also yet to be brought into force.

As I wrote in the Introduction to the ninth edition of the *Manual*:

> ... [H]ousing law is a subject in a state of constant evolution (if not revolution) and, if this history is anything to go by, is probably destined so to remain. ... That makes it difficult to keep up with. Furthermore, law is rarely retrospective. Accordingly, one set of rules does not replace another, so much as two (or ten) sets co-exist for a period. And, as this is about where people live, that can commonly mean decades rather than years.

Concept, complexity and consistency

Although housing law's approach is practical rather than theoretical, that does not mean that there is no underlying concept: its *purpose* was to seek a housing focus for housing cases, however they were categorised in law, to ensure that decisions reflect awareness that what is in issue is someone's home, not merely property, local authority discretion or an abstract interpretation of statute. This is not to say that the subject is one that 'belongs' exclusively to occupiers, although there was undoubtedly a significant element in its origins which was intended to redress an historical imbalance; the idea was to ensure that all those involved in housing share that purpose as a common, guiding principle, not only to enhance the rights of occupiers but to help all the subject's 'clients' or 'constituents' better to understand how housing cases are likely to be treated in the courts and housing law itself is likely to develop.

The exponential growth in the number of statuses, this most fundamental aspect of housing law and its key structural foundation, has, however, posed a continuing problem in terms both of this purpose and of these books; it has complicated the subject and made it more and more difficult to understand, to write about and to apply, especially as tenancies can and do last for a very long time indeed and tenants may remain in the same accommodation not merely for years but for decades, which means that even law which ceased to apply to new tenancies 20–30 years ago may still be applicable to some older tenants (or their successors) and may still need to be considered. Moreover, old laws may sometimes remain applicable to a new tenancy granted to an existing tenant, in the same or different premises, to prevent tenants being talked into exchanging one set of rights for another, less favourable set.

Status is, however, not the only source of complexity and obfuscation. Central governments of all parties have micro-managed housing law, using it both as an economic tool, which may be expected, and as a political football, responding to populist perceptions without regard to its purpose: this has been particularly acute in the areas of immigration and anti-social behaviour. Given that it is only rarely, and only more recently, that this involves the removal of existing rights, this piles more and more layers of law on top of one another, so that rights turn not merely on status, but increasingly on when something occurred, eg the array of rules governing discharge of duty to homeless applicants depending on when an application was made. There is also something of a ping-pong between criminal and civil law: at points in time, functions which may properly be thought to belong to the criminal law – again, in particular in relation to anti-social behaviour – have been passed to local authorities and other social housing providers, while measures to tackle unlawful immigration have been handed out not only to those landlords but to all; at other times, functions which have historically been issues of civil law – eg trespass and unlawful sub-letting – have been criminalised.

Nor is it only governments who have lost sight of any central concept of housing law: courts have increasingly been led by so-called 'merits', that most subjective of approaches, without regard to the need to preserve any kind of over-arching principle or consistency of approach. Sometimes, this has been motivated by the best of intentions – to jettison archaic rules which are unacceptable in a more modern, human rights-oriented climate. Sometimes, it has been solely motivated by consideration of cost to the public purse. Sometimes, it has been motivated by a largely uninformed assumption as to what will advance the interests of housing. Sometimes, a return to abstract interpretation has countered the positive gains that a housing focus has otherwise achieved – for example in relation to the powers of local authorities to enforce standards in the (ever-increasing and much troubled) private sector.

This is not the place to pursue an analysis of these developments. While it has always been true that the outcome of very few cases has ever been capable of certain prediction, it is now the position, more widely than at any time I have known in my career as legal practitioner and writer, that how an issue will be determined by the courts depends predominantly upon who determines it and how the merits are perceived. Even leaving aside the effects of constant legislative change, this undermines consistency and increases the complexity of housing law. Sad to say, housing is being reduced to a set of detailed rules, not dissimilar to the intricacies of social security legislation, a subject with which it is increasingly coming to have in common an absence of access to qualified advice.

Current editions

This, then, is the climate in which these new editions are published and in which they have had to be re-considered. In earlier editions, chapter 1 of the *Manual* tied classes of occupation to their security of tenure, which is their first and foremost concern: by the last edition, the growth of statuses meant that this approach had become too unwieldy and it had proved necessary to separate class of occupation from security and eviction, a problem that further developments would have exacerbated. Moreover, a substantial chunk of *Quiet Enjoyment* – a subject to which status is critical – would need to be given over to describing the numerous different ways in which people occupy rented accommodation, adding to its length, even though much of its readership is sufficiently familiar with most of them not to need more than occasional reference to the issue. Aspects of homelessness law itself also depend on status: in particular, whether someone is homeless (defined in terms of rights of occupation) and whether someone is intentionally homeless (often turning on whether there was a right to remain in accommodation). It is also central to the new assessment and initial help duties which will come in with the Homelessness Reduction Act 2017.

As the books are now all under one roof and published together, it has been possible to introduce an element of rationalisation: status in *Quiet Enjoyment* now relies exclusively on the *Manual*, affording more space for the considerable body of new law which has emerged over the last few years to reflect the resurgence in private renting and to control the abuses to which it has given rise: I no more foresaw that *Quiet Enjoyment*, newly suffixed *Protection from rogue landlords*, would come back into its own any the more than I ever expected to see the term 'rogue landlords' enshrined in statute. *Homelessness and Allocations* also relies on the *Manual* for status where appropriate, as well as for other questions, eg whether a valid section 21 notice has been served on an assured shorthold tenant.

The *Manual* provides an introduction to the new laws protecting tenants from abuse; *Quiet Enjoyment* considers them in close detail. Both have been restructured. The *Manual*, as mentioned, had already separated out classes of occupation from security of tenure and eviction; in addition, protection from rogue landlords has now been separated out from anti-social behaviour, which is more largely about the conduct of occupiers. The *Manual* includes a wholly new chapter on mobile homes and houseboats, a subject which had slipped out of coverage but that needs to be brought back in as more and more people resort to them as a permanent home for want of being able to afford either owner-occupation or even renting. Naturally, the book continues coverage of rents, other rights (such as leasehold enfranchisement and right to buy), domestic breakdown, regulation of social landlords and housing conditions, including contract and tort, housing standards, environmental health, overcrowding, multiple occupation and licensing.

Quiet Enjoyment for the first time separates out eviction and harassment, as the law on the latter grows to reflect increased awareness of the many different ways that some people set out to distress others and seeks to protect victims. Mobile homes and houseboats are also afforded treatment. There are wholly new chapters on tenancy deposits, licensing of landlords, banning orders and a range of additional duties in respect of rented property many of which impact on a landlord's rights to take advantage of reduced security but which, in turn, may in practice give rise to additional unacceptable and unlawful conduct towards tenants when they are enforced, eg duties in relation to gas, fire, electricity and smoke alarms. As before, there are separate chapters on bringing civil and criminal proceedings, and the traditional collection of case reports on awards of damages is retained and updated, albeit now to be found in an appendix.

The *Manual* also outlines homelessness and allocations law, which *Homelessness and Allocations* addresses fully. The structure of the latter has not changed: an introduction to policy, an outline of the law, detailed consideration of the key concepts – eligibility, homelessness, priority need, intentionality, local connection, protection of property – followed by chapters on enquiries and decisions (including review), discharge of homelessness duties, allocations, enforcement by way of appeal to the county court and judicial review, other provisions to which recourse may need to be had in order to secure housing by way of social and child care provisions, strategy, practice, aid and advice, and criminal offences.

The two key changes since the last edition are the separate development of homelessness in Wales under the Housing (Wales) Act 2014 Part 2, and the Homelessness Reduction Act 2017, through which England adopted some of the changes which Wales had already introduced. The new duties in England include the extension from 28 days to 56 of the period during which a person is threatened with homelessness (dating, where appropriate and as qualified, from service of a valid notice under Housing Act 1988 s21), the introduction of a new assessment duty and consideration of support to ensure that applicants have or retain suitable accommodation, including reasonable steps to be taken by authorities to help applicants secure that accommodation does not cease to be available for their occupation, as well as a new initial duty requiring authorities to take reasonable steps for 56 days to help applicants to secure accommodation, regardless of whether they are in priority need. These developments have added to the increasing complexity of the subject and result in significant changes to chapter 10, on discharge.

Otherwise, the book continues the approach taken in previous editions so far as concerns the development of the law: every detail of homelessness and allocations law is recorded, analysed and applied; nothing which has gone before, however revised by the courts, has been wholly abandoned even if relegated to footnote or analysis reduced to reflect current lack of importance; nothing is divorced from its history and evolution. Experience has shown that cases come back again and again – as true as it may well be of other areas of law, homelessness and allocations have a marked tendency to shift with the winds: nothing is ever finally overruled or permanently irrelevant.

In addition to the structural changes and coverage of new law, in both England and Wales, the opportunity has been taken to reconsider the text of each book. Too often, later editions take for granted what has been written previously, focusing instead on the need to bring books up to date: these books have been no less guilty of this than others. It is not merely that it can leave text feeling stale so much as it can cause a loss of focus or even coherence: the branches can so change the tree that it is not the same picture at all. I have therefore undertaken a line by line – and paragraph by paragraph – revision which I hope will recover some of the freshness which I strove to achieve 'back in the day'.

I extend my thanks to my co-authors, to LAG and, in particular, our publisher Esther Pilger, as well as to colleagues in Chambers and on other publications with which I am associated, and, as always, to my very long-standing writing partners – and friends – Professors Martin Partington CBE, QC (Hon) and Caroline Hunter. My wife and daughter have suffered the stresses and strains of my legal writing – including these books – for far too long for either thanks or apology to make up for what it has cost them. Finally, I should like to dedicate this set of books to the late Pat Reddin, since the early

1970s the go-to housing surveyor of choice in housing disrepair cases both for tenants and for social landlords, who died in April 2015: he is missed both as professional colleague and close friend over the whole of the time-span I have been discussing in this Preface; he remains uppermost in my thoughts and emotions.

The law is predominantly stated as at 30 April 2017, although it has been possible to add a small number of subsequent amendments during the publication process. Two key developments which were due prior to the General Election, which these books have therefore been unable to accommodate, are: the commencement of the Homelessness Reduction Act 2017 (for which no date had been set); and, the introduction of banning orders under the Housing and Planning Act 2016 ss14 and 15 (which had been expected to be implemented from 1 October 2017), although the provisions of each have been fully described so far as available.

Andrew Arden QC
Arden Chambers
London

21 May 2017

Contents

Table of cases

Table of statutes

Table of statutory instruments

Table of European legislation

Abbreviations

AHA 1986	Agricultural Holdings Act 1986
ASBA 2003	Anti-social Behaviour Act 2003
ASBI	Anti-social behaviour injunction
ASBO	Anti-social behaviour order
ATA 1995	Agricultural Tenancies Act 1995
BA 1976	Bail Act 1976
CBO	Criminal behaviour order
CCA 1984	County Courts Act 1984
CDA 1998	Crime and Disorder Act 1998
CJA 1967, 1982, 1991, 2003	Criminal Justice Act 1967, 1982, 1991, 2003
CJPA 2001	Criminal Justice and Police Act 2001
CLA 1977	Criminal Law Act 1977
CPA 1974	Control of Pollution Act 1974
CPI	Community protection order
CPO	Crime prevention injunction
CPR 1998	Civil Procedure Rules 1998
CPS	Crown Prosecution Service
C(RTP)A 1999	Contracts (Rights of Third Parties) Act 1999
CSA 1968	Caravan Sites Act 1968
DA 2015	Deregulation Act 2015
DCLG	Department for Communities and Local Government
DPP	Director of Public Prosecutions
DPS	Deposit Protection Service
ECHR	European Convention on Human Rights
EEA	European Economic Area
EPA 1990	Environmental Protection Act 1990
EPC	Energy Performance Certificate
EU	European Union
FLA 1996	Family Law Act 1996
HA 1985, 1988, 1996, 2004	Housing Act 1985, 1988, 1996, 2004
HMOs	houses in multiple occupation
HPA 2016	Housing and Planning Act 2016
HRA 1998	Human Rights Act 1998
H&RA 2008	Housing and Regeneration Act 2008
H(W)A 2014	Housing (Wales) Act 2014
IA 2014, 2016	Immigration Act 2014, 2016

IAA 1999	Immigration and Asylum Act 1999
IANA 2006	Immigration, Asylum and Nationality Act 2006
LAA	Legal Aid Agency
LASPO 2012	Legal Aid, Sentencing and Punishment of Offenders Act 2012
LGA 1972	Local Government Act 1972
LGHA 1989	Local Government Housing Act 1989
LPA 1925	Law of Property Act 1925
LRA 1925, 2002	Land Registration Act 1925, 2002
LTA 1954	Landlord and Tenant Act 1954
MCA 1980	Magistrates' Courts Act 1980
MCR 1981	Magistrates' Courts Rules 1981
MDS	My Deposits Scheme
MH(W)A 2013	Mobile Homes (Wales) Act 2013
NA 1996	Noise Act 1996
NIP	notice of intended proceedings
PACE	Police and Criminal Evidence Act 1984
PCA 2017	Policing and Crime Act 2017
PCC(S)A 2000	Powers of the Criminal Courts (Sentencing) Act 2000
PEA 1977	Protection from Eviction Act 1977
PHA 1997	Protection from Harassment Act 1997
POA 1985	Public Order Act 1985
POA	Prosecution of Offences Act 1985
RA 1977	Rent Act 1977
R(A)A 1976	Rent (Agriculture) Act 1976
RRO	rent repayment order
RSO	rent stopping order
SCA 1981	Senior Courts Act 1981
SOCPA 2005	Serious and Organised Crime and Police Act 2005
TDS	Tenancy Deposit Scheme

Unlawful eviction

continued

Introduction

1.1 This chapter considers the rights of an occupier who has been unlawfully evicted or the subject of an attempted unlawful eviction. There is no singular definition of unlawful eviction. The term is used to refer to the eviction of an occupier by his or her landlord, or someone acting on the landlord's behalf, from residential premises that the occupier has a continuing right to occupy. Eviction includes both being forced out of premises and entry to them being prevented.

1.2 In most cases, it will be unlawful for a landlord to evict – or to try to evict – such an occupier without a court order. Both tenants and licensees may be the subject of unlawful eviction, although their rights may differ. The distinction between tenant and licensee is usually obvious, but can be difficult: the same is true of other differences in 'status', ie the differences between different classes of statutory protection applicable to tenants and licensees. It is not practicable to define these differences here and a brief summary of them can be misleading: reference is therefore made to the *Manual of Housing Law*, paras 1.17–1.47, 1.114–1.130 and 1.159–1.307.[1]

1.3 Unlawful eviction (actual or attempted) may, depending on the status of the occupier and the person carrying out the eviction, give rise to a civil claim for damages and/or constitute a criminal offence.[2] This chapter therefore considers: the circumstances in which an occupier may bring a claim in the county court; the remedies the county court may award him or her; and, the criminal offence and penalties that arise from it.

1.4 While this may seem 'back-to-front' in the sense that criminal offences are in a popular sense more significant than civil orders, what the occupier will usually want is help to get back in to the premises and, if not, to get damages to pay for accommodation elsewhere – sometimes meaning costly, temporary accommodation, eg in a hotel – and for belongings lost or damaged. These remedies (and, in particular, relief by way of an interim order pending a full hearing) will be found most easily – and in some cases, only – through the civil courts, which is why civil proceedings are taken first in order in this chapter.

---

1 Arden & Dymond *Manual of Housing Law* (LAG, 10th edn, 2017).
2 Conduct falling short of unlawful eviction or attempted unlawful eviction may still give rise to a civil claim for damages and/or may constitute a criminal offence. This is considered in chapter 2.

Civil causes of action

1.5   To sue in the civil courts, it is necessary to show that a complaint falls within one of the categories that the law recognises as giving rise to a remedy, known as a 'cause of action'. The facts in unlawful eviction claims can vary widely: there is accordingly a number of causes of action which may arise. This chapter considers the main causes of action from the perspective of eviction but these will commonly overlap with causes arising where the conduct falls short of eviction, eg harassment and assault on their own.[3] It is always important to identify all the causes of action which may be available, both in order to maximise the occupier's prospects of obtaining all the remedies he or she will want and to avoid the risk that a particular cause of action fails for a minor or technical reason.

1.6   The causes of action set out below fall into two broad categories: tort (including breach of statutory duty) and breach of contract. Additionally, in certain circumstances a claimant may have a cause of action arising under the Human Rights Act (HRA) 1998. The causes of action are considered in the order in which they are likely to be of the most immediate value to the evicted occupier, ie those which will give rise to the right to an injunction to prevent an attempted unlawful eviction or reinstate the occupier as quickly as possible. Nine causes of action likely to be applicable in cases of unlawful eviction are considered in this chapter:

1) breach of tenancy or licence agreement;
2) Protection from Eviction Act (PEA) 1977 s3;
3) trespass to land;
4) trespass to goods;
5) deceit or fraudulent misrepresentation;
6) conspiracy or misfeasance in public office;
7) Housing Act (HA) 1988 s27;
8) HRA 1998; and
9) Caravan Sites Act (CSA) 1968 s3 / Mobile Homes (Wales) Act (MH(W)A) 2013 s42.

---

3 See chapter 2.

Breach of tenancy or licence agreement

1.7   Given the working definition referred to at para 1.1,[4] the starting-point is invariably to ask what rights the occupier does have and that, normally, means rights under a tenancy or licence.[5] As we are concerned with residential occupation, the tenancies and licences with which we are concerned will invariably confer a right of occupation: eviction is, it hardly bears saying, a breach of that right; likewise, an attempt to evict will usually comprise a breach.

Covenant for quiet enjoyment

1.8   Where the premises are subject to a tenancy, the right of occupation is embodied in the contractual term, known as the covenant for quiet enjoyment, which comprises an agreement or promise by the landlord to allow his or her tenant possession of the premises, without interference, for as long as the tenancy lasts.[6] It may be expressly stated in the tenancy agreement; if not, it is in any event implied into the agreement by law.

1.9   Many tenancy agreements express the right to quiet enjoyment to be conditional on the tenant performing his or her obligations under the agreement, for example, payment of the rent. Such a clause is of no effect: even if the tenant is in rent arrears the tenant is still entitled to quiet enjoyment.[7]

1.10   The covenant for quiet enjoyment is a covenant that the landlord will not interfere with the tenant's lawful possession of the premises. For there to be a breach of covenant, there must be a substantial interference with the tenant's ability to use the property in any ordinary, lawful way. The most obvious example of a breach of the covenant is where the landlord evicts the tenant by changing the locks. There does not, however, have to be dispossession or physical interference

---

4   Ie eviction of an occupier by his or her landlord, or someone acting on the landlord's behalf, from residential premises that the occupier has a continuing right to occupy.

5   There are exceptions, eg persons left in occupation after the death or departure of the tenant or licensee and, in some cases, there are even constraints on the eviction of trespassers (see chapter 3).

6   See also *Woodfall: Landlord and Tenant* (looseleaf edition, Sweet & Maxwell), para 11.267.

7   See also *Woodfall: Landlord and tenant* (looseleaf edition, Sweet & Maxwell), para 11.280.

with the premises themselves. Interference with the tenant's comfort or the comfort of his or her family is sufficient.[8]

1.11   Accordingly, acts of harassment which fall short of eviction may also breach the covenant: see further chapter 2 where other examples of what comprises breach of the covenant for quiet enjoyment are considered.

Implied term in licence

1.12   A licensee does not have the benefit of the covenant for quiet enjoyment. A licensee can, however, rely on a similar right implied into the contractual licence where the licensee cannot otherwise be expected to use the premises for the purposes for which the right of occupation was granted. Thus, a covenant to similar effect as the covenant of quiet enjoyment has been implied into a licence agreement which gave a student the right to occupy a room in a hall of residence.[9]

Subsisting right of occupation

1.13   A tenant or licensee can only sue for breach of the tenancy or license agreement if, at the date of the unlawful eviction, there was a subsisting tenancy or licence agreement. The sole exceptions to this are statutory tenancies under the Rent Act (RA) 1977 and Rent (Agriculture) Act (R(A)A) 1976, neither of which is a true tenancy (or contract) but a 'status of irremovability',[10] but each of which is subject – so far as consistent with the right of occupation – to the terms of the previous contractual tenancy,[11] which means that such statutory tenants can sue on them as if the tenancy was still in existence.

1.14   It therefore follows that a tenant or licensee whose right of occupation has come to an end cannot bring a claim based on breach of contract itself, although he or she will sometimes be able to rely on – in particular – PEA 1977 s3, considered below.[12]

---

8   *Southwark LBC v Tanner* (also known as *Southwark LBC v Mills*) [2001] 1 AC 1, (2001) 32 HLR 148, HL, approving *Kenny v Preen* [1963] 1 QB 499, CA. See also *Southwark LBC v Long* [2002] EWCA Civ 403, [2002] HLR 56.

9   *Smith v Nottinghamshire CC* (1981) *Times* 7 November, [1981] CLY 1520, 133 NLJ 13, CA.

10   See *Manual of Housing Law*, paras 1.268–269.

11   RA 1977 s3; R(A)A 1976 s10 and Sch 5 para 2.

12   See paras 1.51–1.75.

Termination by occupier

1.15　The tale of an unlawful eviction does not always begin with exclusion from the property. It sometimes starts with the landlord seeking to persuade the occupier to leave, which may indeed lead the occupier to agree, whether out of ignorance of his or her rights or because he or she is pressured or even intimidated into giving some kind of notice; when he or she changes his or her mind – perhaps because of advice taken or because there are no other options available – the landlord then seeks to justify peremptory eviction by reference to the occupier's behaviour. None of this is relevant to the question of whether the occupier has been unlawfully evicted and although it may sometimes be relevant to the question of interim relief,[13] the critical first issue will be whether the occupier has in law actually determined his or her rights of occupation.

1.16　**Notice.** A tenant may determine a periodic tenancy[14] by serving a notice to quit on the landlord. In the case of a joint tenancy, the service of a notice to quit by only one of the joint tenants will determine the joint tenancy.[15] The notice must be for a full period of the tenancy and must expire on the first or last day of a period of the tenancy,[16] and – unless an excluded tenancy under PEA 1977[17] – it must be in writing and must be of at least 28 days' duration.[18]

1.17　If an RA 1977 protected tenant or an R(A)A 1976 protected occupier serves notice to quit, but remains in occupation, there will still be a right of occupation under the statutory tenancy which follows;[19] in the case of other occupiers, a valid notice to quit will terminate the

---

13　Broadly, this will depend on the circumstances in which notice was given or the occupier indicated he or she was leaving and what steps the landlord has taken in consequence, in particular if the premises had then been let to someone else.

14　Eg one that runs from week to week or month to month.

15　*Hammersmith LBC v Monk* [1992] 1 AC 478, (1992) 24 HLR 206, HL; *Dacorum BC v Sims* [2014] UKSC 63, [2015] AC 1336, [2015] HLR 7.

16　*Crane v Morris* [1965] 1 WLR 1104, CA. If the tenancy commenced on a Monday, the notice must expire on a Sunday or a Monday. Sometimes the landlord may not know the period of the tenancy. Most notices to quit include a saving provision to avoid this, eg: 'I give you notice to quit [the address] by [the date] or at the expiration of the period of your tenancy which shall expire next after the expiration of 4 weeks from the service on you of this notice.'

17　Ie the four weeks' notice required by PEA 1977 s5 is the minimum notice period, which applies if the tenancy is weekly or fortnightly. If the tenancy is monthly, a month's notice is required. If the tenancy is quarterly, a quarter's notice is required.

18　PEA 1977 s5(1), (1A), (1B).

19　RA 1977 ss2 and 3; R(A)A 1976 s4.

right of occupation: this normally does not mean that the occupier can be evicted without a court order, but that will turn on the application of PEA 1977 itself, not on contractual (or former contractual) rights.

1.18   A periodic licensee must give notice which conforms to any explicit requirements in the licence agreement;[20] unless an excluded licence under PEA 1977,[21] it must also be in writing and be for at least 28 days.[22] If not an excluded licence, the landlord may still need to seek a court order before evicting but, again, this protection of the occupier relies on PEA 1977 not the contract or former contract itself.

1.19   **Expiry of fixed term.** At common law, a fixed-term tenancy will end when the period for which it was granted comes to an end. A residential tenancy which attracts security of tenure will not normally come to an end in this way, but will be replaced either – in the case of an RA 1977 or R(A)A 1976 protected right of occupation – with a statutory tenancy, or – in the case of an assured (including assured shorthold) tenancy – with a periodic tenancy imposed by statute,[23] so that the landlord will still need to obtain a court order. In the first of these cases, this will only be so if the tenant is still occupying the premises as a home; in the second, so long as the tenancy is still assured, which imports the requirement that they are occupied as an only or principal home.[24] The circumstances in which other kinds of fixed-term tenancy are likely to give rise to any issue of unlawful eviction are so rare that they are not considered here.

1.20   A licence for a fixed-term will also come to an end when the period runs out, and the question of eviction will then be governed by PEA 1977 s3.[25]

1.21   **Surrender.** Surrender is the means by which a landlord and a tenant agree that the tenancy is at an end, in the case of a periodic tenancy without formal notice to quit by the tenant and – in the case of a fixed-term tenancy – before the full term of the tenancy has run its course: in the case of a licence, such an agreement is not known as a surrender, but would comprise mutual agreement for it to end.

---

20   Eg written notice, minimum period.
21   See paras 1.61–1.72.
22   PEA 1977 s5(1), (1A), (1B).
23   RA 1977 ss2 and 3; R(A)A 1976 s4; HA 1988 s5.
24   *Manual of Housing Law*, paras 1.177–1.179, 1.230 and 1.289–1.293.
25   See paras 1.51–1.75.

1.22   Strictly, surrender requires a deed[26] by which the landlord and the tenant record the agreement for the tenancy to end; there is no such requirement for a licence – even an oral agreement can suffice (subject to the terms of the agreement itself). Where there is no such document, however, the law may recognise a surrender by operation of law, where the tenant's intention to end the tenancy is clear and the landlord's agreement to it can be inferred: the essence of it is conduct by one party which is inconsistent with continuation of the tenancy, to which the other party can be seen to have agreed, evidenced by his or her own unequivocal conduct.

1.23   These criteria can be fulfilled by an invalid notice to quit by a tenant, which the landlord accepts.[27] All joint tenants have to be party to a surrender, however, so that an invalid notice to quit by one of them – which would have comprised notice but for the invalidity[28] – cannot give rise to a surrender by them all.[29]

1.24   Nor is a mere indication by a tenant that he or she intends to move and is looking for other accommodation sufficient.[30] Likewise, a tenant's departure does not necessarily show an unequivocal intention to end the tenancy,[31] especially if the tenant has not returned the keys and has left a partner in occupation of the property.[32] On the other hand, the tenant does not have to give up vacant possession in order for there to be a surrender; if he or she has done all he or she can to indicate that the tenancy has come to an end, eg, by returning the keys.[33] If the tenant's absence is prolonged, possessions have been removed and there are substantial rent arrears, an intention to end the tenancy may be inferred.[34]

---

26   Ie a document in writing that is expressed to be a deed and is signed by all parties to it in the presence of a witness attesting to the truth of the signatures: Law of Property (Miscellaneous Provisions) Act 1989 s1.

27   *Elsden v Pick* [1980] 1 WLR 898, CA; *King v Jackson* (1997) 30 HLR 541, CA.

28   See para 1.16.

29   *Hounslow LBC v Pilling* (1993) 25 HLR 305, CA; see *Wandsworth LBC v Osei Bonsu* [1999] 1 WLR 1011, (1999) 31 HLR 515, CA, for a claim for unlawful eviction brought by one joint tenant where the notice to quit was invalid.

30   *Love v Herrity* (1990) 23 HLR 217, CA.

31   *Preston BC v Fairclough* (1982) 8 HLR 70, CA; although if the tenant has left permanently, his or her security of tenure will usually have been lost.

32   *Ealing Family Housing Association v McKenzie* [2003] EWCA Civ 1602, [2004] HLR 21.

33   *Sanctuary Housing Association v Campbell* [1999] 1 WLR 1279, (1999) 32 HLR 100, CA.

34   *R v Croydon LBC ex p Toth* (1986) 18 HLR 493, CA.

1.25   The intention of the tenant is judged objectively on the circumstances as they appeared to the landlord; a tenant's subjective intention to return is irrelevant.[35] The circumstances as they appear to the landlord must, however, be unambiguous, so that where a landlord saw a note in the common parts addressed to those who have written graffiti on my flat stating that he had left, there had been no evidence of a clear intention to give up possession.[36]

1.26   The landlord's act of acceptance must also be unequivocal. Where a tenant has left the property and indicated that he or she will not return, the tenancy will nonetheless continue unless and until the landlord takes a positive step to show that he or she has accepted that the tenancy has ended. Mere inaction (eg, a failure to re-take possession or collect rent) does not amount to such unequivocal conduct.[37]

1.27   Examples of a landlord's unequivocal acts include re-letting the property, changing the locks, closing the rent account,[38] moving his or her family or furniture into the property[39] or notifying the tenant that he or she deems the tenancy to have ended. Securing the property and advertising the property to be re-let will not, however, constitute acceptance of an offer to surrender the tenancy until the property is in fact re-let.[40]

Termination by landlord

1.28   While the earlier form of security of tenure available under RA 1977 and R(A)A 1976 allowed the landlord (or tenant) to terminate the contractual arrangement, leading to a statutory tenancy on the same terms,[41] more modern forms of security – assured tenancy (including assured shorthold), secure tenancy or licence,[42] introductory tenancy or licence, demoted tenancy – function by requiring the landlord to obtain a court order to determine the right of occupation so that a periodic tenancy will continue until the order takes effect; even in

---

35 *R v Croydon LBC ex p Toth* (1986) 18 HLR 493, CA.
36 *Zionmor v Islington LBC* (1997) 30 HLR 822, CA.
37 *Belcourt Estates Ltd v Adesina* [2005] EWCA Civ 208, [2005] 2 EGLR 33.
38 *Ealing Family Housing Association v McKenzie* [2003] EWCA Civ 1602, [2004] HLR 21.
39 *Artworld Financial Corporation v Safaryan and others* [2009] EWCA Civ 303, [2009] L&TR 20.
40 *Padwick Properties Ltd v Punj Lloyd Ltd* [2016] EWHC 502 (Ch), [2016] L&TR 18.
41 See para 1.17.
42 *Manual of Housing Law*, para 1.168.

the case of a fixed-term tenancy, it is followed by a periodic tenancy imposed by statute running until a court orders it to end.[43]

1.29   Subject to the new provision yet to be brought into force allowing a landlord under an assured shorthold tenancy (only) to serve an abandonment notice which does bring the tenancy to an end,[44] landlords' notices to quit are therefore ineffective, so long as the right of occupation retains its statutory status. A periodic tenancy that ceases to be assured, assured shorthold, secure, introductory or demoted because the tenant has ceased to occupy the premises as his only or principal home, however, may still be terminated by a notice to quit; likewise, if the tenant is not in occupation as such at the end of a fixed term, no statutory periodic tenancy will arise.[45] Note, however, (a) that mere temporary absence will not take the tenancy out of protection,[46] and (b) that occupation by a spouse, civil partner or a former cohabitee (who has obtained an occupation order under Family Law Act (FLA) 1996 s36), will continue to be treated as the tenant's own occupation.[47]

1.30   As this book is concerned with *unlawful* eviction, rather than proceedings by court order, it is not necessary to consider the way in which the landlord under any of these categories of tenancy can obtain the order to determine the tenancy: the important point to make here is that as the tenancy will not have determined, all its terms continue, so that it is the tenant who is entitled to occupy and the landlord has no rights to evict or to try to evict (tenant or anyone else in occupation, eg tenant's friends, family or lodger).

1.31   *Notice.* Where the statutory protection has ended, however, the tenancy itself will continue until ended: in the case of a fixed-term tenancy, this will mean until the period has expired or the tenancy has been forfeit;[48] in the case of a periodic tenancy, this will mean that notice to quit must[49] be given to the occupier either by the landlord

---

43 HA 1988 s5(1); HA 1985 s82(1); HA 1996 ss130(2), 143D(1).
44 See paras 1.36–1.42.
45 HA 1988 s5(2); HA 1985 s86(1).
46 *Crawley BC v Sawyer* (1987) 20 HLR 98, CA.
47 FLA 1996 ss30(4) and 36(13).
48 This itself requires the use of court proceedings – see PEA 1977 s2 – and is a relatively complex process; it is not considered further here.
49 Theoretically, even a periodic tenancy can be forfeited, but this is so rare that it is not considered here.

or his or her agent[50] in order to end it. Unless the tenancy is what is known as an excluded tenancy,[51] and provided that the premises were let (or licensed) 'as a dwelling',[52] PEA 1977 s5 requires that the notice to quit must:

- be in writing and contain such information as may be prescribed;[53] and
- be given not less than four weeks before the date on which it is to take effect.

1.32   In addition, the notice to quit must satisfy certain common law requirements:

- the period of the notice must be equivalent to at least one period of the tenancy;[54] and
- the notice must expire on a day which is either the first or the last of a period of the tenancy.[55]

1.33   No notice to quit is required, however, for what is known as a tenancy at will,[56] ie a tenancy which is neither fixed term nor periodic.

1.34   The landlord must serve the notice to quit on the occupier. The general rule is that the notice must be served personally on the tenant. Many tenancy agreements include a clause allowing service of notices either by post or by leaving them at the property. In the absence of such a clause, however, the landlord must prove that the notice came to the occupier's attention.[57]

---

50 In the case of certain tenancies (eg, assured, assured shorthold and secure tenancies), the tenancy cannot be determined by notice to quit and a notice complying with the relevant statutory provisions must (generally) be served before possession proceedings are commenced.

51 PEA 1977 s5(1B); see paras 1.61–1.72.

52 See paras 1.55–1.58.

53 The current information applying to both tenancies and licences is contained in the Notices to Quit etc (Prescribed Information) Regulations 1988 SI No 2201.

54 Ie the four weeks' notice required by PEA 1977 s5 is the minimum notice period, which applies if the tenancy is weekly or fortnightly. If the tenancy is monthly, a month's notice is required. If the tenancy is quarterly, a quarter's notice is required.

55 *Crane v Morris* [1965] 1 WLR 1104, CA. If the tenancy commenced on a Monday, the notice must expire on a Sunday or a Monday. Sometimes the landlord may not know the period of the tenancy. Most notices to quit include a saving provision to avoid this, eg: 'I give you notice to quit [the address] by [the date] or at the expiration of the period of your tenancy which shall expire next after the expiration of 4 weeks from the service on you of this notice.'

56 *Crane v Morris* [1965] 1 WLR 1104, CA.

57 *Wandsworth LBC v Attwell* (1995) 27 HLR 536, CA.

1.35   In the case of a licence which is not an excluded licence,[58] notice likewise has to be in writing, contain the prescribed information,[59] and be for a minimum period of four weeks.[60] Notice will also have to comply with any requirements of the agreement, which could include a longer period, eg a calendar month. If the licence is an excluded licence, the notice does not have to be in writing unless the agreement requires it; moreover, unless the agreement specifies a longer period, the landlord merely has to give reasonable notice.[61] What constitutes reasonable notice depends on all the circumstances of the case: the period of the licence is relevant as is the length of time the occupier has been in occupation; in the case of an ordinary contractual licence it is likely to be weeks as opposed to (on the one hand) days or (on the other) months or years.[62]

1.36   **Abandonment notice.** Once Part 3 of the Housing and Planning Act (HPA) 2016 is brought into force, a private landlord in England,[63] may give a tenant a notice, under HPA 2016 s57, which brings an assured shorthold tenancy to an end on the day on which the notice is given if:

a) the tenancy relates to premises in England;
b) the unpaid rent condition is met;
c) the landlord has given the warning notices under HPA 2016 s59; and
d) no tenant, named occupier or deposit payer has responded in writing to any of those notices before the date specified in the warning notices.[64]

1.37   Where no notice has been served, and/or the conditions are not fulfilled, a landlord who evicts an assured shorthold tenant without a court order still commits an act of unlawful eviction.

1.38   **Form of notice.** HPA 2016 s57 does not require that the notice determining the tenancy be in a prescribed form but it is not effective unless it is served by:

58 See paras 1.61–1.72.
59 See para 1.31.
60 PEA 1977 s5(1B).
61 *Minister of Health v Bellotti* [1944] KB 298, CA.
62 *Gibson v Douglas* [2016] EWCA Civ 1266, [2017] HLR 11. Cf *Parker v Parker* [2003] EWHC 1846 (Ch), in which a licensee was entitled to notice of two years to leave a home he had been occupying for ten years.
63 This means any landlord who is unable to grant secure tenancies: HPA 2016 s62. Accordingly, it does not include local and certain other public authorities.
64 HPA 2016 s57; HPA 2016 Part 3 does not apply to premises in Wales: s57(a).

a) leaving it at, or sending it to, the premises to which the tenancy relates;
b) leaving it at, or sending it to, every other postal address in the UK that the tenant, named occupier or deposit payer has given the landlord as a contact address for giving notices;
c) sending it to every email address that the tenant, named occupier or deposit payer has given the landlord as a contact address for giving notices; and
d) leaving it at or sending it to every postal address in the UK of every guarantor, marked for the attention of the tenant.[65]

1.39   **The unpaid rent condition.** The unpaid rent condition is satisfied if at least eight weeks or two months' rent is unpaid on the date that the notice is served.[66]

1.40   **The warning notices.** Before serving the notice to bring the tenancy to an end, the landlord must have given three warning notices. The first warning notice may be given even if the unpaid rent condition is not yet met. The first notice may be served in the manner as set out at para 1.38[67] and must state:

a) that the landlord believes the premises to have been abandoned;
b) that if the premises have not been abandoned, the tenant, a named occupier or a deposit payer must respond in writing before the day after the end of the period of eight weeks beginning with the day on which the first warning notice is given to the tenant; and
c) that the landlord proposes to bring the tenancy to an end if no tenant, named occupier or deposit payer responds in writing before that date.[68]

1.41   The second warning notice may be given only once the unpaid rent condition has been met and must be given at least two weeks, and no more than four weeks, after the first warning notice.[69] It must contain the same information as was included in the first warning notice (see para 1.40)[70] and be served in the same manner (see para 1.38).[71]

1.42   The third warning notice must be given before the period of five days ending with the date specified in the earlier warning notices, ie

---

65   HPA 2016 s61(1), (3).
66   HPA 2016 s58.
67   HPA 2016 ss59(2) and 61(3).
68   HPA 2016 s59(4)–(5).
69   HPA 2016 s59(7)–(8).
70   HPA 2016 s59(4).
71   HPA 2016 ss59(2) and 61(3).

it must be served at least five days before the end of the period given in the first warning notice during which the tenant has to respond.[72] For example, if the first notice is served on 7 November 2017 the tenant must have responded by 1 January 2018. Accordingly, the third notice must be served no later than 27 December 2017. It must also include the same information given in the first and second warning notices.[73] It must be served by fixing it to some conspicuous part of the premises to which the tenancy relates.[74]

1.43 **Reinstatement.** Where a tenancy is brought to an end by an abandonment notice under HPA 2016 s57 (see para 1.36), the tenant may apply to the county court for an order reinstating the tenancy if the tenant has a good reason for having failed to respond to the warning notices.[75] If the county court finds that the tenant had a good reason for failing to respond, it may make any order it thinks fit for the purpose of reinstating the tenancy.[76]

1.44 An application for reinstatement may not be made after the end of the period of six months beginning with the day on which the notice under HPA 2016 s57 is given.[77]

Claims for breach of contract

1.45 Usually, the appropriate person to be sued for breach of contract is the landlord, as the party to the contract. If, however, the landlord has acted through agents and the landlord's identity is unknown, eg it is the agents' name on the tenancy agreement, the agents themselves can be sued by the occupier.[78] If, ultimately, the landlord was responsible for his or her agents' actions, it well may be the case that the agents will add the landlord as a party to proceedings in any event.

1.46 Likewise, persons other than the tenant, unless they have been assigned or succeeded to the tenancy, will be unable to sue for breach of the tenancy agreement as they are not a party to the agreement. The same is true of licences.

---

72 HPA 2016 s59(9).
73 HPA 2016 s59(4).
74 HPA 2016 s59(3).
75 HPA 2016 s60(1).
76 HPA 2016 s60(2).
77 HPA 2016 s60(3).
78 *Allen v F O'Hearn & Co* [1937] AC 213, PC.

Contracts (Rights of Third Parties) Act 1999

1.47   Sometimes other persons, such as family members, who are not parties to the tenancy or licence may nonetheless enforce the agreement if the Contracts (Rights of Third Parties) Act (C(RTP)A) 1999 applies.

1.48   C(RTP)A 1999 only applies to agreements made on or after 11 May 2000. It does not, however, apply to agreements made on or after that date if the parties did not intend the contract to be enforced by third parties.[79] Many modern tenancy agreements therefore now include a clause excluding the application of C(RTP)A 1999.

1.49   A person who is not a party to a contract can enforce its terms under C(RTP)A 1999 if either:

- the contract expressly provides that a third party may enforce the term; or
- the term purports to confer a benefit on him or her.[80]

1.50   The third party does not have to be identified by name in the contract. It is sufficient if he or she can be identified as 'a member of a class or as answering to a particular description'.[81] For example, if the tenancy agreement provides that the landlord should allow 'the tenant and his family' quiet enjoyment of the premises, a member of the tenant's family could seek to enforce that contractual term.

Breach of Protection from Eviction Act 1977 s3

1.51   Even if the right of occupation has been ended, the landlord will normally need to take court proceedings before evicting and will be liable to civil proceedings on the part of an occupier if he or she does not do so: PEA 1977 s3(1) prevents an owner of residential property from recovering possession against certain occupiers of residential premises, after the end of the tenancy or licence, otherwise than by proceedings in the court, ie by obtaining and then executing a possession order. Breach of PEA 1977 s3 gives rise to a cause of action for breach of statutory duty.[82] The cause of action can also be used for acts of harassment which fall short of actual eviction (see chapter 2). A claim may be made for damages and/or an injunction (see paras 1.105–1.195).

---

79   C(RTP)A 1999 s1(2).
80   C(RTP)A 1999 s1(1).
81   C(RTP)A 1999 s1(3).
82   *Warder v Cooper* [1970] Ch 495, ChD.

1.52   Tenants and licensees[83] of any premises that have been 'let as a dwelling'[84] may claim the protection of PEA 1977 s3 unless the premises were let under either a statutorily protected tenancy[85] or an 'excluded' tenancy/licence.[86] Additionally, 'any person lawfully residing in the premises or part of them' at the moment when the tenancy or licence is terminated may also claim its protection if evicted otherwise than by proceedings in court.[87] Occupiers may 'lawfully reside' in premises even though they are not lawfully present in the UK for immigration purposes.[88]

1.53   There are therefore four issues to consider:

- who is an owner liable under PEA 1977 s3;
- whether the premises in question are let as 'a dwelling' (whether under a tenancy or a licence); and, if so
- whether the provisions are disapplied because the letting is a statutorily protected tenancy or an excluded tenancy or licence; and
- whether the eviction was 'otherwise than by proceedings in the court'.

Owner

1.54   Only an 'owner' can breach PEA 1977 s3,[89] ie the person who, as against the occupier, is entitled to possession of the premises. Accordingly, if persons other than the landlord carry out the eviction, the evicted occupier will have to prove that the eviction was carried out by those persons on behalf of the landlord.[90]

---

83 PEA 1977 s3 applies to any 'premises occupied as a dwelling under a licence': PEA 1977 s3(2B).

84 See paras 1.55–1.58.

85 As defined in PEA 1977 s8, see paras 1.59–1.60.

86 As defined in PEA 1977 s3A, see paras 1.61–1.72.

87 PEA 1977 s3(2). The protection also applies to anyone who had been lawfully living with a deceased statutory tenant under RA 1977 or R(A)A 1976 when the owner's right to recover arises on the death of the statutory tenant: PEA 1977 s3(3).

88 *Akinbolu v Hackney LBC* (1996) 29 HLR 259, CA.

89 PEA 1977 s3(1) and s8(3).

90 *Gibson v Douglas* [2016] EWCA Civ 1266, [2017] HLR 11.

Let as a dwelling

1.55   In *Patel v Pirabakaran*,[91] 'let as a dwelling' was held to apply to premises comprising a flat above a shop, ie mixed user: the phrase applied to what was let wholly or partly as a dwelling.[92]

1.56   In *Uratemp Ventures Ltd v Collins*,[93] the House of Lords considered the meaning of the word 'dwelling' in the context of HA 1988.[94] The word was said not to be a term of art. It is the occupier's residence or home; the place where he or she lives and to which he or she returns and which forms the centre of his or her existence. A dwelling may consist of no more than one room. There is no requirement that any particular facilities be included. Accordingly, the absence of cooking facilities does not prevent premises from being the occupier's home; the occupier may live on take-away food or eat out. It is not even necessary for there to be a bed, although the room probably has to be big enough to sleep in.

1.57   Notwithstanding this, in *R (CN) v Lewisham LBC*,[95] the Supreme Court[96] decided that interim accommodation let to a homeless applicant on a licence by a local housing authority – or by another landlord under an arrangement with the authority – while the authority carries out inquiries into an applicant's homelessness application under HA 1996 Part 7, in performance of its temporary obligation under HA 1996 s188, is not 'let as a dwelling' for the purposes of PEA 1977 s3; the same is assumed to apply to other temporary duties, eg accommodation for the intentionally homeless or pending a local connection referral.[97]

1.58   The Supreme Court left open the possibility that self-contained accommodation provided under a tenancy might be let as a dwelling even if under the temporary duties; and, it appears to have been

---

91 [2006] EWCA Civ 685, [2006] 1 WLR 3112.

92 The decision was under PEA 1977 s2, governing forfeiture, where the same phrase is used.

93 [2002] 1 AC 301, (2001) 33 HLR 4, HL.

94 Ie 'let as a separate dwelling' – the same phrase is used in HA 1985 and HA 1988.

95 *R (CN) v Lewisham LBC* [2014] UKSC 62, [2015] AC 1259, [2015] HLR 6.

96 Following the Court of Appeal decisions in *Mohamed v Manek and Kensington & Chelsea RLBC* (1995) 27 HLR 439, CA and in *Desnousse v Newham LBC* [2006] EWCA Civ 547, [2006] QB 831, [2006] HLR 38. See also *Brouillet v Landless* (1995) 28 HLR 836, CA.

97 See A Arden QC, J Bates and T Vanhegan *Homelessness and Allocations* (LAG, 10th edn, 2017), chapter 10.

accepted that once a 'full' homelessness duty has been accepted,[98] accommodation – even if still temporary (pending permanent rehousing) – would be considered to be let as a dwelling.[99]

Statutorily protected tenancies

1.59   PEA 1977 s3 does not apply where the tenancy is a statutorily protected tenancy, because these all have their own statutory provisions protecting the occupier from peremptory eviction, which allow the occupier to rely either on the terms of the tenancy (paras 1.8–1.14) or other causes of action (paras 1.76–1.104). The following are statutorily protected tenants:[100]

- protected tenants under RA 1977;[101]
- assured tenants, assured shorthold tenants and assured agricultural occupants under HA 1988;
- tenants of long leases of dwellings to which Landlord and Tenant Act (LTA) 1954 Part 1 applies;[102]
- tenants holding over after the expiry of long leases;[103]
- business tenants of premises to which LTA 1954 Part 2 applies;
- protected occupants or statutory tenants as defined in the R(A)A 1976;
- tenants of agricultural holdings as defined in the Agricultural Holdings Act (AHA) 1986; and
- farm business tenants within the meaning of the Agricultural Tenancies Act (ATA) 1995.

---

98 Under HA 1996 s193.

99 This would seem to follow from Lord Hodge at [16] and [45]. Lady Hale referred at [165] to the 'generally accepted view that the protection of section 3 of the 1977 Act *will* apply once the local authority have accepted that they owe the family the "full housing duty"', presumably picking up the local authorities' submission that the 'licences were expressly limited to the period to be taken to provide a decision' (at 1287F) and the Secretary of State's submission that the premises were 'temporary accommodation while the council made inquiries' (at 1288D).

100 PEA 1977 s8(1).

101 A statutory tenant under RA 1977 is a former protected tenant and therefore a statutorily protected tenant for the purposes of PEA 1977.

102 A long lease is for 21 years or more.

103 On the expiry of a long lease, the tenant may entitled to hold over under Local Government and Housing Act 1989 Sch 10, and, depending on when the tenancy commenced, may be entitled to a statutory tenancy under RA 1977 or an assured tenancy under HA 1988. See further *Manual of Housing Law*, paras 2.73–2.83.

1.60   It follows that a former assured (or assured shorthold) tenant who terminated his or her tenancy (paras 1.15–1.27) cannot rely on PEA 1977 s3 if he or she does not vacate and the former landlord evicts without a court order.

Excluded tenancies and licences

1.61   PEA 1977 s3 does not apply if the tenancy or licence is 'excluded': the landlord is therefore entitled to recover possession without a court order. It should not, however, be forgotten that the occupier may still have another cause of action, such as breach of covenant for quiet enjoyment (paras 1.8–1.11) or implied term (para 1.12), or trespass (paras 1.76–1.81) if the tenancy or licence has not been properly determined (whether by the landlord or by the occupier).

1.62   By PEA 1977 s3A, the following categories of tenancies and licences are excluded:

- sharing with a resident landlord;
- sharing with a member of a resident landlord's family;
- temporary expedient to a trespasser;
- holiday accommodation;
- letting other than for money or money's worth;
- accommodation provided to asylum-seekers or displaced persons;
- licence of a public sector hostel; and
- where the landlord has been served with a notice by the secretary of state that the accommodation let under a tenancy or licence is occupied by a person who is disqualified as a result of his or her immigration status from occupying premises under a residential tenancy agreement.

Sharing with a resident landlord

1.63   For this exclusion to apply, the following conditions must be met:

- under the terms of the agreement, the occupier shares accommodation[104] with the landlord; and
- immediately before the occupancy was granted and when it comes to an end, the landlord occupies (as his or her only or principal home) premises which include the shared accommodation.

104 'Sharing' means having the use of the accommodation in common with another person; 'accommodation' is anything other than the common parts (ie, stairs, passageways, etc) or a storage area: PEA 1977 s3A(4) and (5).

Sharing with a member of a resident landlord's family

1.64 For this exclusion to apply, the following conditions must be met:

- under the terms of the agreement, the occupier shares accommodation[105] with a member of the landlord's family;[106]
- immediately before the occupancy was granted and when it comes to an end, the member of the landlord's family occupies as his or her only or principal home premises which include the shared accommodation; and
- immediately before the occupancy was granted and when it comes to an end, the landlord occupies as his or her only or principal home premises in the same building as the shared accommodation (unless the building is a purpose-built block of flats).

Temporary expedient to a trespasser

1.65 This exclusion applies to a tenancy or licence granted as a temporary expedient to an occupier who had entered the premises or any other premises as a trespasser,[107] for example, a squatter who later receives permission to stay in the premises, eg, for a short time until redevelopment or who is offered a short-life property elsewhere.

Holiday accommodation

1.66 A tenancy or licence which confers the right to occupy the premises for a holiday is excluded.[108]

Other than for money or money's worth

1.67 If the occupier is not obliged to pay for the accommodation, nor obliged to provide some other form of consideration for the right to occupy the property, for example, services in lieu of payment, the tenancy or licence is excluded.[109] Examples include family arrangements

---

105 PEA 1977 s3A(4) and (5).
106 'Family member' means a spouse, civil partner, cohabitant, parent, grandparent, child, grandchild, brother, sister, uncle, aunt, nephew or niece: PEA 1977 s3A(5), adopting the definition of family member in HA 1985 s113, as amended. Relationships by marriage are treated as relationships by blood; relationships of half-blood are treated as relationships of whole blood; stepchildren are treated as children; illegitimate children are treated as legitimate: HA 1985 s113.
107 PEA 1977 s3A(6).
108 PEA 1977 s3A(7)(a); if the agreement records that the letting is a holiday let but the agreement is a sham, the letting will not be excluded: see *Buchmann v May* (1983) 7 HLR 1, CA and *R v Rent Officer for Camden LBC ex p Plant* (1980) 7 HLR 15, QBD.
109 PEA 1977 s3A(7)(b).

and weekend guests. A tenancy or licence was not for money's worth where the occupier was only required to pay for utilities, heating, water and food so that there was no payment or consideration for occupation of the land.[110] Conversely, an obligation to keep property repaired and insured, and to pay all relevant taxes, has been held to be a right to occupy for money's worth.[111]

Asylum-seekers or displaced persons

1.68   Tenancies or licences granted to asylum-seekers (and/or their dependants) under Immigration and Asylum Act (IAA) 1999 Part 6 are excluded.[112] IAA 1999 established a system of support for asylum-seekers, provided by the secretary of state through the UK Border Agency. Support may include the provision of accommodation, which may be provided directly, or through arrangements with local authorities or others. Tenancies or licences granted to displaced persons under the Displaced Persons (Temporary Protection) Regulations 2005 are also excluded.[113]

Licences to occupy a public sector hostel

1.69   A licence (but not a tenancy) will be excluded if it is a licence to occupy a hostel provided by a specified public sector landlord.[114] A hostel is a

---

110   *West Wiltshire DC v Snelgrove* (1997) 30 HLR 57, QBD.

111   *Polarpark Enterprises Inc v Allason* [2007] EWHC 1088 (Ch), [2008] 1 P&CR 4.

112   PEA 1977 s3A(7A), added by IAA 1999 Sch 14 para 73 (with effect from 1 April 2000), as amended by Immigration, Asylum and Nationality Act 2006 s43(4).

113   PEA 1977 s3A(7C), added by Displaced Persons (Temporary Protection) Regulations 2005 SI No 1379 Sch 1 para 1 (with effect from 15 June 2005). This applies to any person granted temporary protection as a result of a decision of the Council of the European Union made pursuant to Article 5 of the Temporary Protection Directive who are deemed for the purposes of provision of means of subsistence to have leave to enter or remain in the UK exceptionally, outside the Immigration Rules.

114   A local authority, a private registered provider of social housing or a registered social landlord or housing trust, the regulator of social housing, the secretary of state, a combined authority, a development corporation, an economic prosperity board, an urban development corporation, a mayoral development corporation, a housing action trust, or any other person or body specified by the secretary of state: PEA 1977 s3A(8). To date, the secretary of state has specified the London Hostels Associations Ltd (Protection from Eviction (Excluded Licences) Order 1991 SI No 1943), the Shaftesbury Society (Protection from Eviction (Excluded Licences) (Shaftesbury Society) Order 1999 SI No 1758) and the Royal British Legion Industries Ltd (Protection from Eviction (Excluded Licences) (Royal British Legion Industries Ltd) (England) Order 2003 SI No 2436).

building in which is provided, for persons generally or for a class or classes of persons:

a) residential accommodation otherwise than in separate and self-contained sets of premises, and

b) either board or facilities for the preparation of food adequate to the needs of those persons, or both.[115]

1.70 Accommodation is not separate and self-contained if the terms governing its occupation require the occupier to share facilities with someone with whom he or she has not chosen to share. Whether anyone is actually sharing the accommodation is irrelevant.[116]

The occupier or occupiers are disqualified as a result of their immigration status from occupying premises under a residential tenancy agreement

1.71 From 1 February 2016,[117] it has been unlawful for a landlord[118] in England[119] to authorise an adult to occupy premises under a residential tenancy agreement if the adult is disqualified as a result of his or her immigration status.[120] A person is disqualified[121] if he or she is not a relevant national, ie he or she is not a British or EEA national, or does not have a right to rent, ie does not have leave to remain in the UK.[122]

1.72 The secretary of state may serve a landlord with a notice informing him or her that a named occupier, or named occupiers, of premises let by the landlord is or are disqualified as a result of immigration status from occupying premises under a residential tenancy agreement.[123] A landlord who has received such a notice may terminate the residential tenancy agreement by giving notice in writing – in the prescribed form – to the tenant or, in the case of a joint tenancy, to all

115 PEA 1977 s3A(8), adopting the definition of a hostel in HA 1985 s622.

116 *Rogerson v Wigan MBC* [2005] HLR 10, QBD.

117 A 'pilot' period began on 1 December 2014 in parts of the West Midlands: see Immigration Act 2014 (Commencement No 3, Transitional and Saving Provisions) Order 2014 SI No 2771 article 6.

118 A licensor will be a 'landlord' for these purposes: Immigration Act (IA) 2014 s20(3).

119 IA 2014 does not apply in Wales.

120 IA 2014 s22(1).

121 This is not limited to the tenant or licensee; it may include anyone else who is occupying the premises as their only or main home: IA 2014 s22(4).

122 IA 2014 s21.

123 IA 2014 s33D(2).

of the tenants, specifying the date[124] on which the agreement comes to an end.[125] Once the notice has been received, the tenancy or licence becomes an excluded tenancy or licence and – once the tenancy or licence has come to an end – the landlord can therefore recover possession without a court order[126] irrespective of whether the tenancy or licence was granted before the Immigration Act (IA) 2016 came into force.[127]

Proceedings in the court

1.73   PEA 1977 s3 prohibits the owner of the premises let from recovering possession of the premises otherwise than by 'proceedings in the court'.[128] This requires an owner to do two things: first, obtain a possession order; and, secondly, enforce the possession order by applying for either a writ or warrant of possession. This means that an owner who obtains a possession order, but evicts the occupier personally without applying for a writ or a warrant, is still liable under PEA 1977 s3.

1.74   A writ or warrant once executed may be set aside if it has been obtained by fraud, oppression or by an abuse of process.[129] Examples of warrants being set aside in these circumstances are where:

- six years had elapsed since the date of the possession order and the landlord applies for a warrant without the permission of the court;[130]
- the landlord has transferred enforcement of a possession order, in respect of a premises let under a residential tenancy, to the High Court, using form N293A;[131]
- the landlord has applied for a writ without first notifying the tenant of the application;[132]

---

124 Not being earlier than the end of the period of 28 days beginning with the day specified in the notice as the day on which it is given.

125 IA 2014 s33D(3), (4).

126 PEA 1977 s3A(7D).

127 IA 2016 s40(7). IA 2014 s33D was inserted by IA 2016.

128 PEA 1977 s3(1). Court is defined as the county court and the High Court: PEA 1977 s9(1).

129 *Hammersmith and Fulham LBC v Hill* (1994) 27 HLR 368, CA.

130 *Hackney LBC v White* (1996) 28 HLR 219, CA; *AA v Southwark LBC* [2014] EWHC 500 (QB). Permission of the court is required in such circumstances by CPR 83.3(a).

131 *Birmingham City Council v Mondhlani* [2015] EW Misc B41 (CC).

132 *Nicholas v Secretary of State for Defence* [2015] EWHC 4064 (Ch). Note that the requirement to give notice only applies to writs in the High Court and not warrants in the county court.

- the landlord, when applying for a writ, misled the court by certifying that there were no outstanding appeals against the possession order;[133]
- the landlord has sought to enforce a suspended possession order without first obtaining the permission of the court;[134] and
- there has been an unfair use of the court procedures that gives rise to oppression, eg where the tenant is misled and thereby prevented from applying to stay the execution of a warrant.[135]

1.75 Where a warrant has been set aside for fraud, oppression or an abuse of process, it is likely to be considered that the eviction was not effected by court proceedings so that the landlord will therefore be liable under PEA 1977 s3.[136] A simple and genuine error of procedure will not, however, necessarily result in the warrant being set aside.[137] Even where the possession order is subsequently set aside under Civil Procedure Rules (CPR) 39.3,[138] the eviction is not unlawful.[139]

Trespass to land

1.76 Any unlawful entry by one person onto another person's land constitutes a trespass.[140] An unlawful eviction will therefore amount to a trespass to land if the landlord has re-taken possession from a tenant before the tenancy has ended. In unlawful eviction cases, it is important to plead trespass alongside other contractual claims, eg breach of quiet enjoyment,[141] as it allows the evicted tenant to recover general damages for matters such as anxiety, shock, discomfort or inconvenience, which are not recoverable for breach of contract (see para 1.144).[142]

1.77 A trespass is committed as soon as someone enters on the land of another without permission: so long as a tenancy subsists, the land is in the possession of the tenant so that the landlord who enters

---

133 *Ahmed v Mahmood* [2013] EWHC 3176 (QB).
134 *Cardiff CC v Lee* [2016] EWCA Civ 1034, [2016] HLR 45.
135 *Camden v Akani* (1997) 29 HLR 845, CA; *Lambeth LBC v Hughes* (2001) 33 HLR 33, CA; *Hammersmith & Fulham LBC v Lemeh* (2001) 33 HLR 23, CA.
136 *AA v Southwark LBC* [2014] EWHC 500 (QB).
137 *Cardiff CC v Lee* [2016] EWCA Civ 1034, [2016] HLR 45.
138 Where the tenant did not attend the hearing at which the possession order was made.
139 *Brent LBC v Botu* (2001) 33 HLR 14, CA.
140 *Clerk and Lindsell on Torts* (21st edn, 2016), para 19-01.
141 See paras 1.8–1.11.
142 *Branchett v Beaney* (1992) 24 HLR 348, CA.

without his or her permission is trespassing on the tenant's land. It is also a trespass to fail to leave the land when requested to do so: thus, a landlord who has been invited into property by a tenant will commit a trespass if he or she refuses to leave after being asked to do so. In the same way, if the landlord has a specific right to enter the tenant's premises,[143] but uses it for something that the right does not cover, or if he or she remains on the premises after the right has come to an end, he or she will become a trespasser,[144] eg a landlord who purports to enter in order to carry out repairs but who uses the opportunity to shut the tenant out after completing the repairs will not only have breached the tenant's entitlement to quiet enjoyment but will also have become a trespasser, even though he or she did not enter as such.

1.78   It is not necessary to show any harm in order to sue for damages for trespass: the very fact that there has been a trespass is sufficient to give rise to a claim for damages (although obviously if there is no or little damage then the amount of compensation awarded may be small).

1.79   Anyone with sufficient possession of the land can rely on trespass to land.[145] A tenant clearly has a sufficient interest as the tenancy itself imports a right of exclusive possession, ie the right to exclude everyone, which right extends (subject to any specific rights to enter, for example, to inspect) to excluding the landlord from the premises. Other occupiers with possession can also rely on trespass including a licensee with exclusive occupation[146] and in some cases even a trespasser.[147] The licensee of a person with sufficient interest cannot, however, rely on trespass in his or her own right, but only through the person with possession: accordingly, members of a tenant's family or household have no remedy in trespass against the landlord.[148]

---

143 Eg to inspect for disrepair.
144 *Hillen v ICI (Alkali) Ltd* [1936] AC 65, HL.
145 *Hunter v Canary Wharf Ltd* [1997] AC 655, (1997) 30 HLR 409, HL.
146 *Hunter v Canary Wharf Ltd* [1997] AC 655, (1997) 30 HLR 409, HL.
147 *Hunter v Canary Wharf Ltd* [1997] AC 655, (1997) 30 HLR 409, HL; in the context of residential premises, a squatter is in adverse possession if he or she lives in the property as his or her home and has unequivocally shown his or her intention to exclude the world (including the true owner) from the property, eg by changing the locks to the premises: *Lambeth LBC v Blackburn* (2001) 33 HLR 74, CA.
148 *Hunter v Canary Wharf Ltd* [1997] AC 684, (1997) 30 HLR 409, HL approving *Malone v Laskey* [1907] 2 KB 141, CA.

1.80   A former tenant or licensee may not sue in trespass if evicted after the tenancy or licence has come to an end, eg by surrender or by the serving of a notice to quit (see paras 1.15–1.37).

1.81   A claim for trespass lies against whoever enters or remains without permission: the cause of action is not confined to the landlord, although if someone else is acting on behalf of the landlord in trespassing, the landlord will also be liable. It is a question of responsibility for the trespass: thus, where the police carried out an eviction, the person who had called them was not liable as he had not been responsible for what the police did.[149]

Trespass to goods

1.82   A trespass to goods is a direct interference with another person's belongings. It frequently co-exists with conversion, in which a person entitled to the possession of goods is permanently deprived of that possession and the goods are converted to the use of someone else. In unlawful eviction cases, the landlord commonly interferes with the occupier's belongings, either destroying them or packing them up and placing them outside the premises. These actions are instances of trespass to goods. If the belongings are retained this may also amount to conversion. In either case, an action may be brought under the Torts (Interference with Goods) Act 1977 for the return of the goods, or their value, or damages. Trespass to goods and conversion, like trespass to land, may be committed by anyone, but a landlord will also be liable for the acts of those acting on his or her behalf or for whose actions he or she is responsible.

1.83   If the tenant is in arrears of rent at the time of the eviction, the landlord often refuses to return the tenant's possessions until the rent is paid: this is not permissible;[150] he or she must sue for the arrears in court proceedings.

Deceit or fraudulent misrepresentation

1.84   Deceit consists of a representation of fact, whether made by words or by conduct, by a person who knows that it is false. Silence alone is

---

149 *Gibson v Douglas* [2016] EWCA Civ 1266, [2017] HLR 11.

150 The common law remedy known as distress, under which a landlord could enter premises, seize the tenant's possessions, sell them and recoup rent arrears from the proceeds, was rarely applicable in respect of modern residential tenancies, but has in any event been abolished entirely by Tribunals, Courts and Enforcement Act 2007 s71.

not sufficient. The representation must be made with the intention that it be acted upon. It must have been acted upon and resulted in damage. In *Mafo v Adams*,[151] a landlord who had tricked his tenant into leaving his accommodation by falsely informing him that alternative accommodation was available at another address, was held liable for deceit.

Conspiracy or misfeasance in public office

1.85   The tort of conspiracy occurs where two or more parties use unlawful means to cause harm to another.[152] The tort of misfeasance in public office arises where an officer of a public authority either:

a) maliciously exercises a power with the intent to injure a person or persons; or

b) acts knowing that he has no power to act where to do so will probably injure a third party.[153]

1.86   In *AA v Southwark LBC*,[154] the High Court found that two officers of Southwark had conspired to evict the tenant from his secure tenancy by applying, without first seeking the court's permission, for a warrant to execute a possession order that had been obtained more than six years previously. Moreover, the officers had, in doing so, exercised their powers with an intention of harming the tenant by causing his eviction where there were no reasonable grounds for it.

Housing Act 1988 s27

1.87   HA 1988 s27(1) and (2) creates a cause of action where a landlord[155] or any person acting on his or her behalf:

- unlawfully deprives the residential occupier of any premises of his or her occupation of the whole or part of the premises; or
- attempts unlawfully to deprive the residential occupier of any premises of his or her occupation of the whole or part of the premises; or

---

151 [1970] 1 QB 548, CA.

152 *Customs and Excise Commissioners v Total Network SL* [2008] UKHL 19, [2008] 1 AC 1174.

153 *Three Rivers DC v Bank of England (No 3)* [2003] 2 AC 1, HL.

154 [2014] EWHC 500 (QB).

155 Defined in HA 1988 s27(9) as the person who, but for the occupier's right to occupy, would be entitled to occupation of the premises and any superior landlord under whom that person derives title.

- knowing or having cause to believe that the conduct is either likely to cause the residential occupier of any premises to give up his or her occupation of the premises or any part of them, or else to refrain from exercising any right or pursuing any remedy in respect of the premises or any part of them, does acts calculated to interfere with the peace or comfort of the residential occupier or members of his or her household or persistently withdraws or withholds services reasonably required for occupation of the premises, and, as a result, the residential occupier gives up his or her occupation of the premises as a residence.

1.88   As the majority of tenants in the private sector are now assured shorthold tenants, the relevance of this action has diminished somewhat because landlords can recover possession more easily than when most tenants were fully protected; as a result, the level of damages likely to be awarded is less. It is most relevant if the occupier is a secure, (fully) assured or Rent Act protected or statutory tenant although there will still be cases where the occupier is an assured shorthold tenant and the landlord is unwilling to take court proceedings. Owing to the significant level of damages that may be awarded, it should always be considered.

1.89   HA 1988 s27 is modelled on the criminal offences of unlawful eviction created by PEA 1977 s1, discussed in detail below (see paras 1.197–1.254) and reference is therefore made, where relevant, to the identical provisions under those offences.

1.90   Only a 'residential occupier' may sue under HA 1988 s27. 'Residential occupier' has the same meaning as under PEA 1977 s1 (see paras 1.201–2.244).

1.91   Under HA 1988 s27(3), only the landlord is liable for damages. Where the acts in question have been committed by the landlord's agent, it is the landlord who will be liable for them.[156]

1.92   The measure of damages in an action under HA 1988 s27 is defined in HA 1988 s28 and is discussed below under remedies (see paras 1.168–1.195).

Unlawfully deprives of any premises of his or her occupation

1.93   The meaning of 'unlawfully deprives of any premises of his or her occupation' is discussed in detail at paras 1.246–1.251.

---

156 *Sampson v Wilson* [1996] Ch 39, (1996) 29 HLR 18, CA.

Reinstatement

1.94   There is no liability under HA 1988 s27 if the occupier is reinstated
(whether by agreement with the landlord or because of a court
order) before proceedings are finally disposed of.[157] Proceedings
are not finally disposed of until any appeal has been determined or
abandoned.[158]

1.95   Reinstatement was considered in *Tagro v Cafane*,[159] in which
the landlord handed back the keys to the occupier, only for her to
find that the lock did not work and that her room had been totally
wrecked: unsurprisingly, this was held not to amount to reinstatement. In *Murray v Aslam*,[160] the tenant returned home to find the
locks changed and her belongings in the street. She and her young
child had to stand in the rain. Her possessions were damaged and
her son fell ill. The police were called and they persuaded the landlord to allow her back in. Although the landlord did not harass her
again, two weeks later she decided to leave. The landlord initially
failed to defend the tenant's claim and judgment was entered against
him. The Court of Appeal was only required to decide whether the
landlord should be given the opportunity to defend the proceedings
and so did not rule on whether there had been a reinstatement: Sir
Thomas Bingham MR, however, thought that there was doubt about
whether the tenant was entitled to rely on HA 1988 s27 because she
had in fact been allowed back into the property; Sir Ralph Gibson,
on the other hand, thought that a temporary return to the property
might not be sufficient to amount to reinstatement, which is consistent with the approach taken in *Mehta v Royal Bank of Scotland*.[161]

1.96   If reinstatement is offered before proceedings are commenced,
the occupier is not obliged to accept the offer, although an unreasonable refusal to do so may reduce the level of damages.[162]

No right to re-admission

1.97   HA 1988 s27 cannot be used to obtain an injunction to re-admit the
occupier to the premises. Accordingly, where the occupier wishes to
be re-admitted, one of the other causes of action referred to in this

157 HA 1988 s27(6).
158 HA 1988 s27(6).
159 (1991) 23 HLR 250, CA.
160 (1994) 27 HLR 284, CA.
161 (1999) 32 HLR 45, QBD.
162 HA 1988 s27(7)(b); see *Tagro v Cafane* (1991) 23 HLR 250, CA and paras
1.189–1.191.

chapter needs to be relied on. If the occupier is then re-admitted, there will no longer be any cause of action under HA 1988 s27.

1.98 The most appropriate course for an occupier is therefore to commence proceedings for breach of the covenant for quiet enjoyment (paras 1.8–1.11) and trespass to land (paras 1.76–1.81) as well as breach of HA 1988 s27. If the occupier is re-admitted, the claim under HA 1988 s27 can be withdrawn while if the claim for the injunction fails (for example, because the property has been re-let and the court is unwilling to dispossess the new occupier), the occupier can still pursue the claim under HA 1988 s27.

Defences

1.99 It is a defence to any action that the defendant believed and had reasonable cause to believe that the residential occupier had ceased to reside in the premises at the relevant time. Where liability arises by virtue of the doing of acts, or the withdrawal or withholding of services, it is a defence that the defendant had reasonable grounds for the acts complained of.[163] These defences are also available under PEA 1977 s1 and are discussed at paras 1.252–1.254.

Breach of the Human Rights Act 1998

1.100 By Article 8 of the European Convention on Human Rights (ECHR), enacted in Schedule 1 to the Human Rights Act (HRA) 1998:

> (1) Everyone has the right to respect for his private and family life, his home and his correspondence.
>
> (2) There shall be no interference by a public authority with the exercise of this right except such as is in accordance with the law and is necessary in a democratic society in the interests of national security, public safety or the economic well-being of the country, for the prevention of disorder or crime, for the protection of health or morals, or for the protection of the rights and freedoms of others.

1.101 Damages or an injunction may be awarded for a breach of Article 8 in circumstances where it is just and appropriate to do so.[164] Only a public authority is bound by the Act.[165] Private bodies which exercise

---

163 HA 1988 s27(8); see *Wandsworth LBC v Osei Bonsu* [1999] 1 WLR 1011, (1998) 31 HLR 515, CA.
164 HRA 1998 s8(1) provides that a court may grant any remedy within its powers.
165 HRA 1998 s6.

functions of a public nature – known as hybrid bodies[166] – are deemed to be public authorities unless the act in question is private.[167] Private companies who provide services that are regulated by statute, which would otherwise have been provided by a public authority, are likely to be public authorities, eg, a water company,[168] or a distributor – but not a supplier – of electricity.[169] Critically, a registered social landlord[170] has been held to qualify as a public authority in relation to its provision and management of social housing.[171] Plainly, a local housing authority is. A private landlord, however, is not.[172]

1.102   It follows that an unlawful eviction by such a body will additionally comprise a breach of Article 8 and will be actionable as such (albeit an eviction without a court order, that is otherwise in accordance with the law, will not).[173] Anyone who is a victim of the breach may sue if his or her Article 8 rights have been interfered with.[174] In practice, however, as the amount of damages awarded for breaches of a person's human rights are significantly less than under other causes of action,[175] it is only likely to be of benefit to someone without a sufficient interest to claim for trespass, eg the family member of a tenant or a licensee without exclusive possession. The same loss cannot, however, give rise to two sets of damages so that, eg, a child is unlikely to be entitled to a separate award of damages under Article 8 if his or her parents have successfully claimed.[176]

166 HRA 1998 s6(3)(b). Eg, termination of social housing in *R (Weaver) v London & Quadrant Housing Trust* [2009] EWCA Civ 587, [2010] 1 WLR 363, [2009] HLR 40.

167 HRA 1998 s6(3)(b), (5).

168 *Marcic v Thames Water Utilities Ltd* [2003] UKHL 66, [2004] 2 AC 42.

169 *James v London Electricity Plc* [2004] EWHC 3226 (QB).

170 Now, private registered provider of social housing (in England), see Housing and Regeneration Act 2008 s80.

171 *R (Weaver) v London & Quadrant Housing Trust* [2009] EWCA Civ 587, [2010] 1 WLR 363, [2009] HLR 40.

172 *McDonald v McDonald* [2016] UKSC 28, [2016] 3 WLR 45, [2016] HLR 28.

173 *R (CN) v Lewisham LBC* [2014] UKSC 62, [2015] AC 1259, [2015] HLR 6.

174 *Dobson v Thames Water Utilities Ltd* [2009] EWCA Civ 28, [2010] HLR 9.

175 *R (Greenfield) v Secretary of State for the Home Department* [2005] UKHL 14, [2005] 1 WLR 673. See also *D v Commissioner of Police of the Metropolis* [2014] EWHC 2493 (QB), [2015] 1 WLR 1833, for the approach to quantifying damages under HRA 1998.

176 *Dobson v Thames Water Utilities Ltd* [2009] EWCA Civ 28, [2010] HLR 9.

Caravan Sites Act 1968 / Mobile Homes (Wales) Act 2013

1.103 CSA 1968 Part 1 and the MH(W)A 2013 Part 3 make provision for the protection from eviction for occupiers of mobile homes, ie any structure designed or adapted for human habitation which is capable of being moved from one place to another (whether by being towed, or by being transported on a motor vehicle or trailer) and any motor vehicle so designed or adapted excluding (a) any railway rolling stock which is for the time being on rails forming part of a railway system, or (b) any tent.[177] The provisions apply to an occupier of a mobile home who has a 'residential contract', which is any licence or contract under which a person is entitled either to station a mobile home on a protected site and occupy it as his or her residence, or to occupy as his or her residence a mobile home stationed on the site.[178] The protection is accordingly given both to a mobile home owner who only rents his or her pitch and to an occupier who rents both pitch and mobile home.

1.104 An occupier under a residential contract is given similar protection to that of a residential occupier under PEA 1977 s3 (see paras 1.51–1.75): he or she can only be evicted by court order.[179] Where a residential contract (see para 1.103) permits termination by notice to quit by either party, the notice must be given at least four weeks before the date on which it is to take effect.[180] Unlike under PEA 1977 s5, however, the notice need not be in writing nor contain prescribed information. In England, as under PEA 1977, the perpetrator of an unlawful eviction is liable to damages and an injunction in civil proceedings (paras 1.105–1.167) and to criminal proceedings (paras 1.197–1.256).[181] In Wales, it is unclear whether a breach of MH(W)A 2013 s42 gives rise to liability in civil proceedings as the section does not expressly refer to the right to bring civil proceedings.

---

177 CSA 1968 s16(1); MH(W)A 2013 s60(1).
178 CSA 1968 s1(1); MH(W)A 2013 s40.
179 CSA 1968 ss3(1)(b) and 5; MH(W)A 2013 s42(3).
180 CSA 1968 s2; MH(W)A 2013 s41).
181 CSA 1968 s3(3). Section 3(3) is expressed to be 'without prejudice to any liability or remedy to which [the perpetrator] may be subject in civil proceedings'.

Civil remedies

1.105   There are two civil remedies available to a person who has been unlawfully evicted:

a) an injunction (whether interim or final); and
b) damages.

There is no reason why the court may not award damages and injunction together.[182]

Injunctions

1.106   An injunction is an order of the court requiring someone to do or refrain from doing something, for example, re-admit an evicted occupier. There is no need to prove damage to get an injunction or to await the unlawful act. For example, if a landlord has warned tenants that they will be thrown out of the premises if they do not leave by a certain date, an application can be made to prevent the landlord from carrying out the unlawful eviction.

1.107   An injunction is a discretionary remedy. Nonetheless, where a contract contains covenants that prohibit one of the parties from doing something, eg from breaching a tenant's right to quiet enjoyment, the court will normally grant an injunction prohibiting one party from breaching that to which they have agreed, as a matter of course. The fact that damages would be an adequate remedy is not generally a relevant consideration where the injunction restrains the breach of a covenant not to do something.[183]

1.108   A court will, however, generally refuse to grant a mandatory order where the interference with the claimant's legal rights is small, can be quantified in money, where damages would provide an adequate remedy and where it would be oppressive to grant the injunction.[184] Damages, in the context of an unlawful eviction, are, however, unlikely to provide an adequate remedy where the loss of the occupier's home is at stake and will very rarely prove a bar to an evicted occupier obtaining an injunction requiring his or her re-admission.

---

182 *Raymond v Young* [2015] EWCA Civ 456, [2015] HLR 41.

183 *Araci v Fallon* [2011] EWCA Civ 668, [2011] LLR 440, at [70].

184 *Shelfer v City of London Electric Lighting Co Ltd (No 1)* [1895] 1 Ch 287, CA, per AL Smith LJ at 322–323. While the four-stage test in *Shelfer* has been applied more widely, it was a case concerning nuisance. In that context, the Supreme Court has said that the four-stage test should not be applied as a fetter on the court's discretion to grant an injunction: *Lawrence v Coventry* [2014] UKSC 13, [2014] AC 822, [2014] HLR 21.

Interim and final injunctions

1.109   Injunctions are either final or interim.

1.110   A final injunction is awarded at the end of a trial when the factual disputes between the parties have been resolved. The trial may not take place for some months after the commencement of proceedings and the prospect of a final injunction is of little assistance to someone locked out of his or her home who is sleeping rough or staying with friends. In such circumstances, the victim may apply for an interim injunction at the commencement of proceedings or exceptionally before proceedings have even been issued.[185]

1.111   In deciding whether to grant an interim injunction, the court does not attempt to resolve the dispute between the parties. Rather, the applicant must show that:

- there is a serious dispute between the parties;
- damages would not be an adequate remedy for the applicant; and
- the balance of justice between the parties is in favour of granting the injunction and restoring or maintaining the status quo for the time being.[186]

1.112   If, on the application for an interim injunction, the defendant accepts the applicant's version of events – which is not unknown[187] – there is no serious issue between the parties and no issue of the balance of justice arises. The court should therefore grant the injunction re-admitting the occupier or restraining the eviction and give directions for how the rest of the case should proceed (assuming that damages are still being claimed).[188] In other circumstances, the applicant does not have to show that the claim is a strong one in order to show that there is a serious dispute, merely that the facts asserted disclose that

---

185   CPR 25.2(1)(a).

186   The leading case is *American Cyanamid Co v Ethicon Ltd* [1975] AC 396, CA, in which the House of Lords referred to maintaining the 'balance of convenience' pending the trial. In *Francome v Mirror Group Newspapers* [1984] 1 WLR 892, CA, Sir John Donaldson MR held that it was more appropriate to refer to the 'balance of justice'. In *Nottingham Building Society v Eurodynamics Systems* [1993] FSR 468, ChD, Chadwick J said that this involved considering what course would involve the least risk of injustice if after a trial it transpired that the granting of an interim order had been wrong.

187   The landlord may not have appreciated that the conduct was unlawful; or he or she may admit it anyway, claiming that he or she was 'provoked' (not uncommonly by reference to rent arrears).

188   *Love v Herrity* (1990) 23 HLR 217, CA.

there is a cause of action recognised by the law, ie one of the grounds for proceedings described above.

1.113   Most applications for interim injunctions therefore turn on the question of the balance of justice between the parties. The basic principle in deciding at the interim stage whether granting or withholding an injunction is more likely to produce a just result is that the court should take whichever course seems likely to cause the least irremediable prejudice to one party or the other.[189] In the majority of unlawful eviction cases, where an applicant is seeking an injunction which prevents his or her landlord from evicting him or her, the balance of justice will be heavily in favour of maintaining the status quo, which means allowing the occupier peacefully to remain in the premises in question, enjoying all the normal facilities.[190] Obtaining such an injunction is therefore not difficult.

1.114   Where the occupier has already been evicted, he or she will want a mandatory order which requires the landlord to re-admit him or her to the home. While courts should not ordinarily grant a mandatory injunction on an interim basis unless it has a high degree of assurance that the applicant will succeed at trial, this does not apply where the refusal to make the order would carry a greater risk of injustice.[191] Thus, the balance is likely to favour the interests of a person who will be homeless against the interests of the landlord, who will in any event be able to continue to charge rent to the occupier pending the outcome of the trial.[192]

1.115   The applicant is usually required to give an undertaking to pay damages to the person who is to be subject to the interim injunction, to guard against a decision at trial that there had been no right to the injunction. This could create difficulties for applicants with limited funds but an interim injunction should not be withheld merely because a publicly-funded client cannot give a worthwhile

---

189 *National Commercial Bank Jamaica Ltd v Olint Corpn Ltd* [2009] UKPC 16, [2009] 1 WLR 1405.

190 For the same reason, the balance of justice will normally be in favour of an interim injunction in harassment cases too, see chapter 2.

191 *Nottingham Building Society v Eurodynamics Systems* [1993] FSR 468, Ch D. See also *National Commercial Bank Jamaica Ltd v Olint Corpn Ltd* [2009] UKPC 16, [2009] 1 WLR 1405, where it was said that arguments over whether an injunction should be classified as prohibitive or mandatory are barren: what matters is what the practical consequences of the injunction are likely to be.

192 In *Handley v Halsall* 1978 *LAG Bulletin* 189, the Court of Appeal was extremely critical of a county court judge who had failed to exercise his discretion to issue an injunction in an unlawful eviction case.

undertaking[193] and in most unlawful eviction cases any undertaking should be no more than to pay the rent owed under the tenancy agreement.

New occupier

1.116 The most commonly encountered difficulty which may prevent the grant of both an interim and final injunction in unlawful eviction cases is that the landlord has already re-let the property and is therefore unable to comply with an order to re-admit the occupier without unlawfully evicting someone else.

1.117 In such circumstances, the evicted tenant whose tenancy has not ended has the right to exclusive possession of the premises including as against the new occupier. This is because the new occupier's right of occupation will either be considered void or will take effect as a tenancy[194] subject to that of the evicted tenant, ie the new tenant is treated as having taken over the landlord's interest for the duration of the tenancy so that he or she becomes the existing tenant's landlord and has no more right of possession against the evicted tenant than did the landlord.

1.118 Assuming the new occupier is a tenant, he or she will be a concurrent tenant provided that his or her tenancy granted from the landlord is for less than three years and began when he or she went into possession of the premises; otherwise, the new tenancy will be void.[195]

1.119 In *Love v Herrity*,[196] the Court of Appeal considered the appropriate procedure to follow in such cases, where the evicted occupier seeks an interim order requiring his or her re-admittance. The court should grant a declaration that the evicted occupier remains a tenant of the property and allow the parties to apply for further directions. These will depend on whether the evicted occupier wishes to be re-admitted to the property. Alternatively, the evicted tenant could bring a claim for possession against the new occupier.

---

193 *Allen v Jambo Holdings Ltd* [1980] 1 WLR 1252, CA.

194 Known as a concurrent tenancy.

195 *Sheffield CC v Wall (by her personal representatives)* [2010] EWCA Civ 922, [2011] 1 WLR 1342, [2010] HLR 47; *Haringey LBC v Ahmed* [2016] EWHC 1257 (Ch). A tenancy of more than three years or one that does not take effect in possession will be void because it would have to have been granted by deed: Law of Property Act 1925 s54(2).

196 (1990) 23 HLR 217, CA.

Damages

1.120   There are five different types of damages which can arise in cases of unlawful eviction. The most common are *special* and *general* damages. In addition, there are *aggravated* damages and *exemplary* damages (not available for breach of contract). If the facts justify it, a person may claim under all heads of damages in one action. In the case of trespass to land, which does not require the claimant to establish that any loss has occurred,[197] the claimant may only be awarded *nominal* damages. All of these are categories of damages developed by the common law. In unlawful eviction cases, damages for breach of HA 1988 s27 may be awarded. These have their own particular basis of calculation under HA 1988 s28 and as such are considered under their own heading (see paras 1.168–1.191). Brief accounts of cases on damages for illegal eviction (and harassment) – both higher court cases which lay down principles and county court cases which illustrate their operation – are to be found in appendix A.

1.121   Before addressing each of these categories, it is necessary to understand some of the basic principles on which damages are awarded. The principles are different in respect of claims for breach of contract and claims for the other causes of action (known as torts).

General principles

Breach of contract

1.122   When two people enter into a contractual arrangement, they do so in order to put themselves in a better position than they were before it was made. Each wants something from the other; that is the basis of the exchange. In general, therefore, when there is a breach of contract the law will attempt to put the party who has suffered in the position he or she would have been in had the contract been properly fulfilled.[198]

Tort

1.123   An action for tort arises because one person has done to another something which the law considers ought not to have been done, not being a breach of contract. The action is – and the damages are – therefore intended to restore the party who has suffered loss to the position he or she would have been in had the tort complained of

197 See para 1.78.
198 *Robinson v Harman* (1848) 1 Ex 850.

not taken place.[199] In addition, however, the claimant in an action in tort may be able to recover other types of damages such as exemplary damages, for example, where the tort was committed deliberately anticipating that any award of damages would be less than the gain to be made by the unlawful action.[200]

1.124   In cases of trespass, damages may also be assessed by reference to the benefit received by the trespasser.[201] Accordingly, an evicted tenant may recover in damages the profit the landlord has derived from taking possession unlawfully, eg re-letting the premises, or the benefit of selling with vacant possession.

Mitigation of loss

1.125   Whether in contract or tort, a person who has suffered damage is under a duty to mitigate the loss if it is possible to do so, ie to reduce it. For example, it is common in unlawful eviction cases for the landlord to pack up the occupier's possessions and leave them outside the property. They may have suffered some damage by the time the occupier arrives home. If the occupier has somewhere to leave them, such as with a neighbour or friend, then he or she should do so in order to mitigate the loss.

1.126   On the other hand, if the occupier has nowhere to leave them, he or she cannot be expected to stand guard over them or to carry them all around with him or her. In that case, the occupier cannot mitigate the damage and – if the possessions are lost or damaged as a result of being put into the street – he or she will be entitled to damages for the full loss. It has been held in the county court that the duty to mitigate does not mean that an evicted tenant has to apply for an interim injunction requiring his or her landlord to re-admit him or her to the home.[202]

Causation and remoteness of damage

1.127   A person can only claim for loss that arises directly and naturally from the conduct complained of. For example, a tenant who is forced to take time off work after an unlawful eviction would not be able to claim for loss of earnings if he or she had already booked out to take a holiday that week anyway; the unlawful eviction would not have

---

199 *Livingstone v Raywards Coal Co* (1880) 5 App Cas 25.
200 See paras 1.153–1.167.
201 *Attorney-General v Blake* [2001] 1 AC 268, HL.
202 *Garcia v Khan*, March 2005 *Legal Action* 21, Bow County Court.

been the cause of the missed work. If the holiday was lost as a result, however, he or she would be likely to be able to recover its cost.

1.128   The line can be difficult to draw. By way of further example, where occupiers have been evicted and as a result have to walk the streets through the night during a thunderstorm, they may become ill. Under the duty to mitigate, they are obliged to seek such shelter as they can afford or find. Assuming that they have taken proper steps to try to mitigate the damage but were unable to do so, the landlord will be liable for illness and time off work that follows. (Loss of earnings will constitute special damage; suffering through illness will qualify as general damages, see paras 1.139–1.147.) If the illness was caused, however, not as a natural result of walking the streets but because of a car accident or an assault (by someone unconnected with the landlord and the circumstances of the eviction), the damage suffered will not be recoverable as it was not directly caused by the eviction.[203]

1.129   A claimant is not, however, necessarily entitled to recover all of his or her loss even if he or she can show that it has been caused directly by the unlawful eviction or harassment. The type of losses that will be recoverable will depend upon the damage that has been caused and the causes of action that are relied on.

1.130   Thus, the losses that a tenant may recover for breach of contract (eg breach of quiet enjoyment)[204] are limited to those that the landlord should have realised, when the tenancy was granted, were likely to result from a breach of the tenancy agreement.[205] Therefore, following an unlawful eviction, a tenant should be able to recover the expense of staying in bed and breakfast accommodation because the landlord ought to have realised that by evicting the tenant, he or she would be likely to incur the expense of staying in alternative accommodation.

1.131   In the case of some torts, a person will be able to claim all of his or her losses that have been caused by the harassment or unlawful eviction; in others, he or she will only be able to claim for losses that were reasonably foreseeable.

203 Even this may be too absolute a proposition. If the eviction itself was late at night, and in a particularly dangerous area, might harm to a vulnerable person not be considered the direct consequence?

204 See paras 1.8–1.11.

205 *Czarnikow v Koufos, The Heron II* [1969] 1 AC 350, HL.

1.132   In the torts of trespass to goods (where the taking of goods has been committed honestly)[206] and possibly trespass to land,[207] a person will only be able to recover losses arising from damage that was reasonably foreseeable.[208] Thus, where a landlord has unlawfully evicted a tenant, and accordingly trespassed on the tenant's land, the tenant would be able to recover damages for the shock, anxiety and inconvenience caused by the eviction because it would have been obvious that this would be the result of it.[209] The tenant would, however, be unlikely to obtain damages for the loss of a lucrative business contract he or she failed to take up because he or she was distressed by the eviction.

1.133   In other torts, on the other hand – such as deceit,[210] and trespass to goods[211] (where the tort was committed intentionally)[212] – the person would be able to claim damages for the loss of a lucrative business contract if it could be shown that it arose directly and naturally from the unlawful act.

1.134   In *Kuwait Airways Corp v Iraqi Airways Co*,[213] the House of Lords drew a distinction between someone who dishonestly converts another's goods and someone who does so innocently. Both are liable in damages, but the person acting dishonestly (ie who knows the goods are not his or hers) is liable for all loss that flows directly and naturally from taking another's possessions, while the person who does so innocently (ie is unaware that the goods belong to someone else) is only liable for the loss that was reasonably foreseeable.[214]

1.135   It is arguable that this distinction should apply equally to other torts, which may be committed either honestly or otherwise; this is worth considering as, in many cases of unlawful eviction and harassment, the conduct is likely to be dishonest in this sense.

---

206 *Kuwait Airways Corp v Iraqi Airways Co* [2002] UKHL 19, [2002] 2 AC 883.

207 The editors of *McGregor on Damages* (Sweet & Maxwell, 19th edn, 2014) at para 37-066, take the view that the principles that apply to trespass to goods are likely to apply equally to a trespass to land.

208 The same may be true of nuisance (*Cambridge Water Co v Eastern Counties Leather plc* [1994] 2 AC 264, HL), although that will only be relevant if at all in a case of harassment, ie it is not one of the causes of action identified above as of use in relation to unlawful eviction.

209 See, for example, *Drane v Evangelou* [1978] 1 WLR 455, CA, and paras 1.150–1.152.

210 *Clark v Urquhat* [1930] AC 28, HL.

211 *Kuwait Airways Corp v Iraqi Airways Co* [2002] UKHL 19, [2002] 2 AC 883.

212 *Kuwait Airways Corp v Iraqi Airways Co* [2002] UKHL 19, [2002] 2 AC 883.

213 [2002] UKHL 19, [2002] 2 AC 883.

214 [2002] UKHL 19, [2002] 2 AC 883 at [103]–[104].

Uplift

1.136   Defendants' advisers should be aware of the benefits of making an offer to settle in accordance with CPR Part 36 in an appropriate case.[215] One particular benefit of note is that, if a claimant obtains a judgment that is at least as advantageous to him or her as the Part 36 offer, the court must, unless it considers it unjust to do so, award the claimant an 'additional amount'.[216] The 'additional amount' is ten per cent of the amount awarded by the court.[217]

Interest

1.137   The court has power to award interest on any damages recovered by the claimant.[218] Interest is usually only awarded on special damages rather than on non-pecuniary losses, such as aggravated damages, exemplary damages or general damages,[219] unless they are general damages for pain, suffering and loss of amenity in a personal injury claim, in which case interest is fixed at two per cent per annum.[220] Interest cannot be awarded on damages under HA 1988 s28.[221] The right to interest runs from the date on which the cause of action arises.[222]

Compensation in criminal proceedings

1.138   Where compensation in criminal proceedings is awarded (see paras 9.28–9.35), the amount must be deducted from any damages subsequently awarded in civil proceedings.[223]

215 Ie a written offer which states that it is a Part 36 offer and gives the other party a period of 21 days, or a shorter period if the offer is made less than 21 days before the start of the trial, to accept the offer and that the result of such acceptance will mean that the defendant is liable to pay the claimant's costs.

216 CPR 36.17(1)(b), (4)(d).

217 Ten per cent applies to the first £500,000 awarded by the court; above that level a five per cent uplift applies, subject to a maximum additional amount of £75,000: CPR 36.17(4)(d). Where the court makes no monetary award, the ten per cent uplift is applied to the sum awarded to the claimant in respect of costs.

218 County Courts Act (CCA) 1984 s69; the rate of interest is within the discretion of the court, but is routinely awarded as eight per cent.

219 *Saunders v Edwards* [1987] 1 WLR 1116, CA.

220 *Birkett v Hayes* [1982] 1 WLR 816, CA.

221 *Jones v Miah* (1992) 24 HLR 578, CA.

222 CCA 1984 s69(1)(a).

223 Powers of Criminal Courts (Sentencing) Act 2000 s134.

Types of damages

Special damages

1.139 Special damages are designed to compensate for any identifiable and quantified loss. The critical element is that the loss is quantifiable in money terms. For example, the cost of alternative accommodation or the cost of replacing lost possessions can be quantified. The loss of enjoyment resulting from being deprived of the use of a possession, however, cannot (but may be compensated within general damages, see paras 1.144–1.147).

1.140 Where the loss of or damage to property is the subject of the claim, there are two issues that the occupier must be able to address: the existence of the goods and their value. The landlord may argue that items claimed were not in the premises when the eviction took place and/or that the value placed on them by the claimant is grossly inflated. Evidence from friends or neighbours may assist in establishing what the claimant owned. Proving the value of items can often be difficult, although in *Ayari v Jetha*,[224] the Court of Appeal refused to interfere with an award of £11,500 special damages, some of the value of which was proved with duplicate receipts.

1.141 It is the market value of the item lost, as at the date it was taken, which is recoverable, not its purchase price, so that the damages awarded reflect any decrease or increases since purchase.[225] The cost of buying replacements will be a guide to value, but those figures will be reduced to reflect the actual value of the items or the element of 'betterment' which has crept in, even though the occupier might well not have wished to replace an item, or might have been unable to afford to do so (although this, too, may be compensated for by way of general damages). Nor does it matter whether or not the claimant paid for the item: for example, if the occupier loses a watch which was a family heirloom, the measure of damages will be the cost of buying a replacement.

1.142 Where an item lost was used by the occupier for the purposes of a trade, the loss of business resulting is also claimable[226] as will be the cost of hiring new tools at the market rate. The cost of emergency accommodation may be claimed as a quantifiable item; so also the additional cost of eating in restaurants or cafés over and above the cost of preparing one's own food. Note, however, that only the

---

224 (1991) 24 HLR 639, CA.

225 *Liesbosch Dredger v SS Edison* [1933] AC 449, HL.

226 In *Bodley v Reynolds* (1846) 8 QB 779, a carpenter whose tools were taken obtained the value of the tools and a sum for lost work.

additional cost can be claimed, regardless of whether the claim is in contract or tort, so that, for example, what it would have cost to buy and prepare one's own food has to be deducted.

1.143   The court will only award reasonable, proper and necessary expenditure: the cost of relatively cheap bed and breakfast accommodation will be recoverable but the cost of staying in an expensive hotel will not. The court will, however, take into account the emergency nature of the situation. If an occupier returns home late at night to find that he or she has been evicted, and it is not possible to contact friends or relatives, it may very well be difficult for him or her to find cheap accommodation and the only option may be to stay somewhere expensive. The court may well allow the full cost of the first night, but if the occupier then makes no effort to find somewhere cheaper for the following nights, it will not allow the full cost of those later nights. As with all these issues, however, the key question is what is reasonable: just as an occupier evicted from cheap accommodation cannot expect to be accommodated while out of occupation in markedly superior property, so also would it not be reasonable to expect an occupier evicted from high quality or costly accommodation, used to a particularly good standard, to go and stay in a run-down bed and breakfast just because it is cheaper.

General damages

1.144   General damages are unquantified damages. They can be claimed for, among other things, harm, discomfort, loss of enjoyment, pain and suffering, shock, physical injury and inconvenience. They are, therefore, particularly apt for cases of unlawful eviction. As a general rule, however, such damages are only recoverable in tort and not in contract, save where the purpose of the contract is to provide pleasure, relaxation, peace of mind or freedom from molestation.[227] As the purpose of the covenant for quiet enjoyment is not to provide pleasure, general damages for loss of enjoyment, discomfort and physical injury are not recoverable.[228] It is, therefore, important that, depending on the facts of each case, a tort is, if available, pleaded, ie trespass to land and goods, deceit, conspiracy, misfeasance in public office or breach of PEA 1977,[229] as the level of damages otherwise available to the claimant will be reduced. From 1 April 2013, the proper approach to the assessment of general damages in, inter alia, nuisance and 'all

---

227 *Watts v Morrow* [1991] 1 WLR 1421, (1991) 23 HLR 608, CA.

228 *Branchett v Beaney* (1992) 24 HLR 348, CA.

229 See paras 1.51–1.86.

other torts which cause suffering, inconvenience or distress to individuals' is to reach a view as to what they should be and then increase that sum by ten per cent.[230]

1.145 In unlawful eviction claims, general damages may be awarded for the pain and suffering of the unlawful eviction, any harassment leading up to the eviction and for the resulting loss of occupancy. Courts now commonly award a 'daily rate' to compensate the tenant for the time spent staying in accommodation inferior to that from which he or she was evicted.[231] Where the tenant was fully assured or Rent Act protected, an additional award should be sought to reflect the fact that they will not be able to obtain alternative accommodation with the same security of tenure.[232] When assessing damages, county court judges are usually assisted by considering the levels of damages awarded in other cases; advisers will also be assisted when quantifying claims by considering other similar cases. Summaries of damages cases can be found in appendix A.

1.146 General damages overlap with HA 1988 s28 (see paras 1.168–1.191), which are damages explicitly calculated with reference to the effect of the occupier's interest on the value of the premises. Where such statutory damages are awarded, the occupier will not also be able to recover general damages for loss of occupancy.[233] As, however, assured shorthold tenants will not ordinarily be able to claim substantive damages under HA 1988,[234] general damages may well produce a higher level of compensation for loss of occupancy. General damages should, in any event, always be sought in the alternative, to guard against a failure of the HA 1988 claim.

1.147 Where general damages are claimed for personal injury, the court should assess the quantum of damage with reference to the *Judicial College: Guidelines for the assessment of general damages in personal injury claims.*[235]

---

230 *Simmons v Castle* [2012] EWCA Civ 1039, [2012] EWCA Civ 1288, [2013] 1 WLR 1239. This reflected that it was no longer possible to recover by way of costs an uplift for success within a conditional fee agreement.

231 See, for example, *Daramy v Streeks* June 2007 *Legal Action* 37, Lambeth County Court (para A14).

232 See, for example, *Mafo v Adams* [1970] 1 QB 548 and *Grillo v Cant and Bassairi Ltd* March 1998 *Legal Action* 13, Central London CC.

233 HA 1988 s27(5); see paras 1.192–1.195.

234 See para 1.173.

235 Oxford University Press, 13th revised edn, 2015.

Aggravated damages

1.148   Aggravated damages are awarded to compensate the claimant for injury to his or her feelings of dignity and pride and for aggravation generally.[236] They cannot be awarded for breach of contract.[237] Awards for aggravated damages have been made, however, for the torts of assault, trespass to land and deceit.[238] Where available, therefore, advisers should ensure that the claim includes one of these causes of action.

1.149   Awards are commonly made in cases involving the use or threat of violence, or where the victim has been particularly demeaned, for example, in cases involving sexual or racial abuse. In unlawful eviction cases, aggravated damages are regularly awarded to reflect the suffering of an occupier who finds him or herself locked out on the street with his or her belongings packed up.

1.150   In *Drane v Evangelou*,[239] the tenant returned to his flat to find that entry to the building was barred by one of the landlord's associates. The door to his flat had been bolted on the inside and his belongings, some of which had been damaged, had been put in the back yard. The tenant and his partner were forced to store their belongings in a friend's garage and sleep on their friend's floor until they were eventually re-admitted to the flat ten weeks later. The county court judge awarded the tenant £1,000 exemplary damages.

1.151   On appeal, the level of the award was upheld not only on the basis that exemplary damages were appropriate but also on the basis that even if £1,000 for exemplary damages had been high, the tenant was in any event entitled to aggravated damages which would have justified the award.

1.152   Lawton LJ observed:[240]

> It seems to me that my task here is to look at the facts and to start by asking the question what sort of sum would it have been proper to award for aggravated damages in this case, which undoubtedly was one for aggravated damages. Counsel for the landlord at times seemed to be suggesting that this was a comparatively minor dispute between a landlord and a tenant. I emphatically dissociate myself from that. To deprive a man of a roof over his head is, in my judgment, one of the worst torts which can be committed. It causes stress, worry and

---

236 *Ramdath v Daley* (1993) 25 HLR 273, CA.
237 *Branchett v Beaney* (1992) 24 HLR 348, CA.
238 Aggravated damages are not available for all torts, eg, they cannot be awarded for negligence.
239 [1978] 1 WLR 455, CA.
240 At 461E–G.

anxiety ... I myself would not have regarded the sum awarded ... as excessive for aggravated damages.[241]

Exemplary damages

1.153 Exemplary damages are often confused with aggravated damages.[242] Aggravated damages are compensatory; they reflect the victim's suffering. Exemplary damages are punitive and are awarded to punish the defendant and to deter him or her from similar behaviour in the future. Exemplary damages cannot be awarded for breach of contract.[243] Accordingly, where available, advisers should ensure that a claim in tort is included.

1.154 The leading case of *Rookes v Barnard*[244] sets out the principles on which exemplary damages may be awarded. They may only be awarded in three circumstances:[245]

a) where they are expressly provided for by statute;

b) where there has been oppressive conduct by servants of the government; or

c) where the defendant's conduct has been calculated to make a profit which may well exceed the compensation available to the claimant.

1.155 Exemplary damages are commonly awarded under the third category in cases of unlawful eviction or harassment (see chapter 2) by a landlord, on the basis that the landlord was intending to profit from his or her unlawful actions.

1.156 The need to establish the element of calculation on the part of the landlord would at first appear to make it necessary to establish that the landlord has profited financially from the eviction. In some

---

241 Goff LJ agreed that the level of the award could be justified if aggravated damages were taken into account.

242 The confusion between aggravated and exemplary damages is illustrated in a number of cases of unlawful eviction. In *Ramdath v Daley* (1993) 25 HLR 273, the Court of Appeal quashed an award of exemplary damages but was not prepared to substitute an award for aggravated damages as they have different purposes, and the recorder had already included a sum for aggravated damages in the award of general damages. Contrast *Nwokorie v Mason* (1993) 26 HLR 60, CA, in which an inappropriate award of exemplary damages was treated as aggravated damages. In *Francis v Brown* (1997) 30 HLR 143, CA, the trial judge made awards for both aggravated and exemplary damages, but it was clear from his judgment that he had confused the two.

243 *Addis v Gramophone Co Ltd* [1909] AC 488, HL; *Guppys (Bridport) Ltd v Brookling* (1984) 14 HLR 1, CA.

244 [1964] AC 1129, HL.

245 At 1226–1227.

cases, the profit may be self-evident, for example, where the landlord redevelops the flat to sell it on a long lease or the property is re-let at a higher rent. This will obviously be the case where the evicted tenant had a protected tenancy and paid a Rent Officer determined fair rent and – after the eviction – the landlord is then able to re-let the property at a market rent. The landlord can be compelled to provide a copy of any agreement with a new occupier to show that a higher rent is now being obtained.[246]

1.157   In practice, however, it is not necessary to establish concrete financial advantages of this kind, albeit that the evicted occupier must prove that the landlord's motive was to profit in some way from his or her actions.[247] The category of damages is not confined to money-making in the strict sense but extends to cases in which the defendant is seeking to gain at the claimant's expense some property he or she wanted, which either he or she could not obtain at all or could not obtain at a price greater than he or she is willing to pay.[248] Obtaining vacant possession without resorting to the difficulty and expense of possession proceedings falls within this category.[249]

1.158   In *Cassell & Co Ltd v Broome*,[250] Lord Hailsham commented on the application of exemplary damages to harassment and eviction:

> How ... about the late Mr Rachman, who is alleged to have used hired bullies to intimidate statutory tenants by violence or threats of violence into giving up vacant possession of their residences and so placing a valuable asset in the hands of the landlord? My answer must be that if this is not a cynical calculation of profit and cold-blooded disregard of a claimant's rights, I do not know what is.[251]

1.159   The occupier's conduct is irrelevant to whether exemplary damages should be awarded. The court is only concerned with the landlord's conduct.[252]

---

246 This may be done through the process of disclosure under which the parties are obliged to allow each other the opportunity to see any documents which may be relevant to the issues between the parties: CPR Part 31.
247 *Mafo v Adams* [1970] 1 QB 548, CA.
248 *Cassell & Co Ltd v Broome* [1972] AC 1027, HL.
249 *Drane v Evangelou* [1978] 1 WLR 455, CA.
250 [1972] AC 1027, HL.
251 At 1079.
252 *McMillan v Singh* (1984) 17 HLR 120, CA, in which the fact that the tenant was in arrears was held to be irrelevant.

1.160   Likewise, the fact that the landlord may already have been fined for an offence under PEA 1977 does not prevent an award being made.[253]

1.161   The correct approach is for the court to assess the general and special damages suffered by the claimant and any aggravated damages before going on to assess the amount of any exemplary damages.[254]

1.162   The level of award is not limited to any actual profit made by the landlord[255] but the amount must be kept within reason.[256] Awards of exemplary damages are usually in the region of £1,000 to £2,500. Relevant factors include the seriousness of the conduct complained of – for example, whether violence was used or threatened – and/or the extent to which the landlord may have disregarded warnings from the police, a local authority tenancy relations or similar officer or the claimant's solicitors. Where the landlord has deliberately disobeyed an order for re-admission or has disobeyed other orders of the court relating to the conduct of the proceedings, a larger award ought to be made. It is arguable that the figures commonly awarded in the county court are unreasonably low and do not punish the landlord's unlawful conduct sufficiently.[257]

1.163   *Sufficient interest.* Although it is not necessary to show that the defendant has profited in financial terms before an award can be made, it is necessary to show that the defendant had a sufficient interest in the matter to benefit.

1.164   This can be of significance in cases where both the landlord and his or her agent have been involved. In *Ramdath v Daley*,[258] the Court of Appeal upheld the award of exemplary damages against a landlord. The property was managed by the landlord's son, who had been authorised and encouraged to throw the claimant out of the flat. On this basis, it was found that an award of exemplary damages against the landlord was justified. A separate award of exemplary damages

---

253 *Asghar v Ahmed* (1984) 17 HLR 25, CA; compare *Devonshire and Smith v Jenkins* (1978) 28 April, unreported, CA, in which the Court of Appeal decided that no exemplary damages should be awarded because of the size of the fine in that case.

254 *McMillan v Singh* (1985) 17 HLR 120, CA.

255 *McMillan v Singh* (1985) 17 HLR 120, CA.

256 In *Francis v Brown* (1997) 30 HLR 143, the Court of Appeal held that an award of £40,000 was manifestly excessive. In *Mehta v Royal Bank of Scotland* (1999) 32 HLR 45, QBD, an award of £7,500 was made.

257 See R Calzavara, 'Deterring unlawful eviction: a plea to district judges' (2015) JHL 18(4), 67–72.

258 (1993) 25 HLR 273, CA.

against the son was, however, quashed because it was not shown that he had a sufficient interest in the matter himself to benefit.

1.165   Arguably, however, exemplary damages should not have been awarded at all in that case, since, where a claim for exemplary damages is made against two or more defendants, only a single award should be made, reflecting as a matter of law the lowest figure for which any of the defendants could be held liable.[259]

1.166   Advisers need to consider this issue where a claim is proposed against both the landlord and an agent. The agent may not be profiting from the eviction and, as such, may have no sufficient interest to warrant an award of exemplary damages. By suing both landlord and agent, the occupier may therefore fail to obtain exemplary damages at all. It is perfectly proper for the occupier to sue only the landlord so that the right to exemplary damages is not lost.[260]

1.167   On the other hand, the agent may be holding on to the occupier's possessions, or have committed a serious assault on the occupier, so that the occupier's claim against the agent may be substantial. In such a case, the occupier can avoid the possibility of losing the right to exemplary damages against the landlord by commencing separate proceedings against the landlord and the agent and subsequently having the two claims heard together.[261]

Damages for breach of Housing Act 1988 s27

1.168   Damages under HA 1988 can be sizeable and often the largest element of compensation for unlawful eviction; the benefit where the evicted occupier lacks long-term security of tenure is, however, limited.

Basis of assessment

1.169   The basis of assessment of damages under HA 1988 is the difference, as at the date when the residential occupier left the premises, between the value of the landlord's interest[262] with the occupier still

---

259 *Cassell & Co Ltd v Broome* [1972] AC 1027, HL; *Francis v Brown* (1997) 30 HLR 143, CA.

260 Suing only one of the two joint tortfeasors is a course of action specifically envisaged by Lord Hailsham in *Cassell & Co Ltd v Broome* [1972] AC 1027, HL at 1063H.

261 This course of action was approved by Lord Hailsham in *Cassell & Co Ltd v Broome* [1972] AC 1027, HL.

262 It is only the interest of the landlord in default which is to be valued. Although a superior landlord can be in default, where it is an immediate landlord who is in default it is the value of the intermediate landlord's interest which is relevant: *Jones v Miah* (1992) 24 HLR 578, CA.

enjoying the right to occupy and the value of the landlord's interest without such a right.[263]

1.170 The interest of the landlord to be valued is that of the whole building in which the premises are situated, together with the curtilage[264] of the building.[265] Accordingly, where a landlord owns the whole house but the tenancy is of only a flat in it, it is the difference in the value to the house not the flat which is to be assessed.

1.171 In reaching this valuation certain assumptions must be made:

- the landlord is selling his or her interest on the open market to a willing buyer;[266]
- neither the occupier nor any member of his or her family[267] wishes to buy; and
- it is unlawful to carry out any substantial development of the land in which the landlord's interest subsists or to demolish the whole or any part of any building on that land.

1.172 The landlord's interest in the premises must be valued on the assumption that the residential occupier 'continues to have the same right to occupy' the premises as he or she had before the eviction. Accordingly, where the tenant is a secure tenant it is to be assumed that the landlord is selling his or her interest on the open market subject to the secure tenancy even though in practice the claimant's right of occupation would change[268] as a matter of law on the sale.[269]

1.173 In determining the measure of damages, the legal status of the occupier is therefore central. The greater the statutory protection from eviction, the greater the damages should be. If the occupier is a fully assured tenant, or a statutory tenant under the RA 1977, there may be a significant difference in values with and without the tenant. By contrast, the presence of an assured shorthold tenant whose tenancy

---

263 HA 1988 s28(1).

264 For instance, any garden or yard.

265 HA 1988 s28(2).

266 Where the landlord cannot sell – for example, because of a lease which prohibits assignment – the premises will still be treated as having a saleable value, although it will be assumed that the willing buyer would take a lease subject to the covenant: *Tagro v Cafane* (1991) 23 HLR 250, CA.

267 As defined by HA 1985 s113, ie spouse, civil partner, couple living together as spouse or civil partner, parent, grandparent, child, grandchild, brother, sister, uncle, aunt, nephew or niece.

268 Ie to an assured tenancy: HA 1988 s38.

269 *Lambeth LBC v Loveridge* [2014] UKSC 65, [2014] 1 WLR 4516, [2015] HLR 12. In *Loveridge*, the Supreme Court invited parliament to consider the application of HA 1988 ss27 and 28 to local authorities.

is at a market rent is unlikely to have any – or any real – effect on the value of the property.[270] Similarly, the eviction of a tenant who has only a few days of the tenancy remaining[271] or whose joint tenancy is precarious because the other joint tenant is likely to serve a notice to quit,[272] is unlikely to lead to any significant difference in value.

1.174   The fact that almost all new tenancies in the private sector are assured shorthold tenancies has greatly reduced the number of cases in which damages under HA 1988 s28 are likely to be available or, at any rate, substantial; general and aggravated damages,[273] perhaps backed by exemplary damages (which are not confined by the actual profit),[274] are likely to result in a greater award of damages.

1.175   Where the tenancy was created before 28 February 1997, advisers should check whether the formal requirements were complied with, as what may appear from the tenancy agreement to be an assured shorthold tenancy may in law be fully assured. Even if the tenancy was created after 28 February 1997, there are circumstances in which the tenancy may nonetheless be a fully assured tenancy, and – again – an adviser should always check.[275]

1.176   Even where the occupier's rights of occupation is limited, however, advisers should not necessarily rule out the possibility of a claim under HA 1988 ss27 and 28, for, in the particular circumstances, a valuer may still find that there is a significant difference in value. For example, HA 1988 ss27 and 28 may assist a former occupier if a particularly high price is available during a window of time too short for the landlord lawfully to evict and effect a sale, so that there has been a substantive increase by virtue of evicting without awaiting expiry of tenancy and/or

---

270 See *Melville v Bruton* (1996) 29 HLR 319, CA, in which an award of £15,000 under HA 1988 s28 was quashed and substituted with an award of £500 in general damages. In that case, the valuers had failed to address the tenant's status in their reports.

271 *King v Jackson* (1997) 30 HLR 541, CA, in which the tenant was evicted a few days before the expiry of her notice to quit.

272 *Wandsworth LBC v Osei Bonsu* [1999] 1 WLR 1011, (1999) 31 HLR 515, CA: the Court of Appeal accepted the authority's argument that a joint tenancy was clearly precarious because the claimant joint tenant's wife was anxious to serve a notice to quit at the relevant time so as to obtain new accommodation from the local authority. The Court of Appeal held that an appropriate award of damages would have been £2,000 (had it not been bound by a concession made in the court below).

273 See paras 1.144–1.152.

274 See paras 1.153–1.167.

275 See *Manual of Housing Law*, para 1.248.

court proceedings.[276] It is, however, the open market value which is in issue, not circumstances peculiar to the landlord, ie the circumstances giving rise to the temporary increase in value would have to be of a general order rather than peculiar to the landlord in question.

1.177 As it is the landlord's interest in the whole building which must be valued, not just the part of the building let to the occupier, the valuation must take into account the presence of any other residential occupiers in the building.[277]

1.178 This has the greatest effect in buildings let out as bedsitting-rooms. Where the remainder of the house remains let out at the time of the eviction, the eviction of one occupier may make little if any difference to the value of the property as a whole, because all the landlord can do with the vacancy is to re-let the room. As many unlawful eviction cases concern occupiers of bedsitting-rooms, this is also a substantial restriction on the effective application of HA 1988 ss27 and 28.

Expert evidence

1.179 The level of HA 1988 s28 damages turns on expert evidence, although some of the reported cases illustrate how difficult it can be to reach a valuation in such cases.[278]

1.180 In providing the report, the expert's overriding duty is to help the court on matters within his or her expertise; this duty overrides any obligation to the dispossessed occupier.[279] The valuer may have to provide a number of different valuations reflecting different versions of the facts put forward by the parties, for example, where the occupier claims to be an assured tenant but the landlord claims that only an assured shorthold tenancy was granted, or the tenancy was subject to the mandatory ground for possession available to a returning home owner.[280]

---

276 See *Nwokorie v Mason* (1993) 26 HLR 60, CA, in which the Court of Appeal refused to interfere with an award of £4,500 under HA 1988 s28. The judge had preferred the valuation of the occupier's surveyor, even though the landlord's valuer had found that there would be no difference in value. The occupier had a very limited interest as the defendant was a resident landlord. The valuation took into account the 28 days' notice to quit required, and the time it would have taken for a possession action to come before the court. The case was decided before *Melville v Bruton* (1996) 29 HLR 319, CA, but in principle remains correct. Compare, too, the surprisingly high award given to a licensee in *Mehta v Royal Bank of Scotland* (2000) 32 HLR 45, QBD.

277 *Melville v Bruton* (1996) 29 HLR 319, CA.

278 See, eg, *Jones v Miah* (1992) 24 HLR 578, CA; *Nwokorie v Mason* (1993) 26 HLR 60, CA; *Melville v Bruton* (1996) 29 HLR 319, CA.

279 CPR 35.3.

280 Under HA 1988 Sch 2 Ground 1.

1.181   Expert reports must comply with CPR Part 35 and the practice direction made under it. The report must be addressed to the court[281] and must:[282]

- give details of the expert's qualifications;
- give details of any literature or other materials on which the expert has relied in making the report – for example, details of comparable properties or citations from textbooks;
- where there is a range of opinion on the matters dealt with in the report, summarise that range and give reasons for the expert's own opinion;
- contain a summary of the conclusions reached;
- contain a statement that the expert understands his or her duty to the court and has complied with that duty;
- contain a statement setting out the substance of all material instructions, summarising the facts which are material to the opinions expressed in the report; and
- be verified by a statement of truth.[283]

Reduction of damages

1.182   Damages under HA 1988 s28 may be reduced in two circumstances:

   a) first, on account of the conduct of the former residential occupier or someone living with him or her before the event which gave rise to the liability, eg before eviction; or
   b) second, if the landlord offers reinstatement[284] and it would be (or, if he or she had obtained alternative accommodation before the offer was made, it would have been) unreasonable for the occupier to refuse to accept.[285]

1.183   A landlord who wishes to rely on HA 1988 s27(7) must plead the facts relied on in the defence.[286] Where a landlord neither does so nor makes submissions to that effect at trial, a court is not required to consider, of its own motion, whether damages should be reduced.[287]

1.184   *Residential occupier's conduct.* Mitigation of damages on account of the occupier's conduct before the act giving rise to the liability was

---

281 CPR Part 35 PD 3.1.
282 CPR Part 35 PD 3.2.
283 CPR Part 35 PD 3.3.
284 See paras 1.94–1.96 as to what is meant by reinstatement.
285 HA 1988 s27(7).
286 *Regalgrand v Dickerson* (1996) 29 HLR 620, CA.
287 *Kalas v Farmer* [2010] EWCA Civ 108, [2010] HLR 25.

considered in *Regalgrand v Dickerson*.[288] 'Conduct' means behaviour and is not limited to serious acts. The conduct complained of does not have to be a positive act; it may be a failure to do something. Accordingly, failure to pay rent may justify a reduction in damages, even where the landlord successfully counterclaims for the arrears.

1.185   It is for the court to decide in all the circumstances of the case whether or not it is reasonable to reduce the damages. If it decides that it is, it must go on to decide the extent of the reduction, although where there is a number of factors to be taken into account it does not have to apportion the amount deducted to each act or omission. In *Regalgrand*, the Court of Appeal upheld the judge's decision to reduce the award of damages from £12,000 to £1,500 because the tenants were in arrears of rent and had already decided to leave the property within a short time.

1.186   In *Wandsworth LBC v Osei Bonsu*,[289] the claimant and his wife were joint tenants of a local authority house. The wife fled from the house with their children because of domestic violence. At the authority's suggestion, she served a notice to quit to determine the tenancy. That notice was invalid because it did not give 28 days' notice.[290] Meanwhile, the claimant had been excluded from the house because his wife had obtained an ouster injunction. The authority treated the notice to quit as valid so that, when the claimant asked to be let back into the house once the ouster injunction had been discharged, it refused him re-admission.

1.187   In the county court, the claimant was awarded £30,000 under HA 1988 s28 (by way of a concession as to difference in values). The Court of Appeal, however, held that the husband's conduct was relevant to the level of damages. His violence towards his wife broke up the family and by way of the ouster injunction and the notice to quit led the authority to seek possession with a view to rehousing the wife and the children. The eviction was the culmination of an unbroken chain of events starting with the husband's conduct. The damages were reduced to £10,000.

1.188   The statutory limitation on conduct prior to the act giving rise to the liability means that subsequent conduct, however provocative, cannot affect the level of damages, save so far as it goes to the issue of reinstatement.

288 (1996) 29 HLR 620, CA.
289 [1999] 1 WLR 1011, (1999) 31 HLR 515, CA.
290 See para 1.31.

1.189   *Reinstatement.* As mitigation of damages on account of reinstatement is only available if an offer for reinstatement is (or would have been) unreasonably refused,[291] HA 1988 s27(7)(b) necessarily accepts that sufficiently bad conduct by the landlord will justify (or would have justified) a decision not to return to the property, eg, where the tenant could not reasonably be expected to go back to the location of the events.

1.190   The reference to the possibility of mitigation of damages even once the occupier has found alternative accommodation seems to have been directed to the occupier who has already taken (inferior) alternative accommodation (which he or she could give up in order to return) rather than opening up the possibility of an offer being made safe in the knowledge that the occupier has found somewhere else (suitable) so that he or she is unlikely to return.

1.191   Note that, in order to qualify, an offer must have been made before the occupier commences legal proceedings.[292]

Relationship with common law damages

1.192   HA 1988 s27(4) and (5) make clear that liability under HA 1988 s27 is in addition to any other liability which might arise. Damages may not, however, be awarded twice for the same loss.

1.193   Where an award is made under HA 1988 s28, the tenant is not entitled to any additional award for loss of occupation which may arise under another cause of action, for example, breach of contract, for the loss of the right of occupation.[293]

1.194   It is, however, only the damages relating to the loss of occupation which are set off in this way, not any damages for conversion of goods or physical injury. Likewise, while general or aggravated damages attributable to the loss of right of occupation will be set off,[294] general damages for the landlord's acts of harassment prior to the eviction will not,[295] nor will aggravated damages unconnected with the right of occupation.[296]

1.195   Exemplary damages are not to be awarded in addition to statutory damages.[297]

---

291 See paras 1.94–1.96 and 1.182.

292 Meaning action under HA 1988 s27, not any other action which may be taken in relation to the case: *Tagro v Cafane* (1991) 23 HLR 250, CA.

293 HA 1988 s27(5).

294 *Nwokorie v Mason* (1993) 26 HLR 60, CA.

295 *Kaur v Gill* (1995) *Times* 15 June, CA.

296 *Francis v Brown* (1997) 30 HLR 143, CA.

297 *Nwokorie v Mason* (1993) 26 HLR 60, CA and *Francis v Brown* (1997) 30 HLR 143, CA.

Criminal offences and other sanctions

1.196   Any person who carries out an unlawful eviction, in addition to being potentially liable to a civil claim for damages and injunction, may also commit a criminal offence;[298] any landlord who commits the criminal offence may also be made subject to a rent repayment order.[299]

Breach of PEA 1977 s1

1.197   The offence under PEA 1977 s1(2) is committed by any person who unlawfully deprives, or attempts to deprive, a residential occupier of any premises, or any part thereof, of his or her occupation unless he or she proves that he or she believed, and had reasonable cause to believe, that the residential occupier had ceased to reside in the premises. Accordingly, the offence may be committed by someone who is not the occupier's landlord.

1.198   This gives rise to a number of issues. First, who is the person responsible for carrying out the eviction. Second, whether the person evicted is a 'residential occupier'. Third, whether the residential occupier has been 'deprived of occupying premises'. Fourth, whether the deprivation was 'unlawful'. Fifth, whether the person alleged to have committed the offence believed, or had reasonable cause to believe, that the residential occupier had ceased to reside in the premises.

Any person

1.199   The offence is most likely to be committed by a landlord or a landlord's agent, but the defendant may be 'any person', regardless of relationship to the occupier. Thus, a head landlord who evicts a subtenant or a tenant's licensee commits the offence (as long as that subtenant or licensee is a residential occupier). Equally, it may be committed by, for example, a landlord's agent, a joint tenant, a co-occupier or even a neighbour. There must, however, be proof of actual participation by the person being prosecuted; a landlord cannot be vicariously liable in criminal law for the acts of others.[300]

1.200   The definition extends to other legal persons, for example, companies. Where the offence has been committed by a company any director, manager, secretary or other similar officer may – in addition

---

298 PEA 1977 s1.
299 HPA 2016 s40.
300 *Peterborough CC v Quereshi* [2011] EWCA Crim 1584, [2012] 1 WLR 694, [2011] HLR 34.

to the company itself – be prosecuted, as may be any person 'purporting to act in any such capacity'.[301]

Residential occupier

1.201   A residential occupier is:

> ... a person occupying ... premises as a residence, whether under a
> contract or by virtue of any enactment or rule of law giving him the
> right to remain in occupation or restricting the right of any other per-
> son to recover possession of the premises.[302]

1.202   There are two issues:

a) whether the premises in question are occupied 'as a residence';
and, if so,

b) whether the person has a sufficient right of occupation.

Occupation as a residence

1.203   Residence is not defined by PEA 1977, but has been held to have the
same meaning as in RA 1977.[303] The phrase 'occupying the premises as a residence' is almost identical to that used in RA 1977 when
defining a statutory tenancy[304] or when defining who is a resident
landlord.[305]

1.204   Whether an occupier is resident is a question of fact and degree.
An occupier must have a home at the premises and there must be:

> A substantial degree of regular personal occupation ... of an essen-
> tially personal nature.[306]

1.205   There is no need for constant occupation; residence is preserved
if there is both some evidence of occupation and an intention to
return.[307] Even if there is no intention to return, residence will also
be preserved by the tenant's spouse, civil partner or co-habitant with
an occupation order residing in the premises.[308] It is possible to have
more than one residence.[309]

---

301 PEA 1977 s1(6).
302 PEA 1977 s1(1).
303 *Schon v Camden LBC* (1986) 18 HLR 341, QBD.
304 RA 1977 s2(1) refers to the tenant 'occupying the dwelling house as his
residence'.
305 RA 1977 s12.
306 *Herbert v Byrne* [1964] 1 WLR 519, CA.
307 *Brown v Brash* [1948] 2 KB 247, CA.
308 *Old Gate Estates Ltd v Alexander* [1950] 1 KB 311, CA; *Wabe v Taylor* [1952] 2
QB 735, CA.
309 *Hampstead Way Investments Ltd v Lewis-Weare* [1985] 1 WLR 164, HL.

1.206   In *Uratemp Ventures Ltd v Collins*,[310] it was held that a hotel room without cooking facilities could be let as a 'dwelling'; the term was said[311] to mean more than mere 'residence', the term used in PEA 1977 s1.[312] Moreover, it is possible that transient accommodation that is not occupied as a dwelling may none the less be someone's residence.

Right of occupation

1.207   If the person is resident, the second question is whether he or she occupies:

> … under a contract, or by virtue of any enactment or rule of law, giving him the right to remain in occupation or restricting the right of any other person to recover possession.[313]

1.208   It is necessary to apply this criterion to the various types of occupation arrangement that may have been made.[314]

1.209   **Freeholders.** Freeholders are residential occupiers because they occupy under a rule of law, their ownership of the premises.

1.210   **Tenants.** Tenants occupy under contract until the tenancy comes to an end; the majority will also be able to stay on by statute until a court orders them to leave.

1.211   **Long leaseholders.** A tenant under a long lease[315] is a residential occupier while the contractual tenancy continues. When it comes to an end, whether by the landlord exercising a right of re-entry or forfeiture,[316] or on expiry of the term, the former leaseholder has a statutory right to remain and thus continues to be a residential occupier until the expiry of a possession order.[317]

1.212   **Assured tenants.** A landlord cannot bring a fully assured tenancy to an end except by obtaining and executing a court order.[318] An

---

310 [2002] 1 AC 301, (2001) 33 HLR 85, HL.

311 At [30].

312 This was approved by the Supreme Court in *R (CN) v Lewisham LBC* [2014] UKSC 62, [2015] AC 1259, [2015] HLR 6.

313 PEA 1977 s1(1).

314 See *Manual of Housing Law*, chapter 1.

315 A tenancy for a fixed term in excess of 21 years at a low rent: LTA 1954 s2. For tenancies commencing on or after 1 April 1990, see Local Government and Housing Act (LGHA) 1989 s186 and Sch 10 para 1.

316 Which cannot be exercised other than by court proceedings: PEA 1977 s2.

317 LTA 1954 s3; LGHA 1989 Sch 10 para 3(2).

318 HA 1988 s5(1); *Knowsley Housing Trust v White* [2008] UKHL 70, [2009] 1 AC 636, [2009] HLR 17. In the case of a fixed-term tenancy, a 'statutory periodic tenancy' arises automatically on expiry: HA 1988 s5(2). Note, however, that statutory protection does not apply where the tenancy is brought to an end by the tenant or by surrender, see paras 1.16–1.18 and 1.21–1.27.

assured tenant is, thus, a residential occupier (by contract) until he or she is evicted by a court order.

1.213   **Protected and statutory tenants**. A protected tenant has a right to remain until the contractual tenancy is brought to an end (for example, by notice to quit) and is, thus, a residential occupier. Thereafter and so long as he or she occupies the premises as a residence, the tenant is a statutory tenant, with a statutory right to remain unless and until an order for possession is obtained and executed.[319] A statutory tenant is, therefore, a residential occupier (by RA 1977) until he or she is evicted by a court order.

1.214   **Secure tenants.**[320] A landlord cannot bring a secure tenancy, whether it is for a fixed-term or periodic, to an end except by obtaining and executing a court order.[321] Such a tenant is, thus, a residential occupier (by contract) until he or she is evicted by a court order.

1.215   **Introductory tenants**. A landlord cannot bring an introductory tenancy to an end except by obtaining and executing a possession order.[322] An introductory tenant is therefore also a residential occupier (by contract) until he or she is evicted by a court order.

1.216   **Demoted tenants**. A landlord cannot bring a demoted tenancy to an end except by obtaining and executing a possession order.[323] A demoted tenant is likewise a residential occupier (by contract) until he or she is evicted by a court order.

1.217   **Assured agricultural occupiers**. A landlord cannot bring an assured agricultural occupancy to an end except by obtaining and executing a court order.[324] An assured agricultural occupier is a residential occupier (by contract) until he or she is evicted by a court order.

1.218   **R(A)A 1976 protected occupiers and statutory tenants**. A protected occupier has a right to remain until the contractual tenancy or licence is brought to an end (for example, by notice to quit) and is, thus, a residential occupier. Thereafter, if a statutory tenancy arises,[325] he or

---

319 RA 1977 ss2, 98 and 100.

320 Whether the tenancy is granted before or after amendments made by HPA 2016 Sch 7, pursuant to which all new secure tenancies, subject to limited exceptions, will be for fixed terms.

321 HA 1985 s82(A1), (1A).

322 HA 1996 s127(1).

323 HA 1996 s143D(1).

324 HA 1988 ss5(1), 24 and 25. In the case of a fixed-term tenancy, a 'statutory periodic tenancy' arises automatically on expiry: HA 1988 s5(2). Note, however, that statutory protection does not apply where the tenancy is brought to an end by the tenant or by surrender.

325 It arises automatically on termination of the protected occupancy: R(A)A 1976 s4, provided the landlord is not excepted, eg a local authority (see s5).

she remains a residential occupier until an order for possession is executed.[326]

1.219 **Assured shorthold tenants.** Until Part 3 of HPA 2016 is brought into force, ie the abandonment procedure (paras 1.36–1.44), a landlord cannot bring an assured shorthold tenancy to an end except by obtaining and executing a possession order.[327] Accordingly, and again unless the landlord brings the tenancy to an end by complying with the requirements of the 'abandonment notice' procedure,[328] the tenant is a residential occupier until an order for possession is executed. If the tenancy is ended by the service of an abandonment notice, the landlord may evict without committing an offence under PEA 1977 s1.[329]

1.220 **Protected shorthold tenants.** As a protected shorthold tenancy is a type of protected tenancy, the same provisions apply (para 1.213). Accordingly, a protected shorthold tenant remains a residential occupier until he or she is evicted by a court order.

1.221 **Restricted contract tenants.**[330] A restricted contract tenant is a residential occupier until he or she is evicted by a court bailiff because there is a statutory right to remain.[331]

1.222 **Unprotected tenants.**[332] An unprotected tenant is a residential occupier until a possession order is obtained and executed because there is a statutory right to remain under PEA 1977.[333]

---

326 RA 1977 ss2, 98 and 100.

327 HA 1988 ss5(1) and 21(1).

328 See paras 1.36–1.44.

329 A landlord may nonetheless commit a criminal offence under CLA 1977 s6(1) if he or she uses or threatens violence to secure entry to the premises when there is someone present on those premises that opposes the landlord entering (see paras 3.6–3.36).

330 Particular care should be taken as restricted contracts are now very unusual. In most cases they have been 'converted' into a different type of occupancy, often an excluded tenancy. Subject to limited exceptions, it has not been possible to create a restricted contract from 15 January 1989. The greater body of restricted contract tenancies were those where furniture was provided, most of which became fully protected pursuant to the Rent Act 1974, unless they had resident landlords (or the provision of attendances or board): see RA 1977 s19. This is not an exhaustive description, but it emphasises how rare these cases will be.

331 PEA 1977 s3(1) .

332 This term is used throughout this book to refer to any tenancy which is not protected by LTA 1954, R(A)A 1976, RA 1977, HA 1985, HA 1988 and LGHA 1989 nor is an excluded tenancy.

333 PEA 1977 s3(1); *Haniff v Robinson* [1993] QB 419, (1994) 26 HLR 386, CA.

1.223   **Excluded tenants**. An excluded tenant (see paras 1.61–1.72), whose tenancy began before 15 January 1989, is a residential occupier until a possession order is obtained and executed because there is a statutory right to remain under PEA 1977.[334] An excluded tenant whose tenancy was granted on or after 15 January 1989, however, is only a residential occupier up to the termination of the right to occupy (ie expiry of a notice to quit, by effluxion of time, by forfeiture or by surrender), as there is thereafter no statutory protection nor any other requirement that a court order be sought before he or she is evicted.[335]

1.224   **Licensees**. Licensees occupying premises as a dwelling are residential occupiers by contract until the termination of the licence; thereafter, those who are not excluded licensees (see paras 1.61–1.72) will remain residential occupiers until a possession order is obtained and executed, as they cannot be evicted without a court order.[336] Accordingly, a non-excluded licensee remains a residential occupier until a possession order is obtained and executed. So far as concerns excluded licensees, however, there is no statutory protection nor any other requirement that a court order be sought before he or she is evicted,[337] save in the now extremely rare case of a licensee who had a restricted contract under RA 1977 which was entered into between the commencement of HA 1980 s69,[338] and (subject to exceptions) 15 January 1989, after which few further restricted contracts could be created (see para 1.221 and n330): such a licensee is a residential occupier until a possession order is obtained and executed.[339]

1.225   **Other lawful occupiers**. The benefit of PEA 1977 s3 extends to someone lawfully residing in the premises or part of them when the tenancy or licence is terminated – eg family, friends or lodgers:

---

334   PEA 1977 s3(1) and (2C)(a). Also included within this definition are tenancies which started on or after 15 January 1989 pursuant to a contract made before that date: PEA 1977 s3(2C)(b).

335   They are specifically excluded from PEA 1977 s3(1).

336   PEA 1977 s3(1). See paras 1.51–1.75 as to the ambit of this provision.

337   PEA 1977 s3(1) and (2B). A contractual licence will end in accordance with its terms. Accordingly, a licence for a fixed term cannot be determined during the term by giving one month's notice to quit: *R v H* [2008] EWCA Crim 483. Even a bare licence requires reasonable notice (which will depend on all the circumstances) before it comes to an end.

338   28 November 1980.

339   PEA 1977 s3(1) and (2B).

see para 1.52. Accordingly, they have a statutory right to remain and qualify as residential occupiers protected by PEA 1977 s1.[340]

1.226 **Trespassers.** Some of the residential occupiers described above qualify at common law as trespassers; that is, in the context of this book, somewhat misleading and this subheading is not concerned with them. Other trespassers have neither contractual rights nor rights under the principal Acts providing statutory security of tenure to occupiers of residential accommodation.[341] Owners of property with an immediate right to possession are restricted by law in the way they secure entry to premises and may not use or threaten violence to enter residential premises[342] unless they are occupied by a displaced residential occupier or a protected intending occupier[343] (see chapter 3). Moreover, a trespasser who lives in a residential building and who entered it as a trespasser may be removed by a police officer[344] as he or she is committing a criminal offence.[345]

1.227 In general, a trespasser can only be regarded as a residential occupier if the restriction on entry imposed by the Criminal Law Act (CLA) 1977 s6(1) is interpreted as restricting the right to recover possession. This presents difficulties. There is no case-law[346] on the issue, but mere trespassers are unlikely to be regarded as residential occupiers. Given that CLA 1977 s6(1) has effect only if the trespasser is present at the time of entry to the premises, it would lead, for instance, to the anomalous position of a trespasser being a residential occupier only when he or she was physically on the premises. Furthermore, CLA

---

340 PEA 1977 s3(2). The protection also applies to anyone who had been lawfully living with a deceased statutory tenant under RA 1977 or R(A)A 1976 when the owner's right to recover arises on the death of the statutory tenant: PEA 1977 s3(3).

341 LTA 1954, R(A)A 1976, RA 1977, PEA 1977, HA 1985, HA 1988 and LGHA 1989.

342 CLA 1977 s6.

343 CLA 1977 s6(1A). A protected intending occupier is a person with a freehold interest or a leasehold interest with not less than two years to run, who requires the premises for his or her own occupation as a residence: CLA 1977 s12A.

344 Police and Criminal Evidence Act 1984 (PACE) s17(1)(c)(vi).

345 Legal Aid, Sentencing and Punishment of Offenders Act 2012 (LASPO) s144(1).

346 It is worth noting that, although the point was not argued in *R v Phekoo* [1981] 1 WLR 1117, CA, the court accepted that trespassers were not residential occupiers and held that a genuine belief that an occupier was a trespasser was a defence to a charge of harassment; nor was the point taken in *West Wiltshire DC v Snelgrove* (1997) 30 HLR 57, QBD, when the basis of the defence in *Phekoo* was considered by the court.

1977 s6(1) neither gives a trespasser a right to remain in occupation nor does it restrict the right of the owner to recover possession.[347] It merely makes violent entry unlawful and only then if the occupier opposes the entry.

1.228   A trespasser may, however, in limited circumstances, acquire a right of occupation by adverse possession. This is a difficult area of law and cannot be explored fully or properly here. Adverse possession arises where a trespasser is in possession of a property and intends to exclude everyone else from it (including the true owner of the land). The trespasser must demonstrate this intention by unequivocal acts so that if the owner visited the land, it would be clear to him or her that the trespasser intends to exclude him or her from the property.[348] In the context of residential accommodation, these conditions are satisfied if the trespasser changes the locks to the property and lives in it as his or her home.[349]

1.229   Whether or not a trespasser who is in adverse possession has a right of occupation will depend on the length of their occupation and whether or not the land is registered or unregistered.[350] If the land is unregistered, once the trespasser has been in adverse possession for 12 years, the owner's title is automatically extinguished and the trespasser becomes the owner of the property by virtue of his or her own possessory title.[351] At this point, he or she is therefore a residential occupier because he or she occupies the property under a rule of law.

1.230   If the land is registered, then as a result of the Land Registration Act (LRA) 2002, the question depends on whether the trespasser had been in adverse possession for 12 years prior to 13 October 2003 (ie the date on which the relevant provisions of the LRA 2002 came into force). If he or she had been, then he or she has a statutory right to be registered as the owner,[352] and a defence to any claim for possession.[353] Accordingly, he or she is a residential occupier because he or

---

347 The test under PEA 1977 s1(1).

348 *JA Pye (Oxford) v Graham* [2002] UKHL 30, [2003] 1 AC 419.

349 *Lambeth LBC v Blackburn* (2001) 33 HLR 74, CA.

350 Registered land is land in respect of which the title has been registered with HM Land Registry under LRA 2002 (or its predecessor, Land Registration Act 1925). Most residential land will now be registered. See further C Harpum, S Bridge and M Dixon, *Megarry & Wade: The Law of Real Property* (Sweet & Maxwell, 8th edn, 2012), chapters 7 and 8.

351 Limitation Act 1980 s17; *Tichborne v Weir* (1892) 678 LT 735, CA.

352 LRA 2002 Sch 12 para 18(1).

353 LRA 2002 Sch 12 para 18(2).

she remains in occupation due to a restriction on the right to recover possession against him or her.

1.231   If the trespasser has not been in adverse possession for 12 years before 13 October 2003, however, he or she can only become the registered owner through adverse possession in more limited circumstances. First, after ten years of adverse possession, he or she can apply to be registered as the owner.[354] The owner will be notified of the application and can ask for the application to be dealt with under LRA 2002 Sch 6 para 5.[355] If the owner does not take this option, however, and the trespasser can establish ten years' adverse possession, he or she is entitled to be registered as the owner.

1.232   If the application is dealt with under LRA 2002 Sch 6 para 5, the trespasser has to establish not only that he or she has been in adverse possession for ten years but also that one of a number of very restricted conditions apply.[356] If the trespasser makes this kind of application but is unsuccessful, he or she may make a second application after a further two years.[357] Assuming that he or she can show that he or she has been in adverse possession for the whole 12 years, he or she is entitled to be registered as the owner without needing to establish any of the circumstances required in the first application.[358]

1.233   A trespasser who would be entitled to make the first application set out above and rely on the para 5(4) condition has a defence to a possession action.[359] A trespasser who would be entitled to the make the second application set out above also has a defence to a possession action.[360] Accordingly, such a trespasser is a residential occupier because of a restriction on the right to recover possession against him or her.

---

354 LRA 2002 Sch 6 para 1.

355 LRA 2002 Sch 6 para 3.

356 LRA 2002 Sch 6 para 5. For present purposes, the relevant conditions are that the trespasser can establish an equity by estoppel (para 5(2)) or can show some other reason entitling him or her to be registered as the proprietor (para 5(3)). In practice, however, this will rarely be the case. There is a further condition relating to boundary disputes (para 5(4)), which is unlikely to be relevant in the contexts discussed in this book.

357 LRA 2002 Sch 6 para 6.

358 In practice, this is unlikely as the owner will take steps to evict the trespasser during that two-year period.

359 LRA 2002 s98(1).

360 LRA 2002 s98(3).

Special categories

1.234   There is a number of other circumstances which merit consideration in relation to whether or not someone is a residential occupier, whom it would be an offence under PEA 1977 s1 to evict (otherwise than by way of court order).

1.235   **Joint tenants**. A joint tenancy continues so long as the tenancy subsists. Accordingly, a joint tenant remains a residential occupier until either he or she vacates or until the right to occupy determines. If one joint tenant vacates, that joint tenant ceases to be a residential occupier, but this has no bearing on any other joint tenant who continues to reside in the premises. If one joint tenant gives notice to quit, effective to determine the tenancy (para 1.16), however, a remaining (former) joint tenant occupier will only be a residential occupier if the original tenancy was protected by the RA 1977, R(A)A 1976[361] or PEA 1977.[362] Otherwise, the remaining (former) joint tenant occupier will, on termination of the tenancy, cease to be a residential occupier.

1.236   **Assignees**. Where a tenancy has been assigned, the assignee replaces the assignor (ie the contractual tenant). Accordingly, the assignee is a residential occupier on taking up residence and thereafter is in the same position as the former tenant would have been.

1.237   **Service tenants**. A service tenant is a particular type of tenant. He or she is, therefore, a residential occupier on the same basis as any other tenant (as considered above), even though he or she may be less likely to have security of tenure.

1.238   **Tenants of mortgagors**. The tenant of a mortgagor is in the same position as a tenant of any other landlord so long as the mortgagor is in possession; it does not matter if the tenancy was granted in contravention of the mortgage deed.[363] Where the mortgagee repossesses as against the mortgagor (for example, for mortgage arrears), the tenant becomes the direct tenant of the mortgagee only if the tenancy is binding on the mortgagee; that is rare but if it happens, the tenant remains a residential occupier. If the tenancy is not binding on the mortgagee,[364] the tenant is a trespasser in relation to the

---

361 If a joint tenancy is RA 1977 or R(A)A 1976 protected, one joint tenant can become the statutory tenant in his or her own right: *Lloyd v Sadler* [1978] QB 774, CA.

362 Ie it was let as a dwelling and was neither an excluded or statutorily protected tenancy (see paras 1.55–1.72).

363 *Church of England Building Society v Piskor* [1954] 1 Ch 553, CA.

364 For the circumstances where the tenancy is and is not binding on the mortgagee, see *Manual of Housing Law*, paras 1.100–1.105.

mortgagee after the expiry of the possession order obtained against the mortgagor, when he or she will cease to be a residential occupier. The court may, however, on an application by the tenant, postpone the date on which the mortgagor is to give up possession for a period of up to two months,[365] during which period the tenant will remain a residential occupier.

1.239 **Subtenants.** While the tenancy in relation to which the occupier is a subtenant subsists, ie the tenancy (known as a mesne tenancy) between the landlord (L) and the tenant (T), a subtenant (ST) is in the same position as the tenant of any other landlord. Whether ST is a residential occupier is determined according to his or her right of occupation in relation to T. In general, when the mesne tenancy comes to an end, any subtenancy determines automatically;[366] ST has no right to occupy and is a trespasser. In certain circumstances, when the mesne tenancy comes to an end the ST becomes the direct tenant of L;[367] if so, ST is a residential occupier. Where the mesne tenancy is determined and ST does not become the direct tenant of L, ST remains a residential occupier if, at the time of termination of the mesne tenancy, ST was lawfully residing in the premises and the mesne tenancy itself was neither statutorily protected nor excluded.[368]

1.240 **Rental purchasers.**[369] Rental purchasers are residential occupiers until the expiry of a possession order because they have statutory protection against eviction without a court order.[370]

1.241 **Licensees of tenants.** Provided that his or her licence has not been determined by the tenant, a tenant's licensee is a residential occupier until the tenant's interest has been terminated by the landlord. Where the tenant had a tenancy which was neither statutorily protected nor excluded, and the licensee was lawfully residing in the premises at the time of termination of the tenant's interest, he or she

365 Mortgage Repossessions (Protection of Tenants etc) Act 2010 s1(2).
366 *Moore Properties (Ilford) Ltd v McKeon and others* [1976] 1 WLR 1278, ChD.
367 Ie where the mesne tenancy is surrendered (*Parker v Jones* [1910] 2 KB 32) or where T was a protected, statutory, assured or assured shorthold tenant and the grant of the subtenancy was not a breach of the terms of the mesne tenancy (RA 1977 s137 and HA 1988 s18).
368 PEA 1977 s3(1) and (2); see para 1.225.
369 Ie an agreement for the purchase of a dwelling-house (whether freehold or leasehold property) under which the whole or part of the purchase price is to be paid in three or more instalments and the completion of the purchase is deferred until the whole or a specified part of the purchase price has been paid: HA 1980 s88(4).
370 PEA 1977 s3 is applied to these occupiers by HA 1980 Sch 25 para 61.

remains a residential occupier until the possession order obtained by the landlord is executed.[371]

1.242   **Service occupiers.** A service occupier is a special category of licensee, who occupies accommodation under the terms of a contract of employment and is, thus, a residential occupier until it is terminated. A service occupier with exclusive possession of the premises, who remains in occupation after termination of the contract of employment, is a residential occupier until the possession order is executed, by express provision under PEA 1977.[372] Agricultural workers in tied accommodation who fall outside the protection afforded by the R(A)A 1976 are residential occupiers until a possession order expires, unless they are excluded licensees.[373] The same applies to such workers who do not qualify as assured agricultural occupiers (under HA 1988).[374]

1.243   **Spouses and civil partners.** A spouse or civil partner lacking any other right to occupy the home has 'home rights'.[375] These are statutory rights and, accordingly, he or she is a residential occupier for so long as they subsist. These rights terminate automatically on the dissolution of the marriage or civil partnership. Home rights are also only relevant while the other spouse or civil partner has an entitlement to occupy the dwelling house. Thus, once a tenancy is terminated the home rights also end.[376] In such circumstances, a spouse or civil partner is still likely to be a residential occupier until a possession order is obtained and executed provided that the tenancy was neither statutorily protected nor excluded, and he or she was lawfully residing in the premises at the time of termination of the tenant's interest.[377] A former spouse or civil partner who has been granted an occupation order in respect of the formerly shared home[378] is a residential occupier.

---

371 PEA 1977 s3(1) and (2); see para 1.225.
372 PEA 1977 s8(2).
373 PEA 1977 s4.
374 If they are tenants of an agricultural holding or they are farm business tenants, they are statutorily protected tenants: PEA 1977 s8(1)(d), (g).
375 FLA 1996 s30(2).
376 *Derwent HA Ltd v Taylor* [2016] EWCA Civ 508, [2016] HLR 25.
377 PEA 1977 s3(1) and (2); see para 1.225.
378 FLA 1996 s35.

1.244   **Cohabitants.** A cohabitant[379] who has been granted an occupation order over the shared home[380] is a residential occupier, as it is a statutory right. As with a former spouse or civil partner, a former cohabitant with an occupation order in respect of the formerly shared home[381] is a residential occupier.

Any premises

1.245 The offence may be committed in relation to 'any premises'. This should be given a broad meaning.[382] It includes all types of residential premises. A single room with the shared use of a kitchen and bathroom is 'premises' for these purposes,[383] as are premises let for mixed residential and business purposes.[384] The term was held to include a caravan, which, though not attached to the ground, had been static for ten years and could not easily be towed away.[385]

Deprives

1.246 The occupier must be 'deprived' of occupation of the premises, or there must have been an attempt to deprive the occupier of occupation. Whether or not this has occurred is a question of fact for the court to decide.

1.247   Deprivation of part only of the premises (for example, by locking a lavatory door)[386] is sufficient.[387]

1.248   Deprivation does not have to be violent; changing the locks may satisfy the requirement.[388]

1.249   Although the definition of the offence does not contain the word 'eviction', any unlawful deprivation of occupation must have the character of an eviction.[389] The Court of Appeal regarded the view

---

379 'Cohabitants' are two persons who are neither married to each other nor civil partners of each other but are living together as though they were husband and wife or civil partners: FLA 1996 s62(1).

380 FLA 1996 ss33 and 36.

381 FLA 1996 s36.

382 *Thurrock UDC v Shina* (1972) 23 P&CR 205, QBD.

383 *Thurrock UDC v Shina* (1972) 23 P&CR 205, QBD. A single room with no cooking facilities should therefore also suffice, assuming the 'residence' element: see *Uratemp Ventures Ltd v Collins* [2001] 1 AC 301, HL reversing (2001) 33 HLR 4, CA and para 1.206.

384 *Patel v Pirabakaran* [2006] EWCA Civ 685, [2006] 1 WLR 3112, [2006] HLR 39.

385 *Norton v Knowles* [1969] 1 QB 572, QBD.

386 As in *R v Burke* [1991] 1 AC 135, (1990) 22 HLR 433, HL.

387 See the words of PEA 1977 s1(3).

388 *R v Yuthiwattana* (1984) 16 HLR 49, CA.

389 *R v Yuthiwattana* (1984) 16 HLR 49, CA.

of Lord Evershed MR in *Crown Lands Commissioners v Page*[390] – that eviction must be permanent – as going too far but nonetheless held that a tenant who was locked out of his accommodation for one night only or for a short period of time, and who was allowed to retain his right of occupation over the premises, had not been deprived of the premises; rather, the incident amounted to harassment (see chapter 2).

1.250   In *Costelloe v Camden LBC*,[391] the question was said to be whether the exclusion was designed to evict the tenant from the premises; if it was, then regardless of whether it was short or long, it was unlawful eviction; if, on the other hand, the object was the deprivation of occupation for a short time, which was what had happened, it was not.

Unlawfully

1.251   The deprivation must be 'unlawful'. This means that the person depriving the residential occupier of the premises does not have the legal right to do so, which in turn relates to the occupier's security, whether by common law or by statute.

Reasonable belief that the residential occupier had ceased to reside in the premises

1.252   If the prosecution establishes that the residential occupier has been unlawfully deprived of occupation, it is a defence that the defendant:

> ... believed, and had reasonable cause to believe, that the residential occupier had ceased to reside in the premises.[392]

1.253   The defendant[393] must establish – on a balance of probabilities – both the belief and that it was reasonably held.[394] It follows from the use of the word 'and' that a purely subjective but unreasonable belief that

---

390 [1960] 2 QB 274, 281, CA.

391 [1986] Crim LR 249, QBD.

392 PEA 1977 s1(2); see, for example, *Islington LBC v Clonis and another* (2000) 80 P&CR D24, QBD, in which it was held that the magistrates were entitled to conclude that the defendant believed the tenant had left the accommodation he had occupied under an assured shorthold tenancy, where he was physically absent but had left his possessions at the property.

393 Magistrates' Courts Act (MCA) 1980 s101; *R v Hunt* [1987] AC 352, HL.

394 In *A-G's Ref (No 1 of 2004)* [2004] EWCA Crim 1025, [2004] 1 WLR 2111, the Court of Appeal held that the legal burden imposed on the defendant to prove that he or she had reasonable cause to believe that the residential occupier had ceased to reside in the premises amounted to a very limited infringement of ECHR Article 6(2) but one which was wholly justified.

the occupier had left is not sufficient. The existence of a reasonable belief is a question of fact for the magistrates or the jury to decide.[395]

1.254 It is also a defence that the defendant mistakenly believed that the person who was evicted was not a residential occupier.[396]

Penalties

Criminal offence

1.255 Unlawful eviction can be tried in a magistrates' court or the Crown Court. The maximum penalty for the offence in a magistrates' court is six months' imprisonment and/or an unlimited fine;[397] and in the Crown Court two years' imprisonment and/or an unlimited fine.[398]

1.256 In *R v Brennan*,[399] the Court of Appeal remarked that, at least in cases dealt with by the Crown Court, it was proper for those convicted of unlawful eviction to be sent to prison even for a first offence, although the period of imprisonment should be determined in the light of the defendant's overall record and past behaviour. In *R v Khan (Jahinger)*,[400] a sentence of 15 months was not considered excessive given the threats and intimidation used and damage that had been caused to the victim's property.

Rent repayment order

1.257 Under Chapter 4 of Part 2 of HPA 2016, the First-tier Tribunal has power to make a rent repayment order against a landlord in England[401] who has committed an offence under PEA 1977 s1(2), where the offence took place on or after 6 April 2017.[402]

---

395 *R v Davidson-Acres* [1980] Crim LR 50, CA.

396 *R v Phekoo* [1981] 1 WLR 1117, CA; *West Wiltshire DC v Snelgrove* (1997) 30 HLR 57, QBD; although these were decided in relation to harassment, they apply equally to unlawful eviction.

397 PEA 1997 s1(4); MCA 1980 s32(2), (9), (10); and LASPO s85(2).

398 PEA 1977 s1(4). In *R v Pittard* (1994) 15 Cr App R (S) 108, the Court of Appeal decided that a fine of £1,000 was the appropriate sentence where the defendant broke into his tenant's home, changed the locks and remained there for 12 hours.

399 (1979) 1 Cr App R (S) 103, CA.

400 [2001] EWCA Crim 912, [2001] 2 Cr App R (S) 129.

401 The provisions do not apply in Wales.

402 HPA 2016 s40; Housing and Planning Act 2016 (Commencement No 5, Transitional Provisions and Savings) Regulations 2017 SI No 281 regs 4, 5(1). Note that in relation to HA 2004 ss72(1) and 95(1) offences (discussed at paras

1.258   Either a tenant or a local housing authority may apply for a rent repayment order.[403]

Application by tenant

1.259   A tenant may apply if the offence was committed within the 12 months before the application was made and was related to the housing that was let to the tenant.[404] The tenant may recover the rent for the period of up to 12 months before the date that the landlord committed the offence, less any amount which was paid in respect of the rent by universal credit or housing benefit.[405] The tribunal must, in deciding the amount of the award, have regard to the conduct both of the landlord and of the tenant, the financial circumstances of the landlord and whether the landlord has at any time been convicted of an offence under Chapter 4 of Part 2[406] of HPA 2016;[407] see also para 1.262.

Application by local housing authority

1.260   Where the application is made by a local housing authority, the tribunal may award the universal credit or housing benefit that was paid, directly or indirectly, to the landlord in respect of the rent for the period of up to 12 months before the date that the landlord committed the offence.[408] In deciding the amount of the award, the tri-

5.30–5.31 and 5.36), HPA 2016 does not apply where the commission of the offence began before 6 April 2017 and ended no later than 5 April 2018: reg 5(2). In that case, the HA 2004 provisions will apply: see paras 5.55–5.70.

403   HPA 2016 s41(1).

404   HPA 2016 s41(2).

405   HPA 2016 ss44(1)–(3) and 51. Section 44 refers to universal credit, which is currently implemented only in certain areas and for certain types of claimant; section 51 therefore requires references to universal credit to include a reference to housing benefit, ie where the latter remains the relevant benefit.

406   This includes the PEA 1977 offence referred to at para 1.257, as well as a number of other offences, specified in HPA 2016 s40(3), which includes violent entry into premises (CLA 1977 s6(1) – see paras 3.6–3.36), harassment under PEA 1977 s1(3) and (3A) (see paras 2.52–2.91), failure to comply with certain orders under HA 2004 Part 1, offences related to the control or management of unlicensed houses in multiple occupation (HMOs) or houses under HA 2004 ss72(1) and 95(1) (see paras 5.30–5.31 and 5.36) and will include breach of a banning order under HPA 2016 s21 when banning orders are brought into force (paras 6.2–6.38).

407   HPA 2016 s44(4).

408   HPA 2016 s45(1)–(3) and s51 (see n405, above). The authority may apply any amount recovered under a rent repayment order to meet the costs and expenses incurred in, or associated with, carrying out enforcement functions in relation to the private rented sector: Rent Repayment Orders and Financial

bunal must have regard to the conduct of the landlord, the financial circumstances of the landlord and whether the landlord has been convicted of an offence under Chapter 4 of Part 2[409] of HPA 2016;[410] see also para 1.262.

1.261   While in principle the local housing authority has a discretion whether or not to apply for an order,[411] it is under a duty to consider doing so once it has become aware that any offence under Chapter 4 of Part 2 of HPA 2016[412] has been committed committed on or after 6 April 2017.[413] The authority must, when deciding whether to apply for an order, have regard to guidance given by the secretary of state.[414] The authority may only seek the order if it has first served a notice of intended proceedings informing the landlord of its reasons for doing so, the amount sought and invited the landlord to make representations.[415]

Tribunal order

1.262   The First-tier Tribunal may make a rent repayment order provided it is satisfied, beyond reasonable doubt, that the landlord has committed an offence under PEA 1977 s1(2) (see paras 1.197–1.254); it is not, however, necessary that there should be an actual conviction – only that the offence has been committed on or after 6 April 2017.[416] Although the tribunal has a discretion as to the amount of the order, it may prima facie not reduce the maximum amount that would otherwise be payable[417] where the landlord has been convicted

Penalties (Amounts Recovered) (England) Regulations 2017 SI No 367 reg 3(1). Enforcement functions are defined by reg 2 to mean functions under HA 2004 Parts 1–4, and functions under HPA 2016 Part 2, as well as other functions connected with the law related to housing or landlord and tenant. Any amount not applied in that way must be paid into the Consolidated Fund: reg 3(2).

409 See n406, above.
410 HPA 2016 s45(4).
411 HPA 2016 s41(1).
412 See n406, above.
413 HPA 2016 s48.
414 HPA 2016 s41. The secretary of state has issued guidance: Department for Communities and Local Government, *Rent repayment orders under Housing and Planning Act 2016: Guidance for Local Authorities* (April 2017). The guidance, however, does no more than describe the law.
415 HPA 2016 s42(2).
416 HPA 2016 s43(1).
417 Ie the rent or credit/benefit referable to the 12 months before the offence was committed: paras 1.259–1.260.

of the offence which gives rise to the application.[418] Even so, there is a residual discretion to reduce the amount, if the tribunal considers – by reason of exceptional circumstances – that it would be unreasonable to require the landlord to pay it.[419]

Mobile homes

1.263   Anyone who evicts an occupier of a mobile home[420] who has a residential contract[421] without a court order commits a criminal offence.[422] It is a defence to show that the defendant believed, and had reasonable cause to believe, that the occupier had ceased to reside on the site (see paras 1.252–1.253 for a discussion of the similar reasonable belief defence in PEA 1977).[423]

1.264   The defendant is liable on conviction in the magistrates' court to an unlimited fine and/or to imprisonment for a maximum of six months.[424] On conviction in the Crown Court, a defendant is liable to an unlimited fine and/or imprisonment for a maximum of two years.[425]

---

418   HPA 2016 s46(1).
419   HPA 2016 s46(5).
420   See para 1.103.
421   See paras 1.103–1.104.
422   CSA 1968 s3(1)(a), (b); MH(W)A 2013 s42(2), (3).
423   CSA 1968 s3(4); MH(W)A 2013 s43(1).
424   CSA 1968 s3(3)(a); MH(W)A 2013 s43(3)(a); MCA 1980 s32(2), (9), (10); and LASPO 2012 s85(2).
425   CSA 1968 s3(3)(b); MH(W)A 2013 s43(3)(b).

Harassment

continued

Harassment of an individual or of two or more persons • Harassment of a person in his or her home • Putting another in fear of violence • Stalking • Stalking involving fear of violence or serious alarm or distress • Racially or religiously aggravated harassment • Restraining orders • Breach of an injunction

Introduction

2.1 Chapter 1 addressed the rights of an occupier who has been unlawfully evicted or the subject of an attempted unlawful eviction; this chapter considers an occupier's rights in those cases where the behaviour complained of falls short of unlawful eviction (actually or attempted) but is intended to interfere with a residential occupier's home, referred to generically as harassment, including a number of acts which are likely to give rise to a civil claim for damages under one or other of the civil causes of action considered below, and/or which may amount to a criminal offence. Save so far as statute provides, harassment is not in itself a civil cause of action; and, while the term is used in relation to some criminal offences, there are others where different language is used for what is popularly recognisable as harassment. The terminology and definitions which matter in either case are those which are known to or defined by the law.

2.2 There is a considerable overlap between eviction and harassment, and it is sometimes (perhaps often) unclear (as a matter of fact and law) whether what is in issue is harassment or an attempt at eviction, so that it will be common to make a claim for both, additionally or in the alternative.

2.3 Following the same approach as chapter 1 (for similar reasons),[1] this chapter will deal with civil claims before turning to criminal offences and penalties.

Civil causes of action

2.4 The importance of a 'cause of action' in a civil claim was explained at para 1.5: without a cause of action into which to 'fit' the harassment complained of, there will be no civil claims. The discussion that follows is of civil causes of action under their own heads, one or more of which may be available to remedy an act which, generically (see para 2.1), comprises harassment; as noted, save so far as statute provides, harassment is not in itself a civil cause of action.

2.5 It is important for an adviser to identify all the relevant causes of action which may arise so that the claimant can obtain the remedies

---

1 See paras 1.3–1.4. Here, what the occupier will usually want first is for the harassment to stop. An interim injunction, as part of a civil claim, is usually the quickest way to bring the matter before the courts. Moreover, a civil injunction is a pre-requisite to one of the criminal offences which will be considered (see paras 2.158–2.160).

required. So far as harassment is concerned, the following causes of action are those which are most likely to be relevant:[2]

1) breach of tenancy or licence agreement;
2) nuisance;
3) Protection from Harassment Act (PHA) 1997;
4) trespass to land;
5) trespass to the person;
6) trespass to goods;
7) verbal threats;
8) intimidation;
9) Human Rights Act (HRA) 1998.

Breach of tenancy or licence agreement

2.6   Three causes of action based on the occupation agreement – tenancy or licence – need to be considered:

a) breach of covenant for quiet enjoyment;
b) breach of implied obligation not to derogate from grant; and
c) breach of other contractual terms.

Covenant for quiet enjoyment

2.7   The covenant for quiet enjoyment was discussed in relation to unlawful eviction (see paras 1.8–1.11). In *Kenny v Preen*,[3] letters from the landlord threatening eviction, coupled with calls at the tenant's room, knocking on her door and shouting threats at her, were held to amount to a course of conduct which interfered with the tenant's right of quiet enjoyment. Cutting off gas and electricity supplies has also been held to be capable of being a breach of the covenant,[4] as can regular excessive noise by the landlord.[5]

2.8   The covenant has also been held to have been breached both where the landlord failed to comply with repairing obligations,[6] withholding

---

2 To this list could also be added the torts of deceit or fraudulent misrepresentation and conspiracy or misfeasance in public office, which might also found a cause of action in a harassment case although not commonly: they were addressed at paras 1.84–1.86 and it is not necessary to consider them further here but they should be borne in mind.
3 [1963] 1 QB 499, CA.
4 *McCall v Abelesz* [1976] QB 585, CA.
5 *Southwark LBC v Tanner* [2001] 1 AC 1, (2001) 32 HLR 148, HL.
6 *Gordon v Selico* (1986) 18 HLR 219, CA; *Mira v Aylmer Square Investments* (1989) 21 HLR 284, QBD.

which can comprise a form of harassment in its own right, and where a landlord, while complying with his repairing obligations, failed to take all reasonable steps to minimise the disturbance caused during the works.[7]

Obligation not to derogate from grant

2.9 It is an implied term of any tenancy agreement that a landlord must 'not derogate from' his or her 'grant'. A person who agrees to confer a benefit on another must not act so as to deprive him or her of that benefit. This obligation is primarily applicable where a landlord lets part of his or her land and retains the other part for him or herself, for example, the common parts and may therefore be of particular relevance to tenants of resident landlords.

2.10 The landlord must not do anything on the retained property so as to make the land which has been let unfit, or materially less fit for the particular purpose for which the letting was made, which can likewise be the consequence of harassment.

2.11 The covenant obliges landlords not to take away any 'easements' that were granted (expressly or by implication) when the tenancy was created. Easements include rights of way, the right to use a parking place, or the right to use adjacent premises, often for storage purposes. The cause of action is therefore often applicable where the landlord prevents the tenant gaining access to premises.

Breach of other contractual terms

2.12 Wherever an agreement exists for the occupation of premises and the terms of the agreement are broken, there is a breach of contract for which the courts can give a remedy.

2.13 Terms are usually expressly agreed between the parties and set out in a written agreement. Certain terms are also implied into agreements by law as being necessary to give effect to the parties' intentions.[8]

---

7 *Goldmile Properties Ltd v Lechouritis* [2003] EWCA Civ 49, [2003] 2 P&CR 1.

8 *Liverpool City Council v Irwin* [1977] 2 AC 239, HL; *Marks & Spencer Plc v BNP Paribas Securities Services Trust Company (Jersey) Ltd* [2015] UKSC 72, [2016] AC 742. The courts are only prepared to imply terms into a tenancy agreement in limited circumstances, eg, where something is so obvious that it does not have to be expressed in the agreement, or if it is necessary to do so in order to render the contract effective.

2.14   For example, in *McCall v Abelesz*,[9] cutting off gas and electricity was described as a breach of the implied term that the landlord would supply gas and electricity to the premises as long as the tenancy lasted. A right to use furniture supplied in relation to, or a facility associated with, the tenancy, even though not actually spelled out at the outset of an arrangement, might be implied in all the circumstances, so that its withdrawal would be a breach of contract.

2.15   It can be more difficult to establish a breach of contract where a right has been granted after the beginning of the arrangement and then taken away at a later date, unless the occupier gave something in exchange for the new facility (for example, paying more money or giving up some existing right), in which case it can be argued either that there was a new contract or a variation of the terms of the existing contract.

Nuisance

2.16   A private nuisance is an activity or state of affairs existing on land which unduly interferes with the use or enjoyment of neighbouring land[10] or some right over or in connection with it. The nuisance must generally arise from something emanating from the defendant's land.[11] It is not necessary for the claimant to prove that the defendant caused the nuisance; a land owner is liable in nuisance if he or she fails to take reasonable steps to abate it after he or she becomes, or should have become, aware of it.[12] The wronged person must be able to demonstrate that he or she has suffered loss arising from the nuisance, eg, physical damage to the land or injury to health.[13]

2.17   Common examples include:

- excessive noise;
- bad odours;
- dust;
- smoke;
- vibrations resulting in damage to a neighbouring property;
- blocked drains resulting in an overflow of water; and
- leaks or overflowing baths or basins causing water penetration into the premises below.

9 [1976] QB 585, CA.
10 *Arden and Partington's Housing Law* (looseleaf, Sweet & Maxwell) para 15-171.
11 *Hunter v Canary Wharf Ltd* [1997] AC 655, (1997) 30 HLR 409, HL.
12 *Sedleigh-Denfield v O'Callaghan* [1940] AC 880, HL.
13 Damages can be claimed for losses that were reasonably foreseeable: see paras 1.127–1.135.

2.18 Acts of harassment by or on behalf of a landlord may also be a nuisance if they infringe on the claimant's enjoyment of property. In *Khorasandjian v Bush*,[14] harassing telephone calls made to someone's home were held to be actions capable of amounting to a nuisance because they interfered with enjoyment of the property.[15]

2.19 In a number of so-called 'picketing' cases, it was held that it is a nuisance to stand outside and watch a person's house with the intention of getting that person to do or refrain from doing something within his or her rights.[16] The principle can be extended to anyone who deliberately hangs around a person's home in order to intimidate him or her. These cases were decided before the PHA 1997 and such acts of harassment are now more readily actionable under section 3 of that Act.

2.20 The tort of nuisance also affords a cause of action for interference with easements, for example, rights of way.[17] In the context of residential premises, such complaints often arise from parking disputes where a landlord or person acting on his or her behalf, blocks a right of way or prevents the use of an allocated parking space.

2.21 Apart from interference with easements, the essential basis for an action based on nuisance is unreasonable conduct. Some intrusion, eg, by noise or smell, is inevitable. The law proceeds on the basis that there must be some give and take. The task of the court is to strike a balance between the right of the defendant to use his or her property for his or her own lawful enjoyment and the right of the claimant to the undisturbed enjoyment of his or her property. For example, a resident landlord who plays loud music occasionally for a short time in the early evening may be reasonable but if the music is played for a long time, or played in the early hours of the morning, or if the pattern of behaviour is repeated every day, then there may be a nuisance.

2.22 The question for the court is whether the act complained of is one which would be considered a nuisance according to the standards of the average person (rather than one of undue sensitivity).[18] Whether a state of affairs amounts to a nuisance can only be determined in light of all the circumstances, for example, the locality of the premises.

---

14 [1993] QB 727, (1993) 25 HLR 392, CA.
15 The decision has subsequently been disapproved, but only as to who had the right to sue for nuisance: see para 2.24.
16 *Hubbard v Pitt* [1976] QB 142, CA.
17 See para 2.11.
18 *Robinson v Kilvert* (1889) 41 ChD 88.

2.23   In order to sue in nuisance, the claimant must have a sufficient right in land.[19] An owner of property or a tenant clearly has a sufficient interest because he or she has a proprietary interest. It is not, however, necessary to have a proprietary interest and possession is sufficient. Accordingly, all occupiers with possession can also sue in nuisance including for this purpose a licensee with exclusive occupation[20] or even a trespasser in adverse possession.[21]

2.24   The licensee of a person with a sufficient interest cannot, however, sue in nuisance. Accordingly, members of a tenant's family or household have no remedy in nuisance,[22] although in limited circumstances they may have a cause of action arising from a breach of HRA 1998. In *Khorasandjian v Bush*,[23] the daughter of the owner-occupier of premises was held to be capable of suing in nuisance for persistent, harassing telephone calls but, on this aspect, the case was subsequently overruled.[24] Instead, she could now make a claim for harassment under PHA 1997 s3.[25]

2.25   Whoever causes the nuisance can be sued, including landlords and their agents (if they caused the nuisance). A landlord can, however, only be liable for a nuisance committed by his or her tenant if he or she is taken to have authorised the nuisance by letting the property or has participated directly in the nuisance.[26]

2.26   A landlord will only be taken to have authorised a nuisance through letting a property if there is a virtual certainty or a very high probability that the letting will result in the tenant causing a nuisance.[27] Where it is inevitable that the permitted use of the property will result in a nuisance, the fact that the tenancy agreement prohibits

19 *Hunter v Canary Wharf Ltd* [1997] AC 655, (1997) 30 HLR 409, HL.
20 *Hunter v Canary Wharf Ltd* [1997] AC 655, (1997) 30 HLR 409, HL.
21 *Hunter v Canary Wharf Ltd* [1997] AC 655, (1997) 30 HLR 409, HL; in the context of residential premises, a squatter is in adverse possession if he or she lives in the property as his or her home and has unequivocally shown his or her intention to exclude the world (including the true owner) from the property, eg by changing the locks to the premises: *Lambeth LBC v Blackburn* (2001) 33 HLR 74, CA.
22 *Hunter v Canary Wharf Ltd* [1997] AC 655, (1997) 30 HLR 409, HL approving *Malone v Laskey* [1907] 2 KB 141, CA.
23 [1993] QB 727, (1993) 25 HLR 392, CA.
24 *Hunter v Canary Wharf Ltd* [1997] AC 655, (1997) 30 HLR 409, HL.
25 See paras 2.32–2.36.
26 *Smith v Scott* [1973] Ch 314, ChD; *Mowan v Wandsworth LBC* (2000) 33 HLR 56, [2001] LGR 110, CA; *Lawrence v Coventry (No 2)* [2014] UKSC 46, [2015] AC 106, [2014] HLR 42.
27 *Smith v Scott* [1973] Ch 314, ChD; *Lawrence v Coventry (No 2)* [2014] UKSC 46, [2015] AC 106, [2014] HLR 42.

the tenant from committing a nuisance will not prevent the landlord from being liable for having authorised that nuisance.[28]

2.27 The fact that a landlord does nothing to stop a tenant from causing a nuisance does not amount to participation in it.[29]

2.28 Otherwise, a landlord is only likely to be liable for nuisance committed by his or her tenant if the acts of nuisance are committed on land in the landlord's possession, eg the communal stairway of a flat, and if the landlord has become aware of the nuisance and has refused to take reasonable steps to prevent it recurring or continuing.[30]

2.29 A landlord is also liable if a nuisance, emanating from the land that is subject to a tenancy, arose prior to the letting and continues during the tenancy, if he or she knew, or ought to have known, of it.[31]

2.30 A landlord who lets premises to a tenant does not commit, or authorise, a nuisance, however, even if the physical condition, eg lack of sound insulation, is such that tenants can hear everything their neighbours say or do provided that the defect in the construction of the property existed before the start of the tenancy and it does not amount to a breach of a repairing covenant.[32]

2.31 It is not only a landlord who can, where appropriate, be liable for nuisance caused by others: any owner of land can be liable for nuisance. Thus, in *Lippiatt v South Gloucestershire Council*,[33] the authority was liable in nuisance for the actions of its licensees because it refused to take steps to remove them even though they were using the land as a base from which to trespass on the claimant's land and cause a nuisance. In *Cocking v Eacott*,[34] the owner of a house was liable for nuisance caused by the occupier (her daughter) even though she herself lived elsewhere. The Court of Appeal left open the question of whether a licensor would be potentially liable for the nuisance of a contractual licensee.

---

28 *Lawrence v Coventry (No 2)* [2014] UKSC 46, [2015] AC 106, [2014] HLR 42.
29 *Lawrence v Coventry (No 2)* [2014] UKSC 46, [2015] AC 106, [2014] HLR 42.
30 *Octavia Hill Housing Trust v Brumby* [2010] EWHC 1793 (QB).
31 *Brew Bros Ltd v Snax* [1970] 1 QB 612, CA.
32 *Baxter v Camden LBC; Southwark v Tanner* [2001] 1 AC 1, (2001) 32 HLR 148, HL; *Jackson v JH Watson Property Investment Ltd* [2008] EWHC 14 (Ch), [2008] Env LR 30.
33 [2000] QB 51, CA.
34 [2016] EWCA Civ 140, [2016] QB 1080, [2016] HLR 15.

Breach of the Protection from Harassment Act 1997

2.32   The PHA 1997 was primarily introduced to combat the activities of stalkers but its provisions apply to all campaigns of harassment, including those by landlords. Harassment in contravention of PHA 1997 is an offence.[35]

2.33   The offence of harassment under PHA 1997 is considered in more detail at paras 2.107–2.125. For present purposes it is sufficient to note that the offence can be committed in two ways, set out in s1 as follows.

> (1) A person must not pursue a course of conduct–
>   (a) which amounts to harassment of another, and
>   (b) which he knows or ought to know amounts to harassment of the other.
> (1A) A person must not pursue a course of conduct–
>   (a) which involves harassment of two or more persons, and
>   (b) which he knows or ought to know involves harassment of those persons, and
>   (c) by which he intends to persuade any person (whether or not one of those mentioned above)–
>   (i)   not to do something that he is entitled or required to do, or
>   (ii) to do something that he is not under any obligation to do.

2.34   There are two provisions of PHA 1997 that are relevant in the context of a civil claim: section 3, which creates a civil cause of action, allowing the remedies of an injunction and/or damages; and section 3A, which only allows an injunction to be granted.

2.35   PHA 1997 s3 allows the victim[36] of an actual or apprehended breach of section 1(1) to bring a civil claim, allowing him or her to seek an injunction and damages.[37] It is expressly provided that damages may be awarded for any anxiety caused by the harassment as well as for any financial loss.[38]

2.36   Actions under PHA 1997 s3 commonly overlap with other causes of action considered in this chapter, for example, breach of quiet

---

35 PHA 1997 s2(1).
36 A person 'who is *or may be* the victim of the course of conduct in question': PHA 1997 s3(1) (emphasis added).
37 Note that the normal civil standard of proof (ie the court needs to be satisfied on the balance of probabilities) applies to an application for an injunction under PHA 1997 s3, even though breach of s3 is an offence to which the criminal standard (ie the court needs to be satisfied beyond all reasonable doubt) applies when prosecuted: *Hipgrave v Jones* [2004] EWHC 2901 (QB), [2005] 2 FLR 174.
38 PHA 1997 s3(2); although damages are not limited to these two types of loss.

enjoyment and nuisance. It may be of particular use, however, where the victim is not a tenant, as protection is not limited to persons with an interest in land. Likewise, anyone can be sued for harassment, including but not limited to landlords and their agents.[39] An employer may be vicariously liable for harassment committed by one of its employees in the course of his or her employment.[40] It is also a more attractive cause of action than the tort of nuisance as a tenant may recover damages for all of his or her losses that were actually caused by the campaign of harassment rather than only those which were reasonably foreseeable, because section 3(2) provides that damages may be awarded for 'any financial loss resulting from the harassment'.[41]

2.37   PHA 1997 s3A(2) allows both the victim[42] of an actual or apprehended breach of section 1(1) and someone who it is intended to persuade not to do something that he or she is entitled or required to do or to do something that he or is not under any obligation to do[43] to bring a civil claim, allowing him or her to seek an injunction but not damages.[44]

2.38   Breach of an injunction granted under either PHA 1997 s3 or s3A is itself an offence.[45]

Trespass to land[46]

2.39   In harassment cases, common complaints include dumping refuse or other things in the complainant's garden or through the letter-box, which constitutes trespass to land. Driving a nail into the wall of the land of another has been held to be a trespass,[47] which could apply to a landlord who has nailed up a door or blocked up a lock.

---

39 Although the criminal offences, which are considered at paras 2.107–2.125 can probably not be committed by a company, because of the requirement to prove intention, a company or partnership can be a defendant to a civil claim: *Iqbal v Dean Manson Solicitors* [2011] EWCA Civ 123, [2011] CP Rep 26.

40 *Majrowski v Guy's and St Thomas's NHS Trust* [2006] UKHL 34, [2007] 1 AC 224.

41 *Jones v Ruth* [2011] EWCA Civ 804, [2012] 1 WLR 1495. Cf the discussion of causation and remoteness at paras 1.127–1.135 and see n13 above.

42 Again (see above, n36), a 'person who is *or may be* the victim of the course of conduct in question': PHA 1997 s3A(1) (emphasis added).

43 PHA 1997 s3A(2)(b).

44 In respect of which the civil standard of proof (ie the balance of probabilities) will apply: *Hipgrave v Jones* [2004] EWHC 2901 (QB), [2005] 2 FLR 174 (see para 2.35 and n37, above).

45 Under PHA 1997 s3(6) or s3A(3).

46 See also paras 1.76–1.81.

47 *Lawrence v Obee* (1815) 1 Stark 22.

Assault and battery: trespass to the person

2.40   The use of violence, or threats of violence, against a person are the torts of assault and battery. A battery is any intentional application of direct physical force on another person without lawful excuse. An assault is any act which puts another person in immediate and reasonable fear of a battery.[48] There must be some threatening act; threatening words alone are not usually enough,[49] although the victim may still have a cause of action under PHA 1997 s3.[50]

2.41   Assault and battery commonly go together but they are also actionable separately. Assault and battery are part of the law of trespass to the person. It is therefore not necessary to prove actual damage or harm in order to sustain an action.[51] Where the claimant is seriously injured, he or she may claim general damages for pain, suffering and loss of amenity as well as special damages for such losses as time off work.

Trespass to goods and conversion

2.42   Trespass to goods is addressed at paras 1.82–1.83. This tort may well also be relevant in harassment cases where a perpetrator commits acts of vandalism to the complainant's property, for example, scratching the paintwork of a car.

Verbal threats

2.43   If verbal threats are sufficient to make their victim ill, they amount to an actionable tort.[52] The illness does not have to be physical but may be a recognisable psychiatric illness, although emotional distress falling short of illness is not sufficient. Someone merely suffering distress may, however, have a cause of action under PHA 1997 s3.[53]

Intimidation

2.44   Intimidation consists of any threat, by words or actions, intended to make someone do something that causes damage either to the

---

48 Although technically a separate tort, battery is often referred to as assault.
49 *Meade's Case* (1823) 1 Lew CC 184.
50 See paras 2.35–2.36.
51 See para 1.78 in the context of trespass to land.
52 *Khorasandjian v Bush* [1993] QB 727, (1993) 25 HLR 392, CA, citing *Wilkinson v Downton* [1897] 2 QB 57; and *Janvier v Sweeney* [1919] 2 KB 316.
53 See paras 2.35–2.36.

intimidated person or to some other person.[54] The threat must be intentional and must be a threat to do something unlawful (ie, a crime, breach of contract or a tort).[55] It must be a coercive threat, not mere persuasion, and it must be coupled with a demand. Thus, a landlord who threatens to harass or unlawfully evict a tenant for doing something that the tenant is entitled to do is intimidating the tenant. Similarly, intimidation occurs where the landlord threatens to evict someone else, eg, another occupier in a house in multiple occupation (HMO), if that person does not assist in harassing or evicting the occupier. The threat does not have to be carried out but it must be effective to make the person intimidated comply with the landlord's wishes.

2.45   The person entitled to sue for intimidation is the person who suffers the damage rather than the person intimidated, although that can be the same person.[56]

Breach of the Human Rights Act 1998

2.46   The HRA 1998 is considered at paras 1.100–1.102, in the context of unlawful eviction and Article 8. An unlawful act of harassment by a public authority will additionally comprise a breach of Article 8 and will be actionable as such.[57] In an extreme case, there could even be a breach of Article 3 (the prohibition on torture and inhuman or degrading treatment and punishment).[58]

Remedies

2.47   A victim of harassment has two civil remedies available:

a) an injunction to prevent further harassment; and
b) damages, ie compensation for what they have suffered.

---

54 *Allen v Flood* [1898] AC 1, HL.
55 *Rookes v Barnard* [1964] AC 1129, HL.
56 *Morgan v Fry* [1968] 2 QB 710, CA; *JT Stratford & Son Ltd v Lindley* [1965] AC 307, HL.
57 At a national level, compliance with Article 8 requires there to be accessible civil law remedies, such as injunctions: *Smirnova v Ukraine* App No 1870/05, ECtHR.
58 See, eg, *BV v Croatia* App No 38435/13, ECtHR; *Dordevic v Croatia* App No 41526/10, (2012) 34 BHRC 392, ECtHR; and, *Smirnova v Ukraine* App No 1870/05, [2016] ECHR 873, ECtHR.

2.48   The principles on which an injunction may be awarded have already been discussed in chapter 1, in the context of unlawful eviction,[59] as have the various categories of damages that might be awarded and the principles underpinning them;[60] advisers should also consider the damages cases in appendix A. So far as an interim injunction to prevent harassment is concerned, there can be no injustice to the alleged perpetrator in being prevented from carrying out what are, in any event, unlawful acts.

Criminal offences

2.49   Criminal offences particularly relevant to harassment are to be found in five statutes:[61]

- Protection from Eviction Act (PEA) 1977;
- Caravan Sites Act (CSA) 1968 / Mobile Homes (Wales) Act (MH(W)A) 2013.
- PHA 1997;
- Criminal Justice and Police Act (CJPA) 2001.

2.50   Criminal cases are tried in either a magistrates' court or the Crown Court, as the statute which proscribes the conduct in question provides, detailed below in relation to each offence.

Protection from Eviction Act 1977[62]

2.51   PEA 1977 creates three criminal offences. One of those offences, relating to unlawful eviction, is considered at paras 1.197–1.256. There are also two offences of harassment.[63] Both harassment offences can

---

59 See paras 1.106–1.115.

60 See paras 1.120–1.167. So far as damages under PHA 1997 are concerned, see also paras 2.35–2.36.

61 Depending on the facts, offences in other statutes may also be relevant, eg a particularly serious case of harassment involving violence may give rise to offences under Offences Against the Person Act 1861, but the focus of this book is on those offences that are specifically aimed at harassment, so other, more generally applicable, criminal offences are not considered further here. Advisers should instead consider *Blackstone's Criminal Practice 2017* (Oxford University Press, 2016) or *Archbold: Criminal Pleading, Evidence and Practice 2017* (Sweet & Maxwell, 2016).

62 The relevant provisions of PEA 1977 are set out in appendix B.

63 Note that a landlord who is guilty of either offence may be subject to a rent repayment order: Housing and Planning Act (HPA) 2016 s40. See paras 2.92–2.97.

be tried in a magistrates' court or the Crown Court. The maximum penalty for any of the offences in a magistrates' court is six months' imprisonment and/or an unlimited fine[64] and in the Crown Court two years' imprisonment and/or an unlimited fine.[65]

Harassment

2.52 One of the offences of harassment arises where the defendant is the victim's landlord (or an agent of the landlord);[66] the other may be committed by anyone.[67] Although this book is concerned with protection against rogue landlords, the latter offence may nonetheless be relevant where the conduct cannot be shown to be that of the landlord or the landlord's agent.

2.53 Each offence comprises two elements, both of which must be proved:

a) the culpable behaviour (the 'harassing conduct') and
b) the mental intent to do it (the 'intention').

2.54 The harassing conduct is defined in the same way for both. The difference arises in relation to the intention that needs to be proved.[68]

Harassment by a landlord or a landlord's agent[69]

Landlord

2.55 A landlord is the person who would be entitled to possession but for the residential occupier's right to remain or the restriction on the right to recover possession; the definition includes not only the immediate landlord but also any superior landlord from whom the immediate landlord derives title.[70] There must, however, be proof of actual participation by the person being prosecuted; a landlord cannot be vicariously liable for the acts of others.[71]

---

64 PEA 1997 s1(4); Magistrates' Courts Act (MCA) 1980 s32(2), (9), (10); and Legal Aid, Sentencing and Punishment of Offenders Act 2012 (LASPO) s85(2).
65 PEA 1977 s1(4).
66 PEA 1977 s1(3A).
67 PEA 1977 s1(3).
68 The second offence (under PEA 1977 s1(3A)) was created by Housing Act (HA) 1988 s29, which amended PEA 1977, as it was thought that the requirement to prove specific intent in the original offence (under PEA 1977 s1(3)) enabled guilty landlords to escape conviction by placing too high a burden on the prosecution. As this offence is most likely to be relevant, it is considered here first.
69 PEA 1977 s1(3A).
70 PEA 1977 s1(3C).
71 *Peterborough CC v Quereshi* [2011] EWCA Crim 1584, [2011] HLR 34.

Agent

2.56   An agent is any person who acts on behalf of the landlord. In the absence of a specific definition in PEA 1977, it has the meaning ascribed to it by the general law.[72]

2.57   Agency can be either express or implied. Express agency is specific authorisation by the landlord of another person to act on his or her behalf. There is no requirement that this is evidenced in writing. Agency is implied where the state of affairs gives rise to the implication that one person is acting on behalf of another.

Residential occupier

2.58   As with the offence of unlawful eviction under PEA 1977, this offence can only be committed against a residential occupier (see paras 1.201–1.244).

The harassing conduct

2.59   This may be one of two acts:

(a) ... acts likely to interfere with the peace and comfort of a residential occupier or members of his household; or

(b) ... persistently withdraw[ing] or withhold[ing] services reasonably required for the occupation of the premises ... as a residence.[73]

2.60   **Interfering with peace and comfort**. PEA 1977 does not further define these words: while one can illustrate possible acts, the examples are just that, examples not a comprehensive list. It is also important to bear the issue of intention in mind (paras 2.74–2.75) as the same act may be wholly innocent or accidental and not comprise harassment in any sense of that word.

2.61   Interference with peace and comfort could comprise, by way of example, excessive noise or threats of violence. Other illustrations include: removing fittings, knocking holes in walls and ceilings and leaving rubble about;[74] or ordering a member of a tenant's household to remove his or her clothes from the premises.[75] It is a question of fact in each case whether the behaviour complained about interfered with the peace and comfort of the residential occupier.

2.62   The qualification provided by the word 'likely' (to interfere) injects an element of objectivity but – because there will be a specific residential occupier in mind – it does not allow a defendant to escape

---

72   See generally, *Bowstead and Reynolds on agency* (Sweet & Maxwell, 20th edn, 2014).

73   PEA 1977 s1(3A).

74   *R v Bokhari* (1974) 59 Cr App R 303, CA.

75   *R v Spratt* [1978] Crim LR 102, CA.

conviction on the basis that some other occupier would not have been affected, ie the test is not whether the act would have been likely to interfere with the peace and comfort of some notional 'reasonable' or 'average' occupier, but the actual occupier in question.

2.63　　The question for the court to consider is whether the act or acts alleged by the prosecution was or were likely to interfere with the residential occupier's peace or comfort.[76]

2.64　　The interference may not only be with the occupier's peace and comfort but also with that of members of his or her household. The word 'household' is wider than family and includes lodgers and flat-sharers.

2.65　　Although the statute refers to 'acts' (ie in the plural), a single act is sufficient.[77]

2.66　　Where more than one act of harassment is alleged, they are preferably specified in separate counts on the indictment.[78] Where a count on an indictment consists of more than than one act, a judge should – if he or she believes there is a danger that individual members of a jury may decide, individually rather than collectively, that different acts have been proved – direct the jury that they must be satisfied collectively that at least one of the acts of harassment within a count has been proved if they are to return a guilty verdict.[79]

2.67　　There is no requirement – or precondition – that the act or acts complained of should give the occupier a civil cause of action (for example, breach of contract or tort), provided that, as a matter of fact,

---

76　*R (McGowan) v Brent Justices* [2001] EWHC 814 (Admin), [2002] HLR 55, per Tuckey LJ at [23].

77　*R v Evangelos Polycarpou* (1978) 9 HLR 129, CA, applying Interpretation Act 1978 s6(c), which states: 'In any Act, unless the contrary intention appears ... words in the singular include the plural and words in the plural include the singular' (although the judgment of the Court of Appeal does not consider whether the contrary intention appeared in the relevant statutory provision, the Rent Act 1965 s30(2) as it then was; as, however the House of Lords in *R v Burke* [1991] 1 AC 135, (1990) 22 HLR 433 approved *R v Yuthiwattana* (1984) 16 HLR 49, CA, in which there was only a single act complained of, the decision in *Polycarpou* would seem to be correct).

78　Or in separate charges in summary proceedings.

79　*R v Mitchell* (1993) 26 HLR 394, CA. Although *Mitchell* did not address summary trial, it seems likely that the same approach should apply; as a bench of magistrates reaches a decision by a majority (see *Barnsley v Marsh* [1947] KB 672, DC), it would follow that a majority would need to be agreed on the same act(s). Any difficulty can be avoided by specifying the acts as separate charges, see n78, above.

they are likely to interfere with the occupier's peace or comfort.[80] Thus, while tenants had no contractual right to use a particular bathroom and lavatory (because there were others in the house which they were permitted to use) or to a doorbell, a landlord who prevented tenants from using a bathroom and lavatory on the same floor as their room and disconnected a doorbell had nonetheless performed acts within the prohibition.[81]

2.68   It is, however, necessary to prove positive action rather than mere omission. The offence is not committed if the landlord fails to act. In *R v Zafar Ahmad*,[82] the landlord started works to a flat without the intention required to constitute an offence. The works rendered the tenant's flat uninhabitable and the landlord refused to do the work necessary to make it habitable again. It was held that his omission to take steps to complete the work was not the doing of an act for the purposes of harassment.

2.69   **Persistently withdrawing or withholding services.** 'Services' must be:

> ... reasonably required for occupation of the premises as a residence.[83]

2.70   The term is not defined but the supply of a utility such as gas, electricity or water has been held to be a service.[84]

2.71   The word 'persistently' qualifies both withdrawing and withholding services.[85] It requires more than one incident or some element of 'deliberate continuity'.[86]

2.72   It appears unlikely that a mere failure by a landlord to pay a gas or electricity bill which results in those services being cut off by the supplier, without an intention to harass, amounts to an offence under section 1.[87]

---

80   *R v Yuthiwattana* (1984) 16 HLR 49, CA (contrary to the dictum of Ormrod LJ in *McCall v Abelesz* [1976] QB 585, 591, CA). The landlord refused to supply a replacement key, thereby preventing the tenant who had lost it from getting into his accommodation. This conclusion was approved in *R v Burke* [1991] 1 AC 135, (1990) 22 HLR 433, HL.

81   *R v Burke* [1991] 1 AC 135, (1990) 22 HLR 433, HL.

82   (1986) 18 HLR 416, CA.

83   PEA 1977 s1(3A)(b).

84   *Westminster City Council v Peart* (1968) 19 P&CR 736, QBD.

85   *Westminster City Council v Peart* (1968) 19 P&CR 736, QBD.

86   *R v Abrol* [1972] Crim LR 318, CA. In *Hooper v Eaglestone* (1977) 34 P&CR 311, QBD, the question whether cutting off supplies was persistent was not argued but was assumed to be so; the case was brought under CSA 1968 s3, which contains provisions very similar to PEA 1977 s1(3) and (3A).

87   See *McCall v Abelesz* [1976] QB 585, CA. In *Westminster City Council v Peart* (1968) 19 P&CR 736, QBD, the landlord failed to pay the gas and electricity

2.73   In *McCall v Abelesz*,[88] it was suggested that the offence cannot be committed where the landlord withholds or withdraws a service that he or she had been providing voluntarily, as opposed to one provided contractually under the terms of the letting. This would no longer seem to be good law. First, it conflicts with the wording of the statute, which provides that it is the withdrawal or withholding of any service 'reasonably required' that constitutes the offence; secondly, the House of Lords[89] subsequently held that an interference with peace and comfort could result from an act which did not comprise a breach of contract.

The intention

2.74   The prosecution must prove that the defendant committed the harassing conduct:

> ... know[ing] or [having] reasonable cause to believe either that [the] conduct [was] likely to cause the residential occupier to give up the occupation of the whole or part of the premises or to refrain from exercising any right or pursuing any remedy in respect of the whole or part of the premises.[90]

2.75   Whether the defendant had knowledge of the requisite consequences of his or her actions or had reasonable cause for believing the same is a question of fact for the court to decide. The use of the word 'reasonable' indicates that that belief should be determined objectively.[91]

Defences

2.76   A defendant does not commit the offence if he or she honestly believes that the person harassed was not a residential occupier.[92]

2.77   It is a defence for the defendant to show that he or she had reasonable grounds for interfering with the peace and comfort of the

accounts to the suppliers, which resulted in disconnection; the Divisional Court left open the question whether, in so doing, the landlord had withheld a service. If disconnection occurs, local housing authorities have the power to make arrangements for the restoration or continuation of supplies of water, gas or electricity for the benefit of the occupiers of the premises: Local Government (Miscellaneous Provisions) Act 1976 s33.

88 [1976] QB 585 at 596G–H, CA, per Ormrod LJ.
89 *R v Burke* [1991] 1 AC 135, (1990) 22 HLR 433, HL, see para 2.67.
90 PEA 1977 s1(3A).
91 See also *R (McGowan) v Brent Justices* [2001] EWHC 814 (Admin), [2002] HLR 55, Tuckey LJ at [24]–[25].
92 *R v Phekoo* [1981] 1 WLR 1117, CA; *West Wiltshire DC v Snelgrove* (1997) 30 HLR 57, QBD; although these were decided in relation to charges of harassment by any person (see paras 2.79–2.91), the defence applies equally to harassment by a landlord or an agent.

residential occupier or for withdrawing or withholding the services.[93] Reasonable grounds could not be established where the tenant failed to pay rent, was evasive towards the landlord, refused to allow the landlord to inspect the premises or acted provocatively towards the landlord; nor – on the facts – did the presence of bottles containing urine in the premises establish reasonable grounds, as the defendant was not aware of them until after he had carried out the harassing conduct.[94] In *McGowan*, converting a floor below the occupier's premises into a public house did not amount to reasonable grounds.[95]

2.78　　　Where a defence is raised, it is for the defendant[96] to establish it on the balance of probabilities.[97] Whether this has been done is a matter of fact for magistrates or a jury to decide.

Harassment by any person[98]

Residential occupier

2.79　Although this offence is not confined to a landlord or a landlord's agent, it can also only be committed against a residential occupier (see paras 1.201–1.244).

Any person

2.80　As with unlawful eviction, this offence may be committed by 'any person' (see paras 1.199–1.200).

The harassing conduct

2.81　This is the same as described in relation to the offences committed by a landlord or a landlord's agent (see paras 2.59–2.73).[99]

The intention

2.82　The prosecution must prove that the defendant committed the harassing conduct with the intention of causing the residential occupier either:

93　PEA 1977 s1(3B).
94　*R v Allen* [2013] EWCA Crim 676.
95　*R (McGowan) v Brent Justices* [2001] EWHC 814 (Admin), [2002] HLR 55.
96　MCA 1980 s101; *R v Hunt* [1987] AC 352, HL.
97　*Blackstone's Criminal Practice 2017* (Oxford University Press, 2016), para F3.5.
98　PEA 1977 s1(3).
99　As originally enacted, PEA 1977 s1(3) required the prosecution to prove that the defendant did 'acts calculated to interfere with the peace and comfort … [etc]'. HA 1988 s29 substituted 'likely' for 'calculated'; although it is still necessary to prove intent; s1(3) is strengthened because the requirement of proving an ulterior motive has been removed and the court may decide, objectively, whether acts were likely to interfere with the peace and comfort of the occupier.

(a) to give up occupation of the premises or any part thereof; or
(b) to refrain from exercising any right or from pursuing any remedy
     in respect of the premises or part thereof ...[100]

2.83   The two parts of the subsection do not constitute separate offences. The harassing conduct may be performed with either intention. If it is unclear on the facts whether a case falls within (a) or (b), there is no reason why the offence should not be expressed in one charge with alternative intentions.[101]

2.84   The intention is the same as that required for harassment by a landlord or agent (paras 2.74–2.75) subject to this important difference: the prosecution has to prove that the defendant had specific intent to achieve the stated effect (give up occupation or refrain from exercising right/pursuing remedy), as distinct from knowledge or belief of the likely consequences of his or her actions.

2.85   As a general proposition, where specific intent is an element of an offence, it must be proved that the defendant either intended a particular result or, if not intending it, foresaw it.[102] In the latter case, it cannot be assumed that the defendant intended the natural consequences of his or her actions; the defendant's foresight is to be judged subjectively and:

> ... the probability, however high, of a consequence is only a factor ... to be considered with all the other evidence in determining whether the accused intended to bring it about.[103]

2.86   Intention means that the defendant had the purpose of causing the occupier to give up occupation or to refrain from exercising a right or pursuing a remedy.[104] The court is not entitled to draw the conclusion that the defendant had the necessary intent just because the harassing conduct caused the victim to give up occupation (or refrain from the exercise or pursuit).

2.87   Thus, the carrying out of building works which caused disruption did not of itself demonstrate the presence of the necessary intent, because it did not automatically follow that the defendant intended the occupier to leave.[105]

2.88   Likewise, indifference by a landlord to the plight of an occupier whose gas had been disconnected by the supplier because of the

100 PEA 1977 s1(3).
101 *Schon v Camden LBC* (1986) 18 HLR 341, CA.
102 Criminal Justice Act (CJA) 1967 s8.
103 *R v Hancock* [1986] AC 455, HL, at 474.
104 *R v Burke* [1991] 1 AC 135, (1990) 22 HLR 433, HL.
105 *R v AMK (Property Management) Ltd* [1985] Crim LR 600, CA.

landlord's failure to pay for it was insufficient to establish the necessary intent under PEA 1977 s1(3)(a),[106] nor was an intention to persuade the occupier to leave for a limited period of time to enable works to be done and thereafter to return sufficient.[107] The nature and extent of the harassing conduct is, however, a factor, albeit only *a* factor, to be taken into account when deciding whether the necessary intent was present.

Defences

2.89   In *R v Phekoo*,[108] it was held that a mistaken belief, honestly and reasonably held, that a person was not a residential occupier afforded a defence to a charge of harassment; the mistake was that the defendant believed the occupiers to be trespassers and did not know that they were lawful subtenants of his own tenant.[109] In *West Wiltshire DC v Snelgrove*,[110] the court characterised the mistake in *Phekoo* as a mistake of fact, because a mistake in law does not amount to a defence to a criminal offence.[111]

2.90   Where a defence is raised, it is for the defendant,[112] to establish it on the balance of probabilities.[113] Whether this can be done is a matter of fact for magistrates or a jury to decide.

2.91   Unlike the offence of harassment by a landlord or landlord's agent, there is no defence here that the defendant had reasonable grounds for committing the harassing conduct.

Rent repayment order

2.92   Under Chapter 4 of Part 2 of Housing and Planning Act (HPA) 2016, the First-tier Tribunal has power to make a rent repayment

---

106   *McCall v Abelesz* [1976] QB 585, CA, per Ormrod LJ at 598 (obiter).
107   *Schon v Camden LBC* (1986) 18 HLR 341, CA. It would be sufficient for PEA 1977 s1(3)(b), but the charge did not refer to this and so the defendant was acquitted.
108   [1981] 1 WLR 1117, CA.
109   The decision would apply equally to illegal eviction; see *Wandsworth LBC v Osei Bonsu* [1999] 1 WLR 1011, (1999) 31 HLR 515, CA.
110   (1997) 30 HLR 57, 63, QBD, per Simon Brown LJ.
111   Nevertheless, although ignorance of the criminal law is not a defence, a mistake as to the civil law may have the effect of negating the criminal intent: *Wandsworth LBC v Osei Bonsu* [1999] 1 WLR 1011, (1999) 31 HLR 515, CA, per Simon Brown LJ at 1019H.
112   MCA 1980 s101; *R v Hunt* [1987] AC 352, HL.
113   *Blackstone's Criminal Practice 2017* (Oxford University Press, 2016), para F3.5.

order against a landlord in England[114] who has committed an offence under PEA 1977 s1(3) or (3A), where the offence took place on or after 6 April 2017.[115]

2.93 Either a tenant or a local housing authority may apply for a rent repayment order.[116]

2.94 **Application by tenant.** A tenant may apply if the offence was committed within the 12 months before the application was made and was related to the housing that was let to the tenant.[117] The tenant may recover the rent for the period of up to 12 months before the date that the landlord committed the offence, less any amount which was paid in respect of the rent by universal credit or housing benefit.[118] The tribunal must, in deciding the amount of the award, have regard to the conduct both of the landlord and of the tenant, the financial circumstances of the landlord and whether the landlord has at any time been convicted of an offence under Chapter 4 of Part 2[119] of HPA 2016:[120] see also para 2.97.

2.95 **Application by local housing authority.** Where the application is made by a local housing authority, the tribunal may award the universal credit or housing benefit that was paid, directly or indirectly, to the landlord in respect of the rent for the period of up to 12 months

---

114 The provisions do not apply in Wales.

115 HPA 2016 s40; Housing and Planning Act 2016 (Commencement No 5, Transitional Provisions and Savings) Regulations 2017 SI No 281 regs 4, 5(1). Note that in relation to the HA 2004 ss72(1) and 95(1) offences (discussed at paras 5.30–5.31 and 5.36), HPA 2016 does not apply where the commission of the offence began before 6 April 2017 and ended no later than 5 April 2018: reg 5(2). In that case, the HA 2004 provisions will apply: see paras 5.55–5.70.

116 HPA 2016 s41(1).

117 HPA 2016 s41(2).

118 HPA 2016 ss44(1)–(3) and 51. Section 44 refers to universal credit, which is currently implemented only in certain areas and for certain types of claimant; section 51 therefore requires references to universal credit to include a reference to housing benefit, ie where the latter remains the relevant benefit.

119 This includes the PEA 1977 offences referred to at para 2.92, as well as a number of other offences, specified in HPA 2016 s40(3), which includes unlawful eviction under PEA 1977 s1(2) (see paras 1.197–1.254), violent entry into premises (Criminal Law Act 1977 s6(1) – see paras 3.6–3.36), failure to comply with certain orders under HA 2004 Part 1, offences related to the control or management of unlicensed HMOs or houses under HA 2004 ss72(1) and 95(1) (see paras 5.30–5.31 and 5.36) and will include breach of a banning order under HPA 2016 s21 when banning orders are brought into force (paras 6.2–6.38).

120 HPA 2016 s44(4).

before the date that the landlord committed the offence.[121] In deciding the amount of the award, the tribunal must have regard to the conduct of the landlord, the financial circumstances of the landlord and whether the landlord has been convicted of an offence under Chapter 4 of Part 2[122] of HPA 2016:[123] see also para 2.97.

2.96   While in principle the local housing authority has a discretion whether or not to apply for an order,[124] it is under a duty to consider doing so once it has become aware that any offence under Chapter 4 of Part 2 of HPA 2016[125] has been committed on or after 6 April 2017.[126] The authority must, when deciding whether to apply for an order, have regard to guidance given by the secretary of state.[127] The authority may only seek the order if it has first served a notice of intended proceedings informing the landlord of its reasons for doing so, the amount sought and invited the landlord to make representations.[128]

2.97   *Tribunal Order.* The First-tier Tribunal may make a rent repayment order provided it is satisfied, beyond reasonable doubt, that the landlord has committed an offence under PEA 1977 s1(3) or (3A) (paras 2.52–2.91); it is not, however, necessary that there should be an actual conviction – only that the offence has been committed on or after 6 April 2017.[129] Although the tribunal has a discretion as to the amount of the order, it may prima facie not reduce the maximum amount that would otherwise be payable[130] where the landlord has

121   HPA 2016 ss45(1)–(3) and 51 (see n118, above). The authority may apply any amount recovered under a rent repayment order to meet the costs and expenses incurred in, or associated with, carrying out enforcement functions in relation to the private rented sector: Rent Repayment Orders and Financial Penalties (Amounts Recovered) (England) Regulations 2017 SI No 367 reg 3(1). Enforcement functions are defined by reg 2 to mean functions under HA 2004 Parts 1–4, and functions under HPA 2016 Part 2, as well as other functions connected with the law related to housing or landlord and tenant. Any amount not applied in that way must be paid into the Consolidated Fund: reg 3(2).

122   See n119, above.

123   HPA 2016 s45(4).

124   HPA 2016 s41(1).

125   See n119, above.

126   HPA 2016 s48.

127   HPA 2016 s41(4). The secretary of state has issued guidance: Department for Communities and Local Government, *Rent repayment orders under Housing and Planning Act 2016: Guidance for Local Authorities* (April 2017). The guidance, however, does no more than describe the law.

128   HPA 2016 s42(2).

129   HPA 2016 s43(1).

130   Ie the rent or credit/benefit referable to the 12 months before the offence was committed: paras 2.94–2.95.

been convicted of the offence which gives rise to the application.[131] Even so, there is a residual discretion to reduce the amount, if the tribunal considers – by reason of exceptional circumstances – that it would be unreasonable to require the landlord to pay it.[132]

Caravan Sites Act 1968 / Mobile Homes (Wales) Act 2013

2.98   There are also two offences of harassment of occupiers of mobile homes under residental contracts (see paras 1.103–1.104), modelled on the offences of harassment under PEA 1977 (paras 2.52–2.91). One offence can only be committed by the site owner or his or her agent; the other by anyone. Each offence has two elements:

a) the prohibited harassment; and
b) the perpetrator's state of mind.

Harassment

2.99   Under both offences, the prohibited harassment comprises:

a) acts likely to interfere with the peace and comfort of a residential occupier or members of his or her household; or
b) persistent withdrawal or withholding of services or facilities reasonably required for occupation of the mobile home.[133]

2.100   A person who commits such an act of harassment is guilty of an offence if he or she intended to cause the occupier of the mobile home:

i)   to abandon occupation of the mobile home;
ii) to remove it from the site; or
iii) to refrain from exercising his or her rights or pursuing any remedy in respect of the mobile home.[134]

2.101   If the perpetrator of the harassment is a site owner or his or her agent, an offence is committed if he or she knew, or had reasonable cause to believe, that the actions would have any of those consequences.[135]

---

131 HPA 2016 s46(1).
132 HPA 2016 s46(5).
133 CSA 1968 s3(1)(c), (1A); MH(W)A 2013 s42(4), (5).
134 CSA 1968 s3(1); MH(W)A 2013 s42(4).
135 CSA 1968 s3(1A); MH(W)A 2013 s42(5).

Defences

2.102   It is a defence for the site owner or agent to show that there were reasonable grounds for interfering with the peace or comfort of the residential occupier or for withdrawing or withholding the services or facilities.[136]

Penalty

2.103   The defendant is liable on conviction in the magistrates' court to an unlimited fine and/or to imprisonment for a maximum of six months. [137] On conviction in the Crown Court, a defendant is liable to an unlimited fine and/or imprisonment for a maximum of two years.[138]

Protection from Harassment Act 1997 and Criminal Justice and Police Act 2001

2.104   PHA 1997 and CJPA 2001 prohibit harassment, breach of which is actionable in the civil and criminal courts.[139] The provisions are not specifically directed at landlords (or their agents), but so much of what they provide catches harassment in its general landlord–tenant sense that there is as much reason to consider their applicability in the criminal context as there is in the civil.[140]

2.105   The provisions create eight relevant criminal offences:

1) harassment of an individual;
2) harassment of two or more persons;
3) harassment of a person in his or her home;
4) putting another person in fear of violence;
5) stalking;
6) stalking involving fear of violence or serious alarm or distress;
7) breach of a restraining order; and
8) breach of an injunction.

2.106   Additionally, PHA 1997 gives a criminal court the power to make a restraining order, which has a similar effect to an injunction (and is

---

136 CSA 1968 s3(4A); MH(W)A 2013 s43(2).
137 CSA 1968 s3(3)(a); MH(W)A 2013 s43(3)(a); MCA 1980 s32(2), (9), (10); and LASPO 2012 s85(2).
138 CSA 1968 s3(3)(b); MH(W)A 2013 s43(3)(b).
139 The relevant provisions of both PHA 1997 and CJPA 2001 are set out in appendix B.
140 For the civil cause of action, see paras 2.32–2.37.

required before the offence of breaching a restraining order can be committed).[141]

Harassment of an individual or of two or more persons

2.107 Section 1(1) of PHA 1997 prohibits a person from pursuing a course of conduct:

a) which amounts to harassment of another; and
b) which he or she knows or ought to know amounts to harassment of the other.[142]

2.108 Section 1(1A) of PHA 1997 prohibits a person from pursuing a course of conduct:

a) which involves harassment of two or more persons; and
b) which he or she knows or ought to know involves harassment of those persons; and
c) by which he or she intends to persuade any person (whether or not one of those mentioned above):
i) not to do something that he or she is entitled or required to do; or
ii) to do something that he or she is not under any obligation to do.[143]

2.109 References to a 'person', in the context of the harassment of a person, are references to an individual.[144] The offence does not cover the harassment of a company.[145]

---

141 See paras 2.152–2.157.
142 PHA 1997 s1(1).
143 PHA 1997 s1(1A), as inserted by Serious Organised Crime and Police Act (SOCPA) 2005 s125(2).
144 PHA 1997 s7(5), as inserted by SOCPA 2005.
145 *Daiichi Pharmaceuticals UK Ltd v Stop Huntingdon Animal Cruelty* [2003] EWHC 2337 (QB), [2004] 1 WLR 1503, at [20] per Owen J; and *Director of Public Prosecutions v Dziurzynski* [2002] EWHC 1380 (Admin), [2002] ACD 88. In *Huntingdon Life Sciences v Curtin and others* [1998] Env LR D9, CA, the Court of Appeal held that a person did include a company. This decision, however, was not followed in *Daiichi* or *Dziurzynski* on the basis that it had been reached following an appeal from an ex parte injunction in which there had not been argument from both sides.

2.110   There is no definition of harassment.[146] It includes, but is not limited to, alarming or causing distress to a person.[147] Conduct need not, therefore, cause actual alarm or distress,[148] although it must be targeted at an individual and have been calculated to cause that person alarm or distress.[149] The conduct must be oppressive and unacceptable and sufficiently serious to warrant a criminal conviction; unreasonable conduct that merely irritates, annoys or causes a small measure of upset will not amount to harassment.[150] It is for the court, on the facts of the particular case, to assess whether behaviour is unacceptable and unreasonable. The context in which the conduct occurred is likely to assist the court in determining if the conduct amounted to harassment.[151]

2.111   In *Tuppen and another v Microsoft Corporation Ltd and another*,[152] the PHA 1997 was said to be directed at the prevention of stalking, anti-social behaviour by neighbours and racial harassment. In *Director of Public Prosecutions v Selvanayagam*,[153] however, Collins J observed that, whatever its purpose, the words of PHA 1997 were clear and could cover harassment of any sort. Plainly, the sort of conduct with which this book is concerned could comprise harassment within PHA 1997.

2.112   The prosecution must prove that the defendant was aware that the conduct amounted to or involved harassment or, if not, that he or she 'ought to have known'.

2.113   A person ought to know that a course of conduct amounts to or involves harassment if:

---

146 The government chose not to include one, taking the view that harassment as a concept had been interpreted regularly by the courts under Public Order Act 1986 s4A: Home Secretary, *Hansard*, HC vol 287 col 784, 17 December 1996.

147 PHA 1997 s7(2); *Director of Public Prosecutions v Ramsdale* (2001) *Independent* 19 March, QBD.

148 *Majrowski v Guy's and St Thomas's NHS Trust* [2006] UKHL 34, [2007] 1 AC 224 at [66] per Lady Hale.

149 *Thomas v News Group Newspapers Ltd* [2001] EWCA Civ 1233 at [29]–[30] per Lord Philips MR. (This approach has subsequently been doubted, however, in a dissenting judgment in *Allen v Southwark LBC* [2008] EWCA Civ 1478 at [27] per Arden LJ who held that conduct might be harassment even though no alarm or distress was in fact caused.)

150 *Majrowski* at [30] per Lord Nicholls; and *R v N* [2016] EWCA Crim 92, [2016] 2 Cr App R 10.

151 *Conn v Sunderland CC* [2007] EWCA Civ 1492, [2008] IRLR 324, at [12] per Gage LJ.

152 (2000) *Times* 15 November, QBD.

153 (1999) *Times* 23 June, QBD.

... a reasonable person in possession of the same information would think [it] amounted to or involved harassment of [another].[154]

2.114 This indicates a broadly objective approach without any allowance for the defendant's own mental health,[155] belief or culture.[156]

Course of conduct

2.115 It is an offence to pursue a course of conduct in breach of the prohibition on harassment set out in PHA 1997 s1(1) or s1(1A).[157] At least one of the acts constituting the course of conduct must have been committed in the six months before the complaint to the magistrates' court is made.[158]

2.116 'Conduct' is not defined, but includes speech.[159]

2.117 A 'course of conduct' must involve conduct[160] on a minimum of two occasions.[161] There is no requirement, however, for the conduct to comprise acts of the same nature; it is the course of conduct that must amount to harassment, as opposed to the individual instances of conduct,[162] so that a course of conduct may amount to harassment even if it involves acts that would not in isolation amount to harassment.

2.118 While the number of incidents required to constitute a course of conduct need not exceed two, however, the conduct will need to be more severe to sustain a conviction where there is only a small

---

154 PHA 1997 s1(2), as amended by SOCPA 2005.

155 *R v C* [2001] EWCA Crim 1251, [2001] 2 FLR 757 (the defendant's schizophrenia should not be attributed to the reasonable person).

156 *Crawford v Crown Prosecution Service* [2008] EWHC 148 (Admin) at [64] per Thomas LJ.

157 PHA 1997 s2(1). A racially or religiously aggravated form of the offence is created by Crime and Disorder Act (CDA) 1998 s32(1), see paras 2.146–2.151.

158 MCA 1980 s127; *Director of Public Prosecutions v Baker* [2004] EWHC 2782 (Admin), (2005) 169 JP 140.

159 PHA 1997 s7(4).

160 Acts done on behalf of the Crown, which the Home Secretary has certified relate to national security, the economic well-being of the UK or the prevention or detection of serious crime are excluded from 'conduct' for these purposes: PHA 1997 s12.

161 PHA 1997 s7(3). This is wider than 'persistent', which is used in both offences of harassment under PEA 1977 s1(3) and (3A), in which context it has been held to mean both more than once and one occurrence followed by 'deliberate continuity': *R v Abrol* [1972] Crim LR 318, CA.

162 *Iqbal v Dean Manson Solicitors* [2011] EWCA Civ 123, [2011] CP Rep 26 per Rix LJ at [45].

number of incidents.[163] Likewise, the wider apart the incidents are spread, the less likely it is that a finding of harassment can reasonably be made,[164] although it is conceivable that incidents occurring, say, a year apart could constitute a course of conduct, for example, threats made on the complainant's birthday each year.[165] Acts which are not sufficiently connected in type and context, however, will not constitute a course of conduct.[166]

2.119　　There is no requirement that the course of conduct is communicated to the victim by the perpetrator directly. If a person pursues a course of conduct and the detail of his or her actions is relayed to the victim by a third party, then the perpetrator can still have committed the offence.[167]

2.120　　The course of conduct must, however, affect the victim within the jurisdiction, so that there was no breach of PHA 1997 where the defendant mounted a campaign of abuse in television programmes which were broadcast in England and Wales at a time when the victim was in Dubai.[168] It would seem to follow that a landlord might not commit the offence by sending, eg, threatening text messages, if the tenant is abroad on holiday at the time.

2.121　　Conduct may be directed at more than one person.[169] In such circumstances, there is a course of conduct where there is conduct on at least one occasion in relation to each person,[170] ie there need not be a course in relation to each, but the course can be comprised of conduct across them all.

---

163 *Jones v Director of Public Prosecutions* [2010] EWHC 523 (Admin), [2011] 1 WLR 833 at [35] per Ouseley J.

164 *Baron v Crown Prosecution Service* (CO/1569/00) unreported, QBD.

165 *Lau v Director of Public Prosecutions* [2000] 1 FLR 799, QBD and *R v Patel* [2005] 1 Cr App R 27, CA. In *Pratt v Director of Public Prosecutions* [2001] EWHC 483 (Admin), (2001) *Times* 22 August, the High Court held that two incidents almost three months apart were 'close to the line, but sufficient to establish a course of conduct'. See also *R v Hills* [2001] 1 FLR 580, CA, and *R v Sahin* [2009] EWCA Crim 2616. In *Kelly v Director of Public Prosecutions* [2002] EWHC 1428 (Admin), (2002) 166 JP 621, three telephone calls made in a five-minute period constituted a 'course of conduct'.

166 *Pratt v Director of Public Prosecutions* [2001] EWHC 483 (Admin), (2001) *Times* 22 August.

167 *Kellett v Director of Public Prosecutions* [2001] EWHC 107 (Admin) at [16] per Penry-Davey J.

168 *Shakil-Ur-Rahman v ARY Network Ltd* [2016] EWHC 3110 (QB), [2017] 4 WLR 22.

169 PHA 1997 s1(1A); *Director of Public Prosecutions v Dunn* [2001] 1 Cr App R 22, DC.

170 PHA 1997 s7(3)(b).

2.122 Conduct need not be directed at the person affected, provided that it is targeted at someone; accordingly, where a defendant had harassed a husband, also causing distress to his wife, the defendant had also unlawfully harassed the wife.[171]

2.123 Moreover, where the conduct of one person (D1) is aided, abetted, counselled or procured[172] by another person (D2), D1's conduct is deemed to be the conduct of D2 (as well as remaining D1's own conduct). D2's conduct is to be considered in relation to his or her knowledge and purpose[173] at the time of the aiding, abetting, counselling or procuring.[174]

2.124 A course of conduct does not, however, amount to harassment in any of the following three circumstances.[175]

- It is pursued to prevent or detect crime – this exception is necessary to prevent law enforcement agencies being caught by the provision, but it is not limited to action by the police. So, for example, a tenancy relations officer pursuing a landlord during the course of an investigation into allegations of harassment of a tenant, can rely on it, as can a private individual.

- It is pursued under any statute or rule of law or to comply with a condition or requirement imposed by any person under a statute; if the law permits certain conduct, such as the service of a notice seeking possession, it may not amount to harassment.[176]

- In the particular circumstances, it was reasonable to pursue it – this is an open category allowing a court to decide on the facts of the particular case that the defendant's behaviour was not harassment. For example, the mere reporting of a person's wrongdoing to an employer is likely to be reasonable, but will cease to be reasonable if the person doing the reporting goes beyond the simple reporting of the fact, eg, by adding other unfounded allegations.[177]

171 *Levi v Bates* [2015] EWCA Civ 206, [2016] QB 91.
172 The concepts of aiding, abetting, counselling and procuring are familiar to the criminal law. See *Blackstone's Criminal Practice 2017* (Oxford University Press, 2016), section A4.
173 Including what he or she ought to have known.
174 PHA 1997 s7(3A).
175 PHA 1997 s1(3). The burden is on the person accused of the conduct to show that one of these circumstances applies.
176 The issue of five sets of proceedings against a person seeking possession orders on essentially the same ground might, however, be considered to be conduct that amounted to harassment: *Allen v Southwark LBC* [2008] EWCA Civ 1478.
177 *Kellett v Director of Public Prosecutions* [2001] EWHC 107 (Admin) at [18].

Penalty

2.125   The offence under PHA 1997 s2 is only triable in the magistrates' court. The maximum penalty is six months' imprisonment and/or a fine.[178] *The Magistrates' Court Sentencing Guidelines* set out aggravating features which include: constant contact at night, threatening violence, taking personal photographs, sending offensive material, attempts to enter a victim's home or workplace, use or distribution of photographs, planning, ignoring obvious distress, the involvement of others, where the action is over a long period, where the victim needs medical help or counselling and where children are frightened. In addition, on conviction, the court may make a restraining order[179] (see paras 2.152–2.157).

Harassment of a person in his or her home

2.126   Section 42A of CJPA 2001 provides that:

> (1) A person commits an offence if–
>> (a) that person is present outside or in the vicinity of any premises that are used by any individual ('the resident') as his dwelling;
>> (b) that person is present there for the purpose (by his presence or otherwise) of representing to the resident or another individual (whether or not one who uses the premises as his dwelling), or of persuading the resident or such another individual –
>>> (i) that he should not do something he is entitled or required to do; or
>>> (ii) that he should do something that he is not under any obligation to do.

2.127   In addition, the person must either:

a) intend his or her presence to amount to the harassment of, or to cause alarm or distress to, the resident; or

b) know or ought to know, that his or her presence is likely to result in the harassment of, or to cause alarm or distress to, the resident.[180]

A person ought to know the likely effect of his or her conduct if a reasonable person would think that the person's presence was likely

---

178 PHA 1997 s2(2). PHA 1997 refers to a fine not exceeding level 5 on the standard scale, the effect of which is now an unlimited fine: Criminal Justice Act (CJA) 1982 s37(2) and LASPO 2012 s85(1).

179 PHA 1997 s5(1).

180 CJPA 2001 s42A(1)(c).

to have that effect.[181] The conduct must also amount to, or be likely to result in, harassment, alarm or distress of the resident.[182]

Penalty

2.128 The offence is only triable in the magistrates' court.[183] The maximum penalty is six months' imprisonment or a fine not exceeding level 4 on the standard scale (currently £2,500).[184]

Putting another in fear of violence

2.129 A person commits an offence by pursuing a course of conduct[185] which:

> ... causes another to fear, on at least two occasions, that violence will be used against him ... if he knows or ought to know that his course of conduct will cause the other so to fear on each of those occasions.[186]

2.130 'Course of conduct' has the same meaning as it does in relation to the offence of harassment (see paras 2.115–2.124) subject to the additional requirement that the conduct must have caused another person to fear that violence will be used against him or her.[187]

2.131 A person 'ought to know' that a course of conduct would cause another to fear violence if a reasonable person possessed of the same information would think so.[188] Each act relied on must cause fear that violence will be used.[189] Moreover, the conduct must be such that there is fear that violence *will* be used against another; conduct which causes a person to be frightened about what *might* happen is insufficient.[190] Accordingly, while a fear of violence may be inferred from a person's

---

181 CJPA 2001 s42A(4).
182 CJPA 2001 s42A(1)(d).
183 CJPA 2001 s42A(4).
184 CJA 1982 s37, as amended by CJA 1991 s17.
185 Acts done on behalf of the Crown, which the Home Secretary has certified relate to national security, the economic well-being of the UK or the prevention or detection of serious crime are excluded from being 'conduct' for these purposes: PHA 1997 s12.
186 PHA 1997 s4(1). A racially or religiously aggravated form of the offence is created by CDA 1998 s32(1), see paras 2.146–2.151.
187 *R v Curtis* [2010] EWCA Crim 123, [2010] 1 WLR 2770 at [20] per Pill LJ.
188 PHA 1997 s4(2); ie, the same guidance to the meaning of constructive knowledge as in s1(2) in relation to whether a person knows a course of conduct amounts to harassment (see paras 2.112–2.114).
189 *Kelly v Director of Public Prosecutions* [2002] EWHC 1428 (Admin) at [24] per Burton J.
190 *R v Henley* [2000] Crim LR 582, CA at [13] per Burton J.

conduct, direct evidence is ordinarily needed to prove that a person actually feared that violence would be used against him or her.[191]

Defences

2.132   A defence to a charge of putting a person in fear of violence is available in any of the following three circumstances:[192]

a) the course of conduct was pursued to prevent or detect crime;
b) the course of conduct was pursued under any statute or rule of law or to comply with a condition or requirement imposed by a person under a statute;
c) the pursuit of the course of conduct was reasonable for the protection of the defendant or of another or for the protection of the defendant's or another's property.

2.133   These circumstances are broadly the same as the circumstances in which a course of conduct will not amount to harassment.[193] It is for the defendant[194] to establish the defence on the balance of probabilities.[195] Whether this has been done is a matter of fact for magistrates or a jury to decide.

Penalty

2.134   The offence can be tried in either a magistrates' court or the Crown Court. The maximum penalty in a magistrates' court is six months' imprisonment and/or a fine[196] and in the Crown Court ten years' imprisonment and/or an unlimited fine.[197] On conviction, the court may make a restraining order.[198]

2.135   If the defendant is acquitted by the Crown Court of this offence under PHA 1997 s4, he or she may nevertheless be convicted of harassment or stalking.[199]

---

191 *R (a child) v Director of Public Prosecutions* [2001] EWHC 17 (Admin) at [19] per Newman J.

192 PHA 1997 s4(3).

193 See para 2.124. Note, however, that, in relation to harassment, it is sufficient to show that the conduct was reasonable per se, whereas for this offence it is necessary to prove that it was reasonable specifically for the protection of the person or property.

194 MCA 1980 s101; *R v Hunt* [1987] AC 352, HL.

195 *Blackstone's Criminal Practice 2017* (Oxford University Press, 2016), para F3.5.

196 PHA 1997 s4(4)(b). PHA 1997 refers to a fine not exceeding the statutory maximum, the effect of which is now an unlimited fine: LASPO 2012 s85(1).

197 PHA 1997 s4(4)(a).

198 PHA 1997 s5(1) and see paras 2.152–2.157.

199 PHA 1997 s4(5); but not if acquitted in a magistrates' court.

Stalking

2.136   PHA 1997 s2A creates an offence of stalking.[200] The offence is committed where a person pursues a course of conduct in breach of PHA 1997 s1(1)[201] which course of conduct amounts to stalking.[202]

2.137   A course of conduct amounts to stalking if it is harassment of another person, involving acts or omissions associated with stalking, and the defendant knew or ought to have known that it amounted to harassment of that person.[203]

2.138   There is no comprehensive definition of 'acts or omissions associated with stalking'. Instead, PHA 1997 s2 provides a list of examples of acts or omissions which may be associated with stalking.[204]

a) following a person;
b) contacting, or attempting to contact, a person by any means;
c) publishing any material which relates or purports to relate to a person, or purports to originate from a person;
d) monitoring the use by a person of any form of electronic communication;
e) loitering in any place;
f) interfering with property in the possession of a person; and
g) watching or spying on a person.

Penalty

2.139   The PHA 1997 s2A offence of stalking is only triable in a magistrates' court. The maximum penalty is six months' imprisonment and/or a fine.[205]

Stalking involving fear of violence or serious alarm or distress

2.140   A person (A) commits an offence by pursuing a course of conduct which amounts to stalking (see paras 2.136–2.138) and which:

---

200 Added by Protection of Freedoms Act 2012 s111 with effect from 25 November 2012. An amendment was made to CDA 1998 s32(1) at the same time to create a racially or religiously aggravated form of the offence, see paras 2.146–2.151.
201 See paras 2.115–2.124.
202 PHA 1997 s2(1).
203 PHA 1997 s2(2).
204 PHA 1997 s2(3).
205 PHA 1997 s2(4), (5). PHA 1997 refers to a fine not exceeding the statutory maximum, the effect of which is now an unlimited fine: LASPO s85(1). When Criminal Justice Act (CJA) 2003 s281 is brought into force, the maximum sentence will be increased to 51 weeks' imprisonment: PHA 1997 s2(4), (5).

either–
(i) causes another ('B') to fear, on at least two occasions, that violence will be used against B, or
(ii) causes B serious alarm or distress which has a substantial adverse effect on B's usual day-to-day activities,
... if A knows or ought to know that A's course of conduct will cause B so to fear on each of those occasions or (as the case may be) will cause such alarm or distress.[206]

2.141   The defendant 'ought to know' that his or her course of conduct will cause B to fear that violence will be used if that is what a reasonable person in possession of the same information would think.[207]

2.142   Similarly, the defendant ought to know his or her course of conduct will cause B the necessary alarm or distress if a reasonable person in possession of the same information would think that it would do so.[208]

Defence

2.143   A charge of stalking involving fear of violence or serious alarm or distress can be defended where the defendant can show that any one of the following three conditions is met:[209]

i) the course of conduct was pursued to prevent or detect crime;
ii) the course of conduct was pursued under any statute or rule of law or to comply with a condition or requirement imposed by a person under a statute;
iii) the pursuit of the course of conduct was reasonable for the protection of the defendant or of another or for the protection of the defendant's or another's property.

Penalty

2.144   The offence can be tried in either a magistrates' court or the Crown Court. The maximum penalty in a magistrates' court is six months' imprisonment and/or a fine[210] and in the Crown Court ten years'

---

206 PHA 1997 s4A(1). An amendment was made to CDA 1998 s32(1) at the same time to create a racially or religiously aggravated form of the offence, see paras 2.146–2.151.
207 PHA 1997 s4A(2).
208 PHA 1997 s4A(3)
209 PHA 1997 s4A(4).
210 PHA 1997 s4A(5)(b). PHA 1997 refers to a fine not exceeding the statutory maximum, the effect of which is now an unlimited fine: LASPO s85(1). When CJA 2003 s154 is brought into force, the maximum sentence will be increased to 12 months' imprisonment: PHA 1997 s4A(5)(b), (6).

imprisonment and/or an unlimited fine.[211] On conviction, the court may make a restraining order.[212]

2.145   If the defendant is acquitted by the Crown Court of this offence, he or she may nevertheless be convicted of harassment or stalking.[213]

Racially or religiously aggravated harassment

2.146   CDA 1998 creates a number of offences of racially or religiously aggravated harassment.

2.147   First, CDA 1998 s32(1)(a) provides for racially or religiously aggravated versions of the PHA 1997 s2 and s2A offences.[214]

2.148   Secondly, CDA 1998 s32(1)(b) provides for racially or religously aggravated versions of the PHA 1997 s4 and s4A offences.[215]

2.149   An offence is racially or religiously aggravated if:

(a) at the time of committing the offence, or immediately before or after doing so, the offender demonstrates towards the victim of the offence hostility based on the victim's membership[216] (or presumed[217] membership) of a racial or religious group; or

(b) the offence is motivated (wholly or partly) by hostility towards members of a racial or religious group based on their membership of that group.[218]

2.150   The offences are triable in either the magistrates' court or the Crown Court. If tried in the magistrates' court, the maximum penalty is the same as for the equivalent offences under PHA 1997 ss2, 2A, 4 and 4A.[219] If tried in the Crown Court, the maximum penalty in relation to CDA 1998 s32(1)(a) is two years' imprisonment and/or an unlimited fine,[220] while the maximum penalty in relation to s32(1)(b) is 14 years' imprisonment and/or an unlimited fine.[221]

---

211 PHA 1997 s4A(5)(a).
212 PHA 1997 s5(1); and see paras 2.152–2.157.
213 PHA 1997 s4A(7); but not if acquitted in a magistrates' court.
214 See paras 2.115–2.125 and 2.136–2.139.
215 See paras 2.129–2.135 and 2.140–2.145.
216 Which includes association with members of that group: CDA 1998 s28(2).
217 Ie presumed by the offender: CDA 1998 s28(2).
218 CDA 1998 s28(1).
219 CDA 1998 s32(3)(a), (4)(a). *The Magistrates' Court Sentencing Guidelines* indicate that the magistrates should form a preliminary view of the appropriate sentence and then increase it where the offender has been convicted of the racially or religiously aggravated form of the offence.
220 CDA 1998 s32(3)(b).
221 CDA 1998 s32(4)(b).

2.151   If the defendant is acquitted by the Crown Court of one of the racially or religiously aggravated offences, he or she may nevertheless be convicted of the equivalent PHA 1997 offence.[222]

Restraining orders

2.152   The court may impose a 'restraining order' on a defendant to protect the victim or victims (or any other specified person(s)) from further conduct which may amount to harassment or cause a fear of violence.[223]

2.153   The power arises where:

> A court [is] sentencing or otherwise dealing with the person ... convicted of an offence ...[224]

2.154   A court can impose a restraining order on or after conviction.[225] In addition, a court may impose a restraining order on a person who is acquitted of an offence if it considers it necessary to do so to protect a person from harassment by the defendant.[226] The order must describe the prohibited conduct and may be for a specified period or until a further order is made.[227]

Breach of a restraining order

2.155   It is an offence for a person to do anything prohibited under a restraining order without reasonable excuse.[228] When determining if an individual has breached the terms of a restraining order, the court is required to give the words used in the order their ordinary English meaning and not to construe them narrowly simply because they are being applied in a criminal context.[229]

2.156   Whether an excuse is reasonable is to be determined objectively. It is for the defendant[230] to establish – on the balance of probabilities

---

222 CDA 1998 s32(5), (6); but not if acquitted in a magistrates' court.
223 PHA 1997 s5(1) and (2).
224 PHA 1997 s5(1).
225 Prior to conviction, a similar result can be achieved by the court remanding the defendant on bail, subject to a condition not to interfere with a witness, in this case, the victim: Bail Act 1976 s3(6).
226 In either the magistrates' court or Crown Court: PHA 1997 s5A, as inserted by Domestic Violence, Crime and Victims Act 2004.
227 PHA 1997 s5(2) and (3).
228 PHA 1997 s5(5).
229 *R v Evans* [2004] EWCA Crim 3102, [2005] 1 WLR 1435 at [15] and [18] per Dyson LJ.
230 MCA 1980 s101; *R v Hunt* [1987] AC 352, HL.

– both the excuse and that it was reasonable.[231] The existence of a reasonable excuse is a question of fact for magistrates or a jury to decide.

Penalty

2.157 The offence can be tried in either a magistrates' court or the Crown Court. The maximum penalty in a magistrates' court is six months' imprisonment and/or a fine[232] and in the Crown Court five years' imprisonment and/or an unlimited fine.[233]

Breach of an injunction

2.158 Where a civil court has granted an injunction to prevent further harassment in civil proceedings for breach of the prohibition of harassment,[234] it is an offence if the defendant:

> ... without reasonable excuse ... does anything which he is prohibited from doing by the injunction.[235]

2.159 The penal notice in an injunction must therefore indicate that a failure to comply with the order will constitute a criminal offence under PHA 1997.[236] As to 'reasonable excuse', see paras 2.155–2.156. The defendant cannot be convicted of this offence if he or she has been punished for contempt of court[237] for breach of the injunction.[238]

Penalty

2.160 The offence can be tried in either a magistrates' court or the Crown Court. The maximum penalty in a magistrates' court is six months' imprisonment and a fine not exceeding level 5 on the standard scale (currently £5,000)[239] and in the Crown Court five years' imprisonment and/or an unlimited fine.[240]

---

231 *Blackstone's Criminal Practice 2017* (Oxford University Press, 2016), para F3.5.
232 PHA 1997 s5(6)(a). PHA 1997 refers to a fine not exceeding the statutory maximum, the effect of which is now an unlimited fine: LASPO s85(1).
233 PHA 1997 s5(6)(b).
234 Under PHA 1997 s3(3), and see paras 2.32–2.37. Note that it is not an offence to breach an injunction made in relation to any other cause of action.
235 PHA 1997 s3(6). This is novel. The normal way in which an injunction is enforced is by proceedings for contempt of court in the civil courts, see paras 8.16–8.24.
236 *Jeffries v Robb* [2012] EWCA Civ 1149.
237 See paras 8.16–8.24.
238 PHA 1997 s3(8).
239 PHA 1997 s3(9)(b). PHA 1997 refers to a fine not exceeding the statutory maximum, the effect of which is now an unlimited fine: LASPO s85(1).
240 PHA 1997 s3(9)(a).

Criminal trespass

Introduction

3.1   Before 1977, there was no offence of criminal trespass; it had been a matter solely for the civil law. The genesis of the change was a Law Commission Report,[1] recommending the modernisation of the law on forcible entry, much of which had remained the same since the Forcible Entry Act 1381, and the abolition of the offence of conspiracy to commit a tort.[2]

3.2   The proposals for reform were brought into focus by two contemporary phenomena: residential squatting and 'sit-ins'.[3] The Criminal Law Act (CLA) 1977 created two criminal offences relating to entry to premises, whether by lawful owners or strangers:[4] where land is occupied, an owner with an immediate right to possession against a trespasser is expected to use the summary possession procedure in the county court.[5] The offences can be committed even by a lawful owner (which is why the provisions are relevant to this book and the perspective from which they are addressed).

3.3   The two offences are:

- using violence to secure entry to premises; and
- threatening violence to secure entry to premises.

3.4   Additionally, the Legal Aid, Sentencing and Punishment of Offenders Act 2012 s144 criminalises all those who live in residential buildings without permission.[6] This could therefore include both a landlord

1   Conspiracy and criminal law reform (Law Com No 76 (1976)). For commentaries, see Dashwood and Trice [1976] Crim LR 500 and ATH Smith [1977] Crim LR 139.
2   Thereby reversing the House of Lords decision in *Kamara v Director of Public Prosecutions* [1974] AC 104, HL.
3   The occupation of industrial or academic premises, usually for political reasons.
4   Although there are exemptions for owner-occupiers and certain persons who intend to take up occupation (see paras 3.22–3.33 on 'displaced residential occupiers' and 'protected intended occupiers').
5   Civil Procedure Rules (CPR) Part 55. A claim may be brought in the High Court provided that the claimant files with the claim form a certificate, verified by a statement of truth, stating the reasons for bringing the claim: CPR 55.5(2). Circumstances that may justify bringing a claim in the High Court are where there are points of law of general importance, complicated facts or there is a substantial risk of public disturbance or of serious harm to persons or property which properly requires immediate determination: CPR 55A PD 1.3.
6   CLA 1977 s7(1) also criminalises any person who is present on, and entered, residential premises as a trespasser and who is asked to leave those premises by a displaced residential occupier or a protected intending occupier (see paras 3.22–3.33). As any person who commits the offence under CLA 1977 s7(1)

who moves into residential premises after unlawfully evicting a tenant and someone else to whom a landlord purports to grant a right of occupation following an unlawful eviction.

3.5 The full text of the relevant sections is set out in appendix B.

Criminal Law Act (CLA) 1977

Using violence to secure entry to premises

3.6 It is an offence if:

> ... any person ... without lawful authority, uses ... violence for the purpose of securing entry into any premises for himself or any other person ... provided that–
> (a) there is someone present on those premises who is opposed to the entry which the violence is intended to secure; and
> (b) the person using or threatening the violence knows that that is the case.[7]

3.7 Certain occupiers, known as 'displaced residential occupiers' and 'protected intended occupiers' – and persons acting on their behalf (see paras 3.22–3.33) – are, however, exempt from the provisions of this section.[8]

Lawful authority

3.8 CLA 1977 does not define 'lawful authority'. Instead, it states what is *not* lawful authority, namely, merely being the owner or having a right of possession or occupation of the premises.[9]

3.9 Persons having lawful authority include a displaced residential occupier,[10] a protected intended occupier,[11] a court bailiff executing a possession order, and a police officer entering to exercise a power of arrest or search under the criminal law.

---

will also have committed the offence under LASPO s144 (paras 3.44–3.48) it is unlikely, as the conditions for the offence under LASPO s144 are easier to satisfy, that this offence will be much used in the future.

7 CLA 1977 s6(1).
8 CLA 1977 s6(1A).
9 CLA 1977 s6(2).
10 By virtue of having or having been given a right over the property and they are expressly disapplied from CLA 1977 s6(1) by s6(1A).
11 By virtue of having or having been given a right over the property and they are expressly disapplied from CLA 1977 s6(1) by s6(1A).

3.10   The wording of the section means that the burden lies on the prosecution to prove an absence of lawful authority, rather than on the defendant to prove that he or she had it.

Premises

3.11   The term 'premises' is widely defined. It includes not only buildings, but also land ancillary[12] to a building and even the whole of a site that comprises a building or buildings with ancillary land.[13]

3.12   If parts of a building are separately occupied, however, they constitute different premises,[14] so that a person already lawfully in one part of the building can commit the offence by entering another (separately occupied) part.

3.13   The term also encompasses any fixed structure used for whatever purpose and any movable structure, vehicle or vessel, designed or adapted for use for residential purposes.[15] Thus, caravans, houseboats and converted buses are within the definition.

Violence

3.14   'Violence'[16] is not defined in CLA 1977: it is accordingly a question of fact and degree in any case whether violence was used. It should be construed in its ordinary, everyday sense.

3.15   It is immaterial whether the violence is directed against a person or against property.[17] It is not enough, however, that the person in the premises opposed to entry feared or apprehended violence. The prosecution must prove that actual violence was used.[18]

---

12 For instance, land adjacent to a building and used in connection with its occupation: CLA 1977 s12(2).

13 CLA 1977 s12(1).

14 CLA 1977 s12(1) and (2).

15 CLA 1977 s12(2).

16 This word was chosen rather than 'force', which is perhaps more common in criminal statutes, on the basis that it covers any application of force against the person, but carries a somewhat restricted meaning in relation to property; splintering a door or window would be violent but forcing a window catch would not: Conspiracy and criminal law reform (Law Com No 76 (1976)) at para 2.61.

17 CLA 1977 s6(4)(a).

18 There is, however, the offence of threatening violence to secure entry (see paras 3.34–3.36): conduct falling short of actual violence may be sufficient to constitute a threat.

For the purposes of securing entry to the premises

3.16 The violence must be committed with the objective in the mind of the person acting violently of securing entry to the premises. It is not, however, essential that actual entry into the premises be achieved.

3.17 It is irrelevant whether the purpose of the entry is to acquire possession or otherwise;[19] it is as much an offence to gate-crash a party violently as it is to evict a squatter – all that is needed is the intention to secure entry.

Someone on the premises opposed to the entry

3.18 It does not matter what the status of the person on the premises is: the occupier may be an owner, a tenant, a licensee or a trespasser. As long as there is someone present and opposed to the entry, the person seeking to secure entry violently commits the offence.

3.19 It is unclear whether the person opposed to entry has to know that the defendant is intending to secure entry to the premises. The test is whether he or she opposes the entry. This does not appear to import a requirement for an active display of opposition, merely the factual question whether someone on the premises does oppose entry.[20]

3.20 If nobody is on the premises, however, no offence is committed.[21]

Knowledge that there is someone on the premises

3.21 There is some older authority for the proposition that knowledge includes 'wilfully shutting one's eyes to the truth',[22] but the modern view is that nothing short of actual knowledge will suffice.[23] In the final analysis, it is a question of evidence whether the accused knew that somebody opposed to entry was on the premises.

---

19 CLA 1977 s6(4)(b).

20 It would seem bizarre if no offence was committed where someone was too ill or frail to oppose the entry or, indeed, even asleep or unaware of the entry.

21 See, for example, *Ropaigealach v Barclays Bank Plc* [2000] QB 263, (2000) 32 HLR 234, CA.

22 *Warner v Metropolitan Police Commissioner* [1969] 2 AC 256, HL, 279 per Lord Reid.

23 See, eg, *Westminster City Council v Croyalgrange Ltd* [1986] 1 WLR 674, HL, 682C per Lord Bridge. See generally *Blackstone's Criminal Practice 2017* (Oxford University Press, 2016).

Displaced residential occupier

3.22   CLA 1977 exempts from the offence someone who has been prevented from entering his or her own home. This is not a warrant to commit violence, because an offence against the person of the trespasser could still be committed, but it prevents such a person being caught by this offence.

3.23   For the purposes of CLA 1977, such a person is known as a 'displaced residential occupier' and is defined as:[24]

> ... any person who was occupying any premises as a residence[25] immediately before being excluded by anyone who entered those premises, or any access to those premises,[26] as a trespasser.

3.24   A person remains a displaced residential occupier while excluded from occupation by the trespasser or any subsequent trespasser.[27]

3.25   A trespasser cannot benefit from the privilege given to a displaced residential occupier. A person is not a displaced residential occupier if he or she was occupying the premises as a trespasser immediately before being excluded from occupation.[28] For these purposes, a person who occupies by virtue of any title derived from a trespasser, or permission given by a trespasser,[29] is treated as a trespasser.[30]

3.26   Displaced residential occupiers cannot commit the offence of violent entry; this exemption extends to anyone acting on behalf of a displaced residential occupier.[31]

3.27   It is a question of fact whether one person is 'acting on behalf of' another. There appears to be no need for an express agreement; it can be inferred from the circumstances.

3.28   If a defendant adduces sufficient evidence of being a displaced residential occupier,[32] it creates a rebuttable presumption that he or she is such an occupier which, should the issue arise by way of trial, the prosecution will have to disprove.[33]

---

24 CLA 1977 s12(3).
25 See paras 1.203–1.206 for a discussion on occupying as a residence.
26 'Access' means any part of a site or building in which the premises are situated, which constitutes an ordinary means of access to those premises: CLA 1977 s12(1)(b).
27 CLA 1977 s12(3).
28 CLA 1977 s12(4); *Wakolo v DPP* [2012] EWHC 611 (Admin), [2012] ACD 47.
29 Or from a person who himself or herself derived title from a trespasser.
30 CLA 1977 s12(6).
31 CLA 1977 s6(1A).
32 Or acting on behalf of a displaced residential occupier.
33 CLA 1977 s6(1A).

Protected intended occupier

3.29 The offence can also not be committed by a 'protected intended occupier'.

3.30 Although not resident, a protected intended occupier intends to reside, but cannot do so because he or she is prevented from taking up occupation by a trespasser.

3.31 A 'protected intended occupier' is defined[34] as an individual[35] who requires the premises for his or her own occupation, who is excluded from occupation by a trespasser and who is one of the following:

- a freeholder or a leaseholder (whose lease has at least two years to run) with a sworn statement to this effect;[36]
- a tenant or licensee of a local authority,[37] a registered provider of social housing[38] or a registered social landlord with a certificate[39] from the landlord to this effect;[40]
- any other tenant or licensee of a freeholder or a leaseholder (whose lease has at least two years to run) with a sworn statement to this effect.[41]

3.32 The conditions in CLA 1977 s12A are cumulative, not alternatives: an individual who is a freeholder must require the premises for his own occupation as a residence *and* be excluded from occupation of the premises by a person who entered them, or any access to them, as a trespasser *and* have the necessary written statement.[42] It follows that

---

34 CLA 1977 s12A.

35 Compare the definition of a displaced residential occupier in CLA 1977 s12(3), which refers to 'any person'. Presumably this is to avoid another type of legal person, eg, a company, from benefiting. It is unnecessary to make the distinction for displaced residential occupiers because a company cannot be resident: *Hiller v United Dairies (London) Ltd* [1934] 1 KB 57, CA.

36 CLA 1977 s12A(2). The statement must be sworn by the person whose interest is specified in it before a justice of the peace or a commissioner for oaths: CLA 1977 s12A(3).

37 Or a similar body: see Rent Act (RA) 1977 s14 for the complete list. Tenants and licensees of the Regulator of Social Housing are also covered by this provision.

38 In respect of a profit-making provider of registered provider of social housing, this only applies in relation to premises which are social housing within the meaning of Housing and Regeneration Act 2008 Part 2: CLA 1977 s12A(7)(bb).

39 That is a statement in writing.

40 CLA 1977 s12A(6).

41 CLA 1977 s12A(4) and (5). The statement must be sworn by both landlord and tenant before a justice of the peace or a commissioner for oaths: CLA 1977 s12A(3).

42 *Wakolo v DPP* [2012] EWHC 611 (Admin), [2012] ACD 47.

a husband who was the freehold owner of the matrimonial home but had been locked out by his wife could not rely on CLA 1977 s12A.[43]

3.33   As in the case of a displaced residential occupier, a protected intended occupier cannot commit the offence of violent entry, an exemption which extends to anyone acting on his or her behalf.[44]

Threatening violence to secure entry to premises

3.34   It is also an offence to threaten violence to secure entry to premises.[45] Threats may be made in any number of ways – for instance, spoken to someone in his or her presence or over the telephone, put into writing or implied by behaviour. The offence is committed only where the threat is of violence. Acts which cause the occupier to fear violence but which, on an objective view, do not amount to a threat of violence are not sufficient.

3.35   A general threat of violence towards an occupier is not enough; it must be for the purpose of securing entry to the property.

3.36   All the other elements of the offence – and the exemption of displaced residential occupiers and protected intended occupiers and persons acting on their behalf – are the same as in relation to the offence of using violence to secure entry (see paras 3.6–3.33).

Penalties

Criminal offence

3.37   The offences are triable only in a magistrates' court. The maximum penalty is six months' imprisonment and/or an unlimited fine.[46]

Rent repayment order

3.38   Under Chapter 4 of Part 2 of the Housing and Planning Act (HPA) 2016, the First-tier Tribunal has power to make a rent repayment order against a landlord in England[47] who has committed an offence

---

43   *Wakolo v DPP* [2012] EWHC 611 (Admin), [2012] ACD 47.
44   CLA 1977 s6(1A).
45   CLA 1977 s6(1).
46   CLA 1977 s6(5) and LASPO s85(1).
47   The provisions do not apply in Wales.

under CLA 1977 s6(1), where the offence took place on or after 6 April 2017.[48]

3.39 Either a tenant or a local housing authority may apply for a rent repayment order.[49]

Application by tenant

3.40 A tenant may apply if the offence was committed within the 12 months before the application was made and was related to the housing that was let to the tenant.[50] The tenant may recover the rent for the period of up to 12 months before the date that the landlord committed the offence, less any amount which was paid in respect of the rent by universal credit or housing benefit.[51] The tribunal must, in deciding the amount of the award, have regard to the conduct both of the landlord and of the tenant, the financial circumstances of the landlord and whether the landlord has at any time been convicted of an offence under Chapter 4 of Part 2[52] of HPA 2016:[53] see also para 3.43.

Application by local housing authority

3.41 Where the application is made by a local housing authority, the tribunal may award the universal credit or housing benefit that was paid, directly or indirectly, to the landlord in respect of the rent for the

---

48 HPA 2016 s40; Housing and Planning Act 2016 (Commencement No 5, Transitional Provisions and Savings) Regulations 2017 SI No 281 regs 4, 5(1). Note that in relation to the Housing Act (HA) 2004 ss72(1) and 95(1) offences (discussed at paras 5.30–5.31 and 5.36), HPA 2016 does not apply where the commission of the offence began before 6 April 2017 and ended no later than 5 April 2018: reg 5(2). In that case, the HA 2004 provisions will apply: see paras 5.55–5.70.

49 HPA 2016 s41(1).

50 HPA 2016 s41(2).

51 HPA 2016 s44(1)–(3) and s51. Section 44 refers to universal credit, which is currently implemented only in certain areas and for certain types of claimant; s51 therefore requires references to universal credit to include a reference to housing benefit, ie where the latter remains the relevant benefit.

52 This includes the CLA 1977 offence referred to at para 3.38, as well as a number of other offences, specified in HPA 2016 s40(3), which includes unlawful eviction and harassment under PEA 1977 s1(2), (3) and (3A) (see paras 1.197–1.254, 2.52–2.91), failure to comply with certain orders under HA 2004 Part 1, offences related to the control or management of unlicensed houses in multiple occupation (HMOs) or houses under HA 2004 ss72(1) and 95(1) (see paras 5.30–5.31 and 5.36) and will include breach of a banning order under HPA 2016, s21 when banning orders are brought into force (paras 6.2–6.38).

53 HPA 2016 s44(4).

period of up to 12 months before the date that the landlord committed the offence.[54] In deciding the amount of the award, the tribunal
must have regard to the conduct of the landlord, the financial circumstances of the landlord and whether the landlord has been convicted
of an offence under Part 2 of Chapter 4[55] of the HPA 2016:[56] see also
para 3.43.

3.42   While in principle the local housing authority has a discretion
whether or not to apply for an order,[57] it is under a duty to consider
doing so once it has become aware that any offence under Chapter 4 of Part 2 of the HPA 2016[58] has been committed on or after 6
April 2017.[59] The authority must, when deciding whether to apply for
an order, have regard to guidance given by the secretary of state.[60]
The authority may only seek the order if it has first served a notice
of intended proceedings informing the landlord of its reasons for
doing so, the amount sought and invited the landlord to make
representations.[61]

Tribunal order

3.43   The First-tier Tribunal may make a rent repayment order provided it
is satisfied, beyond reasonable doubt, that the landlord has committed
an offence under CLA 1977 s6(1) (see paras 3.6–3.36); it is not, however, necessary that there should be an actual conviction – only that
the offence has been committed on or after 6 April 2017.[62] Although
the tribunal has a discretion as to the amount of the order, it may

54 HPA 2016 ss45(1)–(3) and 51 (see n51, above). The authority may apply
    any amount recovered under a rent repayment order to meet the costs and
    expenses incurred in, or associated with, carrying out enforcement functions
    in relation to the private rented sector: Rent Repayment Orders and Financial
    Penalties (Amounts Recovered) (England) Regulations 2017 SI No 367 reg 3(1).
    Enforcement functions are defined by reg 2 to mean functions under HA 2004
    Parts 1–4, and functions under HPA 2016 Part 2, as well as other functions
    connected with the law related to housing or landlord and tenant. Any amount
    not applied in that way must be paid into the Consolidated Fund: reg 3(2).
55 See n52, above.
56 HPA 2016 s45(4).
57 HPA 2016 s41(1).
58 See n52, above.
59 HPA 2016 s48.
60 HPA 2016 s41(4). The secretary of state has issued guidance: Department for
    Communities and Local Government, *Rent repayment orders under Housing and
    Planning Act 2016: Guidance for Local Authorities* (April 2017). The guidance,
    however, does no more than describe the law.
61 HPA 2016 s42(2).
62 HPA 2016 s43(1).

prima facie not reduce the maximum amount that would otherwise be payable[63] where the landlord has been convicted of the offence which gives rise to the application.[64] Even so, there is a residual discretion to reduce the amount, if the tribunal considers – by reason of exceptional circumstances – that it would be unreasonable to require the landlord to pay it.[65]

Legal Aid, Sentencing and Punishment of Offenders Act 2012

Trespass in a residential building

3.44   LASPO s144 provides that it is a criminal offence where a person:

a) is in a residential building as a trespasser having entered it as a trespasser;

b) knows or ought to know that he or she is a trespasser; and

c) is living in the building or intends to live there for any period.[66]

3.45   A building is 'residential' if it is designed or adapted, before the time of entry, for use as a place to live.[67]

3.46   A person who remains in a residential building after his or her tenancy or licence has determined is not guilty of the offence.[68]

3.47   A person who remained as a trespasser in a residential building at the time section 144 was brought into force[69] committed the offence.[70]

---

63 Ie the rent or credit/benefit referable to the 12 months before the offence was committed: paras 3.40–3.41.

64 HPA 2016 s46(1).

65 HPA 2016 s46(5).

66 LASPO s144(1).

67 LASPO s144(3).

68 LASPO s144(2).

69 1 September 2012 (Legal Aid, Sentencing and Punishment of Offenders Act 2012 (Commencement No 1) Order 2012 SI No 1956 Article 2).

70 LASPO s144(7). Note, however, that a person trespassing in a residential building may, if left alone for long enough, establish a sufficient period of adverse possession to apply to the Land Registry under Land Registration Act 2002 in order to obtain title, even though he or she will have been committing an offence: *R (Best) v Chief Land Registrar* [2015] EWCA Civ 17, [2016] QB 23, [2015] HLR 17.

Penalties

3.48   The offence is triable only in the magistrates' court. The maximum penalty is a sentence for imprisonment of six months[71] and/or an unlimited fine.[72]

---

71 If Criminal Justice Act 2003 s281(5) is brought into force, the maximum sentence will be 51 weeks' imprisonment: LASPO s144(5), (6).
72 LASPO ss85(1) and 144(5), (6).

Tenancy deposits

Introduction

4.1   Chapter 4 of Part 6 of the Housing Act (HA) 2004 requires land-lords of assured shorthold tenancies in England and Wales to deal with any tenancy deposit in accordance with an authorised tenancy deposit scheme. A landlord who fails to do so can be penalised in one of three ways, depending on to which requirements he or she has failed to adhere to – he or she can be:

a) forced to return the deposit to the tenant; and/or
b) forced to pay the tenant a sum of money; and/or
c) prevented from serving the tenant with a notice under HA 1988 s21 to bring the tenancy to an end.

4.2   It is necessary first to consider the requirements, before considering the circumstances in which the landlord can be penalised.

Requirements relating to tenancy deposits

4.3   Any person paid a tenancy deposit in connection with an assured shorthold tenancy, must, from the time it is received, deal with the deposit within an authorised scheme.[1] If the person is a landlord, there are two additional requirements:

a) he or she must comply with the initial requirements of which-ever scheme is used within 30 days of the deposit being received;[2] and
b) he or she must give the tenant and any relevant person details of the scheme which is protecting the deposit, confirmation that the landlord has complied with its initial requirements and any other such information as may be prescribed.[3]

Authorised scheme

4.4   An authorised scheme is one which has been approved by the sec-retary of state or Welsh Ministers.[4] There are two types of scheme: custodial and insurance. If a landlord chooses to protect a deposit

---

1 HA 2004 s213(1).
2 HA 2004 s213(3).
3 HA 2004 s213(5).
4 HA 2004 s212(1), (8). There are three authorised schemes: Deposit Protection Service; My Deposits Scheme; and Tenancy Deposit Scheme.

within a custodial scheme, he or she is required to pay the amount of the deposit into a designated account held by the scheme.[5] Under an insurance scheme, the landlord is required to enter into an agreement to undertake to reimburse the scheme administrator for the amount of the deposit if it, or part of it, is returned by the scheme administrator to the tenant.[6]

Landlord

4.5 A landlord includes an agent, or any person, acting on behalf of the landlord.[7]

Relevant person

4.6 A relevant person means any person who, in accordance with any arrangements made with the tenant, paid the deposit on behalf of the tenant.[8]

In connection with an assured shorthold tenancy

4.7 In the vast majority of cases it will be a term of the tenancy agreement that a deposit be paid. The provisions of HA 2004 also apply however wherever a deposit is paid in *connection* with an assured shorthold tenancy; the provisions are not confined to deposits which have to be paid under the terms of a tenancy agreement. For example, the requirements will apply to a deposit that has been paid after it has been demanded of a tenant orally by a landlord as a condition of entering into the tenancy.

4.8 The tenancy must be an assured shorthold tenancy within the meaning of Chapter 2 of Part 1 of HA 1988.[9] These provisions therefore do not apply to licences or other residential tenancies which are exempt from being assured by Part 1 of Schedule 1 to HA 1988.

---

5 HA 2004 Sch 10 para 2.
6 HA 2004 Sch 10 para 3.
7 HA 2004 s212(8).
8 HA 2004 s213(10).
9 HA 2004 s212(8). See, generally, Arden & Dymond, *Manual of Housing Law* (LAG, 10th edn, 2017), paras 1.246–1.250.

Tenancy deposit

4.9   A tenancy deposit means any money intended to be held by the landlord or otherwise as security for the performance of any obligations
of the tenant or the discharge of any liability of the tenant arising
under or in connection with the tenancy.[10] Money means 'cash or
otherwise'.[11] In another context, the House of Lord has held that a
definition of money can include money held in a bank, cheques,
postal orders, stocks or shares.[12] Money, under the Act, does not,
however, include property.[13]

4.10   Rent payable in advance is not a tenancy deposit provided that
the sum of money is not intended, by the terms of the tenancy, to be
held by the landlord as security for the performance of the tenant's
obligations or for the discharge of any liability of the tenant.[14] Likewise, a holding deposit, eg a payment taken by a letting agent which
is forfeited in the event that the potential tenant chooses not to enter
into a tenancy, is unlikely to be a 'tenancy deposit' because it is not
security for the performance of any obligations arising under or in
connection with the tenancy.

Paid and received

4.11   Any tenancy deposit that has been paid to *any* person, in connection
with an assured shorthold tenancy, must be dealt with in accordance
with a scheme.[15] This includes deposits that were paid or received
before HA 2004 came into force on 6 April 2007[16] (although in such
a case, the tenant would not be entitled to recover the deposit or
receive a penalty payment, see paras 4.27–4.31). It is also immaterial
whether the deposit was paid to the landlord, or paid by the tenant,
provided that it was paid in connection with the assured shorthold
tenancy; accordingly, a deposit paid by someone else and a deposit
paid to someone else will qualify.

4.12   An existing tenant, who has already paid a deposit to a landlord,
is treated as having paid the amount of the deposit to the landlord in
respect of any new, or replacement, tenancy, including a statutory

10   HA 2004 s212(8).
11   HA 2004 s212(8).
12   *Perrin v Morgan* [1943] AC 399, HL.
13   HA 2004 s213(7).
14   *Johnson v Old* [2013] EWCA Civ 415, [2013] HLR 26.
15   HA 2004 s213(1).
16   *Charalambous v Ng* [2014] EWCA Civ 1604, [2015] 1 WLR 3018, [2015] HLR 15.

periodic tenancy following a fixed-term (unless the landlord returns the deposit at the end of the previous tenancy). This deemed payment will arise wherever the landlord does not seek the payment out of the prior deposit for the consequences of any prior breach of the tenancy agreement.[17]

Initial requirements of a scheme

4.13 The initial requirements of each scheme are governed by the terms of each scheme.[18]

4.14 The initial requirements of the Tenancy Deposit Scheme (TDS) are that all of the details about the deposit, as may be requested by the TDS, are entered onto the TDS' tenancy database unless the deposit is already protected, ie there is no initial requirement to enter the details of the deposit again if the tenancy is renewed or becomes a statutory periodic tenancy after a fixed-term.[19]

4.15 The initial requirements of the My Deposits Scheme (MDS) are that the deposit is protected, ie the fee is paid and all necessary information about the deposit is provided, and the prescribed information (see paras 4.17–4.20) is provided to the tenant.[20]

4.16 The initial requirements of the Deposit Protection Service (DPS) are that an application for the deposit to be protected, is be made, in accordance with the scheme's rules, within 30 days of the deposit being received.[21]

The prescribed information

4.17 HA 2004 s213(6) requires that the landlord provide the tenant the details of the scheme being used, the prescribed information and confirmation that the initial requirements have been complied with in 'the prescribed form'. To date, however, no form has been prescribed.

4.18 Instead, the Housing (Tenancy Deposits) (Prescribed Information) Order 2007[22] sets out the information that must be given to the

---

17 *Superstrike Ltd v Rodrigues* [2013] EWCA Civ 669, [2013] 1 WLR 3848, [2013] HLR 42.
18 HA 2004 s213(4).
19 Tenancy Deposit Scheme Rules 6.1–6.3.
20 My Deposits Scheme Rules C1 and C2.
21 Deposit Protection Service Rules 9–13.
22 2007 SI No 797.

tenant within 30 days of the deposit being received. Article 2 prescribes the following for the purposes of HA 2004 s213(6):

(a) the name, address, telephone number, e-mail address and any fax number of the scheme administrator of the authorised tenancy deposit scheme applying to the deposit;

(b) any information contained in a leaflet supplied by the scheme administrator to the landlord which explains the operation of the provisions contained in sections 212 to 215 of, and Schedule 10 to, the Act;

(c) the procedures that apply under the scheme by which an amount in respect of a deposit may be paid or repaid to the tenant at the end of the shorthold tenancy ('the tenancy');

(d) the procedures that apply under the scheme where either the landlord or the tenant is not contactable at the end of the tenancy (even if their whereabouts are known);

(e) the procedures that apply under the scheme where the landlord and the tenant dispute the amount to be paid or repaid to the tenant in respect of the deposit;

(f) the facilities available under the scheme for enabling a dispute relating to the deposit to be resolved without recourse to litigation; and

(g) the following information in connection with the tenancy in respect of which the deposit has been paid–

(i)   the amount of the deposit paid;

(ii) the address of the property to which the tenancy relates;

(iii) the name, address, telephone number, and any e-mail address or fax number of the landlord;

(iv) the name, address, telephone number, and any e-mail address or fax number of the tenant, including such details that should be used by the landlord or scheme administrator for the purpose of contacting the tenant at the end of the tenancy;

(v)   the name, address, telephone number and any e-mail address or fax number of any relevant person;

(vi) the circumstances when all or part of the deposit may be retained by the landlord, by reference to the terms of the tenancy; and

(vii) confirmation (in the form of a certificate signed by the landlord) that–

(aa) the information he provides under this sub-paragraph is accurate to the best of his knowledge and belief; and

(bb) he has given the tenant the opportunity to sign any document containing the information provided by the landlord under this article by way of confirmation that the information is accurate to the best of his knowledge and belief.

4.19   Where the initial requirements of an authorised scheme have been complied with in relation to the deposit by a person ('the initial agent') acting on the landlord's behalf, the references in paragraph (b), (g)(iii) and (vii) to the landlord are to be read as references to either the landlord or the initial agent and references in paragraphs (d), (e), (g)(iv) and (vi) to the landlord are to be read as references to either the landlord or to a person who acts on the landlord's behalf in relation to the tenancy.[23]

4.20   In the event that a statutory periodic tenancy arises after the expiry of a fixed-term, there is no requirement that the prescribed information be served within 30 days of it arising provided that the initial requirements of the scheme have been complied with and the prescribed information was originally provided to the tenant within 30 days of the deposit first being received.[24]

Within 30 days

4.21   Both the initial requirements of the scheme and the prescribed information must be completed within 30 days of the deposit being received.[25] Likewise, the landlord must notify the tenant of the scheme being used, the prescribed information and confirm that the initial requirements have been complied with within 30 days of the receipt.[26]

4.22   These requirements do not, however, apply to any deposit that was received before 6 April 2012. In these cases, the initial requirements of the scheme must have been complied with and the prescribed information given to the tenant by 5 May 2012.[27]

4.23   Nor do the requirements (paras 4.18–4.19) apply where the following conditions are all satisfied:

a) a deposit was received before 6 April 2007;
b) the fixed term has come to an end and a statutory periodic tenancy has arisen;
c) all or part of the deposit is held in connection with the statutory periodic tenancy;

---

23 Housing (Tenancy Deposits) (Prescribed Information) Order 2007 Article 2(3).
24 HA 2004 s215B(1), (2).
25 HA 2004 s213(3), (6).
26 HA 2004 s213(5), (6).
27 Localism Act 2011 (Commencement No 4 and Transitional, Transitory and Savings Provisions) Order 2012 SI No 628 Article 16.

d) the deposit, as at 26 March 2015, was protected, but the landlord did not comply with the initial requirements of the scheme within 30 days of the deposit being received or had failed to provide the tenant with the prescribed information; and

e) the landlord has complied with the initial requirements of a scheme and provided the tenant with the prescribed information by 23 June 2015.[28]

4.24　Where all of para 4.23a)–d) are satisfied, but the tenancy is no longer in existence or the deposit is no longer held in connection with the periodic tenancy, the requirements are treated as having been complied with.[29]

Contracting out

4.25　The requirements of HA 2004 Part 6 Chapter 4 apply even if the terms of the tenancy agreement seek to exclude them.[30]

Deposit not including money

4.26　No person may, in connection with an assured shorthold tenancy, require a deposit which consists of property other than money.[31] In the event that such a deposit is taken, it is recoverable by the person who gave it from whomever is holding it.[32]

Circumstances relating to tenancy deposits in which the landlord can be penalised

Return of deposit and penalty payment

4.27　Where a tenancy deposit was paid in connection with an assured shorthold tenancy after 6 April 2007, and the following conditions apply, the court must, on an application by a tenant or any relevant person, order that the landlord, and/or his or her agent, pay the applicant a sum of money which is not less than the amount of the deposit

28　HA 2004 s215A(1), (3).
29　HA 2004 s215A(4).
30　HA 2004 s213(2).
31　HA 2004 s213(7). For these purposes 'property' means 'moveable property': s213(10).
32　HA 2004 s214(5).

and not more than three times its amount ('the penalty payment') and/or order the deposit to be repaid to the claimant or paid into the designated account of a scheme administrator. The conditions are:

a) the deposit is not being held in accordance with an authorised scheme; or

b) either the initial requirements of the scheme or the prescribed requirements were not complied with within 30 days.[33]

4.28　Such an application may be made after the tenancy has ended[34] although if it has done so, the court cannot order the deposit to be paid into the designated account of a scheme administrator.[35]

4.29　While the sanctions are not expressed to apply to tenancies that were granted before 6 April 2007, they do apply to deposits that are deemed to be received (para 4.12) in connection with statutory periodic tenancies that came into existence after that date, but which followed the end of a fixed-term that was granted before it.[36]

4.30　Within the parameters of one and three times the amount of the deposit, the court has a discretion as to the amount of the penalty payment. In *Okadigbo v Chan*,[37] Males J said that the question of culpability is the most relevant factor in determining what order to make. In that case, the court had been entitled to award only the amount of the deposit because the error had been corrected during the tenancy, it had been the fault of managing agents (not the landlord), the defendants were not professional landlords and the breach had been admitted.

4.31　Where a statutory periodic tenancy has arisen after the expiry of a fixed-term and the landlord has failed to comply with the initial requirements of the scheme or provide the prescribed information within 30 days of the deposit being received (or of the deposit being deemed to have been received at the beginning of the statutory periodic tenancy, see para 4.12), it is arguable that a tenant is entitled to a penalty payment in respect of each tenancy.

33　HA 2004 s214(1), (2), (3), (4).

34　HA 2004 s214(2A), which was inserted to reverse the effect of *Gladehurst Properties Ltd v Hashemi* [2011] EWCA Civ 604, [2011] HLR 36.

35　HA 2004 s214(2A), (3A).

36　*Superstrike Ltd v Rodrigues* [2013] EWCA Civ 669, [2013] 1 WLR 3848, [2013] HLR 42.

37　[2014] EWHC 4729 (QB).

Prohibition on serving a Housing Act 1988 s21 notice

4.32   If a tenancy deposit has been paid in connection with a shorthold tenancy and the following conditions apply, a HA 1988 s21 notice may not be given:

a) the deposit is not being held in accordance with an authorised scheme (see para 4.4); or

b) the landlord has protected the deposit but did not comply with the initial requirements of the scheme within 30 days of the deposit being received (see paras 4.13–4.16); or

c) the landlord has failed to provide the tenant with the prescribed information (see paras 4.17–4.20),

unless:

a) the deposit has been returned to the tenant in full or with deductions that are agreed by the tenant; or

b) the tenant has made an application to the court for an order under HA 2004 s214(1) – ie for a penalty payment or for the deposit to be returned or protected – and that application has either been determined by the court, been withdrawn or settled.[38]

4.33   The date that the deposit is returned to the tenant can therefore be of crucial importance. It has been held in the county court that a deposit is deemed to be returned to the tenant once the tenant receives a cheque[39] or on the date that the sum is received in the tenant's bank account, rather than the date it is transferred.[40]

4.34   The fact that the deposit was received before 6 April 2007 is immaterial to the question of whether it needs to be held in accordance with an authorised scheme (see paras 4.3–4.4).

---

38   HA 2004 s215(1), (2), (2A).

39   *Yeomans v Newell*, County Court at Canterbury, 25 May 2016.

40   *Chalmiston Properties Ltd v Boudia*, County Court at Barnet, 27 October 2015.

Licensing of landlords and agents

Introduction

5.1   There are three schemes under which landlords may be required to be licensed. The first relates to houses in multiple occupation (HMOs).[1] The second is selective licensing of other residential accommodation.[2] Finally, in Wales, there is a licensing scheme for most residential lettings and management activity.[3]

5.2   The focus of this chapter is on the remedies available where a licence is required but has not been obtained. It is, however, first necessary to consider the circumstances in which a licence is required.

Circumstances in which a licence is required

Licensing of houses in multiple occupation

Houses in multiple occupation

5.3   Licensing of HMOs is provided for by Housing Act (HA) 2004 Part 2. An HMO is a building, or part of a building, that either:

a)   meets the standard test;
b)   meets the self-contained flat test;
c)   meets the converted building test;
d)   has an HMO declaration in force (see para 5.12); or
e)   is a converted block of flats to which HA 2004 s257 applies.[4]

5.4   *The standard test* is satisfied by a building or part of a building where the following conditions are all met.[5]

a)   It consists of one or more units of living accommodation not consisting of a self-contained flat or flats.[6]

---

1   HA 2004 Part 2.
2   HA 2004 Part 3. 'Other' accommodation means residential accommodation that is not an HMO required to be licensed under HA 2004 Part 2: HA 2004 s85(1)(a).
3   Housing (Wales) Act (H(W)A) 2014 Part 1. Agents are also required to be licensed under this scheme.
4   HA 2004 s254(1). This list is subject to exceptions in Sch 14, see paras 5.8–5.9.
5   HA 2004 s254(2).
6   A self-contained flat is a separate set of premises (whether or not on the same floor) which forms part of a building, either the whole or a material part of which lies above or below some other part of the building, and in which all three basic amenities are available for the exclusive use of its occupants: HA 2004 s254(8). The 'basic amenities' are defined by HA 2004 s254(8), see n10, below.

b) That living accommodation is occupied by persons who do not form a single household.[7]

c) That living accommodation is occupied by those persons as their only or main residence.[8]

d) Their occupation of the living accommodation is the only use of it.

e) Rent is payable[9] in respect of occupation of the living accommodation.

f) Two or more of the households share basic amenities[10] or the living accommodation is lacking in basic amenities.

5.5 *The self-contained flat test* is satisfied by a part of a building where it consists of a self-contained flat and conditions b)–f) of para 5.4 apply to it, save that the references to living-accommodation should be read as references to the flat.[11]

5.6 *The converted building test* is satisfied by a building or part of a building where the following conditions are all met.

---

7 Persons are not to be regarded as forming a single household unless they are members of the same family: HA 2004 s258(2)(a). For these purposes, 'family' is defined by HA 2004 s258(3), (4). There is also a power in section 258(2)(b) to specify circumstances in which persons are to be treated as a single household. In England, this power has been used to make the Licensing and Management of Houses in Multiple Occupation and Other Houses (Miscellaneous Provisions) (England) Regulations 2006 SI No 373. In Wales, it has been used to make the Licensing and Management of Houses in Multiple Occupation and Other Houses (Miscellaneous Provisions) (Wales) Regulations 2006 SI No 1715. Under reg 3 of both Regulations, certain live-in employees are to be treated as part of the main household. This covers au pairs, nannies, etc. A person receiving care and his or her carer are also to be treated as single household in the circumstances set out in reg 4 of each set of Regulations.

8 Or where they are to be treated as occupying it as their only or main residence: HA 2004 s254(2)(c). A person is treated as occupying a building as their only or main residence if he occupies it as his residence for the purpose of undertaking a full-time course of further or higher education (but see para 5.8), as a refuge, or in circumstances specified in regulations: HA 2004 s259(2). Provision is made for a property to be treated as the only or main residence of migrant workers, seasonal workers and asylum seekers by reg 5 of the Licensing and Management of Houses in Multiple Occupation and Other Houses (Miscellaneous Provisions) (England) Regulations 2006 SI No 373 and the Licensing and Management of Houses in Multiple Occupation and Other Houses (Miscellaneous Provisions) (Wales) Regulations 2006 SI No 1715.

9 Or some other consideration is provided: HA 2004 s254(2)(f).

10 A toilet, personal washing facilities or cooking facilities: HA 2004 s254(8).

11 HA 2004 s254(3).

a) The building or part of a building consists of living accommodation in which one or more units of such accommodation have been created since the building or part was constructed.[12]
b) It contains one or more units of living accommodation that do not consist of a self-contained flat or flats.[13]
c) Conditions b)–e) of para 5.4 apply to the building or part of a building.[14]

5.7   A *'converted block of flats'* is a building, or part of a building, which has been converted into, and consists of, self-contained flats,[15] if the conversion work does not comply with the appropriate building standards and less than two-thirds of the flats are owner-occupied.[16]

5.8   A building, or part of a building, is *not* an HMO for these purposes if it is:

- managed or controlled by a public sector body;[17]
- regulated under one of a list of other enactments;[18]
- occupied solely or principally for the purpose of undertaking a full-time course of higher or further education at a specified educational establishment and managed or controlled by the educational establishment;[19]

---

12   HA 2004 ss254(4)(a), (8).
13   Whether or not the building (or part of a building) also contains any such flat or flats: HA 2004 s254(4)(b).
14   HA 2004 s254(4).
15   HA 2004 s257(1). 'Self-contained flat' has the same meaning as in HA 2004 s254, see n6, above.
16   HA 2004 s257(2). The 'appropriate building standards' are defined by HA 2004 s257(3).
17   A local housing authority, a non-profit registered provider of social housing, a registered social landlord and various other bodies: HA 2004 Sch 14 para 2(1). Also excluded are buildings managed and controlled by a profit-making registered provider if the building is social housing under Housing and Regeneration Act 2008 Part 2, and some buildings managed or controlled by a co-operative society: Sch 14 paras 2A, 2B.
18   HA 2004 Sch 14 para 3 and Sch 1 para 1 to the Licensing and Management of Houses in Multiple Occupation and Other Houses (Miscellaneous Provisions) (England) Regulations 2006 SI No 373 and the Licensing and Management of Houses in Multiple Occupation and Other Houses (Miscellaneous Provisions) (Wales) Regulations 2006 SI No 1715. These enactments relate to buildings which are not occupied by choice, eg young offender institutions.
19   HA 2004 Sch 14 para 4. The specified educational establishments are set out in the Houses in Multiple Occupation (Specified Educational Establishments) (England) Regulations 2016 SI No 420 and Houses in Multiple Occupation (Specified Educational Establishments) (Wales) Regulations 2006 SI No 1707. This has the effect of taking university-controlled halls of residence out of scope.

- occupied by a religious community;[20]
- occupied by the owner;[21] or
- occupied by only two persons forming two households.[22]

5.9 Subject to exceptions,[23] HMOs falling with a prescribed description require a licence from a local housing authority.[24] The secretary of state and the National Assembly for Wales have both specified descriptions of HMOs which require a licence in the Licensing of Houses in Multiple Occupation (Prescribed Descriptions) (England) Order 2006 and the Licensing of Houses in Multiple Occupation (Prescribed Descriptions) (Wales) Order 2006.[25]

5.10 By Article 3 of both the English and Welsh Orders, an HMO is of a prescribed description (and therefore requires a licence) where it satisfies all of the following conditions.

a) The HMO, or any part of it, comprises at least three storeys.[26]
b) It is occupied by at least five people.
c) It is occupied by persons living in at least two households.

---

20 HA 2004 Sch 14 para 5. This applies where the building is occupied principally for the purposes of a religious community whose principal occupation is prayer, contemplation, education or the relief of suffering. The exception does not, however, apply to a converted block of flats to which HA 2004 s257 applies, see para 5.7.

21 Provided that no more than two people occupy the building with the owner and his or her household: HA 2004 Sch 14 para 6 and reg 6(2) of the Licensing and Management of Houses in Multiple Occupation and Other Houses (Miscellaneous Provisions) (England) Regulations 2006 SI No 373 and the Licensing and Management of Houses in Multiple Occupation and Other Houses (Miscellaneous Provisions) (Wales) Regulations 2006 SI No 1715. Again, this exception does not apply to a converted block of flats to which s257 applies, see para 5.7.

22 HA 2004 Sch 14 para 7.

23 The exceptions are where either a temporary exemption notice or a management order is in force: HA 2004 s61(1). A temporary exemption notice may be given by an authority where premises are required to be licensed under Part 2 but the person having control or managing the premises (see nn38 and 39, below) notifies the authority that he intends to take steps so that the premises do not need to be licensed: HA 2004 s62. Management orders are provided for by HA 2004 Part 4 Chapter 1.

24 HA 2004 ss55(2)(a), 61(1).

25 2006 SI No 371 and 2006 SI No 1712.

26 The Government has announced that it intends to extend mandatory licensing to cover all relevant HMOs, regardless of the number of storeys: Department for Communities and Local Government (DCLG), *Extending mandatory licensing of Houses in Multiple Occupation: A Government Response Document* (2016).

5.11   Article 3(3) makes provision for the storeys of the building which should be taken into account. The purpose of Article 3(3) is to bring within the calculation of the number of storeys business premises and certain premises used with the HMO which would otherwise be excluded; it is, however, the HMO that must comprise the three storeys rather than the building in which it is to be found,[27] so that where an HMO which is a self-contained flat is situated above other residential accommodation, the storeys comprised in that other accommodation are not taken into account in calculating the number of storeys in the HMO.[28]

HMO declaration

5.12   An authority may serve an HMO declaration declaring a building (or part of a building) in its area to be an HMO if it is satisfied that a building or part of a building meets either the standard test, the self-contained flat test or the converted building test.[29] An HMO declaration must meet requirements set out in HA 2004 s255(4) and may be appealed to the First-tier Tribunal (in England) or a residential property tribunal (in Wales).[30] An HMO declaration may also be revoked by the authority which served it.[31]

Local designation

5.13   In addition to the HMOs specified in the English and Welsh Orders, a local housing authority may designate their district, or part of it, as being subject to additional licensing in relation to such other descriptions of HMO as they may specify, of which they consider that a significant proportion is 'being managed sufficiently ineffectively as to give rise, or to be likely to give rise, to one or more particular problems either for those occupying the HMOs or for members of the public'.[32]

---

27   *Islington LBC v Unite Group Plc* [2013] EWHC 508 (Admin), [2013] HLR 33.
28   See also *Bristol CC v Digs (Bristol) Ltd* [2014] EWHC 869 (Admin), [2014] HLR 30.
29   For these purposes, the 'sole use' criterion (ie HA 2004 s254(2)(d), (4)(e), see para 5.4) is replaced by a requirement that occupation by persons who do not form a single household is a 'significant' use: HA 2004 s255(2).
30   HA 2004 s255(9), (13).
31   HA 2004 s256.
32   HA 2004 s56. Before doing so, the authority must carry out consultation and the designation must be approved by the secretary of state or the National Assembly for Wales: HA 2004 ss56(3), 58(1); see also *R (Regas) v Enfield LBC* [2014] EWHC 4173 (Admin), [2015] HLR 14.

5.14   Once a designation has been made in respect of an area, any HMO in that area which falls within any description of HMO specified in the designation requires a licence from the authority.[33]

Application for licence

5.15   Application for a licence must be made to the local housing authority.[34] Before granting a licence, the authority must be satisfied that, among other things, the house is reasonably suitable for occupation by not more than a particular maximum number of households or persons.[35] Where the authority grants a licence, it must attach conditions to it.[36]

Appeal

5.16   There is a right of appeal, to the First-tier Tribunal in England or a residential property tribunal in Wales, against the grant or refusal of a licence, which includes a right of appeal against the terms on which a licence is granted.[37] The right of appeal may be exercised by the applicant or a 'relevant person'. A relevant person is any person having an estate or interest in the HMO, any person managing[38] or having control of the HMO,[39] or any person on whom any restriction or obligation is imposed by the licence.[40]

---

33 HA 2004 ss55(2)(b), 61(1). This is subject to the same exceptions as HMOs covered by mandatory licensing, see n23, above.

34 HA 2004 s63(1).

35 HA 2004 s64(2)(a).

36 HA 2004 s67. Conditions that must be attached to all licences are set out in Sch 4 but the authority has power to attach other conditions.

37 HA 2004 s261(8), Sch 5 para 31.

38 A 'person managing' an HMO is the person who receives (whether directly or through an agent or trustee) rents or other payments from persons who are in occupation as tenants or licensees of *parts* of the premises where that person is either the owner or lessee of the premises or collects the rents or other payments under an agreement with the owner or lessee to do so: HA 2004 s263(3).

39 A 'person having control' of an HMO is the person who receives the rack-rent (ie a rent which is not less than two-thirds of the full net annual value of the premises) of the premises (whether on his own account or as agent or trustee of another person), or who would so receive it if the premises were let at a rack-rent: HA 2004 s263(1), (2).

40 HA 2004 Sch 5 para 36. The applicant for the licence, the licence holder (if different) and a tenant under a lease with an unexpired term of three years or less are not relevant persons: Sch 5 para 36(3).

Sanctions

5.17   The potential sanctions for failure to obtain a licence for an HMO are considered at paras 5.28–5.76 and 5.84–5.85.

Selective licensing of other residential accommodation

5.18   HA 2004 Part 3 also makes provision for local housing authorities to introduce selective licensing for houses which are not HMOs. The definition of 'house' includes flats.[41] An authority may designate its district, or part of it, as being subject to selective licensing.[42]

5.19   Subject to exceptions,[43] a licence is required for any house that is within an area designated as subject to selective licensing and which is occupied under a tenancy or licence which is not an exempt tenancy or licence.[44]

5.20   An application for a licence must be made to the local housing authority.[45] Where the authority grants a licence, it must attach conditions to it.[46]

5.21   There is a right of appeal to the First-tier Tribunal in England or a residential property tribunal in Wales against the grant or refusal of a licence, which includes a right of appeal against the terms on

41   HA 2004 s99: '"house" means a building or part of a building consisting of one or more dwellings'.

42   HA 2004 s80(1). Before doing so, the authority must carry out consultation and the designation must be approved by the secretary of state or the National Assembly for Wales: HA 2004 ss80(9), 82(1); see also *R (Regas) v Enfield LBC* [2014] EWHC 4173 (Admin), [2015] HLR 14.

43   The exceptions are where either the house is an HMO to which HA 2004 Part 2 applies, a temporary exemption notice is in force or a management order is in force: HA 2004 s85(1). A temporary exemption notice may be given by an authority where premises are required to be licensed under Part 3 but the person having control or managing the premises (see nn38 and 39, above) notifies the authority that he intends to take steps so that the premises do not need to be licensed: HA 2004 s86. Management orders are provided for by HA 2004 Part 4 Chapter 1.

44   HA 2004 ss79(2), 85(1). An exempt tenancy or licence is one granted by a non-profit registered provider of social housing, a profit-making registered provider if the house is social housing under Housing and Regeneration Act 2008 Part 2, or a registered social landlord: HA 2004 s79(3). Various other types of tenancy and licence are exempted by Article 2 of the Selective Licensing of Houses (Specified Exemptions) (England) Order 2006 SI No 370 and of the Selective Licensing of Houses (Specified Exemptions) (Wales) Order 2006 SI No 2824.

45   HA 2004 s87(1).

46   HA 2004 s90. Conditions that must be attached to all licences are set out in Sch 4 but the authority may attach other conditions.

which a licence is granted.[47] The right of appeal may be exercised by the applicant or a 'relevant person'. A relevant person is any person having an estate or interest in the house, any person managing or having control of the house,[48] or any person on whom any restriction or obligation is imposed by the licence.[49]

Licensing of lettings activities and property management activities in Wales

5.22   From 23 November 2016, most private sector landlords of residential property in Wales are required to be registered and licensed. Agents are required to be licensed.

5.23   A landlord must be registered and licensed in respect of any dwelling subject to, or marketed or offered for let under, a 'domestic tenancy'. A domestic tenancy is an assured tenancy (including an assured shorthold tenancy) or a regulated tenancy under Rent Act (RA) 1977.[50]

5.24   A landlord is not required to be registered if one of six[51] exceptions applies, and is not required to be licensed if one of the, substantively identical, exceptions[52] applies. The exceptions are as follows.[53]

a) The landlord has applied to the licensing authority to be registered/licensed in relation to that dwelling and the application has not been determined.

b) Where the landlord's interest in the dwelling is assigned to him or her, there is an exception for a period of 28 days.

---

47 HA 2004 s261(8), Sch 5 para 31.
48 See nn38 and 39, above.
49 HA 2004 Sch 5 para 36. The applicant for the licence, the licence holder (if different) and a tenant under a lease with an unexpired term of three years or less are not relevant persons: HA 2004 Sch 5 para 36(3).
50 H(W)A 2014 s 2(1). See further Arden & Dymond *Manual of Housing Law* (LAG, 10th edn, 2017), para 14.75. An assured tenancy is not a domestic tenancy if it is a long lease for the purposes of Leasehold Reform, Housing and Urban Development Act 1993 Part 1 Chapter 1, or of it is a shared ownership lease which would be such a long lease if the tenant's share were 100 per cent: H(W)A 2014 s2(1)(a). There is power for the Welsh Minister to specify other types of tenancy as a domestic tenancy: H(W)A 2014 s2(1)(c).
51 Specified in H(W)A 2014 s5.
52 Specified in H(W)A 2014 s8.
53 H(W)A 2014 ss5 and 8. The only difference between the exceptions is that s5(a) refers to an application to be registered, while s8(a) refers to an application to be licensed.

c) Where the landlord's interest in the dwelling is assigned to him or her and he or she takes steps to recover possession within the period of 28 days, there is an exception for so long as he or she continues to pursue diligently the recovery of possession.

d) The landlord is a registered social landlord.

e) The landlord is a fully mutual housing association.

f) The landlord is of a description specified for the purposes of H(W)A 2014 s5 in an order made by the Welsh Ministers.

5.25   Application for registration and application for a licence must be made to the licensing authority.[54] The Welsh Ministers have designated Cardiff Council as the licensing authority for the whole of Wales.[55] Cardiff Council carries out its licensing functions under the H(W)A 2014 through Rent Smart Wales.[56]

5.26   Provided that certain conditions are met,[57] the licensing authority must grant a licence.[58] Where a licence is granted, it must be subject to a condition that the licence holder complies with any code of practice issued by the Welsh Ministers and may be subject to such further conditions as the licensing authority considers appropriate.[59]

5.27   There is a right of appeal to a residential property tribunal against a decision to refuse an application for a licence and a decision to grant a licence on any condition other than the requirement to comply with the code of practice.[60]

Sanctions

5.28   A range of sanctions is available where a licence should have, but has not been, obtained. Both HA 2004 and H(W)A 2014 create a number of criminal offences. Under both Acts, authorities and tenants can apply for a rent repayment order.

---

54 H(W)A 2014 ss15 and 19.

55 Regulation of Private Rented Housing (Designation of Licensing Authority) (Wales) Order 2015 SI No 1026 Article 2, made under H(W)A 2014 s3.

56 Also known as Rhentu Doeth Cymru. See www.rentsmart.gov.wales.

57 Set out in H(W)A 2014 ss19 and 20; and Regulation of Private Rented Housing (Training Requirements) (Wales) Regulations 2015 SI No 1366.

58 H(W)A 2014 s21(1).

59 H(W)A 2014 s22. The Code of Practice for Landlords and Agents licensed under Part 1 of the H(W)A 2014 was approved by the Welsh Assembly on 3 November 2015 and can be downloaded from http://gov.wales/docs/desh/publications/151110-rent-smart-code-of-practice-en.pdf.

60 H(W)A 2014 s21(2)(a), (b).

Criminal offences

Housing Act 2004

Housing Act 2004 Part 2

5.29 There are three offences created by HA 2004 Part 2 in relation to licensing of HMOs.

5.30 **The first offence** is committed by a person who has control of, or manages, an HMO[61] which is required to be licensed under HA 2004 Part 2 but is not so licensed.[62] This offence is punishable on summary conviction by an unlimited fine.[63]

5.31 There are three statutory defences. First, there is a defence of reasonable excuse.[64] Secondly, it is a defence if notification had been given to the local housing authority of an intention to take steps so that the premises do not need to be licensed, and that notification was still 'effective'.[65] Thirdly, it is a defence if an application for a licence had been made and the application was still 'effective'.[66] A notification or an application is effective if the authority had not decided whether to serve a temporary exemption notice or to grant a licence,[67] or, if it had decided not to do so, that the time for appealing against that decision had not elapsed or that any appeal had not been finally determined or withdrawn.[68]

5.32 **The second offence** created by HA 2004 Part 2 is committed by a person who has control of, or manages, an HMO[69] which is licensed

---

61 See nn38 and 39, above.

62 HA 2004 s72(1).

63 HA 2004 s72(6). From 6 April 2017, an authority may, as an alternative to prosecution, impose a financial penalty of up to £30,000: HA 2004 s249A, as inserted by HPA 2016 Sch 9 para 7. The authority may apply any financial penalty recovered to meet the costs and expenses incurred in, or associated with, carrying out enforcement functions in relation to the private rented sector: Rent Repayment Orders and Financial Penalties (Amounts Recovered) (England) Regulations 2017 SI No 367 reg 4(1). Enforcement functions are defined by reg 2 to mean functions under HA 2004 Parts 1–4, and functions under HPA 2016 Part 2, as well as other functions connected with the law related to housing or landlord and tenant. Any amount not applied in that way must be paid into the Consolidated Fund: reg 4(2).

64 HA 2004 s72(5)(a).

65 HA 2004 s72(4)(a).

66 HA 2004 s72(4)(b).

67 HA 2004 s72(8)(a).

68 HA 2004 s72(8)(b).

69 See nn38 and 39, above.

under HA 2004 Part 2 where two conditions are met:[70] the first condition is that he or she knowingly permits another person to occupy the HMO;[71] the second condition is that the other person's occupation results in the house being occupied by more people or households than permitted by the license.[72] Subject to a statutory defence of reasonable excuse,[73] this offence is punishable on summary conviction by an unlimited fine.[74]

5.33   **The final offence** created by HA 2004 Part 2 is committed by a licence holder, or a person on whom restrictions or obligations have been imposed under a licence, if he or she fails to comply with any condition of the licence.[75] There is a statutory defence of reasonable excuse.[76] The offence is punishable on summary conviction by an unlimited fine.[77]

Housing Act 2004 s234

5.34   Furthermore, HA 2004 s234 creates an offence of failing to comply with regulations made by the secretary of state or the Welsh Ministers[78] in relation to management of HMOs.[79] Regulations have been made in both England and Wales, placing duties on managers to provide information to occupiers; take safety measures; maintain water supply and drainage; supply and maintain gas and electricity; maintain common parts etc; maintain living accommodation; and provide waste disposal facilities.[80] There is a statutory defence of reasonable

---

70 HA 2004 s72(2)(a).
71 HA 2004 s72(2)(b).
72 HA 2004 s72(2)(c).
73 HA 2004 s72(5)(b).
74 HA 2004 s72(6). From 6 April 2017, an authority may, as an alternative to prosecution, impose a financial penalty of up to £30,000: HA 2004 s249A, as inserted by HPA 2016 Sch 9 para 7. For the purposes to which any financial penalty may be put, see n63, above.
75 HA 2004 s72(3).
76 HA 2004 s72(5)(c).
77 HA 2004 s72(7). HA 2004 refers to a fine not exceeding level 5 on the standard scale, the effect of which is now an unlimited fine: Criminal Justice Act (CJA) 1982 s37(2) and Legal Aid, Sentencing and Punishment of Offenders Act 2012 (LASPO) s85(1).
78 HA 2004 refers to regulations made by the National Assembly for Wales. Under Government of Wales Act 2006 Sch 11 para 30(2)(c), functions formerly exercisable by the National Assembly became exercisable by the Welsh Ministers.
79 HA 2004 s234(3).
80 Management of Houses in Multiple Occupation (England) Regulations 2006 SI No 372; Management of Houses in Multiple Occupation (Wales) Regulations

excuse.[81] The offence is punishable on summary conviction by an unlimited fine.[82]

Housing Act 2004 Part 3

5.35   There are also two offences created by HA 2004 Part 3. These are very similar to the first and third offences under Part 2.

5.36   **The first Part 3 offence** is committed by a person who has control of, or manages,[83] a house which is required to be licensed under Part 3 but is not so licensed.[84] This offence is punishable on summary conviction by an unlimited fine.[85] As with the equivalent Part 2 offence, there are three statutory defences, which are in the same terms (see para 5.31).[86]

5.37   **The second Part 3 offence** is committed by a licence holder, or a person on whom restrictions or obligations have been imposed under a licence, if he or she fails to comply with any condition of the licence.[87] As with the equivalent Part 2 offence, this is punishable on summary conviction by an unlimited fine and there is a statutory defence of reasonable excuse.[88]

2006 SI No 1713; Licensing and Management of Houses in Multiple Occupation (Additional Provisions) (England) Regulations 2007 SI No 1903; and, Licensing and Management of Houses in Multiple Occupation (Additional Provisions) (Wales) Regulations 2007 SI No 3229.

81   HA 2004 s234(4).

82   HA 2004 s234(5). HA 2004 refers to a fine not exceeding level 5 on the standard scale, the effect of which is now an unlimited fine: CJA 1982 s37(2) and LASPO 2012 s85(1). From 6 April 2017, the authority may, as an alternative to prosecution, impose a financial penalty of up to £30,000: HA 2004 s249A, as inserted by HPA 2016 Sch 9 para 7. For the purposes to which any financial penalty may be put, see n63, above.

83   See n38 and 39, above.

84   HA 2004 s95(1).

85   HA 2004 s95(5). From 6 April 2017, the authority may, as an alternative to prosecution, impose a financial penalty of up to £30,000: HA 2004 s249A, as inserted by HPA 2016 Sch 9 para 7. For the purposes to which any financial penalty may be put, see n63, above.

86   HA 2004 s95(3), (4)(a), (7) and (8).

87   HA 2004 s95(2).

88   HA 2004 s95(4)(b), (6). HA 2004 refers to a fine not exceeding level 5 on the standard scale, the effect of which is now an unlimited fine: CJA 1982 s37(2) and LASPO s85(1). From 6 April 2017, the authority may, as an alternative to prosecution, impose a financial penalty of up to £30,000: HA 2004 s249A, as inserted by HPA 2016 Sch 9 para 7. For the purposes to which any financial penalty may be put, see n63, above.

Housing (Wales) Act 2014

Offences

5.38 In Wales, H(W)A 2014 has created a series of other offences. The most significant ones are addressed below.

5.39 **The first offence** is committed by an unregistered landlord of a dwelling which is subject to a domestic tenancy or is marketed or offered for let under a domestic tenancy, unless an exception in H(W)A 2014 s5 applies.[89] This offence is punishable on summary conviction by a fine not exceeding level 3 on the standard scale.[90] There is a defence of having a reasonable excuse for not being registered.[91]

5.40 **The next offence** is committed by a landlord of a dwelling marketed or offered for let under a domestic tenancy if he or she carries out any of four types of conduct, unless either the landlord is licensed to do so, he or she is arranging for an authorised agent to do something on his or her behalf[92] or an exception in H(W)A 2014 s8 applies.[93]

5.41 The four types of prohibited conduct are as follows.[94]

a) arranging or conducting viewings with prospective tenants;
b) gathering evidence for the purpose of establishing the suitability of prospective tenants;
c) preparing or arranging the preparation of a tenancy agreement;
d) preparing or arranging the preparation of an inventory or schedule of condition.

5.42 This offence is punishable on conviction by an unlimited fine.[95] A landlord has a defence if he or she has a reasonable excuse for not being licensed.[96]

5.43 **A particularly important offence**, which can be committed by an unlicensed landlord in two different ways, is created by H(W)A 2014 s7(5).[97]

---

89 H(W)A 2014 s4(1). For the exceptions in s5, see para 5.24.
90 H(W)A 2014 s4(2). Level 3 is currently set at £1,000: CJA 1982 s37(2).
91 H(W)A 2014 s4(3).
92 An authorised agent is a person licensed to carry out lettings work and property management work, a local housing authority, or (in relation to the preparation of a tenancy agreement) a solicitor: H(W)A 2014 s6(6).
93 H(W)A 2014 s6(1). For the exceptions in s8, see para 5.24.
94 H(W)A 2014 s6(2).
95 H(W)A 2014 s6(4).
96 H(W)A 2014 s6(5).
97 The significance of the H(W)A 2014 s7(5) offence is that, when committed the first way, it can be relied on to obtain a rent repayment order under H(W)A 2014 s32: see paras 5.77–5.79.

5.44   First, the offence is committed by an unlicensed landlord of a dwelling subject to a domestic tenancy who carries out any of six types of conduct.[98] The six types of prohibited conduct in relation to this offence are as follows.[99]

a) collecting rent;

b) being the principal point of contact for the tenant in relation to matters arising under the tenancy;

c) making arrangements with a person to carry out repairs or maintenance;

d) making arrangements with a tenant or occupier of the dwelling to secure access to the dwelling for any purpose;

e) checking the contents or condition of the dwelling, or arranging for them to be checked;

f) serving notice to terminate a tenancy.

5.45   The offence is also committed by an unlicensed landlord of a dwelling where a domestic tenancy has ended, if he or she checks the contents or condition of the dwelling, or arranges for them to be checked, for any purpose connected with the former tenancy.[100]

5.46   The offence is not committed where the landlord is licensed to do the conduct that would otherwise be prohibited or if he or she arranges for an authorised agent to do something on his or her behalf.[101] It is also not committed where an exception in H(W)A 2014 s8 applies.[102]

5.47   This offence is punishable on conviction by an unlimited fine.[103] A landlord has a defence if he or she has a reasonable excuse for not being licensed.[104]

5.48   H(W)A 2014 also creates **offences in respect of agents**.

5.49   First, it is an offence for a person acting on behalf of the landlord of a dwelling marketed or offered for let under a domestic tenancy to carry out lettings work in respect of it,[105] unless he or she is licensed

---

98 H(W)A 2014 s7(1), (5).

99 H(WA) 2014 s7(2).

100 H(W)A 2014 s7(3), (5).

101 H(W)A 2014 s7(1)(a), (b), (3)(a), (b). An authorised agent is a person licensed to carry out lettings work and property management work, a local housing authority, or (in relation to serving notice to terminate a tenancy) a solicitor: H(W)A 2014 s7(7).

102 H(W)A 2014 s7(1)(c), (3)(c). For the exceptions in s8, see para 5.24.

103 H(W)A 2014 s7(5).

104 H(W)A 2014 s7(6).

105 Lettings work is defined by H(W)A 2014 s10. Note that lettings work does not include anything done by a local housing authority: s10(4)(c).

to do so.[106] This offence is punishable on conviction by an unlimited fine.[107] An agent has a defence if he or she has a reasonable excuse for not being licensed.[108]

5.50   Secondly, it is an offence for a person acting on behalf of the land-lord of a dwelling subject to a domestic tenancy to carry out property management work in respect of that dwelling,[109] unless he or she is licensed to do so.[110] This offence is also committed by a person acting on behalf of a landlord of a dwelling where a domestic tenancy has ended, if he or she checks the contents or condition of the dwelling, or arranges for them to be checked, for any purpose connected with the former tenancy, unless licensed to do so.[111] The offence is punishable on conviction by a summary fine.[112] There is a defence of a reasonable excuse for not being licensed.[113]

5.51   Thirdly, it is an offence for a landlord to appoint an unlicensed agent. This offence can be committed in two ways. First, by appointing, or continuing to allow, a person to undertake lettings work in relation to a dwelling marketed or offered for let under a domestic tenancy;[114] secondly, by appointing, or continuing to allow, a person to undertake property management work in relation to a dwelling subject to a tenancy.[115] In either case, an offence is committed if the agent is not licensed to undertake that work and the landlord knows, or should know, that he or she does not hold a licence.[116] This offence is punishable on conviction by a fine not exceeding level 4 on the standard scale.[117]

---

106 H(W)A 2014 s9(1), (2).

107 H(W)A 2014 s9(2).

108 H(W)A 2014 s9(3).

109 Property management work is defined by H(W)A 2014 s12. Note that property management work does not include anything done by a local housing authority: s12(3)(c).

110 H(W)A 2014 s11(1), (3).

111 H(W)A 2014 s11(2), (3).

112 H(W)A 2014 s11(3).

113 H(W)A 2014 s11(4).

114 H(W)A 2014 s13(1).

115 H(W)A 2014 s13(2).

116 H(W)A 2014 s13. This is an important offence because, if committed by a landlord breaching s13(2) it can be relied on to obtain an RRO under H(W)A 2014 s32, see paras 5.77–5.79.

117 H(W) 2014 s13(3). Level 4 is currently set at £2,500: CJA 1982 s37(2). Note the absence of a reasonable excuse defence.

Prosecution

5.52   Prosecution of the H(W)A 2014 offences is by a licensing authority or local housing authority.[118] A local housing authority may, if authorised in writing by a licensing authority, offer persons suspected of committing most of the H(W)A 2014 offences considered above the opportunity to discharge any liability by paying a fixed penalty.[119] A fixed penalty notice cannot be imposed in relation to an offence under H(W)A 2014 s13(3) (appointing an unlicensed agent).[120] The fixed penalties are £250 for any offence punishable by an unlimited fine and £150 for all other offences.[121]

Reasonable excuse

5.53   Neither HA 2004 nor H(W)A 2014 defines what a 'reasonable excuse' might be. Clearly, what is reasonable may vary from person to person and will depend on the particular circumstances of the case.[122]

Rent repayment orders

5.54   A failure to obtain a licence does not affect the legality of any tenancy granted, nor does it otherwise invalidate any such tenancy.[123] In particular, any provision requiring the payment of rent is enforceable by the landlord. A new remedy was introduced by HA 2004, however, in the form of a rent repayment order (RRO).[124] In England, RROs are now governed by HA 2004 or Housing and Planning Act (HPA) 2016,[125] while in Wales RROs are available under HA 2004 and H(W)A 2014.

118 H(W)A 2014 s28. Where a local housing authority is not the licensing authority for its area, it requires the consent of the licensing authority to bring criminal proceedings: H(W)A 2014 s28(2). The licensing authority for all of Wales is Cardiff Council, see para 5.25.

119 H(W)A 2014 s29(1).

120 H(W)A 2014 s29(1). A fixed penalty notice also cannot be used in relation to an offence under s38(4) (failure to produce documents or provide information when requested).

121 H(W)A 2014 s29(4). These amounts may be amended by the Welsh Ministers: s29(5).

122 *R v Nicholson* [2006] EWCA Crim 1518, [2006] 1 WLR 2857.

123 HA 2004 ss73(3) and 96(3); H(W)A 2014 s43(1).

124 An order can be made in respect of other periodical payments, such as a licence fee.

125 The relevant provisions of HPA 2016 Part 2 Chapter 4 were brought into force on 6 April 2017: Housing and Planning Act 2016 (Commencement No 5, Transitional Provisions and Savings) Regulations 2017 SI No 281. From that

Application under Housing Act 2004

5.55 Although the RRO provisions of HA 2004 are replaced in England by the equivalent provisions in HPA 2016, they remain relevant where the offence under HA 2004 s72(1) or s95(1) was wholly committed before 6 April 2017 or where the commission of the offence started before that date and ended no later than 5 April 2018.[126] The HA 2004 provisions will also continue to apply in Wales.

5.56 Under HA 2004, an application for an RRO may be made in respect of an 'unlicensed HMO' or an 'unlicensed house'.[127] An 'unlicensed HMO' is a HMO that is required to be, but is not, licensed under HA 2004 Part 2,[128] save where either a notification has been given to the local housing authority of an intention to take steps so that the premises do not need to be licensed, which notification is still 'effective',[129] or an application for a licence has been made which is still effective.[130] An 'unlicensed house' is defined in similar terms by reference to HA 2004 Part 3.[131]

5.57 Application for an RRO may be made by a local housing authority or by an occupier of a part of an HMO or of the whole or part of a Part 3 house. The application is made to the First-tier Tribunal in England and a residential property tribunal in Wales.[132] Where the tribunal is satisfied of certain matters, it may make an RRO.[133]

5.58 On an application made by a local housing authority, the matters that the tribunal must be satisfied of before it can make an RRO are as follows.

a) the authority had served a notice of intended proceedings (NIP) on the appropriate person,[134] informing him or her of the authority's

date, rent repayment orders in respect of HA 2004 offences committed after 6 April 2017 are dealt with under HPA 2016 rather than HA 2004, except where the commission of the offence started before 6 April 2017 and ended no later than 5 April 2018, in which case the HA 2004 provisions still apply: reg 5(2).

126 See Housing and Planning Act 2016 (Commencement No 5, Transitional Provisions and Savings) Regulations 2017 SI No 281 reg 5(2).

127 HA 2004 ss73 and 96.

128 HA 2004 s73(1).

129 HA 2004 s73(2)(a), and see para 5.31.

130 HA 2004 s73(2)(b), and see para 5.31.

131 HA 2004 s96(1), (2).

132 HA 2004 ss73(5)(a), 95(5)(a), 261(8).

133 HA 2004 ss73(5) and 96(5).

134 The 'appropriate person' is the person entitled to receive on his or her own account periodical payments payable in connection with occupation of the premises: HA 2004 ss73(10) and 96(10).

intention to apply for an RRO, its reasons for doing so, the amount that it will seek to recover, and inviting representations within a specified period of not less than 28 days;[135] and

b) the period specified in the NIP has expired and the authority has considered any representations made to it within that period;[136] and

c) at any time within the period of 12 months ending with the date of the NIP, the appropriate person has committed an offence under HA 2004 s72(1) in respect of the HMO or HA 2004 s95(1) in respect of the Part 3 house;[137] and

d) either universal credit or housing benefit has been paid in respect of periodical payments in connection with occupation of the premises.[138]

5.59 On an application made by an occupier, the matters that the tribunal must be satisfied of before it can make an RRO are as follows.

a) the appropriate person has either been convicted of an offence under HA 2004 s72(1) in respect of the HMO or s95(1) in respect of the Part 3 house, or he or she has been the subject of an RRO;[139] and

b) the occupier paid, to a person having control of or managing the HMO or house,[140] periodical payments in respect of occupation of those premises during any period in which it appears to the tribunal that an offence under HA 2004 s72(1) or s95(1) was being committed in relation to the premises;[141] and

c) the application is made within 12 months of the date of the conviction or RRO.[142]

---

135 HA 2004 s73(6)(c), (7)(a) and s96(6)(c), (7)(a). The authority must ensure that a copy of the NIP is received by the housing benefit department responsible for administering the relevant housing benefit and that the department is kept informed of any matters relating to the proceedings likely to be of interest in connection with the administration of housing benefit: HA 2004 ss73(9) and 96(9).

136 HA 2004 s73(6)(c), (7)(b), (c) and s96(6)(c), (7)(b), (c).

137 HA 2004 ss73(6)(a) and 96(6)(a): there is no requirement that the appropriate person has been convicted or even charged.

138 HA 2004 ss73(6)(b) and 96(6)(b).

139 HA 2004 ss73(8)(a) and 96(8)(a).

140 See nn38 and 39, above.

141 HA 2004 ss73(8)(b) and 96(8)(b).

142 HA 2004 ss73(8)(c) and 96(8)(c). If there are both a conviction and an RRO, the 12 months runs from the later.

5.60   Calculation of the amount payable under an RRO depends on whether or not the application is made by an authority and there has been a conviction.

5.61   On an application by a local housing authority, where the tribunal is satisfied that there has been a conviction under HA 2004 s72(1) or s95(1), and that either housing benefit or the housing element of universal credit have been paid during any period in which it appears to the tribunal that an offence was being committed, the tribunal must – save as qualified (see paras 5.62–5.64) – make an RRO requiring the appropriate person to pay to the authority the amount of housing benefit or housing element of universal credit paid in respect of the premises.[143]

5.62   There are three exceptions or adjustments. First, if the total amount of rent received by the appropriate person is less than the total amount of housing benefit or housing element of universal credit, the amount required to be paid under the RRO is limited to the total rent received.[144]

5.63   Secondly, the RRO may not require the payment of an amount which, by reason of exceptional circumstances, it would be unreasonable to pay.[145]

5.64   Thirdly, the RRO may not require the payment of any amount in respect of any period outside of the 12 months before the date of the NIP.[146]

5.65   In any other circumstances, including when the application is made by the occupier, the amount required to be paid by an RRO is such amount as the tribunal considers to be reasonable in the circumstances.[147]

5.66   In determining what this amount should be, the tribunal must take into account the following matters.[148]

a) The total amount paid in connection with occupation of the HMO or Part 3 house during any period in which it appears to the tribunal that an offence was being committed.

b) The extent to which that amount consisted of, or derived from, payments of housing benefit or the housing element of universal

---

143 HA 2004 s74(2), (2A) and s97(2), (2A).
144 HA 2004 ss74(3) and 97(3).
145 HA 2004 ss74(4) and 97(8).
146 HA 2004 ss74(8)(a) and 97(8)(a).
147 HA 2004 ss74(5) and 97(5).
148 HA 2004 ss74(6) and 97(6).

credit, and the extent to which it was actually received by the appropriate person.

c) Whether the appropriate person has been convicted of an offence under HA 2004 s72(1) or HA 2004 s95(1).

d) The appropriate person's conduct and financial circumstances.

e) The occupier's conduct (on an application made by the occupier).

5.67 Where the application is made by an authority, the RRO must not require the payment of any amount in respect of any period outside of the 12 months before the date of the NIP,[149] or where made by an occupier in respect of any period outside of the 12 months before application.[150]

5.68 The purposes of RROs, in relation to occupiers, are to enable a penalty in the form of a civil sanction to be imposed in addition to the fine payable for the criminal offence of operating an unlicensed HMO or Part 3 house, to help prevent a landlord from profiting from renting properties illegally, and to resolve the problems arising from the withholding of rent by tenants.[151]

5.69 When deciding what amount would be reasonable in the circumstances, the tribunal should bear the following in mind.[152]

a) The landlord is liable to suffer two penalties, *i.e.* a fine and an RRO: the tribunal should have regard to the total amount that the landlord would have to pay by way of a fine and an RRO.

b) There is no presumption that the RRO should be for the total amount received by the landlord during the relevant period unless there are good reasons why it should not be: the tribunal must take an overall view of the circumstances in determining what amount would be reasonable.

c) While the RRO can only be made in relation to amounts received in a 12-month period, the tribunal should also have regard to the total length of time during which the offence was being committed, which bears upon the seriousness of the offence.

---

149 HA 2004 ss74(8)(a) and 97(8)(a).

150 HA 2004 ss74(8)(b) and 97(8)(b).

151 *Parker v Waller* [2012] UKUT 301 (LC), at [26]. The Upper Tribunal was only concerned in that case with an unlicensed HMO, but the same purposes must also apply in respect of unlicensed Part 3 houses.

152 *Parker v Waller* [2012] UKUT 301 (LC), at [26]. In *Parker*, the Upper Tribunal held that it was not appropriate to impose an RRO amount which exceeded the landlord's profit.

d) The fact that the occupier will have had the benefit of occupying the premises during the relevant period is not a material consideration.

e) While an RRO may relate to payments made as part of the rent for utilities, it is only in the most serious cases that they should be included, as the landlord will not have benefited from them.

f) The circumstances in which the offence was committed are always likely to be material. A deliberate flouting of the requirement to register will obviously merit a larger RRO than instances of inadvertence (although all landlords ought to know the law). A professional landlord is likely to be more harshly dealt with than a non-professional landlord.

5.70   Any money received by an authority under an RRO made under HA 2004 may be applied for specific purposes relating to its functions under HA 2004.[153]

Application under Housing and Planning Act 2016 (England only)

5.71   Under Chapter 4 of Part 2 of HPA 2016, the First-tier Tribunal has power to make a rent repayment order against a landlord in England[154] who has committed an offence under HA 2004 s72(1) or s95(1), where the offence took place on or after 6 April 2017, save where the commission of the offence started before 6 April 2017 and ended no later than 5 April 2018 (in which case the HA 2004 RRO provisions, discussed at paras 5.56–5.70, apply).[155]

5.72   Either a tenant or a local housing authority may apply for a rent repayment order.[156]

Application by tenant

5.73   A tenant may apply if the offence was committed within the 12 months before the application was made and was related to the housing that was let to the tenant.[157] The tenant may recover the rent for

---

153 The permitted purposes are specified in reg 3(2) of the Rent Repayment Orders (Supplementary Provisions) (England) Regulations 2007 SI No 572 and the Rent Repayment Orders (Supplementary Provisions) (Wales) Regulations 2008 SI No 254. Any surplus must be paid into the Consolidated Fund or the Welsh Consolidated Fund, as the case may be: reg 4 of both orders.

154 The provisions do not apply in Wales.

155 HPA 2016 s40; Housing and Planning Act 2016 (Commencement No 5, Transitional Provisions and Savings) Regulations 2017 SI No 281 regs 4, 5.

156 HPA 2016 s41(1).

157 HPA 2016 s41(2).

the period, not exceeding 12 months, during which the landlord committed the offence, less any amount which was paid in respect of the rent by universal credit or housing benefit.[158] The tribunal must, in deciding the amount of the award, have regard to the conduct both of the landlord and of the tenant, the financial circumstances of the landlord and whether the landlord has at any time been convicted of an offence under Chapter 4 of Part 2[159] of HPA 2016:[160] see also para 5.76.

Application by local housing authority

5.74   Where the application is made by a local housing authority, the tribunal may award the universal credit or housing benefit that was paid, directly or indirectly, to the landlord in respect of the rent for the period, not exceeding 12 months, during which the landlord committed the offence.[161] In deciding the amount of the award, the tribunal must have regard to the conduct of the landlord, the financial circumstances of the landlord and whether the landlord has been convicted of an offence under Chapter 4 of Part 2[162] of HPA 2016:[163] see also para 5.76.

---

158 HPA 2016 s44(1)–(3) and s51. Section 44 refers to universal credit, which is currently implemented only in certain areas and for certain types of claimant; s51 therefore requires references to universal credit to include a reference to housing benefit, ie where the latter remains the relevant benefit.

159 This includes the HA 2004 ss72(1) and 95(1) offences referred to at paras 5.30–5.31 and 5.36, as well as a number of other offences, specified in HPA 2016 s40(3), which includes unlawful eviction and harassment under Protection from Eviction Act (PEA) 1977 s1(2), (3) and (3A) (see paras 1.197–1.254 and 2.52–2.91), violent entry into premises (Criminal Law Act (CLA) 1977 s6(1) – see paras 3.6–3.36), failure to comply with certain orders under HA 2004 Part 1, and will include breach of a banning order under HPA 2016 s21 when banning orders are brought into force (paras 6.2–6.38).

160 HPA 2016 s44(4).

161 HPA 2016 ss45(1)–(3) and 51 (see n158, above). The authority may apply any amount recovered under a rent repayment order to meet the costs and expenses incurred in, or associated with, carrying out enforcement functions in relation to the private rented sector: Rent Repayment Orders and Financial Penalties (Amounts Recovered) (England) Regulations 2017 SI No 367 reg 3(1). Enforcement functions are defined by reg 2 to mean functions under HA 2004 Parts 1–4, and functions under HPA 2016 Part 2, as well as other functions connected with the law related to housing or landlord and tenant. Any amount not applied in that way must be paid into the Consolidated Fund: reg 3(2).

162 See n159, above.

163 HPA 2016 s45(4).

5.75　　　While in principle the local housing authority has a discretion whether or not to apply for an order,[164] it is under a duty to consider doing so once it has become aware that any offence under Chapter 4 of Part 2 of HPA 2016[165] has been committed on or after 6 April 2017.[166] The authority must, when deciding whether to apply for an order, have regard to guidance given by the secretary of state.[167] The authority may only seek the order if it has first served a notice of intended proceedings informing the landlord of its reasons for doing so, the amount sought and invited the landlord to make representations.[168]

Tribunal order

Housing Act 2004

5.76　The First-tier Tribunal may make a RRO provided it is satisfied, beyond reasonable doubt, that the landlord has committed an offence under HA 2004 s72(1) or s95(1) (paras 5.30–5.31 and 5.36); it is not, however, necessary that there should be an actual conviction – only that the offence has been committed on or after 6 April 2017.[169] Although the tribunal has a discretion as to the amount of the order, it may prima facie not reduce the maximum amount that would otherwise be payable[170] where the landlord has been convicted of the offence which gives rise to the application.[171] Even so, there is a residual discretion to reduce the amount, if the tribunal considers

---

164　HPA 2016 s41(1).

165　See n158, above.

166　HPA 2016 s48. This does not apply where the commission of an offence under HA 2004 s72(1) or s95(1) started before 6 April 2017 and ended no later than 5 April 2018: Housing and Planning Act 2016 (Commencement No 5, Transitional Provisions and Savings) Regulations 2017 SI No 281 reg 5(2)(b).

167　HPA 2016 s41(4). The secretary of state has issued guidance: DCLG, *Rent repayment orders under Housing and Planning Act 2016: Guidance for Local Authorities* (April 2017). The guidance, however, does no more than describe the law.

168　HPA 2016 s42(2).

169　HPA 2016 s43(1). This is again subject to an exception where the commission of an offence under HA 2004 s72(1) or s95(1) started before 6 April 2017 and ended no later than 5 April 2018, in which case any RRO would need to be made under the equivalent HA 2004 RRO provisions discussed at paras 5.56–5.70: Housing and Planning Act 2016 (Commencement No 5, Transitional Provisions and Savings) Regulations 2017 SI No 281 reg 5(2)(b).

170　Ie the rent or credit/benefit referable to the period (not exceeding 12 months) during which the offence was committed: paras 5.73–5.74.

171　HPA 2016 s46(1).

– by reason of exceptional circumstances – that it would be unreasonable to require the landlord to pay it.[172]

Application under Housing (Wales) Act 2014

5.77 An application for an RRO under H(W)A 2014 may be made to a residential property tribunal by the licensing authority, the local housing authority for the area, or a tenant of the dwelling.[173]

5.78 The circumstance in which an application and an RRO can be made are the same as under HA 2004, save that the relevant trigger offences are under H(W)A 2014 s7(5) and H(W)A 2014 s13(3).[174] The amount payable under an RRO is calculated in accordance with H(W)A 2014 s33, which, so far as material, is in the same terms as HA 2004 ss74 and 97 (see paras 5.61–5.69).

5.79 Money received by an authority under an RRO made under H(W)A 2014 may only be used to fund the making of the application for an RRO, dealing with any application for a licence under H(W)A 2014 Part 1, or prosecuting offences under ss7(5) and 13(3).[175]

Rent stopping order (Wales)

5.80 A further possibility, only available in Wales, is a rent stopping order (RSO). An application for an RSO may be made to a residential property tribunal by the licensing authority or the local housing authority for the area.[176]

5.81 Before making an RSO the tribunal must be satisfied that an offence is being committed under H(W)A 2014 s7(5) or H(W)A 2014 s13(3).[177] The tribunal must also be satisfied of the following matters.

---

172 HPA 2016 s46(5).

173 H(W)A 2014 s32(1). A local housing authority may only make such an application with the consent of the licensing authority: H(W)A 2014 s32(2).

174 H(W)A 2014 s32(5)(a), (7)(a). For these purposes, the s7(5) offence is not sufficient if it is committed by breaching s7(3) and the s13(3) offence is not sufficient if it is committed by breaching s13(1): s32(8). The rationale for this is, presumably, that a breach of s7(3) takes place after the tenancy has ended, while a breach of s13(1) takes place before the tenancy has begun, see paras 5.43–5.47 and 5.51.

175 Regulation of Private Rented Housing (Rent Repayment Orders) (Supplementary Provisions) (Wales) Regulations 2016 SI No 1022 reg 3(2). Any surplus must be paid into the Welsh Consolidated Fund: reg 4.

176 H(W)A 2014 s30(1). A local housing authority may only make such an application with the consent of the licensing authority: s30(2).

177 H(W)A 2014 s30(5). For these purposes, the s13(3) offence is not sufficient if it is committed by breaching s13(1): s30(9). There is no need to exempt the s7(5) offence when committed in breach of s7(3), as that offence can only take

a) that the authority has given the landlord and the tenant an NIP, explaining that it is proposing to apply for an RSO, its reasons for doing so, the effect of an RSO, how an RSO can be revoked, and inviting the landlord to make representations within a specified period of not less than 28 days;[178] and

b) that the period specified in the NIP has expired and the authority has considered any representations made to it within that period.[179]

5.82   If the tribunal makes an RSO it must specify a 'stopping date'. The effect of the RSO is that periodical payments payable in connection with a domestic tenancy of the dwelling which relate to a period, or part of a period, falling after the stopping date no longer need to be paid and an obligation under the tenancy to pay a stopped amount is treated as being met.[180] An RSO has no effect on any other rights and obligations under the tenancy.[181]

5.83   An RSO may be revoked by a residential property tribunal on application by the licensing authority, the local housing authority for the area or the landlord, provided that it is satisfied that the offence is no longer being committed.[182] Where the tribunal revokes an RSO, periodical payments in connection with a domestic tenancy of the dwelling become payable again but only from a specified date,[183] ie there are no arrears attributable to the period during which rent was stopped.

Prohibition on serving a Housing Act 1988 s21 notice

5.84   Landlords in breach of their registration and licensing obligations may not give notice under HA 1988 s21,[184] ie notice of seeking possession.

---

place when the tenancy has come to an end, in which case no rent is payable (cf s32(8), considered at n174, above).

178   H(W)A 2014 s30(6)(a).

179   H(W)A 2014 s30(6)(b), (c).

180   H(W)A 2014 s30(3)(a), (b).

181   H(W)A 2014 s30(3)(c).

182   H(W)A 2014 s31(2). A local housing authority may only make such an application with the consent of the licensing authority: s31(3).

183   H(W)A 2014 s31(4). Note that the specified date may be earlier than the date on which the RSO is actually revoked.

184   HA 2004 ss75 and 98; H(W)A 2014 s44.

5.85 So far as HMOs are concerned, no HA 1988 s21 notice may be given in relation to an assured shorthold tenancy of a part of an unlicensed HMO so long as it remains an unlicensed HMO.[185]

5.86 In relation to an unlicensed house (under HA 2004 Part 3), no HA 1988 s21 notice may be given in relation to an assured shorthold tenancy of the whole or part of the house so long as it remains an unlicensed house.[186]

5.87 Under H(W)A 2014, no HA 1988 s21 notice may be given in relation to a domestic tenancy which is an assured shorthold tenancy if either the landlord is not registered in respect of the dwelling or he or she is not licensed under H(W)A 2014 and has not appointed a person who is licensed to carry out all property management work on the landlord's behalf.[187]

5.88 Note that, while the prohibition under H(W)A 2014 only affects the validity of a HA 1988 s21 notice and not a HA 1988 s8 notice, it is nonetheless likely to amount to an offence under H(W)A 2014 s7(1) to serve a HA 1988 s8 notice (or indeed any notice to terminate the tenancy).[188] Likewise, while there is no express prohibition on serving notice to end a Rent Act 1977 regulated tenancy, such action is likely to be an offence under H(W)A 2014 s7(1).

---

185 HA 2004 s75. For 'unlicensed HMO' see para 5.56. It has been held at county court level that a tenant cannot rely on his or her own unlawful acts in allowing more occupiers into the property, in breach of his or her tenancy agreement, to frustrate the service of a HA 1988 s21 notice by turning the property into an HMO: *Howell v Hughes and Hughes*, 10 September 2015, County Court at Central London, unreported.

186 HA 2004 s98. For 'unlicensed house' see para 5.56.

187 H(W)A 2014 s44. The prohibition on giving a HA 1988 s21 notice does not apply for a period of 28 days beginning on the day on which the landlord's interest in the dwelling is assigned to him: H(W)A 2014 s44(2).

188 See H(W)A 2014 s7(2)(f) and para 5.44.

CHAPTER 6

Banning orders and database of rogue landlords

continued

Introduction

6.1   Part 2 of the Housing and Planning Act (HPA) 2016, once in force,[1] will provide English local housing authorities with the power to apply to the First-tier Tribunal for an order banning a residential landlord, letting agent or property manager, who has been convicted of a banning order offence, from letting housing in England, engaging in English letting agency work and/or engaging in English property management work.[2] This chapter considers banning orders; and the database of rogue landlords, including the circumstances in which a person may be included on the database and who has access to it.

Banning orders

Introduction

6.2   A banning order is an order, made by the First-tier Tribunal, which bans a landlord or property agent from letting housing in England, engaging in English letting agency work and/or engaging in English property management work.[3] A banning order may also ban the person subject to the order from being involved in a body corporate that carries out an activity that the person is banned from carrying out.[4] A banning order may contain exceptions.[5]

6.3   A local housing authority may apply for a banning order against any person, including any body corporate, who has been convicted of a banning order offence.[6] Where an authority make an application against a body corporate, it must also make an application against any officer[7] who was convicted of the same offence in respect of the

---

1   The government has suggested that HPA 2016 Part 2 will be brought fully into force on 1 October 2017: Department for Communities and Local Government (DCLG), *Proposed banning order offences under the Housing and Planning Act 2016: A consultation paper* (December 2016), p8.

2   HPA 2016 ss14(1) and 15(1).

3   HPA 2016 ss14(1) and 16(1). A 'property agent' is a letting agent or property manager: s56.

4   HPA 2016 ss18 and 56. A person is 'involved' if he or she acts as an officer of the body corporate or takes part or is concerned in its management: s18(2).

5   HPA 2016 s17(3). See further para 6.21.

6   HPA 2016 s15.

7   An 'officer' of a body corporate is defined as any director, secretary or other similar officer, and any person who was purporting to act in such a capacity: HPA 2016 s56.

same conduct.[8] A banning order may be made by the First-tier Tribunal against any person who has been convicted of a banning order offence and who was a residential landlord or property agent when the offence was convicted.[9]

Definitions

Residential landlord

6.4 A residential landlord is a 'landlord of housing'.[10] Housing is defined as 'a building, or part of a building, occupied or intended to be occupied as a dwelling or as more than one dwelling'.[11]

Property agent

6.5 A property agent is a letting agent or property manager.[12] A letting agent is a person who engages in letting agency work otherwise than in the course of his or her employment under a contract of employment.[13] Similarly, a property manager is a person who engages in property management work otherwise than in the course of his or her employment under a contract of employment.[14] For letting agency work and property management work, see further paras 6.9–6.17.

Letting housing in England

6.6 Letting housing in England is defined as letting a building, or part of a building, intended to be occupied as a dwelling, under a tenancy or licence which is for a term of less than 21 years.[15]

Building

6.7 HPA 2016 does not define what is meant by a 'building'. In other statutory contexts[16] it has been held to be a built structure or permanent erection which has been annexed to and changed the physical

---

8 HPA 2016 s15(2).
9 HPA 2016 s16(1). So far as officers of a body corporate are concerned, there is no requirement that they were a residential landlord or property agent at the time of the offence: see para 6.34.
10 HPA 2016 s56.
11 HPA 2016 s56. See further paras 6.7–6.8.
12 HPA 2016 s56.
13 HPA 2016 s54(1), (2).
14 HPA 2016 s55(1), (2).
15 HPA 2016 s56.
16 Leasehold Reform Act 1967 and Town and Country Planning Act 1990.

character of the land.[17] It is a question of fact and degree in each case, but can include any building, such as a chalet, that has been erected with a prospect of permanence.[18] A caravan, houseboat or boathouse are therefore unlikely to be 'buildings'.

Occupied as a dwelling

6.8 HPA 2016 does not define what is meant by a 'dwelling'. As in other statutory contexts (see paras 1.55–1.58), it will include any accommodation that is intended to be occupied as someone's home, ie the place where the occupier is to live.[19]

English letting agency work

6.9 English letting agency work is extremely broadly defined: it means things done by a person; in the course of a business; in response to instructions received from a prospective landlord or tenant; and which relates to housing in England.[20]

Housing

6.10 Housing has the same meaning as at paras 6.4, and 6.6–6.8. Accordingly, a banning order does not prevent a letting agent from undertaking commercial letting agency work or letting agency work in respect of premises that are not a building, eg caravans or other movable structures.

In the course of a business

6.11 A banning order does not prevent the person subject to it from introducing a prospective tenant to a prospective landlord otherwise than in the course of a business, eg a tenant introducing a possible replacement as part of an arrangement to leave. HPA 2016 does not define what is meant by 'in the course of a business', but in other statutory contexts the phrase has been given a wide meaning. An organisation can carry on a business without a commercial motive or an intention to make a profit if it is carrying on a 'serious occupation' or profession.[21]

---

17 *Malekshad v Howard de Walden Estates Ltd (No 1)* [2002] UKHL 49, [2003] HLR 31; *Cheshire CC v Woodward* [1962] 2 QB 126, DC.

18 *R v Swansea City Council ex p Elitestone Ltd* (1993) 66 P&CR 422, CA.

19 *R (CN) v Lewisham LBC* [2014] UKSC 62, [2015] AC 1259, [2015] HLR 6; *Uratemp Ventures Ltd v Collins* [2001] UKHL 43, [2002] 1 AC 301, (2001) 33 HLR 85.

20 HPA 2016 s54(3), (5).

21 *Customs and Excise Commissioners v Morrison's Academy Boarding Houses Association* 1977 SC 279, Court of Session; *Town Investments Ltd v Department of the Environment* [1978] AC 359, HL.

In response to instructions received from a prospective landlord or tenant

6.12   A prospective landlord is a person who is seeking to find another person to whom to let housing.[22] A prospective tenant is a person seeking to find housing to rent.[23]

Exclusions

6.13   Letting agency work does not, however, include publishing advertisements or disseminating information or providing a means by which prospective tenants and landlords can make contact and communicate with each other and respond to advertisements.[24] Accordingly, a banning order could not prevent a person from operating a website that allows landlords to advertise residential premises to let to prospective tenants.

English property management work

6.14   English property management work is defined as things done by a person; in the course of a business; in response to instructions received from a client who wishes that person to arrange services, repairs, maintenance, improvements, insurance or to deal with any other aspect of management in respect of premises consisting of housing in England let under a tenancy.[25]

Housing

6.15   Housing has the same meaning as set out in paras 6.4, and 6.6–6.8. A banning order cannot prevent a property manager from undertaking commercial property management work or property management work in respect of premises that are not a building, eg caravans or other movable structures.

In the course of a business

6.16   This has the same meaning as for letting agency work (see para 6.11).

---

22   HPA 2016 s54(3)(a). This will include a person who is seeking to find another person to whom to grant a licence to: HPA 2016 s56. It will not include situations where the tenancy or licence will be for a term of more than 21 years: HPA 2016 s56.

23   HPA 2016 s54(3)(b). It is not clear from HPA 2016 ss54 and 56 but this will presumably also include prospective licensees and will not apply where the tenancy or licence will be for a term of more than 21 years: see n22, above.

24   HPA 2016 s54(4).

25   HPA 2016 s55(3).

Let under a tenancy

6.17 A tenancy includes a licence, but does not include a tenancy or licence for a term of more than 21 years.[26]

Duration

6.18 The length of each ban must be specified in the banning order and must be for at least 12 months.[27] An order, once made, may be varied or revoked on an application to the First-tier Tribunal.[28] The First-tier Tribunal must revoke an order if all of the convictions giving rise to the order have been overturned on appeal.[29] Otherwise, the First-tier Tribunal has the power to vary or revoke the order if some, but not all, of the convictions have either been overturned on appeal or become spent.[30] The power to vary the order includes power to vary the banned activities, the length of the ban and any existing exceptions to the ban.[31] The power may also be exercised by the tribunal adding new exceptions to the ban.[32]

Anti-avoidance

6.19 A person who is subject to banning order may not, without the consent of the First-tier Tribunal, seek to avoid the consequences of the order by transferring any estate of land, to any of the following categories of people.[33]

a) a person associated[34] with the landlord;
b) a business partner[35] of the landlord;
c) a person associated with a business partner of the landlord;
d) a business partner of a person associated with the landlord;

---

26 HPA 2016 s56.
27 HPA 2016 s17(1), (2).
28 HPA 2016 s20(1).
29 HPA 2016 s20(2).
30 HPA 2016 s20(3), (4). Convictions become spent in accordance with Rehabilitation of Offenders Act 1974.
31 HPA 2016 s20(5).
32 HPA 2016 s20(5).
33 Any such transfer made without the tribunal's consent is void: HPA 2016 s27(2).
34 Defined by reference to Housing Act 1996 s178 (broadly, family members): HPA 2016 s27(5).
35 Defined by reference to Deregulation Act 2015 s34(5): HPA 2016 s27(5).

e) a body corporate of which the landlord or a person mentioned in paras a)–d) is an officer,[36]

f) a body corporate in which the landlord has a shareholding or other financial interest; or

g) in a case where the landlord is a body corporate, any body corporate that has an officer in common with the landlord.[37]

Entry onto database of rogue landlords

6.20   Any person made subject to a banning order must be entered onto the database of rogue landlords (see paras 6.51–6.60).[38]

Effect on existing and new tenancies

6.21   A banning order does not bring an existing tenancy or licence to an end. Accordingly, an order may include exceptions to deal with cases where there are existing tenancies which the landlord does not have the power to bring to an immediate end.[39]

6.22   A breach of a banning order does not affect the validity or enforceability of any tenancy entered into.[40]

When can a banning order be made?

6.23   A local housing authority may apply for a banning order against a residential landlord, letting agent or property manager who has been convicted of a banning order offence.[41]

Banning order offences

6.24   'Banning order offence' is not defined by HPA 2016, but will include any offence of a description specified in regulations by the secretary of state.[42]

6.25   While the relevant regulations have not yet been made, the government has consulted on four categories of banning order offence:

---

36 For 'officer' see n7, above.

37 HPA 2016 s27.

38 HPA 2016 s29(1).

39 HPA 2016 s17(4)(a). If the banning order does not contain such an exception, the landlord is liable to be in breach immediately. The banning order should therefore contain an exception in respect of such tenancies for such period of time as it should take for the landlord lawfully to bring them to an end.

40 HPA 2016 s24.

41 HPA 2016 s15(1).

42 HPA 2016 s14(3).

1) relevant housing offences;
2) immigration offences;
3) serious criminal offences; and
4) other criminal offences.[43]

6.26   The proposed *relevant housing offences* are as follows.[44]

a) unlawful eviction or harassment contrary to the Protection from Eviction Act 1977 or the Criminal Law Act 1977;[45]

b) failure to comply with an improvement notice, prohibition order or emergency prohibition order served under Housing Act (HA) 2004;[46]

c) offences under HA 2004 in relation to houses in multiple occupation (HMOs) or HA 2004 Part 3 houses;[47]

d) an offence under Gas Safety (Installation and Use) Regulations 1998 SI No 2451 reg 36;[48]

e) an offence under Regulatory Reform (Fire Safety) Order 2005 SI No 1541 Article 32;[49]

f) the proposed offence of letting agents charging fees to tenants.

6.27   The only proposed *immigration offence* is letting to someone disqualified from renting because of his or her immigration status.[50]

6.28   The proposed *serious criminal offences* are as follows.

a) fraud, contrary to the Fraud Act 2006;

b) drugs offences;

c) serious violent and sexual offences.[51]

---

43 DCLG, *Proposed banning order offences under the Housing and Planning Act 2016: A consultation paper* (December 2016) and DCLG, *Banning letting agent fees paid by tenants* (April 2017).

44 It is suggested that these offences will not be banning order offences where the offender receives an absolute or conditional discharge: DCLG, *Proposed banning order offences*, p13.

45 See paras 1.197–1.254, 2.52–2.91 and 3.6–3.36.

46 Arden & Dymond *Manual of Housing Law* (LAG, 10th edn, 2017), paras 12.18–12.29 and 12.33–12.45.

47 See paras 5.29–5.37.

48 See paras 7.3–7.13.

49 The 2005 Order imposes fire safety duties which, while widely applicable in relation to non-domestic premises, have limited relevance to domestic premises. The fire safety duties will, however, apply to common parts (as these are not "domestic premises' as defined by Article 2) and a landlord will therefore need to take general fire precautions, carry out a risk assessment, put fire safety arrangements in place, etc. Failure to do so is an offence under Article 32. See further paras 7.17–7.22.

50 Immigration Act 2014 Part 3.

51 Those specified in Criminal Justice Act 2003 Sch 15.

6.29   The criminal offences will only qualify as a serious criminal offence for these purposes if the following conditions are all met.

i)   the offence was committed at (or in the local area[52] of) residential premises in England or in relation to residential premises;

ii) the offender (or an associated person) was involved in the management of residential premises when the offence was committed; and

iii) neither the offender nor any associated person was occupying the premises as his or her main residence.

iv) The offence related to the occupier of the premises.

6.30   *'Other' criminal offence* is intended to be any offence for which the offender is sentenced in the Crown Court, so long as it was committed against, or in conjunction with, any person who was residing at the property owned by the offender (other than a person associated with the offender).

Applications for banning orders

6.31   Before making an application for a banning order against a person, a local housing authority must give him or her a notice of intended proceedings (NIP). The NIP must:

a)   inform the person that the authority is proposing to apply for a banning order and explain why;

b)   state the length of each proposed ban; and,

c)   invite the person to make representations within a period of not less than 28 days specified in the notice ('the notice period').[53]

6.32   The authority may not make the application before the notice period has expired and must consider any representations made during it.[54] The NIP may not be given more than six after the person was convicted of the banning order offence.[55]

Provision of information

6.33   An authority may require any person to provide specified information for the purpose of enabling it to decide whether to apply for a

---

52   A five-mile radius is suggested: DCLG, *Proposed banning order offences*, p14.

53   HPA 2016 s15(3).

54   HPA 2016 s15(4), (5).

55   HPA 2016 s15(6).

banning order against that person.[56] It is an offence for the person to fail to comply with the request, without a reasonable excuse for failing to do so.[57] It is also an offence to provide false or misleading information if the person either knows that it is false or misleading or is reckless as to whether it is false or misleading.[58] Both offences are punishable on summary conviction by an unlimited fine.[59]

Landlord, letting agent or property manager

6.34   The First-tier Tribunal may make a banning order against a person who has been convicted of a banning order offence and who was a residential landlord, letting agent or property manager at the time that it was committed.[60] Where the person convicted of a banning order offence is an officer of a body corporate, the tribunal may make the banning order even if he or she was not a residential landlord, letting agent or property manager at the time of the offence, eg where the landlord is a body corporate.

Residential landlord

6.35   A residential landlord is a landlord of housing (see paras 6.4 and 6.6–6.8).[61]

Letting agent

6.36   A letting agent is a person engaged in letting agency work (see paras 6.9–6.13).[62] This does not, however, include someone who engages in letting agency work in the course of his or her employment under a contract of employment.[63]

Property manager

6.37   A property manager is a person engaged in property management work (see paras 6.14–6.17).[64] This does not, however, include

---

56 HPA 2016 s19(1).
57 HPA 2016 s19(2).
58 HPA 2016 s19(3).
59 HPA 2016 s19(4).
60 HPA 2016 s16(1).
61 HPA 2016 s56.
62 HPA 2016 s54(1).
63 HPA 2016 s54(2).
64 HPA 2016 s55(1).

someone who engages in property management work in the course of his or her employment under a contract of employment.[65]

Factors that are relevant to the making of an order

6.38   The First-tier Tribunal must, before making an order, consider:

a) the seriousness of the offence of which the person has been convicted;

b) any previous convictions that the person has for a banning order offence;

c) whether the person is or has at any time been included in the database of rogue landlords and property agents; and

d) the likely effect of the banning order on the person and anyone else who may be affected by it.[66]

Sanctions for breaching a banning order

6.39   There are four sanctions available where a *residential landlord* breaches a banning order. They are:

a) a civil penalty;

b) criminal offence;

c) rent repayment order; and

d) being banned from holding a licence under HA 2004 Parts 2 or 3 (see chapter 5).

There are three possible sanctions for *letting agents* and *property managers*: a), b) and d) above; they cannot be made subject to a rent repayment order.

Civil penalty

6.40   A local housing authority may, if satisfied beyond reasonable doubt that a person has breached a banning order, impose a financial penalty on the person guilty of the offence provided that the person has not already been convicted of the offence (see paras 6.42–6.43).[67] If the person subject to the banning order continues not to comply with the terms of the banning order, then a further financial penalty may

65 HPA 2016 s55(2).
66 HPA 2016 s16(4).
67 HPA 2016 s23(1), (6).

be imposed after six months and for each six-month period thereafter for so long as the breach continues.[68]

6.41   The financial penalty can be up to £30,000.[69] The authority must, before imposing the penalty, give notice of its proposal to do so within six months of becoming aware that the offence has been committed.[70] The notice must set out the amount of, and reasons for, the proposed penalty and inform the person of the right to make representations.[71] The person served with the notice may make representations within 28 days. After that period has expired, the authority must decide whether or not to impose the penalty by serving a final notice.[72] Once the final notice is served, the penalty must be paid within 28 days.[73] The penalty is enforceable as if it were obtained as a money judgment in the county court.[74] There is a right of appeal to the First-tier Tribunal against the decision to impose the penalty and as to its amount.[75]

Criminal offence

6.42   A person, who has not been made subject to a financial penalty under HPA 2016 s23 (see paras 6.40–6.41), may be convicted of a criminal offence if he or she breaches a banning order that has been made against him or her.[76] That person is liable on summary conviction to imprisonment for a period of up to six months and/or an unlimited fine.[77] He or she commits a further offence if the breach of the banning order continues after the first conviction when he or she will be liable on summary conviction to a fine not exceeding one-tenth of level 2[78] on the standard scale for each day or part of a day on which the breach continues.[79]

6.43   Where the criminal offence is committed by a body corporate with the consent or connivance of, or is attributable to any neglect on the

68 HPA 2016 s23(4).
69 HPA 2016 s23(5).
70 HPA 2016 Sch 1 paras 1–2.
71 HPA 2016 Sch 1 para 3.
72 HPA 2016 Sch 1 paras 4–6.
73 HPA 2016 Sch 1 para 7.
74 HPA 2016 Sch 1 para 11.
75 HPA 2016 Sch 1 para 10.
76 HPA 2016 s21(1), (3).
77 HPA 2016 s21(2), (6).
78 £50. The current maximum level 2 fine is £500: Criminal Justice Act 1982 s37.
79 HPA 2016 s21(4).

part of, any officer of the body corporate, that officer also commits an offence.[80] The offence is also committed by a member of a body corporate whose affairs are managed by its members.[81]

Rent repayment order

6.44   Once Chapter 4 of Part 2 of HPA 2016 is brought fully into force,[82] the First-tier Tribunal will have power to make a rent repayment order against a landlord in England[83] who has committed an offence under HPA 2016 s21 (ie breach of a banning order).[84] The First-tier Tribunal does not have power to make such an order against a letting agent or property manager.

6.45   Either a tenant or a local housing authority may apply for a rent repayment order.[85]

Application by tenant

6.46   A tenant may apply if the offence was committed within the 12 months before the application was made and was related to the housing that was let to the tenant.[86] The tenant may recover the rent for a period, not exceeding 12 months, during which the landlord committed the offence, less any amount which was paid in respect of the

---

80   HPA 2016 s22(1). An 'officer' of a body corporate is defined as being any director, secretary or other similar officer, and any person who was purporting to act in such a capacity: HPA 2016 s56.

81   HPA 2016 s22(2). Under Companies Act 2006 s112, the members of a company are the subscribers of the company's memorandum of association and any other person who has agreed to become a member and whose name is entered in the company's register of members. This is likely to include, eg, the members of a housing co-operative, although whether the members are managing the affairs will depend on the circumstances in any individual case.

82   Housing and Planning Act 2016 (Commencement No 5, Transitional Provisions and Savings) Regulations 2017 SI No 281 brought the relevant provisions into force on 6 April 2017 for other offences (see n88, below) but not for breach of a banning order: reg 4(a). Note that in relation to the HA 2004 ss72(1) and 95(1) offences (discussed at paras 5.30–5.31 and 5.36), HPA 2016 does not apply where the commission of the offence began before 6 April 2017 and ended no later than 5 April 2018: reg 5(2). In that case, the HA 2004 provisions will apply: see paras 5.55–5.70.

83   The provisions do not apply in Wales.

84   HPA 2016 s40. This includes landlords who have been made subject to a civil penalty and who are therefore precluded from being convicted of the criminal offence.

85   HPA 2016 s41(1).

86   HPA 2016 s41(2).

rent by universal credit or housing benefit.[87] The tribunal must, in deciding the amount of the award, have regard to the conduct both of the landlord and of the tenant, the financial circumstances of the landlord and whether the landlord has at any time been convicted of an offence under Chapter 4 of Part 2[88] of HPA 2016;[89] see also para 6.49.

Application by local housing authority

6.47   Where the application is made by a local housing authority, the tribunal may award the universal credit or housing benefit that was paid, directly or indirectly, to the landlord in respect of the rent for a period, not exceeding 12 months, during which the landlord committed the offence.[90] In deciding the amount of the award, the tribunal must have regard to the conduct of the landlord, the financial circumstances of the landlord and whether the landlord has been convicted of an offence under Chapter 4 of Part 2[91] of HPA 2016;[92] see also para 6.49.

6.48   While in principle the local housing authority has a discretion whether or not to apply for an order,[93] it is under a duty to consider doing so once it has become aware that any offence under Chapter 4

---

87   HPA 2016 ss44(1)–(3) and 51. Section 44 refers to universal credit, which is currently implemented only in certain areas and for certain types of claimant; s51 therefore requires references to universal credit to include a reference to housing benefit, ie where the latter remains the relevant benefit.

88   This includes HPA 2016 s21, as well as a number of other offences, specified in HPA 2016 s40(3), which includes unlawful eviction and harassment under PEA 1977 s1(2), (3) and (3A) (see paras 1.197–1.254 and 2.52–2.91), violent entry into premises (Criminal Law Act 1977 s6(1) – see paras 3.6–3.36), failure to licence premises under HA 2004 ss72(1) and 95(1) (see paras 5.30–5.31 and 5.36) and the failure to comply with certain orders under HA 2004 Part 1.

89   HPA 2016 s44(4).

90   HPA 2016 ss45(1)–(3) and 51 (see n87, above). The authority may apply any amount recovered under a rent repayment order to meet the costs and expenses incurred in, or associated with, carrying out enforcement functions in relation to the private rented sector: Rent Repayment Orders and Financial Penalties (Amounts Recovered) (England) Regulations 2017 SI No 367 reg 3(1). Enforcement functions are defined by reg 2 to mean functions under HA 2004 Parts 1–4, and functions under HPA 2016 Part 2, as well as other functions connected with the law related to housing or landlord and tenant. Any amount not applied in that way must be paid into the Consolidated Fund: reg 3(2).

91   See n88, above.

92   HPA 2016 s45(4).

93   HPA 2016 s41(1).

of Part 2 of HPA 2016[94] has been committed.[95] The authority must, when deciding whether to apply for an order, have regard to guidance given by the secretary of state.[96] The authority may only seek the order if it has first served a notice of intended proceedings informing the landlord of its reasons for doing so, the amount sought and invited the landlord to make representations.[97]

Tribunal order

6.49   The First-tier Tribunal may make a rent repayment order provided it is satisfied, beyond reasonable doubt, that the landlord has committed an offence under HPA 2016 s21 (paras 6.42–6.43); it is not, however, necessary that there should be an actual conviction – only that the offence has been committed.[98] Although the tribunal has a discretion as to the amount of the order, it may prima facie not reduce the maximum amount that would otherwise be payable[99] where the landlord has been convicted of the offence which gives rise to the application.[100] Even so, there is a residual discretion to reduce the amount, if the tribunal considers – by reason of exceptional circumstances – that it would be unreasonable to require the landlord to pay it.[101]

Banned from holding a licence

6.50   A person who is made subject to a banning order may not be granted a licence under HA 2004 Part 2 (HMOs)[102] or Part 3 (selective and additional)[103] (see paras 5.3–5.21). A local housing authority must revoke a licence that is held by a person subject to a banning order.[104]

---

94 See n88, above.
95 HPA 2016 s48.
96 HPA 2016 s41(4). The secretary of state has issued guidance: DCLG, *Rent repayment orders under Housing and Planning Act 2016: Guidance for Local Authorities* (April 2017). The guidance, however, does no more than describe the law.
97 HPA 2016 s42(2).
98 HPA 2016 s43(1).
99 Ie the rent or credit/benefit referable to the period (not exceeding 12 months) during which the offence was committed: paras 6.46–6.47.
100 HPA 2016 s46(1).
101 HPA 2016 s46(5).
102 HA 2004 s64(3)(aa).
103 HA 2004 s88(3)(aa).
104 HA 2004 ss70A and 93A.

Database of rogue landlords

Introduction

6.51 The secretary of state must establish and operate a database of property agents[105] and rogue landlords.[106] It is, however, the responsibility of local housing authorities to maintain and update its content,[107] ie those persons who are entered onto the database. Each authority is entitled to have access to all of the information contained within the database, not just that which it has entered.[108] This allows authorities to be aware of rogue landlords who have moved into their areas from other parts of the country after being made subject to banning orders or after being convicted of housing-related offences and therefore to have sufficient information to bring prosecutions or other enforcement actions against them.

6.52 To that end, local housing authorities may use the information contained within the database:

a) for any purpose connected with their functions under HA 2004;
b) for the purpose of a criminal investigation or criminal proceedings;
c) for the purpose of promoting compliance with the law relating to housing or landlord and tenant;
d) for investigating or bringing proceedings in relation to any contravention of the law of housing or landlord and tenant; and
e) for statistical or research purposes.[109]

6.53 The secretary of state may not, however, disclose information in the database to any other person otherwise than in anonymised form,[110] so it will not be possible for a tenant or a letting agent to find out if a prospective landlord is on the database otherwise than by approaching the local authority. Accordingly, unless a tenant complains to the authority about a particular landlord's conduct (eg unlawful eviction, harassment or the poor condition of the premises) which would lead to the authority making its own investigations, it is not entirely clear how local housing authorities will become aware of rogue landlords who are on the database and start operating within their areas.

---

105 Ie letting agents and property managers: HPA 2016 s56.
106 HPA 2016 s28(1).
107 HPA 2016 ss28(2) and 34.
108 HPA 2016 s38.
109 HPA 2016 s39(4).
110 HPA 2016 s39(2).

Persons subject to banning orders

6.54   Local housing authorities must make an entry onto the database if a banning order has been made against a person[111] and must ensure that it is removed once the banning order has expired or is revoked.[112]

Persons not subject to banning orders

6.55   Local housing authorities may also make an entry on the database in respect of a person who has been convicted of a banning order offence at a time when he or she was a residential landlord, letting agent or property manager or who has twice, within a period of 12 months, received a financial penalty for breaching a banning order offence but who has not been made subject to a banning order.[113]

6.56   The authority may not do so unless:

a) the entry is made within six months of the person being convicted of the banning order offence;

b) the authority has provided the person who it intends to enter onto the database with a decision notice which:

    i) explains that the authority has decided that it will make the entry in the database after the end of the period of 21 days beginning with the day on which the notice is given ('the notice period');[114]

    ii) specifies the period for which the person's entry will be maintained, which must be at least two years beginning with the day on which the entry is made;

    iii) summarises the person's right to appeal against the decision to enter him or her on the database;

---

111 HPA 2016 s29(1).

112 HPA 2016 s29(2).

113 HPA 2016 s30(1), (2).

114 Although HPA 2016 only expressly says 'explain that the authority has decided to make the entry in the database' (s31(2)(a)), it is likely that this imports a requirement to give a reason, particularly as the common law is moving to the position that, whilst there is no universal obligation to give reasons in all circumstances, in general they should be given unless there is a proper justification for not doing so; reasons will be required where fairness requires it, or a particular decision is aberrant, where the failure to give reasons may frustrate a right of appeal, because without reasons a party will not know whether there is an appealable ground or not and where a party has a legitimate expectation that reasons will be given: *Oakley v South Cambridgeshire DC* [2017] EWCA Civ 71, [2017] 2 P&CR 4 at [30]–[31].

c) the notice period has expired; and

d) the person has not appealed against the decision to enter him or her onto the database or the appeal has been determined or withdrawn and there is no possibility of a further appeal.[115]

6.57 A person who has been given a decision notice may appeal to the First-tier Tribunal against the decision to enter him or her on the database and/or against the period for which the entry will remain on the database.[116]

6.58 Once the entry is made onto the database, a person who is not subject to a banning order may apply to the local housing authority for the entry to be removed and/or for the period in which it is to remain on the database to be reduced.[117] An entry must be removed if all of the convictions on which the entry is based are overturned on appeal.[118] Where some, but not all, of the convictions have been overturned on appeal or become spent, the authority has a discretion to remove the entry or to reduce the period for which the entry is to remain on the database (even if this results in the entry being on the database for less than two years).[119] The same discretion applies where the entry was based on the person receiving two or more financial penalties and at least one year has elapsed since the last of them.[120]

6.59 The authority must, where a request is made to revoke or vary the database and the authority decides not to comply with the request, give the person affected a notice which includes the reasons for its decision and summarises the rights of appeal to the First-tier Tribunal.[121] Any appeal must be made within 21 days of the date that the notice was given.[122] On an appeal, the First-tier Tribunal may order the authority to remove the entry or reduce the period for which entry must be maintained.[123]

---

115 HPA 2016 s31.

116 HPA 2016 s32.

117 HPA 2016 s37(1).

118 HPA 2016 s36(2).

119 HPA 2016 s36(3), (4), (6). Convictions become spent in accordance with Rehabilitation of Offenders Act 1974.

120 HPA 2016 s36(5), (6).

121 HPA 2016 s37(3), (4).

122 HPA 2016 s37(6). The First-tier Tribunal may extend the 21-day period if satisfied that there is a good reason for the failure to appeal within time and for any further delay: s37(7).

123 HPA 2016 s37(8).

Power to require information

6.60 A local housing authority may require any person to provide specified information for the purpose of enabling the authority to decide
whether to make an entry in respect of that person on the database.[124]
An authority proposing to make any entry, or which has made an
entry, in respect of a person may also require that person to provide
information to complete the entry or to keep it up-to-date.[125] It is an
offence for the person to fail to comply with such a requirement without a reasonable excuse for failing to do so.[126] It is also an offence to
provide false or misleading information if the person either knows
that it is false or misleading or is reckless as to whether it is false or
misleading.[127] Both offences are punishable on summary conviction
by an unlimited fine.[128]

---

124 HPA 2016 s35(1).
125 HPA 2016 s35(2).
126 HPA 2016 s35(3).
127 HPA 2016 s35(4).
128 HPA 2016 s35(5).

CHAPTER 7

Additional duties

Introduction

7.1   This chapter addresses a number of miscellaneous statutory provisions which concern rented property and whose purpose is to regulate the behaviour of residential landlords so as to protect occupiers and, ultimately, to prevent 'rogue landlordism'. There is a very large number of provisions which could fall into this category but which it is not possible to address, eg failure to get planning permission; failure to comply with repairing obligations; and/or the requirements of building control. This chapter therefore focuses on what might be characterised as the most immediate duties, eg those offences which may give rise to banning orders;[1] restrictions on a landlord's ability to serve a Housing Act (HA) 1988 s21 notice;[2] and other concerns that directly impinge on tenants' safe and comfortable enjoyment of their premises.

7.2   This chapter accordingly comprises an overview of provisions, so far as they relate to the relationship between landlord and tenant, relating to:

a) gas safety;
b) fire safety;
c) smoke and carbon monoxide alarms;[3]
d) electrical safety; and
e) energy efficiency,

and also:

f) the provision of guidance to prospective tenants on their legal rights; and
g) retaliatory eviction.

Gas safety

Gas Safety (Installation and Use) Regulations 1998

7.3   Regulation 36 of the Gas Safety (Installation and Use) Regulations 1998,[4] imposes a duty on landlords to ensure that any relevant gas

---

1 See paras 6.24–6.30.
2 The inability of a landlord to rely on a 'no fault' ground for possession sometimes being a trigger for unlawful eviction and/or harassment.
3 While this might be thought to be a subset of the previous two areas, it is included here separately because such alarms are, in England, the subject of specific regulation (see paras 7.23–7.34) and because the risks from carbon monoxide poisoning may arise from appliances using fuels other than gas (see para 7.27).
4 1998 SI No 2451.

fitting and any flue serving a relevant gas fitting are maintained in a safe condition so as to prevent the risk of injury to any person in lawful occupation of relevant premises.[5]

7.4 For the purposes of reg 36, the landlord is the person entitled to the reversion on the lease.[6] In turn, 'lease' means a lease for a term of less than seven years or a periodic tenancy.[7]

7.5 Where the premises are occupied under a licence, the 'landlord' is the licensor, except where the licensor is a subtenant, in which case it is his or her landlord.[8]

7.6 The duty in reg 36 applies to 'relevant premises', ie premises (or any part of premises) occupied for residential purposes under a lease or a licence, provided that the occupation is in consideration of money or money's worth.[9]

7.7 The landlord's duty is to ensure that, inter alia, any 'relevant gas fitting' is maintained in a safe condition. Any gas appliance installed in any relevant premises (other than one which the tenant[10] is entitled to remove from the premises) is a relevant gas fitting, as is any installation pipework installed in the premises.[11]

7.8 The definition of 'relevant gas fitting' also includes any gas appliance or installation pipework which, directly or indirectly, serves the relevant premises if it is either installed in any part of premises in which the landlord has an estate or interest, or it is owned by the landlord or is under his or her control.[12]

7.9 A 'gas appliance' is:

... an appliance designed for use by a consumer of gas for heating, lighting, cooking or other purposes for which gas can be used but

---

5 Reg 36(2). The regulations refer to 'the risk of injury to any person in lawful occupation *or* relevant premises' (emphasis added) but it is clear that the word 'of' should be substituted in place of 'or'. This would be in keeping with the predecessor to reg 36: Gas Safety (Installation and Use) Regulations 1994 SI No 1886 reg 35A(2).

6 Reg 36(1).

7 Reg 36(1). The definition of lease includes statutory tenancies: where the premises are occupied under a statutory tenancy (ie under Rent Act 1977 or Rent (Agriculture) Act 1976 – see Arden & Dymond *Manual of Housing Law* (LAG, 10th edn, 2017), paras 1.269 and 1.304) then the landlord is the person who, but for the statutory tenancy, would be entitled to possession of the premises: reg 36(1).

8 Reg 36(1).

9 Reg 36(1). For the meaning of lease, see para 7.4.

10 Or licensee: reg 36(1).

11 Reg 36(1).

12 Save for any gas appliances or installation pipework exclusively used in a part of premises occupied for non-residential purposes: reg 36(1).

it does not include a portable or mobile appliance supplied with gas from a cylinder, or the cylinder, pipes and other fittings used for supplying gas to that appliance, save that ... it does include a portable or mobile space heater supplied with gas from a cylinder, and the cylinder, pipes and other fittings used for supplying gas to that heater.[13]

7.10   The landlord's duty also extends to any flue serving a relevant gas fitting. A flue is:

... a passage for conveying the products of combustion from a gas appliance to the external air and includes any part of the passage in a gas appliance duct which serves the purpose of a flue.[14]

7.11   The general duty in reg 36(2) is developed by a number of specific duties, as follows:

a) Any gas appliance (and any flue serving a relevant gas fitting) must be checked for safety within 12 months of being installed and at intervals of no more than 12 months.[15]

b) A record of each safety check must be kept for at least two years from the date of the check.[16]

c) A copy of the safety check record must be given to any existing tenant[17] within 28 days of the date of the check.[18]

d) A copy of the last safety check record must be given to any new tenant[19] before he or she occupies the premises.[20]

---

13 Reg 2. Portable or mobile space heaters are not included within the definition of a gas appliance for all purposes within the 1998 regulations but they are for the purposes of reg 36, which is with what we are concerned here.

14 Reg 2.

15 Reg 36(3)(a). The Health and Safety Executive has consulted on introducing 'flexibility in the timing of landlords' annual gas safety checks' so that if, for example, a check is carried out after 11 months, the next check will not need to be carried out for a further 13 months: Health and Safety Executive, *Consultation on amendments to the Gas Safety (Installation and Use) Regulations 1998 (GSIUR)* (November 2016).

16 Reg 36(3)(c). The record is required to include certain information, including the date of the check, a description and location of each appliance and flue checked, any defects identified, and any remedial action taken.

17 Or licensee: reg 36(1).

18 Reg 36(6)(a). Where there is no relevant gas appliance in any room occupied by the tenant, the landlord may instead ensure that there is displayed in a prominent position in the premises a copy of the record: reg 36(7).

19 Or licensee: reg 36(1).

20 Reg 36(6)(b). Instead of the requirement to give a copy of the record to a new tenant, it may instead be prominently displayed in the premises if the tenant's right to occupy the premises is only for a period not exceeding 28 days or if there is no relevant gas appliance in any room to be occupied by the tenant: reg 36(6)(b), (7).

e) The safety check record must be made available on request and on reasonable notice for inspection by any person in lawful occupation of relevant premises who may be affected by the use or operation of any appliance to which the record relates.[21]

f) Any work done to, or safety check carried out on, a gas appliance or flue is carried out by someone approved by the Health and Safety Executive;[22] this means a Gas Safe registered engineer.[23]

7.12   Landlords are also required, by reg 36(11), to make sure that a relevant gas fitting is not fitted in any room occupied, or to be occupied, as sleeping accommodation by a tenant[24] in relevant premises if it would contravene reg 30(2) or (3),[25] which provide as follows.

(2) No person shall install a gas fire, other gas space heater or a gas water heater of more than 14 kilowatt gross heat input in a room used or intended to be used as sleeping accommodation unless the appliance is a room-sealed appliance.[26]

(3) No person shall install a gas fire, other gas space heater or a gas water heater of 14 kilowatt gross heat input or less in a room used or intended to be used as sleeping accommodation and no person shall install an instantaneous water heater unless (in each case)–

(a) it is a room-sealed appliance; or

(b) it incorporates a safety control designed to shut down the appliance before there is a build-up of a dangerous quantity of the products of combustion in the room concerned.

7.13   A breach of reg 36 is an offence under Health and Safety at Work etc Act 1974 s33(1)(c), unless the defendant can show that he or she took all reasonable steps to prevent the breach.[27] The offence is punishable on summary conviction by imprisonment for up to six months

---

21 Reg 36(5).

22 Reg 36(4).

23 Gas Safe replaced the previous CORGI scheme (which was run by the Council for Registered Gas Installers) in April 2009. The Gas Safe Register can be searched at www.gassaferegister.co.uk.

24 Or licensee: reg 36(1).

25 This does not apply to any room which has been occupied, or intended to be occupied, as sleeping accommodation since before 31 October 1998: reg 36(12).

26 A 'room-sealed appliance' is 'an appliance whose combustion system is sealed from the room in which the appliance is located and which obtains air for combustion from a ventilated uninhabited space within the premises or directly from the open air outside the premises and which vents the products of combustion directly to open air outside the premises': reg 2.

27 Reg 39.

and/or a fine,[28] and on indictment by imprisonment for up to two years and/or a fine.[29] It is also a proposed banning order offence.[30]

7.14   A landlord who is in breach of the requirement to give a copy of the safety check record to the tenant may not give notice under HA 1988 s21 (ie notice of seeking possession) in relation to an assured shorthold tenancy of a dwelling-house in England which was granted on or after 1 October 2015.[31]

Housing Act 2004

7.15   As previously noted,[32] licences granted under HA 2004 Part 2 or Part 3 are required to include certain conditions. One such condition is an annual requirement for the licence holder to produce to the local housing authority a gas safety certificate obtained in respect of the house within the previous 12 months.[33]

7.16   Failure to comply with a condition of a Part 2 or Part 3 licence is an offence,[34] punishable on conviction by a fine (see paras 5.33 and 5.37). It is also a proposed banning order offence.[35]

28 The maximum term of imprisonment on a summary conviction will increase to 12 months when Criminal Justice Act 2003 s154 is brought into force.

29 Health and Safety at Work etc Act 1974 Sch 3A para 1. An immediate custodial sentence at, or close to, the two-year maximum may be justified where there has been an element of blatant disregard or a desire for financial gain: *R v Martindale* [2014] EWCA Crim 1232.

30 See paras 6.24–6.26.

31 HA 1988 s21A(1) and Assured Shorthold Tenancy Notices and Prescribed Requirements (England) Regulations 2015 SI No 1646) regs 1(3), 2(1)(b). A section 21 notice may, however, be given if a copy of the safety check record is given to the tenant late (ie after the 28-day period provided for by the 1998 regulations): 2015 regulations reg 2(2). The safety check record must presumably still be a valid one, ie less than 12 months old.

32 Paras 5.15 and 5.20.

33 HA 2004 Sch 4 para 2. The licence holder is only required to comply with this condition if gas is supplied to the house.

34 HA 2004 ss72(3) and 95(2).

35 See paras 6.24–6.26.

Fire safety

Regulatory Reform (Fire Safety) Order 2005

7.17 The Regulatory Reform (Fire Safety) Order 2005[36] imposes fire safety duties in relation to premises.[37] While those duties are expressed not to apply to domestic premises,[38] the definition of 'domestic premises' does not include parts of premises which are used in common by the occupants of more than one private dwelling.[39] In practice, the 2005 order therefore applies to the common parts within a blocks of flats and any house that has been converted into flats.

7.18 The fire safety duties are imposed on the responsible person in relation to the common parts of domestic premises,[40] such as the communal parts of a block of flats.[41] The responsible person will be either:

a) the person who has control of the premises (as occupier or otherwise) in connection with the carrying on by him or her of a trade, business or other undertaking; or

b) where the person in control of the premises does not have control in connection with the carrying on by that person of a trade, business or other undertaking, the 'owner', ie the person for the time being receiving the rack rent of the premises, or who would so receive the rack rent if the premises were let at a rack rent.[42]

7.19 The concept of 'general fire precautions' is a key part of the 2005 order. Such precautions are, inter alia, measures:

a) to reduce the risk of fire and the spread of fire on the premises;

b) in relation to the means of escape;

c) for securing that the means of escape can be safely and effectively used;

d) in relation to the means for fighting fires;

e) in relation to the means for detecting fire on the premises and giving warning in case of fire; and

---

36 SI No 1541.
37 Article 5.
38 Article 6(1)(a).
39 Article 2.
40 Article 5(2).
41 See *R (Southwark LBC) v London Fire and Emergency Planning Authority* [2016] EWHC 1701 (Admin), in relation to a fire at a block of flats, known as Lakanal House, in which six people died.
42 Article 3.

f) in relation to the actions to be taken in the event of a fire on the premises.[43]

7.20 The responsible person is required, inter alia, to:

a) take such general fire precautions[44] as may reasonably be required to ensure that the premises are safe in relation to relevant persons;[45]

b) undertake an assessment of the risks to which relevant persons are exposed so as to identify the general fire precautions that the responsible person needs to take;[46]

c) make and give effect to arrangements for the effective planning, organisation, control, monitoring and review of preventive and protective measures;[47]

d) so far as reasonably practicable eliminate or reduce the risk to relevant persons of any dangerous substance present in or on the premises;[48]

e) ensure that the premises are equipped with appropriate fire-fighting equipment and fire detectors/alarms;[49]

f) ensure that routes to emergency exits, as well as such exits, are kept clear;[50]

g) establish and give effect to appropriate procedures such as safety drills;[51] and

h) ensure that the premises and any facilities, equipment and devices provided, are maintained in an efficient state, in efficient working order, and in good repair.[52]

7.21 These duties are imposed on any other person who has control of the premises, to the extent that they relate to matters within his or

---

43 Article 4(1).

44 See para 7.19.

45 Article 8(1)(b). A relevant person is any person who is or may be lawfully on the premises and any person in the immediate vicinity of the premises who is at risk from a fire on the premises: Article 2. Subject to limited exceptions, a firefighter who is carrying out his or her duties is not a relevant person: Article 2.

46 Article 9(1).

47 Article 11(1).

48 Article 12(1).

49 Article 13(1).

50 Article 14(1).

51 Article 15(1)(a).

52 Article 17(1).

her control.[53] For these purposes, any person who, by virtue of any contract or tenancy, has an obligation in relation to the maintenance, repair or safety of premises, is treated as a person who has control of the premises.[54]

7.22   Failure to comply with any of these duties is an offence.[55] The offence is punishable on summary conviction by a fine,[56] or by a fine and/or two years' imprisonment on conviction on indictment.[57] It is also a proposed banning order offence.[58]

Smoke and carbon monoxide alarms

Smoke and Carbon Monoxide Alarm (England) Regulations 2015

7.23   Regulation 4 of the Smoke and Carbon Monoxide Alarm (England) Regulations 2015[59] requires a relevant landlord of a specified tenancy to ensure that smoke and carbon monoxide alarms are fitted.

7.24   Subject to exceptions, a specified tenancy is a tenancy (or licence)[60] of residential premises in England[61] which grants one or more persons the right to occupy all or part of the premises as their only or main residence and which provides for payment of rent.[62] The exceptions are tenancies of a type specified in the Schedule to the regulations, which include where the occupier shares any accommodation with the landlord or a member of the landlord's family, long leases, accommodation within student halls of residence, rights of

---

53 Article 5(3).

54 Article 5(4).

55 Article 32(1)(a).

56 Article 32(3)(a).

57 Article 32(3)(b).

58 See paras 6.24–6.26.

59 2015 SI No 1693. The regulations were made by the secretary of state under Energy Act 2013 s150.

60 See Energy Act 2013 s150(10).

61 The 2015 regulations do not apply in Wales but the *Code of Practice for Landlords and Agents licensed under Part 1 of the Housing (Wales) Act 2014* recommends as 'best practice' the provision of carbon monoxide alarms in all rooms where a gas, oil or solid fuel appliance is present and the fitting of smoke detectors on every floor of a property (see para 5.26).

62 Reg 2. This does not include a house in multiple occupation (HMO) or house which requires a licence under HA 2004 Parts 2 or 3, but see paras 7.35–7.38.

occupation in a hostel, refuge, hospital, hospice or in other accommodation relating to healthcare provision.

7.25   A 'relevant landlord' is a landlord who is the immediate landlord in respect of a specified tenancy (ie the person entitled to the reversion), provided that the landlord is not a registered provider of social housing.[63] Where the premises are occupied under a licence, the 'landlord' is the licensor, except where the licensor is a subtenant, in which case it is his or her landlord.[64]

7.26   From 1 October 2015, a relevant landlord must ensure that, during any period when the premises are occupied under a specified tenancy, a smoke alarm is equipped on each storey of the premises on which there is a room used wholly or partly as living accommodation.[65]

7.27   From 1 October 2015, a relevant landlord must also ensure that, during any period when the premises are occupied under a specified tenancy, a carbon monoxide alarm is equipped in any room of the premises which is used as living accommodation and which contains a solid fuel burning combustion appliance.[66] There is no definition of 'solid fuel burning combustion appliance' in the regulations, but it is likely to include a coal fire or a wood-burning stove.[67]

7.28   A duty is also placed on a relevant landlord to see that checks are made to ensure that such alarms are in proper working order on the day that a new tenancy begins.[68]

7.29   Enforcement of the 2015 regulations is by local housing authorities. Where an authority has reasonable grounds to believe that a relevant landlord is in breach of reg 4(1), the authority must serve a remedial notice on him or her.[69] The notice must, inter alia, specify the remedial action that the landlord is required to take within 28

---

63   Reg 3(1), (2)(a).

64   Reg 3(2)(b).

65   Reg 4(1)(a)(i). Any bathroom or lavatory is to be treated as being used for living accommodation: reg 4(2). A hall or landing is counted as a room: reg 4(2).

66   Reg 4(1)(a)(ii). Reg 4(2) applies: see previous footnote.

67   See Department for Communities and Local Government (DCLG), *The Smoke and Carbon Monoxide Alarm (England) Regulations 2015: Q&A Booklet for the Private Rented Sector – landlords and tenants* (September 2015).

68   Reg 4(1)(b). A 'new tenancy' is a tenancy granted on or after 1 October 2015, except: where the tenancy is granted in pursuance of an agreement entered into before that date; it arises under HA 1988 s5; or it is a tenancy coming into being at the end of an earlier tenancy of the same premises and between the same parties: reg 4(4).

69   Reg 5(1).

days.[70] When the remedial notice is served on the landlord, he or she is under a duty to take the specified remedial action within 28 days.[71]

7.30   Where the authority is satisfied that a landlord is in breach of the duty to take remedial action, the authority must itself carry out the remedial action (provided that the occupier of the premises grants consent).[72]

7.31   The authority may also require the landlord to pay a penalty charge of up to £5,000.[73] In order to do so, the authority must serve a penalty charge notice on the landlord within six weeks of the day on which the authority becomes satisfied that he or she is in breach of the duty to take remedial action.[74] The penalty charge notice must state, inter alia, the following matters.[75]

a) the reasons for imposing the charge;
b) the premises to which it relates;
c) the amount of the charge;
d) that the landlord must within a specified period either pay the penalty charge or request a review of the penalty charge notice.[76]

7.32   Where the landlord requests a review within the specified period, the authority must consider any representations made by the landlord and decide whether to confirm, vary or withdraw the penalty charge notice.[77] The authority's review decision must be notified to the landlord,[78] who must also be informed of his or her right to appeal against a decision confirming or varying a penalty charge notice.[79]

---

70 Reg 5(2)(c), (d).
71 Reg 6(1). A landlord is not in breach of this duty if he or she can show that all reasonable steps, other than legal proceedings, have been taken to comply with the duty: reg 6(2).
72 Reg 7. Any remedial action is taken by an 'authorised person', which means a person authorised in writing by the authority for this purpose: regs 2(1), 7.
73 Reg 8.
74 Reg 8(3).
75 Reg 9(1).
76 The specified period must be not less than 28 days from the date of service of the notice: reg 9(3).
77 Reg 10(1), (2)(a), (b).
78 Reg 10(2)(c).
79 Reg 10(3).

7.33   A landlord may appeal to the First-tier Tribunal against a decision to confirm or vary a penalty charge notice.[80] An appeal may only be brought on the following grounds.[81]

a) the decision was based on an error of fact;
b) the decision was wrong in law;
c) the amount of the penalty charge is unreasonable;
d) the decision was otherwise unreasonable.

7.34   A notice of appeal must be sent or delivered to the First-tier Tribunal so that it is received within 28 days of the date that the authority's review decision was sent to the landlord.[82] The First-tier Tribunal may quash, confirm or vary the penalty charge notice but it cannot increase the amount of the penalty.[83]

Housing Act 2004

7.35   The duties imposed by the 2015 regulations do not apply in respect of premises which require a licence under either Part 2 or Part 3 of HA 2004. Instead, the 2015 regulations amended the mandatory conditions which form part of any licence granted under Parts 2 and 3.[84]

7.36   Any licence granted or renewed on or after 1 October 2015 in England must include conditions requiring the licence holder to:

a) ensure that a smoke alarm is installed on each storey of the house on which there is a room used as living accommodation;
b) ensure that a carbon monoxide alarm is installed in any room which is used for living accommodation and which contains a solid fuel burning combustion appliance;
c) keep any such alarm in proper working order; and
d) supply to the local housing authority, on demand, a declaration as to the condition and position of any such alarm.[85]

---

80 Reg 11.
81 Reg 11(2).
82 Tribunal Procedure (First-tier Tribunal) (General Regulatory Chamber) Rules 2009 SI No 1976 r22(1)(b).
83 Reg 11(4).
84 Paras 5.15 and 5.20.
85 HA 2004 Sch 4 para 1(4), (4A). Any bathroom or lavatory is to be treated as being used for living accommodation: para 1(7). A hall or landing is counted as a room, so far as the carbon monoxide alarm requirements are concerned: para 1(6).

7.37 In Wales,[86] any licence must include conditions requiring the licence holder to:

a) ensure that smoke alarms are installed in the house;
b) keep any such alarm in proper working order; and
c) supply to the local housing authority, on demand, a declaration as to the condition and position of any such alarm.[87]

7.38 Failure to comply with a condition of a Part 2 or Part 3 licence is an offence,[88] punishable on conviction by a fine (see paras 5.33 and 5.37). It is also a proposed banning order offence.[89]

Electrical safety

7.39 There is, at present, no generally applicable requirement for landlords to carry out electrical safety testing (cf the gas safety provisions discussed at paras 7.3–7.13).

7.40 When brought into force, however, Housing and Planning Act (HPA) 2016 s122 will give power to the secretary of state to make regulations imposing duties on a private landlord of residential premises in England for the purposes of ensuring that electrical safety standards are met during any period when the premises are occupied under a tenancy. Any such regulations may provide for covenants to be implied into the tenancy, so as to enable enforcement by a tenant, and for enforcement functions to be conferred on local housing authorities.[90]

7.41 In the specific context of licences granted under either HA 2004 Part 2 or Part 3, [91] any such licence must include a condition requiring the licence holder to:

a) keep electrical appliances made available by him or her in the house in a safe condition; and
b) supply to the authority, on demand, a declaration as to the safety of any such appliances.[92]

---

86 And, in England, in relation to licences granted or renewed on or before 30 September 2015.
87 HA 2004 Sch 4 para 1(4).
88 HA 2004 ss72(3) and 95(2).
89 See paras 6.24–6.26.
90 HPA 2016 s123.
91 Paras 5.15 and 5.20.
92 HA 2004 Sch 4 para 3.

7.42   Failure to comply with a condition of a Part 2 or Part 3 licence is an offence,[93] punishable on conviction by a fine (see paras 5.33 and 5.37). It is also a proposed banning order offence.[94]

Energy efficiency

Introduction

7.43   Energy efficiency has been identified as a particular issue in the private rented sector. Properties in the private rented sector are more likely to be in the two lowest ratings for energy performance than properties in the owner-occupier sector, while around 21 per cent of households in the private rented sector are estimated to be in fuel poverty, compared to 8.5 per cent of households in the owner-occupier sector.[95]

7.44   The provisions with which we are concerned here relate to a certificate grading properties into bands, known as an Energy Performance Certificate (EPC). There are seven bands, from A to G, with A representing the most efficient properties (in terms of energy usage) and G the least.

Energy Performance of Buildings (England and Wales) Regulations 2012

7.45   Landlords of most residential properties which are to be rented out are required by the Energy Performance of Buildings (England and Wales) Regulations 2012[96] to have an EPC for the property.[97]

7.46   Part 2 of the 2012 Regulations imposes duties in relation to EPCs on the 'relevant person'. In relation to a building that is to be rented out, the 'relevant person' is the prospective landlord.[98]

---

93   HA 2004 ss72(3) and 95(2).
94   See paras 6.24–6.26.
95   Department of Energy and Climate Change, *Private Rented Sector Energy Efficiency Regulations (Domestic) (England and Wales): Consultation on implementation of the Energy Act 2011 provision for energy efficiency regulation of the domestic private rented sector* (2014), p12.
96   2012 SI No 3118.
97   The 2012 Regulations repealed and replaced similar provisions in Energy Performance of Buildings (Certificates and Inspections) (England and Wales) Regulations 2007 SI No 991, with effect from 9 January 2013: 2012 Regulations reg 46 and Sch 3.
98   Reg 2(1).

7.47   For the purposes of the 2012 Regulations, a building is a 'roofed construction having walls, for which energy is used to condition the indoor climate'.⁹⁹ A reference to a building includes a reference to any building unit within the building, ie a section, floor or apartment within the building which is designed or altered to be used separately.¹⁰⁰ Accordingly, Part 2 does not apply to individual rooms that are let within an HMO.¹⁰¹

7.48   Part 2 does not apply to residential buildings which are used or intended to be used for less than four months of the year.¹⁰² It does not apply to residential buildings which are used or intended to be used for a limited time each year and with an expected energy consumption of less than 25 per cent of that which would result from being used all year.¹⁰³ Certain small buildings are excluded, being 'stand-alone buildings with a total useful floor area of less than 50m²'.¹⁰⁴

7.49   Where a building is to be rented out,¹⁰⁵ the relevant person must make available, at no charge, an EPC to any prospective tenant at the earliest opportunity.¹⁰⁶ Where a person requests information about the building, the relevant person must make the EPC available no later than the time at which he or she first makes available to that person any information in writing about the building.¹⁰⁷ Where a person makes a request to view the building, the EPC must be made available before he or she views the building.¹⁰⁸

7.50   This requirement does not apply where the relevant person believes on reasonable grounds that the prospective tenant is either:

a) unlikely to have sufficient means to rent the building;
b) not genuinely interested in renting a building of a general description which applies to the building; or

---

99 Reg 2(1).
100 Reg 2(1); this is subject to exceptions which are not relevant for present purposes.
101 DCLG, *Energy Performance Certificates (EPCs) and renting homes: A landlord's guide* (November 2010). It is, however, likely that Part 2 applies to the whole or part of the building comprising the HMO.
102 Reg 5(1)(f)(i).
103 Reg 5(1)(f)(ii).
104 Reg 5(1)(g).
105 Unless the building is to be demolished: regs 6(1), 8.
106 Reg 6(2)(a).
107 Reg 6(2)(b)(i).
108 Reg 6(2)(b)(ii).

c) is not a person to whom the relevant person is likely to be prepared to rent the building.[109]

7.51 A person becomes a prospective tenant of a building when he or she does any of the following:[110]

a) requests any information about the building from the relevant person or the relevant person's agent for the purpose of deciding whether to rent the building;

b) makes a request to view the building for the purpose of deciding whether to rent it;

c) makes an offer to rent the building.[111]

7.52 The relevant person is also required to make sure that an EPC is given, without charge, to the person who ultimately becomes the tenant.[112]

7.53 Where a building with a valid EPC is offered for rent on or after 9 January 2013, the relevant person (or a person acting on his or her behalf) must ensure that the energy performance rating is stated in any advertisement of the rental in commercial media.[113]

7.54 Part 7 of the 2012 Regulations governs enforcement, which is the responsibility of local weights and measures authorities.[114] An authorised officer of an enforcement authority may require a person who appears to be, or to have been, subject to the reg 6 duties (ie to provide an EPC to a prospective tenant and to the person who becomes the tenant)[115] to produce for inspection a copy of, inter alia, a valid EPC.[116] Unless he or she has a reasonable excuse for not doing so, that person must comply within seven days.[117]

7.55 If an authorised officer of an enforcement authority believes that a person has committed a breach of the duties mentioned above,[118]

---

109 Reg 6(3).
110 Reg 3.
111 The offer may be oral or written.
112 Reg 6(5). See para 7.58 for one of the consequences for failure to comply with this requirement.
113 Reg 11(2).
114 Reg 34(1). In England, local weights and measures authorities are county councils, metropolitan district councils, London borough councils, the Common Council of the City of London, and the Council of the Isles of Scilly: Weights and Measures Act 1985 s69(1). In Wales, they are county councils and county borough councils: s69(2).
115 See paras 7.46–7.52.
116 Reg 35(1).
117 Reg 35(5), (6).
118 See paras 7.49, 7.52–7.53.

he or she may give that person a penalty charge notice.[119] A penalty charge notice may only be given during the period of six months beginning with the day on which the breach of duty was committed and must state, inter alia, the following matters:[120]

a) the officer's belief that the person has committed a breach of duty;
b) such particulars of the circumstances as may be necessary to give reasonable notice of the breach;
c) the amount of the charge (£200 for each of the duties identified above[121]);
d) that the landlord must within a specified period either pay the penalty charge or request a review of the penalty charge notice.[122]

7.56   Where a review is requested within the specified period, the authority must consider any representations made by the recipient of the notice, and all other circumstances of the case, and decide whether to confirm or withdraw the penalty charge notice.[123] The authority's review decision must be notified to the recipient of the notice,[124] who must also be informed of his or her right to appeal against a decision confirming a penalty charge notice.[125]

7.57   There is a right of appeal to the county court against a penalty charge notice which has been confirmed on review.[126] An appeal may only be brought on the following grounds.[127]

a) the recipient did not commit the breach of duty;
b) the notice was not given within the six-month period after the breach of duty was committed or does not comply with some other requirement imposed by the 2012 Regulations;
c) in the circumstances of the case, it was inappropriate for the notice to have been given.

---

119 Reg 36(2).
120 Reg 36(2), (3). In the case of a continuing breach, a penalty charge notice may not be given after the end of the period of six months beginning with the last day on which that continuing breach was committed.
121 Reg 38(1)(a)(i), (1)(e).
122 The specified period must be not less than 28 days beginning with the day after the day on which the notice is given: reg 36(4).
123 Reg 39(1)(a), (b).
124 Reg 39(1)(c).
125 Reg 39(2).
126 Reg 40(1).
127 Reg 40(3).

7.58   A landlord who is in breach of the reg 6(5) requirement to provide an EPC to the tenant[128] may not give notice under HA 1988 s21 (ie notice of seeking possession) in relation to an assured shorthold tenancy of a dwelling-house in England which was granted on or after 1 October 2015.[129]

Energy Efficiency (Private Rented Property) (England and Wales) Regulations 2015

7.59   The 2012 regulations do not impose any minimum energy efficiency requirements. That will change when Part 3 of the Energy Efficiency (Private Rented Property) (England and Wales) Regulations 2015[130] is brought into force. The 2015 Regulations will require residential properties in the private rented sector to have an energy efficiency rating of A to E; subject to exceptions,[131] a private sector landlord will not be able to let a residential property if the property's energy efficiency rating is F or G.

7.60   From 1 April 2018, a landlord of a 'domestic PR property' in England or Wales must not grant a new tenancy, or let the property as a result of an extension or renewal of an existing tenancy, if the property is 'sub-standard',[132] ie it has an energy performance indicator of below E.[133] From 1 April 2020, the landlord must not continue to let

---

128   See para 7.49.

129   HA 1988 s21A(1) and Assured Shorthold Tenancy Notices and Prescribed Requirements (England) Regulations 2015 SI No 1646 regs 1(3), 2(1)(a). While reg 6(5) does not explicitly state that the requirement must be complied with before the tenancy is granted, it is clear that this is what is meant, cf 'ultimately becomes the … tenant': para 7.52. On the one hand, there is nothing about the regulation to suggest that the requirement can be complied with later, and a s21 notice then served and, unlike the requirement to provide a copy of the gas safety certificate (see para 7.14 and n31, above), the 2015 regulations do not disapply any time limit in relation to the EPC, which would suggest that a s21 notice cannot be given if the EPC is provided late; on the other hand, this construction would effectively convert an assured shorthold tenancy into a fully assured tenancy and it seems unlikely that the courts will consider this to have been parliament's intention.

130   2015 SI No 962.

131   The prohibition on letting does not apply if the landlord has made all relevant energy efficiency improvements (as defined by reg 24), or if there are no relevant improvements that can be made: regs 23(1), 25. Further exemptions to the prohibition on letting are contained in 2015 Regulations Part 3 Chapter 4: see para 7.62.

132   Reg 23(1), (2)(a).

133   Reg 22.

the property if it is substandard.[134] Any breach of these prohibitions does not affect the validity or enforceability of any provision of the tenancy.[135] A landlord would, therefore, need to bring any tenancy to an end in one of the normal ways.

7.61   A 'domestic PR property' is a property which is let under an assured tenancy, a regulated tenancy, or a tenancy which has been specified by the secretary of state.[136] A property is not, however, a domestic PR property if it is low cost rental accommodation (Housing and Regeneration Act 2008 s69) let by a private registered provider of social housing, low cost home ownership accommodation (Housing and Regeneration Act 2008 s70, or let by a by a body registered as a social landlord (HA 1988 Part 1 Chapter 1).[137]

7.62   The 2015 Regulations provide three exemptions from the prohibition on letting. *First,* there is a consent exemption, which applies where the landlord has not been able to carry out improvements to raise the energy efficiency level above F because either the tenant or a third party has not granted the landlord any necessary consent.[138] *Secondly,* there is a devaluation exemption if carrying out improvements to raise the energy efficiency level above F would result in a reduction of more than five per cent in the market value of the property.[139] *Thirdly,* there is a temporary exemption, which, in general, applies for the six months after the landlord first obtains an interest in the property.[140] In order to rely on any of these exemptions, the landlord must register on a PRS Exemptions Register maintained by the secretary of state.[141]

134 Reg 23(1), (2)(b).

135 Reg 26.

136 Reg 19(1); Energy Act 2011 s42(1)(a). The secretary of state has specified assured agricultural occupancies (HA 1988 s24), protected occupancies (Rent (Agriculture) Act 1976 s3(6)) and statutory tenancies (Rent (Agriculture) Act 1976 s4(6)): Energy Efficiency (Domestic Private Rented Property) Order 2015 SI No 799 Article 2. A property is also not a domestic PR property if no EPC is required: see reg 19(2) and Energy Performance of Buildings (Certificates and Inspections) (England and Wales) Regulations 2007 SI No 991, Building Regulations 2010 SI No 2214 and Energy Performance of Buildings (England and Wales) Regulations 2012 SI No 3118.

137 Reg 19(1); Energy Act 2011 s42(2).

138 Reg 31.

139 Reg 32.

140 Reg 33.

141 Regs 31(2), 32(3), 33(5), 36.

7.63   Breach of the prohibition on letting does not affect the validity or enforcement of any provision of the tenancy.[142] Instead, the 2015 Regulations are enforced, so far as domestic PR property is concerned, by local authorities,[143] who may impose a compliance notice and/or a penalty notice.[144]

7.64   A compliance notice may be served on a landlord on or after 1 April 2018 where the landlord appears to the authority to be, or to have been within the preceding 12 months, in breach of the prohibition on letting sub-standard domestic PR property.[145]

7.65   A compliance notice may request such information as the authority considers necessary to monitor compliance with 2015 Regulations Part 3, including a request for the landlord to produce for inspection originals, or copies, of any energy performance certificate for the property and any current tenancy agreement under which the property is let.[146] The landlord must comply with the compliance notice and allow the local authority to take copies of any original document.[147]

7.66   A penalty notice may be served on a landlord where the authority is satisfied that the landlord is, or in the preceding 18 months has been, in breach of the prohibition on letting sub-standard domestic PR property or has failed to comply with a compliance notice.[148]

7.67   A penalty notice must state, inter alia, the following matters:[149]

a) which regulation the landlord is alleged to have breached;
b) such particulars as the authority considers necessary to identify the matters constituting the breach;
c) the amount of any financial penalty imposed;
d) whether the publication penalty has been imposed;[150]
e) that the landlord may request a review within a specified period.[151]

7.68   The amount of any financial penalty is a maximum of £2,000 or £4,000 depending on whether the breach of the prohibition on letting

---

142 Reg 26.
143 Reg 34(1)(a).
144 Regs 37 and 38.
145 Reg 37(1)(a).
146 Reg 37(2).
147 Reg 37(4).
148 Reg 38(1).
149 Reg 38(2).
150 Under reg 39, the publication penalty means publication of various matters relating to the breach on the PRS Exemptions Register maintained by the secretary of state.
151 The period must be not less than one month, beginning with the day on which the penalty notice is served: reg 38(3).

sub-standard domestic PR property lasted for less than three months or for a period of three months or more.[152] The maximum penalty for failing to comply with a compliance notice is £2,000.[153]

7.69   Where a review is requested within the specified period, the authority must consider any representations made by the landlord and all other circumstances of the case, and decide whether to confirm or withdraw the penalty charge notice and may waive a penalty, allow the landlord additional time to pay any penalty, or substitute a lower financial penalty.[154] The authority's review decision must be notified to the landlord,[155] who must also be informed of his or her right to appeal against a decision confirming a penalty notice.[156]

7.70   A landlord may appeal to the First-tier Tribunal against a decision to confirm a penalty notice.[157] On appeal, the First-tier Tribunal may quash the penalty notice or affirm it (with such modification as the tribunal thinks fit).[158] An appeal may only be brought on the following grounds.[159]

a) the issue of the penalty notice was based on an error of fact;
b) the issue of the penalty notice was based on an error of law;
c) the penalty notice does not comply with any requirement of the 2015 Regulations;
d) in the circumstances of the case, it was inappropriate for the penalty notice to be served on the landlord.

How to rent: the checklist for renting in England

7.71   In England, the Department for Communities and Local Government (DCLG) has published guidance on their legal rights for prospective assured shorthold tenants, under the title *How to rent: the checklist for renting in England*.[160] In England, a landlord under a tenancy granted

---

152 Reg 40(2), (3).
153 Reg 40(5).
154 Reg 42(2)(a), (b), (5). The authority may also modify any publication penalty (see n150, above).
155 Reg 42(2)(c).
156 Reg 42(4).
157 Reg 43.
158 Reg 44(2).
159 Reg 43.
160 DCLG, February 2016.

on or after 1 October 2015,[161] who does not provide a tenant with a copy of the booklet in its current form (from time to time)[162] is prohibited from serving a HA 1988 s21 notice so long as he or she is in breach of the requirement.[163]

7.72   The information can be provided in a hard copy or, if the tenant has notified the landlord or the landlord's agent of an email address at which he or she is content to accept service of notices and other documents under or in connection with the tenancy, by email.[164] The provisions do not apply where the landlord is a private registered provider of social housing, or – if the version of the document has not changed – where the tenancy is a replacement tenancy[165] and the landlord provided the tenant with a copy under the previous tenancy.[166]

Retaliatory eviction

7.73   In England, landlords of assured shorthold tenancies granted on or after 1 October 2015 may not serve a HA 1988 s21 notice within six months[167] of the landlord being served by a local authority with an improvement notice[168] or a notice of emergency remedial action[169] under HA 2004,[170] whether in relation to the premises themselves or any common parts of a building of which the premises form part in which the landlord has a controlling interest and the condition of which is such as to affect the tenant's enjoyment of his or her

---

161   On 1 October 2018, this prohibition will also apply to tenancies granted before 1 October 2015: Deregulation Act (DA) 2015 s41(3).

162   There is no obligation to supply a further copy each time a different version is published during the tenancy: Assured Shorthold Tenancy Notices and Prescribed Requirements (England) Regulations 2015 SI No 1646 reg 3(4).

163   HA 1988 s21B; Assured Shorthold Tenancy Notices and Prescribed Requirements (England) Regulations 2015 SI No 1646.

164   Reg 3(3).

165   HA 1988 s21(7).

166   Reg 3(5).

167   Time runs from service of the notice of, if the notice is suspended, beginning with the day on which the suspension ends.

168   HA 2004 ss11, 12. See *Manual of Housing Law*, paras 12.18–12.29.

169   HA 2004 s40. See *Manual of Housing Law*, paras 12.30–12.32.

170   DA 2015 s33(1). The provisions do not apply if, before the HA 1988 s21 notice is given, the relevant works notice had been revoked or quashed, or a refusal by the authority to revoke the notice or a decision to take the action has been reversed, under specified provisions of HA 2004: DA 2015 s33(8).

dwelling-house or of any common parts which he or she is entitled to use.[171]

7.74   A notice under HA 1988 s21 is also invalid in the following circumstances:[172]

a) the tenant complained in writing[173] to the landlord, or his or her managing agent, about the condition of the dwelling and either the tenant received no response within 14 days, or if there was a response, it did not tell the tenant what the landlord proposed to do and did not set out a reasonable timescale for taking action;
b) the tenant then complained to the local authority about the same defect in the condition of the dwelling;
c) the authority served an improvement notice (para 7.73) or a notice of emergency remedial action (para 7.73) under HA 2004;[174] and
d) if the HA 1988 s21 notice was not given before the tenant's complaint to the local housing authority, the landlord gave the notice requiring possession before being served with the authority's notice.[175]

7.75   Where the notice is invalid under these provisions, the court must strike out possession proceedings based on it;[176] but if a possession order has been made before the local authority notice is served and an application is made to set it aside, these provisions do not provide a basis for doing so.[177]

7.76   The retaliatory eviction provisions do not apply in any of the following circumstances:[178]

a) the defective condition of the dwelling giving rise to the authority's notice is caused by the tenant's failure to use the dwelling in a tenant-like manner,[179] whether pursuant to the implied duty to do so or to an express requirement in the tenancy agreement;

171 DA 2015 s33(10), (11).
172 DA 2015 s33(2).
173 The requirement for a complaint to be in writing does not apply if the tenant does not know the landlord's postal or email address: DA 2015 s33(4).
174 This condition will not be fulfilled – so that the HA 1988 s21 notice will not be invalid – if the notice requiring works has been suspended: DA 2015 s33(9).
175 If the tenant made reasonable efforts to contact the landlord to complain about the condition of the dwelling-house but was unable to do so, the first two requirements need not be met: DA 2015 s33(5).
176 DA 2015 s33(6).
177 DA 2015 s33(7).
178 DA 2015 s34.
179 See *Manual of Housing Law*, para 4.111.

b) when the notice requiring possession is given, the dwelling is genuinely on the market for sale;[180]

c) the landlord is a private registered provider of social housing;

d) the landlord has a mortgage, the lender is entitled to exercise a power of sale conferred by the mortgage or by Law of Property Act 1925 s101, and the lender requires possession to sell the dwelling with vacant possession.

---

180 Proposed sales to defined persons associated with the landlord, or the landlord's business partners, are disqualified: DA 2015 s34(3)–(5).

CHAPTER 8

Bringing civil proceedings

continued

8.72   Example documents

Particulars of claim (1): Unlawful eviction of assured shorthold tenant

Particulars of claim (2): Unlawful eviction of secure tenant

Particulars of claim (3): Harassment by landlord

Application notice for interim injunction

Draft order

Witness statement (1): Unlawful eviction of assured shorthold tenant

Witness statement (2): Tenancy deposit

Introduction

8.1 This chapter describes the steps necessary to start civil proceedings in the county court. In particular, the chapter concentrates on how to get the most immediate remedy needed in cases of harassment or unlawful eviction, ie a 'without notice interim injunction'. Examples are offered of the documents required to apply for a without notice interim injunction in an unlawful eviction claim (see paras 8.72 and following). This chapter will also briefly address how to start proceedings in respect of a tenancy deposit.

8.2 Civil proceedings are governed by the Civil Procedure Rules (CPR) 1998 SI No 3132, a 'procedural code with the overriding objective of enabling the court to deal with cases justly and at proportionate cost'.[1] As far as possible, advisers should ensure that they always comply with the rules although failure to comply does not invalidate any step in proceedings (unless the court so orders) and the court has power to remedy any defect.[2] Note, however, that some rules contain a sanction for non-compliance.[3] While the court may grant relief from sanctions,[4] reforms to the CPR in April 2013 had the effect of making it harder to obtain.[5] This means that it is even more important for advisers to comply with the rules (as well as practice directions (PDs) and court orders).[6]

8.3 There are two ways of commencing proceedings: under CPR Part 7 or CPR Part 8. Part 8 is not appropriate where there is a dispute of fact between the parties.[7] Accordingly, claims involving harassment

---

1 CPR 1.1(1).

2 CPR 3.10.

3 Eg, a party who fails to file a costs budget where costs management applies is treated as having filed a budget comprising only any applicable court fees (CPR 3.14), severely limiting the ability to recover costs (CPR 3.18 and PD 44); and a defendant to a Part 8 claim who fails to file an acknowledgment of service (see para 8.69) may not take part in the hearing of the claim without the court's permission (CPR 8.4(2)).

4 CPR 3.9.

5 See *Mitchell v News Group Newspapers Ltd* [2013] EWCA Civ 1537, [2014] 1 WLR 795; and *Denton v TH White Ltd* [2014] EWCA Civ 906, [2014] 1 WLR 3926.

6 Where it becomes apparent that it will not be possible to comply with a rule, practice direction or order, advisers should be alert to take appropriate action sooner rather than later. For example, an application to extend time for compliance is (all other things being equal) more likely to be granted if made before the time has elapsed rather than later when there is already a breach (not least because such an application is not for relief from sanctions: see *Hallam Estates Ltd v Baker* [2014] EWCA Civ 661, [2014] CP Rep 38).

7 CPR 8.1(2).

or unlawful eviction are usually commenced under CPR Part 7. The person who brings a claim is called a 'claimant' and the person against whom the claim is brought is the 'defendant'.

Injunctions – an overview

Introduction

8.4   The primary concern of a victim of harassment is to ensure that the harassment ceases. An evicted occupier usually wants to get back into his or her home as soon as possible.

8.5   As already noted, this can be achieved by an interim injunction (see paras 1.106–1.115). Such an application can be made without notice to the defendant where it is urgent or where alerting the defendant to the application beforehand would defeat its aim, for example where there is a risk of reprisals if papers are served and there is no injunction in place to protect the victim.[8] Both circuit judges and district judges have the jurisdiction to make such an order.[9]

8.6   Given that the claimant is without a home, the courts are usually prepared to hear an application in an unlawful eviction case without notice.[10] In harassment cases, the courts may be prepared to hear the application without notice if sufficiently urgent, eg, where violence is likely to occur in the near future.

8.7   The most common reason for refusing to hear an application without notice is that there has been a delay before making the application. The claimant's witness statement filed in support of the application should explain any reason for this, eg, inability to obtain advice over a weekend, illness or particular vulnerability. In cases where the claimant is, or will be, street homeless, the court is likely to hear the matter unless the delay has been significant. If the judge refuses to grant the injunction, the application will be adjourned for notice to be given to the defendant rather than dismissed. In those such cases where it is beneficial or necessary to get the matter back before to court as soon

---

8   CPR 25.3(3).

9   CPR 2.4; and see CPR PD 2B.

10   Note, however, that many courts no longer operate a full counter service so that it is necessary to make an appointment to attend the court office in order to issue the application.

as possible, the court can be asked to abridge time for service so that the usual three days' notice[11] is not required.[12]

8.8   While proceedings should normally be commenced before the application for an interim injunction is made, the court has power to hear the application beforehand,[13] ie, where there is insufficient time; if this happens, the court will usually require the proceedings to be properly commenced the following day.[14]

8.9   If the court makes an order without notice, it must fix a date for a further hearing at which the defendant can be present.[15] This second hearing is called the 'return date' and is usually held a few days after the without notice hearing.

8.10   Whether the injunction ought to continue until the trial is not decided by resolving the factual disputes between the parties. It is, rather, a question of where the balance of justice between the parties lies.[16] If the order is continued, it will usually be until the trial or further order.

8.11   After an injunction has been granted, the order must be served on the defendant and will have no effect until it is. This is best done by the use of a professional process server. If more than one person is subject to the injunction, they must each be served with their own separate copy. A certificate of service should be completed (by the person who served the order) to prove that the defendant has been served. Without this evidence, a court will be unable to commit the defendant for contempt of court or – in the event that the defendant fails to attend court for the return date – make a final order.

8.12   The order should be served together with all documents which supported the application. If the landlord is evading service, so that it proves impossible to serve the order, it is possible to apply to the judge for an order allowing service by a substituted method[17] or dispensing with service.[18] An application to dispense with service can itself be made without notice.[19]

---

11 CPR 23.7(1)(b).

12 CPR 23.7(4).

13 CPR 25.2(1)(a).

14 CPR Part 25 PD 25A para 5.1(4), (5).

15 CPR Part 25 PD 25A para 5.1(3).

16 See *American Cyanamid Co v Ethicon Ltd* [1975] AC 396, HL, referring to a 'balance of convenience'; and *Francome v Mirror Group Newspapers* [1984] 1 WLR 892, CA, preferring 'balance of justice'; see also para 1.113.

17 CPR 6.15.

18 CPR 6.9(1).

19 CPR 6.9(2).

Undertakings

8.13   On the return date, it will be unnecessary to have a full hearing if the defendant is willing to submit to the terms of the injunction. In this case, the appropriate course is normally for the defendant to give an 'undertaking' in the same terms as those sought under the injunction. If the defendant is unwilling to give an undertaking, there will need to be a hearing into the merits of the application, even if the defendant does not oppose it.

8.14   By giving an undertaking, the defendant does not make any admission as to the truth of any events which are alleged to have taken place. The defendant is making a promise to do, or to restrain from doing, certain acts in the future. In a harassment case which does not involve unlawful eviction, the defendant will commonly give an undertaking, as he or she is only promising not to do acts which are in any event unlawful.

8.15   An undertaking should be made on the appropriate court form[20] and should set out precisely what the defendant is promising to do or not to do. The court may refuse to accept the undertaking unless the person giving it has signed a statement to the effect that he or she understands the terms of the undertaking and the consequences of failure to comply.[21]

Committal proceedings

8.16   A person who disobeys an order which has been served, or who has breached an undertaking, may be committed to prison for contempt of court, ie for refusing to obey a court order.[22] The committal procedure[23] must be followed carefully, as the court is reluctant to waive any irregularity where a person's liberty is at stake.

---

20 Form N117; this should be readily available from the court office and can be downloaded from https://formfinder.hmctsformfinder.justice.gov.uk/n117-eng.pdf (English only) or https://formfinder.hmctsformfinder.justice.gov.uk/n117-bil.pdf (English and Welsh).

21 CPR PD 81 para 2.2(1). Form N117 contains a statement to this effect, along with a signature box.

22 Contempt of court is punishable in the county court by imprisonment for up to two years, a fine, or seized of property: Contempt of Court Act 1981 s14; CPR 81. See also *Wookey v Wookey* [1991] Fam 121, CA. As a minor cannot be sent to prison and because an injunction needs to be capable of being effectively enforced, a court will not make an injunction against a minor unless there is evidence that the minor has income or property: *Wookey*; and *Harrow LBC v G* [2004] EWHC 17 (QB).

23 Set out in CPR PD 81.

8.17   Before applying to commit the defendant, advisers should check that the court has endorsed the order with a penal notice (a formal warning to the recipient of the order that if it is not obeyed imprisonment may result).[24] A failure to include the correct penal order will not necessarily prevent the court from committing the defendant to prison, provided it is otherwise made clear that the defendant is at risk of being sent to prison if he or she breaches the order.[25] The terms of the order should also be carefully scrutinised to ensure that the act which the landlord has done, or failed to do, is in fact in breach of the terms of the order.

8.18   If the order drawn up by the court inaccurately records the order, application may be made to cure the defect under what is known as 'the slip rule'.[26] The amended order must, however, then be served personally on the person who is subject to the injunction, giving him or her an opportunity to comply before any question of committal recurs.

8.19   An application to commit is made by an application notice.[27] The notice must identify what parts of the injunction have been broken, give details of the way in which the breaches have occurred, identifying each alleged act of contempt separately and numerically, and generally set out sufficient information to show all the allegations being made against the person sought to be committed.[28] The application must also contain a prominent notice stating the possible consequences of the court making a committal order and of the respondent not attending the hearing.[29]

8.20   The application must be supported by an affidavit[30] from the claimant setting out the facts relied on. Two other affidavits are necessary:

---

24 The penal notice should be: 'If you the within-named [...] do not comply with this order you may be held to be in contempt of court and imprisoned or fined, or your assets may be seized' (or words to substantially the same effect): CPR PD 81 para 1.

25 *Jolly v Hull* [2000] 2 FLR 69, CA. The power to dispense with the need for the penal notice (by, in effect, dispensing with the need for service of the order) should not be exercised too readily: *Jolly*. A missing or insufficient penal notice might also be a defect that the court can waive, provided that the court is satisfied that it has not caused any injustice to the respondent: CPR PD 81 para 16.2.

26 CPR 40.12; the application can be made without notice.

27 CPR 81.10(1); form N244.

28 CPR 81.10(3)(a).

29 CPR PD 81 para 13.2(4).

30 CPR 81.10(3)(b). An affidavit is a witness statement sworn on oath or affirmed. See CPR PD 32 paras 2–10.

one to show that the original order was served, the other to show that the defendant was served with the notice to commit and the affidavit in support.[31]

8.21   If the defendant is not legally represented at the committal hearing, the judge should warn him or her about the seriousness of the proceedings and an adjournment may be allowed for legal advice to be taken.[32] In cases of an allegation of breach of an interim injunction, some judges prefer to adjourn the committal application to the trial of the action. On the hearing of the committal application, the standard of proof is higher than for other civil proceedings, ie, the allegations have to be proved beyond reasonable doubt rather than on a balance of probability.[33]

8.22   In exceptional circumstances, an application for committal can be made without notice to the defendant. Such a course should be adopted only where there is no alternative in order to protect the claimant's position and to uphold the order of the court.[34]

8.23   The court takes a very serious view of any breach of an order, unless there is a good reason for non-compliance. This is particularly so where the order is to re-admit an occupier, as the consequences for someone who has been unlawfully evicted are serious.

8.24   In *Saxby v McKinley*,[35] a landlord unlawfully evicted his tenants. He ignored a warning from their solicitor that he was not allowed to do this, and then deliberately evaded service of a without notice interim injunction to re-admit the tenants. Bearing in mind the consequences to the tenants of being kept out of the property and the cynical disregard for the court displayed by the landlord, the Court of Appeal upheld the imposition of an immediate, 28-day custodial sentence as fully justified.

Starting civil proceedings: unlawful eviction and harassment

8.25   Against this background, the steps necessary to launch civil proceedings are now considered in more detail, as follows:

---

31 Unless the court dispenses with service of the order (CPR 81.8(1)) or service of the committal application (CPR 81.10(5)(a)).
32 See *Brown v Haringey LBC* [2015] EWCA Civ 483, [2015] HLR 30.
33 CPR PD 81 para 9.
34 *Wright v Jess* [1987] 1 WLR 1076, CA.
35 (1996) 29 HLR 569, CA.

a) taking a statement;
b) identifying the landlord;
c) applying for public funding;
d) notifying the court;
e) drafting forms;
f) starting proceedings in the court;
g) getting an interim order;
h) serving the order; and
i) after service.

Taking a statement

8.26   When a client comes to the office, it is necessary to take a statement which identifies the causes of action which may be available and the remedies to which the client may be entitled (chapters 1 and 2).

8.27   In unlawful eviction cases, it is necessary to identify:

a) *the premises* – the address; room, flat or house; whether facilities were shared with others; who else lived there;
b) *the status of the occupier* – eg, tenancy or licence; assured, assured shorthold or protected tenancy;
c) *details of the tenancy or licence* – when it began, whether there is a written agreement, the amount of the rent, whether it is weekly, monthly or fixed-term, whether notice has been given;
d) *the landlord's name* (and the names of any other persons involved, eg, landlord's agent or employee);
e) *what has been done, by whom, to whom and when*;
f) *the effect on the occupier* – eg, distress, personal injury, no cooking facilities, no heating, nowhere to sleep, how many people affected (such as family, flatmates); property damaged or taken;
g) *evidence of occupation* – eg, rent book, tenancy agreement, letters from housing benefit department, bills in occupier's name, etc (which, if available, should be copied and exhibited to the witness statement).

8.28   In harassment cases, it is necessary to identify:

a) *the premises* – as above;
b) *the status of the occupier* – as above, but note that it is particularly relevant to identify whether the occupier was a tenant rather than licensee if the tort relied on requires the claimant to have possession of land, for example, nuisance (see paras 2.23–2.24);
c) *the defendant's name* (and the names of any other persons involved) – as above;

d) *what has been done, by whom, to whom and when;*
e) *the effect on the occupier* – as above.

8.29   At this stage, unless there is reason to believe that letting the defendant know that advice has been sought may result in harm to the occupier (eg may exacerbate the situation), it is sensible to try to contact the defendant, personally or by telephone, to make sure that the dispute has not arisen through misunderstanding (eg because the landlord thought that the tenant had left the property or was wholly unaware of the occupier's rights). If public funding is being sought, advisers are usually required to make contact with the landlord, managing agent or defendant.[36] If a local authority tenancy relations or other officer is involved, or could usefully be brought in to help, contact should also be made at this stage, to see whether he or she may be able to secure a solution (subject to the issue of harm).

8.30   If the landlord has already made clear – or at this stage makes clear – that he or she has no intention of allowing the tenant back in, this can be set out in a witness statement to show that an injunction is justified. Any telephone conversations should be confirmed by letter, which should include the suggestion that the defendant seek independent advice.

Identifying the landlord

8.31   A tenant may not always know who the landlord is, or how to locate him or her. An agent or person who receives rent may be served with notice requiring him or her to disclose the full name and place of abode or business address of the landlord in order to bring proceedings[37] under the Protection from Eviction Act (PEA) 1977.[38] For these purposes, the notice must be served with the fixed intention of bringing proceedings, not merely in contemplation of the possibility of bringing proceedings in the future.[39]

8.32   'Landlord' is not defined, but includes:[40]

- any person from time to time deriving title under the original landlord;

---

36   See para 8.42.
37   Criminal or civil.
38   PEA 1977 s7(1).
39   *Lewisham LBC v Ranaweera* [2000] JHL D70, Crown Court.
40   PEA 1977 s7(3).

- in relation to any dwelling house, any person other than the tenant who is entitled to possession of the dwelling house;[41] and
- any person who grants to another the right to occupy the dwelling in question as a residence and any person directly or indirectly deriving title from the grantor.

8.33 A failure or refusal to comply with a notice seeking the identity of the landlord is a criminal offence, unless the accused can show that he or she did not know the information sought and could not have acquired it with reasonable diligence.[42] It is triable only in the magistrates' court, and the maximum penalty is a fine not exceeding level 4 on the standard scale (currently £2,500).[43]

Public funding

8.34 It is not possible to deal with public funding in detail,[44] but some general points may be made.

8.35 The Legal Aid, Sentencing and Punishment of Offenders Act 2012 (LASPO) governs applications for legal aid from 1 April 2013. Under LASPO, the Lord Chancellor has assumed responsibility for the provision of public funding. Most functions in respect of legal aid are the responsibility of the Director of Legal Aid Casework, although in practice this means the Legal Aid Agency (LAA).[45] The effect of LASPO has generally been to reduce the availability of legal aid.[46] Funding does, however, remain available for civil legal services[47] for unlawful eviction cases.[48] Funding is also available in relation to an injunction under either Protection from Harassment Act (PHA)

---

41 Or – in the case of a protected tenancy – would be entitled to possession but for the security of tenure afforded by the Rent Act (RA) 1977.

42 PEA 1977 s7(2).

43 Criminal Justice Act (CJA) 1982 s37, as amended by CJA 1991 s17.

44 See V Ling and S Pugh (eds), *LAG Legal Aid Handbook 2017/18* and its supporting website, https://legalaidhandbook.com (accessed 19 April 2017) for full details. See also the *Lord Chancellor's Guidance*, available at www.gov.uk/government/uploads/system/uploads/attachment_data/file/540158/lord-chancellor_s-guidance.pdf.

45 LASPO s4. See www.gov.uk/government/organisations/legal-aid-agency.

46 See the 7th edition of this work at paras 7.31–7.40 of for a brief overview of the pre-LASPO 2012 position.

47 As defined by LASPO s8. In effect, 'civil legal services' means advice, assistance and representation in non-criminal matters.

48 LASPO Sch 1 Part 1 para 33.

1997 s3 or s3A.[49] It follows that funding is not available for harassment under PEA 1977 unless brought within the 1997 Act.

8.36   The availability of funding also depends on means and merits testing, as set out in the Civil Legal Aid (Financial Resources and Payment for Services) Regulations 2013[50] and the Civil Legal Aid (Merits Criteria) Regulations 2013,[51] respectively. Procedure is governed by the Civil Legal Aid (Procedure) Regulations 2012.[52]

8.37   Civil legal services may take several forms. The most important for present purposes is 'legal representation'.[53] Legal representation means the provision of civil legal services[54] to an individual[55] in particular proceedings where that individual is either a party, wishes to be joined as a party, or is contemplating issuing the proceedings. Legal representation may be full or investigative. Investigative representation is limited to investigating the strength of contemplated proceedings and (to a limited extent) to the issue and conduct of proceedings.[56] Full representation is any other legal representation.[57] It is therefore the most comprehensive form of civil legal service.

8.38   In order to qualify for full representation in relation to unlawful eviction or in relation to an injunction under PHA 1997 (to the extent that it relates to the interference with an individual's enjoyment of their home), the Director of Legal Aid Casework must be satisfied that the applicant meets six standard criteria for determinations for legal representation and a prospects of success test.[58]

---

49 LASPO Sch 1 Part 1 para 37(1)(a).
50 2013 SI No 480.
51 2013 SI No 104.
52 2012 SI No 3098.
53 Civil Legal Aid (Merits Criteria) Regulations 2013 SI No 104 reg 18. The other defined forms of civil legal services are legal help; help at court; family help; family mediation; help with family mediation; and other legal services: see 2013 regulations Part 2.
54 Other than acting as a mediator or arbitrator.
55 Or 'legal person', although this is unlikely to be relevant in the context of areas covered by this book.
56 Civil Legal Aid (Merits Criteria) Regulations 2013 SI No 104 reg 18(3). Investigative representation includes the issue and conduct of proceedings only so far as is necessary to obtain disclosure of information relevant to the prospects of success, to protect the position of the applicant for representation in relation to an urgent hearing, or to protect the position of the applicant for representation in relation to the time limit for issuing proceedings (which is unlikely to arise in the context of an application for an injunction).
57 Civil Legal Aid (Merits Criteria) Regulations 2013 SI No 104 reg 18(4).
58 Civil Legal Aid (Merits Criteria) Regulations 2013 SI No 104 reg 62(1).

8.39 The six standard criteria are as follows.

(a) the individual does not have access to other potential sources of funding (other than a conditional fee agreement) from which it would be reasonable to fund the case;

(b) the case is unsuitable for a conditional fee agreement;

(c) there is no person other than the individual, including a person who might benefit from the proceedings, who can reasonably be expected to bring the proceedings;

(d) the individual has exhausted all reasonable alternatives to bringing proceedings including any complaints system, ombudsman scheme or other form of alternative dispute resolution;

(e) there is a need for representation in all the circumstances of the case including–

(i) the nature and complexity of the issues;

(ii) the existence of other proceedings; and

(iii) the interests of other parties to the proceedings; and

(f) the proceedings are not likely to be allocated to the small claims track.[59]

8.40 For the prospects of success test to be met, the Director of Legal Aid Casework must be satisfied that the prospects are very good, good or moderate.[60] The test is also met where the Director is satisfied that the prospects are only borderline or marginal, but only if the Director is also satisfied that the case is either of significant wider public interest or of overwhelming importance to the individual.[61]

8.41 There are two further conditions. First, the Director of Legal Aid Casework must be satisfied that the proportionality test is met.[62] The proportionality test is met where the likely benefits of the proceedings justify the likely costs (having regard to the prospects of success and all other circumstances).[63]

8.42 Secondly, the Director must be satisfied that the landlord (or other person responsible for the matter complained of) has been notified of the complaint, except where this is impracticable. Presumably it

---

59 Civil Legal Aid (Merits Criteria) Regulations 2013 SI No 104 reg 39.

60 Civil Legal Aid (Merits Criteria) Regulations 2013 SI No 104 reg 43(b). 'Very good' means an 80 per cent or greater chance of obtaining a successful outcome; 'good' is 60–79 per cent; moderate is 50–59 per cent: Civil Legal Aid (Merits Criteria) Regulations 2013 SI No 104 reg 5(1). A 'borderline' case is one where it is not possible to classify the prospects because of disputed law, fact or expert evidence; 'marginal' means a 45 per cent or more chance, but less than 50 per cent, of obtaining a successful outcome: Civil Legal Aid (Merits Criteria) Regulations 2013 SI No 104 reg 5(1).

61 Civil Legal Aid (Merits Criteria) Regulations 2013 SI No 104 reg 43(b).

62 Civil Legal Aid (Merits Criteria) Regulations 2013 SI No 104 reg 62(2)(a).

63 Civil Legal Aid (Merits Criteria) Regulations 2013 SI No 104 reg 8.

will be considered to be impracticable where the matter is urgent, such as cases where the claimant is homeless, or the situation is so serious that contact would be inappropriate, eg, if to do so would increase the likelihood of violence.[64] Where notice has been given, the landlord (or other person) must have had a reasonable opportunity to respond.

8.43   So far as investigative representation is concerned, the standard criteria for determinations for legal representation must be satisfied.[65] The Director of Legal Aid Casework must also be satisfied that the prospects of success are unclear and that substantial investigative work is required before those prospects can be determined, and that there are reasonable grounds for believing that, once investigative work has been carried out, the case will satisfy the criteria for full representation.[66] Moreover, if the claim is primarily for damages which do not exceed £1,000 (for unlawful eviction cases) or £5,000 (for other cases), the case must be of significant wider public interest.[67] This last criterion is unlikely to cause much difficulty in the context of an application for an injunction, as the claim will not be primarily one for damages.[68]

8.44   The Lord Chancellor has issued guidance aimed at the Director of Legal Aid Casework and the LAA,[69] although unlike the *Funding Code* (the guidance issued under the pre-LASPO public funding regime), the *Lord Chancellor's Guidance* does not specifically address either unlawful eviction or harassment.

Notifying the court

8.45   If a without notice application for an interim injunction is to be made, the county court must be notified in advance to ensure that there is a

---

64 As was the position under *Funding Code* (the guidance issued under the pre-LASPO 2012 public funding regime), para 19.9.

65 Civil Legal Aid (Merits Criteria) Regulations 2013 SI No 104 regs 40(1), 63(1)(a). See para 8.39.

66 Civil Legal Aid (Merits Criteria) Regulations 2013 SI No 104 regs 40(1)(a), (b), 63(1)(a).

67 Civil Legal Aid (Merits Criteria) Regulations 2013 SI No 104 regs 40(1)(c), 63(2).

68 So far as concerns harassment cases, there will need to be a claim for an injunction under PHA 1997 to qualify for public funding at all (see para 8.35).

69 *Lord Chancellor's Guidance under Section 4 of the Legal Aid, Sentencing and Punishment of Offenders Act 2012* (July 2016) ('*Lord Chancellor's Guidance*'), available at www.gov.uk/government/uploads/system/uploads/attachment_data/file/540158/lord-chancellor_s-guidance.pdf.

judge available to hear the application. In some courts it may also be necessary to make an appointment to attend the court office in order to have the application issued.

Drafting documents

8.46   To commence proceedings, the following documents are required:
a)   claim form (form N1); and
b)   particulars of claim.

8.47   If an application for an interim injunction is also to be made, the following additional documents are required:
a)   application notice (form N16A);
b)   witness statement; and
c)   draft order (form N16).

8.48   Three copies of all the documents are required, one for each side and one for the court. Guidance on drafting these documents and examples of some of them appear at the end of this chapter from para 8.72 onwards.

Starting the proceedings at the court

8.49   In unlawful eviction and harassment cases there is no restriction on which county court may be used. Obviously, the claimant will, for convenience, normally wish to use his or her local court, but in an eviction case he or she may have had to move some distance away and wish to use another court, local to where he or she is currently staying.

8.50   At the court office, an issue fee must be paid.[70] The claim is then allotted a claim number. This is stamped on all the documents referred to above and is used in all future documents. If it is late in the day and not possible to issue the claim, the court has power to hear the application but will insist on the proceedings being issued on the following day.[71]

---

70   Fees vary depending on the size of the claim and are subject to frequent change.
71   CPR PD 25A para 5.1(4), (5).

Obtaining a 'without notice' order

8.51   The hearing itself is usually brief and in private. The judge reads the documents (normally before the hearing). As the documents should show an entitlement to the injunction, the only issues which usually arise are: delay; the precise wording of the order; and the return date. The judge may also ask the occupier some questions, either informally or on oath.

8.52   If an order is granted by the judge, it will remain in force until the return date, which will be specified by the judge. If an order is not made, the judge will fix a return date for the injunction to be heard with the other side present.

Serving the order

8.53   To be effective, an order must be served on the landlord or other person subject to the injunction. Where there is more than one defendant, the order must be served on each of them. It is necessary to obtain enough copies of the order so that one can be served on each defendant and one retained for further reference by the applicant.

8.54   In urgent cases, the court office usually types the order at once, or within a matter of hours. Although service can be effected by the court (on payment of an additional fee), this is unlikely to be of assistance in an urgent case because it may take several days. Accordingly, a process server should be used. Advisers should warn the process server in advance of the hearing that his or her services are expected to be needed.

After service

8.55   Unless there is to be an application for committal, the next stage is the hearing on the return date. At this, the other side is given an opportunity to be heard and to argue that the injunction should not be continued until trial. If the defendant is unwilling to give an undertaking, the application will be heard and determined according to the principles considered in chapters 1 and 2.[72]

8.56   At the return date, the judge will issue directions as to the procedure to be adopted before the trial. It is not possible here to describe county court procedure in detail. The order will, however, usually provide for the following steps:

72 See paras 1.106–1.115 and 2.48.

a) allocation of the claim to a track;[73]
b) the defendant to file a defence (an answer to the particulars of claim);
c) both parties to provide disclosure of their documents by list;[74]
d) the parties to exchange witness statements of the facts to be relied on at trial;
e) the parties to exchange (or agree) expert evidence on which they intend to rely (eg in a case involving damages under Housing Act (HA) 1988 s28, or general damages for loss of right of occupation);[75]
f) a date to be fixed for the trial, or that the parties file 'listing questionnaires' by a certain date (documents which show whether the parties have complied with the directions and dates on which the trial should not be held because witnesses are unavailable).

8.57   Alternatively, the judge may simply order that the defendant file a defence. Once this is done, the court sends out 'directions questionnaires', which the parties must complete and return to the court. The district judge then decides to which track the claim should be allocated and makes directions at that stage, or he or she may order that there is a cost and case management conference at which the directions can be made.

8.58   The directions order should contain specific dates by which each of these steps must be completed. Advisers should note the importance of ensuring that both parties comply with the directions. If it is clear that the claimant needs extra time, an application should be made to the court to extend time.[76] Conversely, if the defendant fails to comply with a direction, it is possible to apply to the court for 'an unless order', ie, an order that unless the defendant complies within a specified time, he or she will not be allowed to defend the action at all.[77]

---

73 There are three tracks (Small Claims Track, Fast Track, and Multi-track), which are, broadly speaking, based on the value of the claim (see CPR 26.6–26.8).
74 Disclosure is the process by which the parties provide each other with all documentation relevant to the case. This does not include communications between adviser and client. It is usually done by a list of the documents followed by an opportunity to look at those documents and obtain copies.
75 See paras 1.179–1.181.
76 The court has the power to extend time under CPR 3.1(2). It is far better to make an application to extend time *before* time has elapsed, as the application is then not to be treated as one for relief from sanctions: *Hallam Estates Ltd v Baker* [2014] EWCA Civ 661, [2014] CP Rep 38. See also para 8.2 and n6.
77 The power to attach conditions to an order is set in CPR 3.1(3).

8.59   If the defendant fails to comply with the order an application can be made to debar him or her from defending the action. The matter can then be set down for an assessment of damages. The defendant will not be able to dispute liability although he or she can still challenge the amount of the compensation sought.

The forms used

Claim form

8.60   The claim form (form N1) is a simple document, the completion of which is straightforward; no example is therefore needed. The parties' names need to be inserted. Information is also set out which assists the court in allocation of the claim. Brief details of the claim are required, for example: 'claim for damages and an injunction in a case of unlawful eviction and harassment of a residential tenant'.

8.61   There is space for an estimate of the value of the claim. This need not be completed if the claim is for unlawful eviction or harassment by a landlord.

8.62   Form N1 also includes space for the particulars of claim to be set out, but the space provided is small and it is usual to insert 'see particulars of claim attached' and to set out the particulars of claim in a separate document.

Statement of truth

8.63   The claim form, particulars of claim, witness statement and application notice must all contain a statement of truth. If the document is signed by the claimant, the standard form is: 'I believe that the facts stated in this [insert the type of document] are true'. A solicitor may sign the statement of truth on the claimant's behalf, in which case the statement commences: 'The claimant believes ...'.

8.64   If a person without an honest belief in its truth makes a false statement in a document verified with a statement of truth, proceedings may be brought for contempt of court.[78] While this is rare, it emphasises the importance of ensuring that the claimant fully understands what has been written on his or her behalf in all the documents, in particular, the witness statement and the particulars of claim. Firstly, there is a duty not to mislead the court. Secondly, inconsistencies

---

78 CPR 32.14.

between the documents and the claimant's subsequent evidence provide ammunition for cross-examination at trial which may seriously undermine the witness's credibility.

Starting civil proceedings: tenancy deposits

Housing Act 2004 s214

8.65 Under Housing Act (HA) 2004 s214, a tenant may bring a claim in respect of a tenancy deposit where the landlord has failed to protect the deposit or otherwise failed to deal with it properly (see chapter 4).

8.66 A claim under HA 2004 s214 must be brought using the CPR Part 8 procedure. It therefore differs in some respects from the procedure set out above.

8.67 The CPR Part 8 procedure requires a claimant to use form N208.[79] This does not require the same level of detail that would be set out in form N1 (or particulars of claim attached to form N1). Form N208 should be used to set out the facts, the issue and the remedy in summary form. The claimant must, however, file any written evidence when he or she files the claim form.[80] Clearly, the full factual detail will be set out in the witness statement.

8.68 Proceedings may be issued in any county court hearing centre, but will be sent to the county court hearing centre that serves the address.[81] It is therefore best practice to issue in the hearing centre that serves the address, so as to avoid delay.[82]

8.69 The defendant must file an acknowledgement of service on form N210, and any witness evidence on which he or she wishes to rely, not more than 14 days after service of the claim form.[83] The claimant may serve any evidence in reply within 14 days.[84]

---

79 Available at http://formfinder.hmctsformfinder.justice.gov.uk/n208-eng.pdf (English only) and http://formfinder.hmctsformfinder.justice.gov.uk/n208-bil.pdf (English and Welsh).

80 CPR 8.5(1). The claimant may rely on matters set out in the claim form as evidence, provided that the claim form is verified by a statement of truth: CPR 8.5(7), and see paras 8.63–8.64.

81 CPR 56.2(1) and CPR PD 56 para 2.2(2).

82 See CPR PD 56 para 2.2(2): 'A claimant should consider the potential delay which may result if a claim is not sent to the appropriate County Court hearing centre in the first instance.'

83 CPR 8.3(1) and 8.5(3).

84 CPR 8.5(5).

8.70   The court will fix a first hearing date, at which the court may either hear and dispose of the claim or give case management directions.[85] Where there are disputes of fact, the court may give directions for the claim to proceed as a Part 7 claim.

8.71   Legal aid will not be available for proceedings under HA 2004 s214 (save that legal aid may be available, subject to means and merits, where HA 2004 s214 is relied upon for a defence and counterclaim to a possession claim).[86]

Example documents

8.72   The following documents are examples of documents required. They are not intended to lay down detailed or exhaustive rules on drafting. In particular, they are not reproductions of the court forms, which must always be used where applicable. (There is no court form for particulars of claim or witness statements.) All that have been omitted, however, are marginal notes to assist completion of the forms and certain formal parts, which are completed by the court staff.

8.73   Examples are offered of:

- Unlawful eviction:
  a) particulars of claim;
  b) application notice;
  c) draft order; and
  d) witness statement.
- Harassment:
  a) particulars of claim.
- Tenancy deposit:
  a) witness statement.

8.74   There are three sets of particulars of claim. The first is for an unlawful eviction claim against an assured shorthold tenant; the second, for an unlawful eviction claim against a secure tenant; the third is for a claim in harassment. Witness statements are offered for the first unlawful eviction claim and for the tenancy deposit claim. The other example documents all relate to the first unlawful eviction claim, but it will readily be observed how other documents can be adapted to other situations.

---

85 CPR PD 8A para 8.1.
86 LASPO Sch 1 Part 1 para 33.

PARTICULARS OF CLAIM (1)
UNLAWFUL EVICTION OF ASSURED SHORTHOLD TENANT

<u>IN THE COUNTY COURT SITTING AT ANYTOWN</u>

<u>Claim No (see note 1)</u>

B E T W E E N:

(1) JANE FIELDS
(2) JOHN JONES

<u>Claimants</u>

-and-

WARDEN DRANE

<u>Defendant</u>

PARTICULARS OF CLAIM

---

1 At all material times the claimants have been the joint assured shorthold tenants of the premises known as 16A Maxwell Square, Anytown AT16 1AB ('the flat'). The defendant is their landlord. (see note 2)

2 The premises are a self-contained one-bedroomed flat situated in the basement of a terraced house. The defendant is the freehold owner of the house.

3 The said assured shorthold tenancy commenced on 19 January 2016 and was for a fixed term of 12 months at a monthly rent of £700. On its expiry, it became a statutory monthly periodic tenancy. It is evidenced by a written tenancy agreement. (see note 3)

4 It is an implied term of the tenancy that the defendant would allow the claimants quiet enjoyment of the flat. (see note 4)

5 By reason of the matters hereinafter set out, the defendant has been in breach of the said term and has trespassed to the claimants' flat, property and persons, and has pursued a course of conduct which he knew amounted to harassment of the claimants in breach of s1 of the Protection from Harassment Act 1997.

PARTICULARS (see note 5)

(i) On 25 January 2017, during a telephone conversation, the defendant told the first claimant that the claimants had to leave the flat. When the first claimant told the defendant that the claimants were legally entitled to remain in the premises until evicted by court order, the defendant became angry and swore at the first claimant. He told the first claimant that he was coming round to 'sort the matter out'.

(ii) At about 8 pm on the same day, the defendant attended the flat. The first claimant explained to the defendant that the claimants were in

financial difficulties but that they hoped to pay the rent arrears soon. The defendant became extremely angry and swore at the first claimant. He threatened the first claimant and said that he 'knew people'. The defendant refused to leave the premises when asked to do so.

(iii) On 28 January 2017, the defendant telephoned the first claimant in response to a letter from the claimants' solicitors informing him of the claimants' rights. He told her that the claimants had to leave 'or else'.

(iv) On approximately ten occasions between 28 January 2017 and 15 March 2017, the defendant telephoned the claimants. Some of the telephone calls were made in the early hours of the morning when the claimants were asleep. On the first occasion, the defendant said 'As you sow so shall you reap'. On the subsequent occasions, the defendant did not say anything but put the telephone down without speaking. The defendant was identifiable because his number was displayed on the claimants' phone. The claimants felt threatened by the telephone calls.

(v) On 20 March 2017, the defendant in the company of two other men entered the flat by breaking down the front door. They packed the claimants' belongings into black bin liners. One of the men punched the second defendant in the face. The claimants were in fear of a further assault and left the flat.

(vi) On their return to the flat, the claimants were unable to secure entry because the locks had been changed. The claimants found that their possessions had been placed outside the flat. Some items were missing.

6   By reason of the matters aforesaid the claimants have suffered loss, damage, distress, discomfort and inconvenience.

PARTICULARS OF GENERAL DAMAGES (see note 6)

(a) The claimants were obliged to sleep on a friend's floor for the night of 20 to 21 March 2017.

(b) The claimants were distressed and frightened by the defendant's conduct. The second claimant had to attend hospital because of the blow to his face. His face was severely bruised and he was prescribed pain-killers.

PARTICULARS OF SPECIAL DAMAGES (see note 7)

The following items have not been returned to the claimants:
(a) flat-screen television £500
(b) laptop computer £400
(c) various items of jewellery £380

7   The claimants claim to be entitled to exemplary and/or aggravated damages. (see note 8)

PARTICULARS

(i) The defendant was warned of the illegality of his actions by a letter from the claimants' solicitors dated 28 January 2017. Despite the warning, and in cynical disregard of the claimants' legal rights, the defendant acted in a way calculated to obtain vacant possession without incurring the cost of bringing a claim for possession in the courts. In the circumstances, the defendant has sought to profit from his own unlawful acts and the claimant is entitled to exemplary damages.

(ii) The manner of the eviction was very distressing and demeaning to the claimants. In the circumstances, the claimants claim aggravated damages.

8 The claimants claim to be entitled to interest on such damages as the court may award in respect of their claim pursuant to s69 of the County Courts Act 1984, at such rate and for such period as the court thinks fit. (see note 10)

AND the claimants claim: (see note 11)

(1) An injunction requiring the defendant forthwith to re-admit the claimants to the flat and restraining the defendant by himself, his servants or agents, or otherwise from further interfering with the claimants' quiet enjoyment of the flat or further trespassing on the claimants' premises, persons or goods, or in any way harassing the claimants.

(2) An order for the delivery up of their property or special damages in the sum of £1,280.

(3) Damages including general, special, aggravated and exemplary damages.

(4) Interest.

(5) Costs.

The claimants believe that the facts set out in these particulars of claim are true. (see note 12)

Signed ....

Dated: 22 March 2017

....

Leo and Nevil
242–4 Nashville Road, Anytown AT5 6UN
Solicitors for the Claimant
who will accept service at this address

PARTICULARS OF CLAIM (2)
UNLAWFUL EVICTION OF SECURE TENANT

IN THE COUNTY COURT SITTING AT ANYTOWN

Claim No (see note 1)

B E T W E E N:

JOHN SMITH

Claimant

-and-

ANYTOWN DISTRICT COUNCIL

Defendant

PARTICULARS OF CLAIM

---

1   At all material times the claimant has been the secure weekly periodic tenant of a one-bedroom flat situated at 16c Grove Park, Anytown AT7 4XY ('the flat'). The defendant is his landlord. (see note 2)

2   The said secure tenancy commenced on 13 May 1995.

3   On 7 July 2016, the claimant's mother became seriously ill.

4   On 12 July 2016, the claimant left the flat and went to stay with his mother in Newtown so as to care for her. The claimant did not tell the defendant that he was staying with his mother. At all material times, the claimant intended to return to the flat.

5   On 6 January 2017, the claimant's mother died.

6   It is an implied term of the tenancy that the defendant would allow the claimant quiet enjoyment of the flat. (see note 4)

7   By reason of the matters hereinafter set out, the defendant has been in breach of the term for quiet enjoyment and has trespassed to the claimant's flat and property.

PARTICULARS (see note 5)

(i)   On 2 April 2017, the claimant, after his mother had died on 6 January 2017 and he had settled her affairs and her landlord had indicated an intention to recover possession of her property, returned to the flat. On his return he discovered that the locks had been changed and he could not gain entry to the flat.

(ii)   At 4pm that day, the claimant telephoned the defendant and spoke to Mr Jones, the housing officer responsible for the flat. Mr Jones told the claimant that, on 2 February 2017, the defendant had recovered possession of the flat because the claimant was presumed to have abandoned it. All of the claimant's belongings had been stored for

14 days before being disposed after the claimant had failed to contact the defendant for their return.

(iii) Mr Jones said that the defendant would not provide the claimant with alternative accommodation as he had abandoned his property and, as the claimant did not have a priority need, nor would he be provided with temporary accommodation under Part 7 of the Housing Act 1996.

8 By reason of the matters aforesaid the claimants have suffered loss, damage, distress, discomfort and inconvenience.

PARTICULARS OF GENERAL DAMAGES (see note 6)

(i) On 2 April 2017, the claimant was forced to stay in bed and breakfast accommodation.

(ii) From 3 April 2017, until the date of the claim, he has been forced to sleep on a friend's sofa.

PARTICULARS OF SPECIAL DAMAGES (see note 7)

(i) The cost of bed and breakfast accommodation on 2 April 2017: £75.

(ii) The following items, which were disposed of by the defendant:
  (a) Bed: £400.
  (b) Sofa: £500.
  (c) Table: £100.
  (d) 4 Chairs: £100.
  (e) Television: £300.
  (f) Blu-ray player: £100.
  (g) Digital radio: £100.
  (h) Hi-fi system: £200.
  (i) Kitchen utensils: £50.
  (j) Linen: £50.
  (k) Collection of out-of-print crime novels: £100.

9 The claimant is entitled to aggravated and exemplary damages. (see note 8)

PARTICULARS

(i) The defendant has obtained possession of the flat in a way calculated to obtain vacant possession without incurring the cost of bringing a claim for possession in the courts. In the circumstances, the defendant has sought to profit from its own unlawful act and the claimant is entitled to exemplary damages.

(ii) The defendant's actions have caused the claimant stress, anxiety and worry.

10 Further or in the alternative, by reason of the matters set out in paragraph 7 herein the defendant has unlawfully deprived the claimant of his occupation of the premises in breach of section 27 of the Housing Act 1988. In the event that the claimant is not reinstated to the flat, the claimant will claim damages to be assessed in accordance with section 28 of the Housing Act 1988. (see note 9)

11 The claimant claims to be entitled to interest on such damages as the court may award in respect of his claim pursuant to section 69 of the County Courts Act 1984, at such rate and for such period as the court thinks fit. (see note 10)

AND the claimant claims:

   (1) An injunction requiring the defendant to re-admit the claimant to the flat forthwith.

   (2) An order for the delivery up of his property or special damages in the sum of £2,000.

   (3) General, aggravated, special or exemplary damages.

   (4) Damages under Housing Act 1988 s28.

   (5) Interest.

   (6) Costs.

The claimant believes that the facts set out in these particulars of claim are true. (see note 12)

Signed...............................

Dated: 18 April 2017

....

Leo and Nevil
242–4 Nashville Road, Anytown AT5 6UN
Solicitors for the Claimant
who will accept service at this address

PARTICULARS OF CLAIM (3)
HARASSMENT BY LANDLORD

IN THE COUNTY COURT SITTING AT ANYTOWN

Claim No (see note 1)

B E T W E E N:

MEG M SWADDLEY

Claimant

-and-

RON B B TROWER

Defendant

PARTICULARS OF CLAIM

---

1   At all material times, the claimant has been the sole assured shorthold tenant of a flat known as 74 Finton Court, Anytown AT5 0DX ('the flat'). The defendant is her landlord. (see note 2)

2   The premises are a self-contained one-bedroom flat situated on the top floor of a terraced house, which includes a car parking space at the front of the building. The defendant is the freehold owner of the house and lives in the ground-floor flat.

3   The assured shorthold tenancy commenced on 21 May 2010 and was for a fixed term of 12 months at a monthly rent of £800. On its expiry, it became a statutory monthly periodic tenancy. It is evidenced by a written tenancy agreement. (see note 3)

4   By reason of the matters hereinafter set out, the defendant has, in breach of section 1 of the Protection from Harassment Act 1997, pursued a course of conduct which he knew amounted to harassment of the claimant. (see note 4)

PARTICULARS OF HARASSMENT (see note 5)

(i)   On 14 February 2017, the claimant returned home from work to find the defendant filling her parking space with car parts. When the claimant pointed out that the parking space was hers to use under the terms of the tenancy agreement, the defendant became abusive and threatened to hit her with a spanner.

(ii)   On 15 February 2017, the claimant removed the car parts from the parking space and was able to park her car in it. Later that day, she found that the bonnet of her car had been badly scratched. The claimant believes that it was the defendant who scratched the car.

(iii) On 17 February 2017, the claimant took her car to the garage to be resprayed. Later that day, the defendant put the car parts back in the parking space. Despite numerous requests to remove them, the defendant has refused to remove the car parts which remain in the parking space as of today's date.

(iv) On 18 February 2017, the claimant found notes which had been posted through her letter box stating 'Watch yourself'. The claimant believes that the defendant posted the notes.

(v) On 19 February 2017, the claimant asked the defendant whether he had posted the notes. The defendant replied 'What if I have?'. The defendant then became abusive and threatened the claimant.

(vi) On at least seven occasions during the following week, the claimant was woken in the early hours of the morning by telephone calls from the defendant.

(vii) On the evenings of 20, 22, 23 and 24 February 2017, the defendant stood outside the claimant's flat in the communal area, staring through the window of the front door for several hours at a time.

(viii) On 25 February 2017, the defendant once again stood outside the claimant's flat. The claimant went out to confront the defendant. The defendant was abusive and pushed the claimant in the chest.

5   Additionally or alternatively, by reason of the matters set out at paragraph 4, above, the defendant has assaulted and/or intimidated and/or trespassed to the goods of the claimant.

6   By reason of the matters aforesaid, the claimant has suffered loss, damage, distress, discomfort and inconvenience.

PARTICULARS OF GENERAL DAMAGES (see note 6)

(a) The claimant has been distressed and frightened by the defendant's conduct. She tries to stay away from her home because she is frightened of meeting the defendant.

(b) As result of the defendant's blocking of the claimant's parking space, the claimant has had to park her vehicle two streets away from her flat. The claimant drives to and from work every weekday.

PARTICULARS OF SPECIAL DAMAGES (see note 7)

(c) Cost of respraying bonnet of the car: £300

7   The claimant claims aggravated damages. The claimant has been very distressed by the defendant's conduct, in particular, the assault. The claimant no longer feels safe in her own home. (see note 8)

8   The claimant is entitled to interest on such damages as the court may award in respect of her claim pursuant to section 69 of the County Courts Act 1984, at such rate and for such period as the court thinks fit. (see note 10)

AND the claimant claims: (see note 11)

(1) An injunction restraining the defendant by himself, his servants or agents, or otherwise from trespassing on the claimant's premises, persons or goods, or in any way harassing or abusing the claimant.

(2) An injunction requiring the defendant forthwith to remove any items which he has placed in the claimant's parking space and restraining the defendant from in any way interfering with the claimant's right to park her car in the parking space.

(3) Damages including aggravated damages.

(4) Interest.

(5) Costs.

I believe that the facts set out in these particulars of claim are true. (see note 12)

Signed..............................

Dated: 27 February 2017

....

Leo and Nevil
242–4 Nashville Road, Anytown AT5 6UN
Solicitors for the Claimant
who will accept service at this address

Notes to particulars of claim

Note 1 – Heading to form

Fill in the name of the appropriate county court. Leave the case number blank until one is provided by the court. There may be more than one claimant or defendant, in which case the names should all be set out on separate lines and the parties identified by putting a number in brackets before them showing who is the first claimant, second claimant, first defendant, second defendant and so on. It may not be possible to identify a defendant, for example, an agent, except by one name. It is perfectly permissible to identify someone by a forename or surname alone and gender, if that is all that is known.

Note 2 – Introductory paragraphs

The purpose of the introductory paragraphs is to set out the relationship between the parties, which forms the basis of the causes of action (see paras 1.5–1.6 and 2.4–2.5). In unlawful eviction cases, this involves identifying the basis of the agreement under which the claimant occupies the premises and the claimant's status, for example, assured tenant, assured shorthold tenant, secure tenant or licensee (see Arden & Dymond *Manual of Housing Law* (LAG, 10th edn, 2017) chapter 1). In some cases, this may not be straightforward and may have to be set out in separate paragraphs. If there is likely to be a dispute between the parties, for example, assured tenant versus assured shorthold tenant or tenant of resident landlord, assert the claimant's best case.

If the claimant only occupied a single room, or a flat in a house, do not give just the address of the house, but identify clearly the subject matter of the agreement – for example, first floor flat, flat 2, middle room on the second floor, attic room or back room.

In some harassment cases, the status of the parties and their relationship is irrelevant. There may be no contractual relationship between the parties and torts such as assault or harassment under PHA 1997 do not depend on the status of the parties. Information about any relationship between the parties may, however, assist in explaining how the acts complained of arose. In certain torts – for example, nuisance – the status of the claimant is significant and must be included (see paras 2.23–2.24).

Note 3 – Pleading the whole claim

Remember that the particulars of claim form the basis of the whole action. These details may not be necessary for the immediate hearing but will be relevant later.

Note 4 – Causes of action

In this and the first part of the next paragraph, the 'causes of action' are introduced (see note 2). There may be several causes of action. State them all – for example, breach of the covenant for quiet enjoyment; trespass to goods, property and person; nuisance.

Note 5 – Particulars

Using particulars makes the claim more easily understood. Here, set out in a sequence of numbered subparagraphs the actual events which constitute the breach. It is helpful to use different numerals to those already in use for the principal paragraphs. The sequence of events should be set out logically and in chronological order from the first act complained of to the point at which all remedies short of turning for help to the civil courts have been attempted.

Lawyers differ about the need for detail. The document is intended to assist the court, not to confuse it. Brevity is therefore important and reduces the risk of annoying the court. It also reduces the possibility of including inaccuracies which may subsequently be exposed when the claimant gives evidence, thereby undermining his or her credibility. On the other hand, graphic details make a strong impression, both on the judge and the other side, revealing the strength of the claimant's case from the outset and creating a picture in the judge's mind, which the other side may well find hard to shift. A balance must be struck between the desirable aim of imposing a vivid picture upon the court from the outset and the danger associated with lengthy papers. On any approach, however, the key or critical details cannot be omitted, even if the claim is made in haste, and their omission may also undermine the claim at a later date.

Much of the detail, for example, the actual words spoken as opposed to the substance of what they mean, should appear in the witness statement rather than these particulars. It is appropriate to use the actual words if they are central to the case – for example, to make clear the threatening nature of the defendant's actions, or to establish a claim for exemplary or aggravated damages (see paras 1.148–1.167).

Note 6 – Particulars of general damages

Set out any distress, inconvenience or injury suffered (see paras 1.144–1.147). If the injunction is not granted, the inconvenience suffered will increase. The particulars of claim may subsequently be amended to plead any further losses.

Note 7 – Particulars of special damages

Here, set out the particulars of special damages, which must be pleaded, listing each item and value or cost as in the example. The basis for an award of special damages depends on whether the possessions have been either lost or damaged beyond repair, or are capable of repair. If they have been lost, the measure of damages is the value of the possessions, taking into account their condition at the time. If the possessions can be repaired, the measure of damages is the cost of repair. In a case of emergency, occupiers will often not be able to give precise details of special damages, in which case the particulars of claim should say: 'a schedule of special damages will be served in due course'. See generally paras 1.139–1.143. Alternatively, where numerous items have been damaged or removed, it will be appropriate to attach a schedule of special damages to the particulars of claim rather than plead each item in the body of the pleading. In such circumstances, the claimant should indicate that they are claiming special damages for the losses set out in attached schedule of special damages.

Note 8 – Exemplary and aggravated damages

If exemplary and/or aggravated damages are to be sought (see paras 1.148–1.167), a specific claim must be made and the facts on which the claim is based must be stated: CPR 16.4(1)(c).

Note 9 – Housing Act 1988 s27

A claimant is entitled to damages under HA 1988 ss27 and 28 only where he or she has been permanently deprived of occupation (see paras 1.168–1.191). For this reason, the cause of action is pleaded in the alternative to cover the eventuality that an injunction may be refused or proves, in practical terms, to be unenforceable.

If the occupier is reinstated into the premises, the claim under HA 1988 ss27 and 28 will have to be abandoned. If the claim proceeds for damages only, then both types of damages can be claimed, although there could only be one award under the head of damages for loss of home (see paras 1.192–1.195).

Note 10 – Interest

The claim for interest must be pleaded: CPR 16.4(2)(a). The form of words used here is that usually adopted. Interest is normally only available on special damages, not general damages (unless they are damages for personal injury) nor damages in respect of HA 1988 ss27 and 28 (see para 1.137).

Note 11 – The prayer

This part of the particulars of claim is called 'the prayer'. It contains all the elements of the relief or remedy the occupier is seeking from the court.

Note 12 – Statement of truth

The particulars of claim must contain a statement of truth: CPR PD 16 para 3.4. If the document is signed by the claimant, the standard form is: 'I believe that the facts stated in these particulars of claim are true.' A solicitor may sign the statement of truth on the claimant's behalf, in which case the statement of truth is: 'The claimant believes that the facts stated in these particulars of claim are true.'

APPLICATION NOTICE FOR INTERIM INJUNCTION
(see note 1)

IN THE COUNTY COURT SITTING AT ANYTOWN

Claim No

B E T W E E N:

(1) JANE FIELDS
(2) JOHN JONES

Claimants

-and-

WARDEN DRANE

Defendant

By an application in pending proceedings X (see note 2)

Under Statutory provision

This application raises issues under the Human Rights Act 1998 Yes/No (see note 3)

The Claimants Jane Fields and John Jones

apply to the court for an injunction order in the following terms:

That the Defendant Warden Drane

be forbidden (whether by himself or by instructing or encouraging any other person (see note 4)
   (1)   assaulting or threatening or otherwise harassing the first and/or second claimants,
   (2)   interfering with the claimants' quiet enjoyment of 16A Maxwell Square, London AT16 1AB ('the premises').

And that the Defendant:
   (3)   forthwith re-admit the first and second claimants to the premises;
   (4)   forthwith provide the first and second claimants with keys to the premises.

And that:
   (5)   this order remain in force until further order;
   (6)   costs reserved.

The grounds of this application are set out in the written evidence of Jane Fields

signed on 22 March 2017

This written evidence is served with this application

This application is to be served upon Warden Drane

This application is filed by

Leo and Nevil Solicitors
the solicitors for the Claimant
whose address for service is
242–4 Nashville Road,
Anytown AT5 9UN

Signed Leo and Nevil
Dated 22 March 2017

Notes to application notice

Note 1 – Prescribed form

This application is based on the county court prescribed form N16A
(application for injunction). Marginal notes and certain formal parts
are omitted for convenience. The prescribed form must be used.

Note 2 – Basis of application

The form requires the claimant to state whether the injunction is
sought in proceedings which have been commenced or under a specific statutory provision.

Note 3 – Human rights

Unlawful eviction may be a breach of a person's right to respect for
the home under Article 8 of the European Convention on Human
Rights (ECHR). This is only likely to be the case where the eviction is
by a social landlord who qualifies as a public authority.[87]

Note 4 – Terms of the injunction

Set out clearly the terms of both the prohibitory part of the order
sought (ie, restraining the defendant from specified actions), and
the mandatory part of the order (ie, telling the defendant what he
or she must do). The terms should specify a time within which the
defendant is to comply with the order. Here, as in most unlawful
evictions, the order is to be carried out forthwith. Costs of a without
notice application are usually reserved to the return date to allow the
defendant to make representations.

---

87 See para 1.101.

DRAFT ORDER
(see note 1)

IN THE COUNTY COURT SITTING AT ANYTOWN

Claim No

B E T W E E N

(1) JANE FIELDS
(2) JOHN JONES

Claimants

-and-

WARDEN DRANE

Defendant

If you do not obey this order you will be guilty of contempt of court and you may be sent to prison. (see note 2)

On 22 March 2017 the court considered an application by the claimants for an injunction

The Court ordered that Warden Drane (see note 3)
is forbidden whether by himself or by instructing or encouraging any other person from
  (1) assaulting or threatening or otherwise harassing the first and/or second claimants,
  (2) interfering with the claimants' quiet enjoyment of 16A Maxwell Square, London AT16 1AB ('the premises').

This order shall remain in force until the 27 March 2017 at 10 o'clock unless before then it is revoked by a further order of the court.

And it is ordered that Warden Drane shall: (see note 4)
  (3) re-admit the first and second claimants to 16A Maxwell Square, London SE16,
  (4) provide the first and second claimants with keys to 16A Maxwell Square

forthwith on service of this order.

It is further ordered that costs are reserved.

Notice of further hearing

The court will reconsider the application and whether the order should continue at a further hearing at the County Court sitting at Anytown, Belmont Road, Anytown AT12 5BW on the 27 March 2017 at 10 o'clock.

If you do not attend at the time shown the court may make an injunction order in your absence.

You are entitled to apply to the court to re-consider the order before that day.

The claimants gave an undertaking promising to pay any damages ordered by the court if it later decides that the defendant has suffered loss or damages as a result of this order. (see note 5)

Notes to draft order

Note 1 – Prescribed form

This draft order is based on the county court prescribed form N16 (interim injunctions), although marginal notes and certain formal parts are omitted for convenience. An applicant for an interim injunction should provide the court with a draft order.

Note 2 – Penal notice

This part of the order is known as the penal notice. It is included to warn the defendant(s) of the possible consequences of disobeying the order. A defendant cannot be committed for contempt of an order unless he or she knows about the possibility (see para 8.17); the normal means of ensuring this, and the best evidence of it, is to include a penal notice in the order and, therefore, it should be included in the draft order. An order can be addressed to more than one person (or one or more people and/or one or more companies or corporate bodies), but each must be served with a copy. If the defendant is a corporate body, the order can be addressed to either the company or to a suitable individual in the company: *R v Wandsworth County Court ex p Munn*.[88]

Note 3 – Restraining injunction

This is the prohibitory part of the order, ie, restraining the defendant from specified actions.

Note 4 – Mandatory injunction

This is the mandatory part of the order, ie, telling the defendant what he or she must do. The order should specify a time within which the defendant is to comply with the order. Here, as in most unlawful evictions, the order is to be carried out forthwith. Any order for an injunction must set out clearly what the defendant must or must not do: CPR PD 25A para 5.3.

---

88 (1994) 26 HLR 697, QBD.

Note 5 – Undertaking

The court has a discretion whether or not to require this undertaking from a claimant: CPR PD 25A para 5.1(1). The promise by the claimant is that he or she will pay damages if it emerges on further consideration that the injunction should not have been granted and the defendant has suffered loss in consequence. Where a claimant is publicly funded, such an undertaking may be disproportionately onerous, and if necessary it should be submitted that the claimant's financial position ought not to affect the position in regard to what is the essential justice of the case: *Allen v Jambo Holdings Ltd* [1980] 1 WLR 1252, CA. Alternatively, if the claimant has been unlawfully evicted and the court insists that such an undertaking be given, it can be argued that the undertaking should go no further than to require the claimant to pay the defendant a sum equivalent to the rent.

WITNESS STATEMENT (1)
UNLAWFUL EVICTION OF ASSURED SHORTHOLD TENANT

Witness statement on behalf of the claimants
Witness: J Fields
First Statement
Exhibits: JF1, JF2
Date: 22 March 2017
(see note 1)

IN THE COUNTY COURT SITTING AT ANYTOWN

Claim No

BETWEEN

(1) JANE FIELDS
(2) JOHN JONES

Claimants

-and-

WARDEN DRANE

Defendant

WITNESS STATEMENT OF JANE FIELDS

(see note 2)

I JANE FIELDS, unemployed, of 16A Maxwell Square, London AT16 1AB, say as follows:

1. I am the first claimant and make this statement in support of the application for an interim injunction to enable us to move back into our home. The facts stated in this witness statement are made from my own knowledge, unless indicated. (see notes 3 & 4)

2. I and my partner, the second claimant, have been the joint tenants of the above property since 19 January 2016. The property is a self-contained, one-bedroom, basement flat. We responded to an advertisement online and met the defendant, who is our landlord. We agreed to take the flat for a fixed term of 12 months and to move in the following Wednesday. This was 19 January 2016. The rent was agreed to be £700 per month, payable in advance. We were provided with a written tenancy agreement. I refer to a true copy of the tenancy agreement marked 'JF1'.

3. At the start of the tenancy we were able to pay the rent with no difficulties. In November 2016, however, I lost my job. The second claimant is a builder who works on short-term contracts. In January 2017, he had serious cash-flow problems and it was difficult for us to pay the rent. (see note 5)

4. During the last week of January 2017, the defendant telephoned and told us that we would have to be out of the property as our tenancy had expired and we were no longer paying the rent. I was very disappointed and thought that we could not be made to leave straightaway.

5. I spoke to a former work colleague and from our conversation it appeared that we were now periodic assured shorthold tenants and that the defendant would have to serve a section 21, Housing Act 1988 notice and then get a court order if he wanted us to leave. On 25 January 2017, I telephoned the defendant to tell him that we would not be leaving and that it was our legal right to stay in the flat. He became extremely angry and shouted and swore at me. He told me he was coming round to sort the matter out.

6. The defendant came round to the flat that evening at about 8pm. The second claimant was out and I was alone and nervous about letting him in. When he arrived, he was perfectly polite and apologised for sounding so angry over the telephone. I let him in and he started to talk about how he really needed the rent because he had a few debts to pay. I explained to him that we were also having financial difficulties but that we hoped to pay the arrears soon. He then suddenly flew into a rage and started swearing. He said that that was not good enough and that he 'knew people'. During the course of his shouting and swearing, he repeated this a number of times in a threatening manner. I asked him to leave. He replied that he would leave when he wanted to as it was his flat. I became very nervous, but eventually he left and slammed the door behind him.

7. We were worried about what our rights were, so we decided to check the legal position. I went to a solicitor who told us that we were assured shorthold tenants and that the defendant needed a court order to evict us. She said that she would write a letter to the defendant informing him of our rights. I refer to the true copy of the letter dated 26 January 2017 marked 'JF2'.

8. On 28 January 2017, the defendant telephoned me. He was in a rage and told me in no uncertain terms what my solicitor could do with her letters. He said that he did not care what the law was, he needed the rent and he already had a tenant lined up who would be able to pay in a proper manner. I was very frightened by the call.

9. After that occasion, we received a number of very strange telephone calls, sometimes very late at night. On the first occasion, someone who I am sure was the defendant, because his number appeared on my phone, said 'As you sow, so shall you reap'. The caller then just put the telephone down. On the other occasions, the caller did not say anything, there was just silence. I am sure that these calls were made by the defendant because his number appeared on my phone on each occasion. These calls happened about every three days during February and the first two week of March. They were very inconvenient because they often woke us up in the early hours of the morning, but we also found them very disturbing.

10. On 14 March 2017, a man came round to the flat. He looked through the windows and generally looked over the outside. I went out and asked him what he was doing. He was perfectly friendly and said that he hoped that I did not mind but he was moving in soon. From our conversation, it became clear that the defendant had told him we were going on 20 March 2017. (see note 6)

11. We were really worried about what might happen on 20 March and both stayed in. At about midday, the defendant came round to the flat. Two men were with him. He banged on the door and demanded to be let in. We shouted through the door and asked him to go away. He said that we 'should not be stupid' and told us we had to be out. The two men with him then broke down the front door. The defendant told us to get out and the two men started to pile our belongings into black bin liners. By this stage, I was in tears. The second claimant tried to stop the two men. One of them punched him in the face. We were very scared and went to the local police station.

12. About an hour later, we returned with a police officer but found that the locks to the front door of the flat had been changed and we could not get in. The police officer told us to see our solicitor. When we saw our solicitor later that afternoon, she tried to telephone the defendant but could not get any reply. Most of our belongings were piled outside the door but it now appears that our television set, our laptop computer and my jewellery are missing.

13. The second claimant's face was hurting very badly and was swelling up alarmingly so we decided to go to the hospital. The hospital treated the bruise which was now very apparent and prescribed some strong painkillers. We had to wait a long time at the hospital and by the time we had got the prescription it was too late to see our solicitor.

14. Our application for an injunction is being made without giving notice to the defendant because we spent last night on a friend's floor and have nowhere to sleep tonight. If we are not re-admitted to the flat we will be street homeless. (see note 7)

15. I therefore ask that the court order grant an order requiring Mr Drane to re-admit us to the flat as soon as possible. Given the circumstances of the eviction, I would also ask that the court grant the orders we seek restraining the defendant from further unlawful conduct.

I believe that the facts stated in this witness statement are true. (see note 8)

Signed: *Jane Fields*

Dated: 22 March 2017

WITNESS STATEMENT (2)
TENANCY DEPOSIT

Witness statement on behalf of the claimant
Witness: A Smith
First Statement
Exhibits: AS1–AS3
Date: 30 March 2017

(see note 1)

IN THE COUNTY COURT SITTING AT ANYTOWN

Claim No

B E T W E E N

ALAN SMITH

Claimant

-and-

PAUL STEWART

Defendant

WITNESS STATEMENT OF ALAN SMITH

(see note 2)

I ALAN SMITH, retired, of 29 Acacia Road, Anytown, London AT11 9LF, say as follows:

1. I am the first claimant and make this statement in support of my claim for the return of a tenancy deposit I paid to my former landlord and for a statutory penalty due to my former landlord's failure to protect the deposit in a deposit scheme. The facts stated in this witness statement are made from my own knowledge, unless indicated. (see notes 3 & 4)

2. I was the tenant of a property at 17 Cherry Tree Lane, Anytown, from 15 April 2015. I saw an advert for the property in a newsagent's window in late March or early April 2015. I called the defendant, who was advertising the property, and we arranged to meet. On or around 8 April 2015, I met the defendant at the property. I explained that I was interested in taking a tenancy of the property. He told me that the rent would be £1,000 per month and that he needed a deposit of £3,000. He also said that there was a lot of interest in the property and so if I wanted the tenancy I would need to pay the deposit very soon.

3. As I was quite keen to move out from my previous property, I reluctantly agreed, even though I though that the deposit was a lot of money. The defendant gave me his bank details. The next day, I transferred £4,000 to his account, which was to cover the first month's rent and the deposit.

I refer to a copy of my bank statement for April 2015, which shows the transfer of £4,000, marked '**AS1**'.

4. The defendant then provided me with a tenancy agreement, which was headed 'Assured Shorthold Tenancy Agreement'. I refer to a true copy of the tenancy agreement marked '**AS2**'. I did ask the defendant on a couple of occasions for a receipt for my payment. He kept telling me that I did not need to worry and that I could trust him. Eventually I gave up asking.

5. The property was fine, but during the summer of 2016 I decided I wanted to move somewhere else. I discussed it with the defendant and we agreed that my tenancy would end on 12 September 2016, and I then moved out on that day.

6. Before I moved out, I asked the defendant when he would return the deposit. He told me that he would sort it out once he had inspected the property.

7. I did not hear from the defendant, so by the end of the month, I was a bit concerned. I wrote to him on 30 September, asking for the money back and giving him my bank account details so that he could pay it. I refer to a copy of this letter, which is marked '**AS3**'.

8. The defendant did not respond until 23 November, when he rung me up and said 'you never paid me no deposit, you liar'. I told him that I had done and that he knew that I had. He then said 'well, where's the receipt, you mug?' and hung up.

9. I was quite put off by this and gave up on the money for a while. A friend told me that I should speak to a solicitor about it, which I did earlier this year. My solicitor advised me that the defendant should have protected this deposit within a statutory scheme. As far as I am aware the defendant did not protect the £3,000 with a scheme.

10. I am also advised that the defendant should have provided me with some prescribed information about the deposit. I am absolutely certain that he did not do this. I kept all of my paperwork about that tenancy in a folder and there is nothing in there about protecting the deposit.

I believe that the facts stated in this witness statement are true. (see note 8)

Signed: *Alan Smith*

Dated: 30 March 2017

Notes to witness statements

Note 1

The top right-hand corner of the witness statement must set out five matters (CPR PD 32 para 17.2): a) the party on whose behalf the witness statement is made; b) the initials and surname of the witness;

c) the number of the statement in relation to the witness, ie whether the first, second, third, etc; d) identifying initials and number of each exhibit referred to; and e) the date the statement was made.

Note 2

The same remarks on the title apply as under the particulars of claim. A statement may be made by a party or by a witness. Although it is unusual and often impractical, given time constraints, to put in more than one statement on an application for a without notice interim injunction, there is no limit on the number of statements.

Note 3

The witness statement must indicate which of the statements in it are made from the witness's own knowledge and which are matters of information or belief: CPR PD 32 para 18.2(1). The source for any matters of information or belief must also be indicated: CPR PD 32 para 18.2(2). This means that the witness does not have to have had direct experience of everything in the statement. It is perfectly acceptable to include evidence which the witness has heard from other sources, although this should be made clear in the statement, for example: 'I was told by X that ...'.

Note 4

Here, set out the evidence in a sequence of logical statements, in numbered paragraphs, using a new paragraph for each new matter: CPR PD 32 para 19.1–19.2. If the witness is the claimant or other occupier then it is best to set out the details of occupation in the early part of the statement.

If the claimant has a written agreement or any other evidence of the arrangement – for example, a rent book or housing benefit statements – this should be produced as an exhibit to the witness statement, as in the example. The number of the exhibit includes the initials of the person making the witness statement. Each new exhibit is likewise known by the initials of the person making the witness statement and its number, ie, a new number in sequence for each new exhibit. Other relevant exhibits may include letters from the landlord telling the occupier to get out, notes found on doors, notices to quit and so on. Any document can be produced. Each reference to an exhibit should be in bold type: CPR PD 32 para 19.1(7).

The comments made in relation to the particulars of claim on how much detail to include apply here with the same reservations and qualifications. Some people draft extremely lengthy particulars of claim for their clients and short witness statements swearing that the details in the particulars of claim are true. Others draft extremely short particulars of claim and fill out the whole of the detail in the witness statement. There is no single correct method. A balance must be sought so as not to put off the judge or provide too much room for inconsistency but on the other hand to show that there is a strong case and make an impact on the court.

Note 5

When applying for an interim injunction, it is important always to include any facts which may militate against the claimant's case – for example, rent arrears or any occasions when the occupier behaved in such a way as to give the landlord reason for complaint. This applies in particular to without notice applications where the court is asked to take the claimant's case on trust. In any event, it is tactically better to anticipate the defendant's case than to have to respond to allegations at a later date.

Note 6

The conversation with the stranger is hearsay evidence but such evidence may be included (see note 2). Note that this information supports any claim for exemplary damages.

Note 7

Applications for without notice injunctions will only be considered if there is a good reason for not giving notice: CPR 25.3(1). The urgency of the situation or the danger to the occupier will justify an order being made in the absence of the defendant. The statement should therefore include a factual explanation of these matters. In the absence of such an explanation, the court will adjourn the application to allow notice to be given to the defendant.

Note 8

A witness statement must be verified by a statement of truth: CPR PD 32 para 20.1. The form of statement used here is that required by CPR PD 32 para 20.2.

Criminal proceedings

Introduction

9.1 This chapter provides an outline of criminal procedure so far as relevant to the offences discussed in the previous chapters. It is primarily aimed at those advisers who are unfamiliar with the criminal court process and is not intended to be a comprehensive guide.

9.2 The most serious criminal offences ('indictable offences') must be heard by a Crown Court, where trial is by jury. Less serious cases ('summary offences') may only be heard by a magistrates' court. There are other offences ('either way offences') which may be dealt with by either court: the magistrates' court may decide that trial on indictment is more suitable[1] and the defendant has a right to elect it.[2]

9.3 Unlawful eviction and harassment under the Protection from Eviction Act (PEA) 1977 are either way offences, as are putting another in fear of violence and breach of a restraining order or an injunction under the Protection from Harassment Act (PHA) 1997. The other offences discussed in this book are summary offences.

Who may prosecute?

9.4 As a general rule, there is no restriction on who may institute criminal proceedings.[3] In practice, however, a magistrates' court is unlikely to issue proceedings unless the person has a sufficient interest in the offence. In general, therefore, prosecutions are usually taken by the police, the victim or another body empowered to take proceedings including a local authority, whether because a power to prosecute is statutorily conferred or because it is considered to have an interest (see para 9.8 onwards).

The police

9.5 Although the police are commonly thought of as responsible for enforcing the totality of the criminal law, they have a wide discretion

---

1 Based, among other things, on possible sentence and views of prosecution and defence (Magistrates' Courts Act (MCA) 1980 s19).

2 Even if the magistrates decide that summary trial is more suitable, the defendant may still elect to be tried on indictment (MCA 1980 s20) although if the magistrates decide that trial on indictment is more suitable, the defendant cannot elect summary trial (s21).

3 They can be started by 'any person': Prosecution of Offences Act (POA) 1985 s6.

as to both the investigation and prosecution[4] of criminal offences. The exercise of this discretion varies significantly between police areas, reflecting different local priorities.

9.6   The police rarely, if ever, take action in relation to offences under PEA 1977, which, although criminal, tend to be perceived as disputes between landlords and occupiers and therefore more suitable for civil proceedings. That is not to say that the police should not be encouraged to bring criminal proceedings; they are, however, unlikely to participate beyond keeping opposing parties apart, eg where there is a risk of a breach of the peace, or worse.[5]

The victim

9.7   It is always open to a victim of any crime to take a private prosecution. This is not, however, recommended for a number of reasons.[6]

Local authorities

9.8   Certain local authorities[7] are authorised to institute criminal proceedings for harassment or unlawful eviction under PEA 1977.[8]

9.9   Local authorities also have the power, under Local Government Act (LGA) 1972 s222, to bring prosecutions if they 'consider it expedient for the promotion or protection of the inhabitants of their area'. This power therefore allows authorities to bring prosecutions, despite having no express power to do so, against persons for using violence to enter premises under the Criminal Law Act (CLA) 1977 or any offence created by PHA 1997 or Criminal Justice and Police Act (CJPA) 2001 s42A.

---

4   All police prosecutions in England and Wales are now conducted by the Crown Prosecution Service: POA 1985 ss1 and 3.

5   In *Cowan v Chief Constable of Avon and Somerset* [2001] EWCA Civ 1699, [2002] HLR 44, the Court of Appeal held that the police did not owe a tenant a duty of care to prevent his unlawful eviction.

6   In particular: public funding is not available to prosecute; the victim must prove the case beyond reasonable doubt; if the landlord is found guilty, any penalty may be low; and, although the court can award compensation, such an award is unlikely to compensate the victim for all his or her losses.

7   District councils, London borough councils, Welsh county councils, Welsh county boroughs, the Common Council of the City of London and the Council of the Isles of Scilly: PEA 1977 s6. A unitary authority which is a county council has the powers of a district council: Local Government Changes for England Regulations 1994 SI No 867 reg 5(7).

8   PEA 1977 s6.

9.10   It will be rare that an authority will not be able to justify prosecuting under LGA 1972 s222, particularly if the police have declined to take action.[9]

9.11   Local housing authorities are under a duty to take reasonable steps to ensure that accommodation does not cease to be available for occupation by a person who has become unintentionally threatened with homelessness.[10] As homelessness may often be the result of unlawful eviction or harassment, the swift institution of criminal proceedings by a local authority may comprise exactly the reasonable steps or appropriate assistance which are needed.

9.12   Although authorities possess the legal powers to investigate and prosecute alleged incidents, they are not under a duty to do so.[11]

9.13   In many cities and large towns, however, where unlawful eviction and harassment tend to be more prevalent, councils employ officers (commonly called 'harassment' or 'tenancy relations officers'), whose job is to deal with the problem.

9.14   Those councils which do treat these incidents seriously nonetheless only prosecute in a small percentage of cases. Reasons for this include victims' reluctance to give evidence against their landlords; internal council procedures; and the hesitation of many local authority legal departments to issue proceedings unless certain of a conviction.

9.15   Regardless of whether civil proceedings are also to be taken, it is almost invariably advisable to contact the relevant official or department and invite the local authority to investigate and prosecute.

Starting proceedings

9.16   Criminal proceedings must be commenced in the magistrates' court for the area in which the offence is alleged to have been committed.

---

9   Where the police are willing to act, it might be more difficult to argue that it was 'expedient' for the authority to prosecute but it is certainly not impossible or implausible.

10   Housing Act (HA) 1996 s195(2); Housing (Wales) Act (H(W)A) 2014 s66. A person is threatened with homelessness if 'it is likely that he will become homeless within 28 days': HA 1996 s175(4) (this will increase to 56 days one the Homelessness Reduction Act 2017 is brought into force). The period is 56 days in Wales: HWA 2014 s55(4).

11   Advice to local authorities on these issues is set out in DoE Circular 3/89 (Housing Act 1988: Protection of Residential Occupiers), reproduced in *Encyclopaedia of Housing Law and Practice*, Part IV, para 4-1651 (Sweet & Maxwell).

This applies whether or not the offence will eventually be tried in that court or the Crown Court.

9.17   A person accused of an offence may be brought before a court in one of three ways: by charge, which is only available to the police; by summons; or by warrant. The last two methods can be used whoever prosecutes.

By charge

9.18   This is how the police formally accuse a person of an offence and require him or her to attend court. They are not required to obtain the prior approval of the court to start proceedings.

By summons

9.19   An 'information' must be laid before a magistrate (or more commonly a magistrates' court clerk) by the prosecutor.[12] It must give:

- details of both the prosecutor and the accused;
- brief particulars of the alleged offence; and
- if the alleged offence is contrary to statute, details of that provision.[13]

The information can be provided orally or in writing, but need not be under oath.[14]

9.20   The decision to issue a summons is judicial, not merely administrative. The magistrate or clerk issuing the summons must be satisfied that the information alleges an offence known to the law, that it has been served within any time limits, that the court has jurisdiction and that the prosecutor has the authority to lay the information. There is, however, no requirement that the magistrate or clerk should inquire into whether there is a prima facie case or examine the evidence upon which the allegation is based.[15] There is a discretion to refuse to issue a summons, but this may only be exercised if there is a compelling reason to do so.[16]

---

12 An officer, member or employee of the prosecutor may serve the information: Criminal Procedure Rules (Crim PR) 46.1(2)(a).

13 Crim PR 7.3(1).

14 Crim PR 7.2(1).

15 *R v Gateshead Justices ex p Tesco Stores Ltd* [1981] QB 470, CA.

16 There is a discretion to refuse to issue a summons if the magistrate or court clerk believes that the application is frivolous, vexatious or an abuse of process: *R v Bros* (1901) 66 JP 54, QBD.

9.21   The summons is usually sent to the accused by post, to an address where it is reasonably believed that he or she will receive it,[17] requiring attendance at the magistrates' court on a given date to answer the accusation. This procedure is available for the prosecution of any offence and is the most common way for harassment and unlawful eviction proceedings to be commenced.

By warrant

9.22   Wherever there is jurisdiction to issue a summons, a magistrate may instead issue a warrant for the arrest of the person named in the information provided the information is in writing and the offence is either indictable or is punishable with a sentence of imprisonment, or if the defendant's address is not sufficiently established for a summons to be served on him or her.[18]

9.23   The warrant directs the police to bring the person before the court as soon as possible when the court may either hear the matter or adjourn the case. The magistrate has a power to 'back the warrant for bail', in which case, having been arrested, the accused will be released by the police to attend court on a particular date.[19]

9.24   Harassment and unlawful eviction are offences which carry a sentence of imprisonment,[20] as does an offence for harassment of a person in his or her home,[21] any offence under PHA 1997,[22] violent entry to premises[23] and breaching a banning order.[24] Warrants can, accordingly, be issued in respect of these offences.

9.25   The advantage of using the warrant procedure is that the police are obliged to arrest the accused, even if he or she is subsequently released on bail.

17 Crim PR 4.4(1), (2)(a). Service may also be effected by leaving it at this address or personally: Crim PR 4.3(1)(a).
18 MCA 1980 s1(1), (3), (4).
19 MCA 1980 s117.
20 Up to six months in a magistrates' court and two years in the Crown Court: PEA 1977 s1(4).
21 Up to six months: CJPA 2001 s42A(4).
22 See chapter 2.
23 Up to six months: CLA 1977 s6(5).
24 Up to six months: Housing and Planning Act (HPA) 2016 s21(2), (6).

The hearing

9.26 If the defendant pleads not guilty, the case is unlikely to be tried at the first hearing and will be adjourned to another date. It may be adjourned more than once because of a shortage of time, or because of the absence of witnesses.

9.27 At the trial, the prosecution must prove the case on the criminal standard of proof (ie, 'beyond reasonable doubt')[25] and is responsible for putting the evidence before the court. This can include any witnesses, such as police officers, local authority officials or an adviser who attempted to persuade the landlord to readmit the occupier or desist from harassing him or her. The occupier's evidence is likely to be of prime importance.

Compensation

9.28 On conviction, the court can order the defendant to pay compensation to the victim for 'personal injury, loss or damage resulting from [an] offence'.[26]

9.29 The power has been described[27] as 'a convenient and rapid means of avoiding the expense of resort to civil litigation when the criminal clearly has means that would enable the compensation to be paid'. Magistrates' courts are encouraged to order compensation wherever possible. In deciding whether to make an award, justices should not have regard to the availability of other sources of compensation, such as civil litigation or the Criminal Injuries Compensation scheme.[28]

9.30 When making a compensation order, the court may order such amount as it considers appropriate having regard to any evidence and any representations made by the offender or prosecutor. The court must, however, have regard to the means of the person against whom the order is to be made.[29] Where the offender is of limited means, the amount of compensation may need to be reduced or make provision for the offender to pay the total amount over a period of up to three

---

25 *Woolmington v DPP* [1935] AC 462, HL. Commonly the standard of proof is now expressed to be whether justices are sure that the defendant is guilty.
26 Powers of Criminal Courts (Sentencing) Act (PCC(S)A) 2000 s130(1).
27 Scarman LJ in *R v Inwood* (1974) 60 Cr App 70, 73, CA, of the previous provisions of the Powers of Criminal Courts Act 1973 s35.
28 Magistrates' Courts Sentencing Guidelines (July 2016) ('Sentencing Guidelines'), para 4, p155.
29 Sentencing Guidelines para 5 p155; *R v Daly* [1974] 1 WLR 133, CA.

years.[30] Where the court considers it appropriate both to impose a fine and to make a compensation order, but the defendant has insufficient means to pay both, the compensation order should be made in preference to the fine.[31]

9.31   In the magistrates' court, there is no longer a statutory limit on the amount of compensation that may be imposed in respect of offences for an offender aged 18 or over.[32] The Magistrates' Courts Sentencing Guidelines ('Sentencing Guidelines') afford general guidance as to the amount to be awarded for certain injuries.[33] There is also no limit in the Crown Court.

9.32   In *Bond v Chief Constable of Kent*,[34] it was held that anxiety and distress directly caused by the defendant's offence could be either 'personal injury' or 'damage' for the purposes of a compensation order. The Sentencing Guidelines provide that a court may award financial loss sustained as a result of the offence and pain and suffering caused by the injury (including terror, shock or distress) and any loss of facility.[35]

9.33   Compensation is not restricted to personal injury and may therefore also be suitable for losses such as the cost of emergency accommodation or the value of damaged or destroyed belongings. Any award must, however, be based on evidence before the court,[36] which may include medical evidence, the victim's age and other personal circumstances.[37] The victim should be advised to bring to court supporting evidence, such as photographs and bills for repairs to damaged goods or for temporary accommodation, as appropriate. It is not the role of a criminal court, however, to embark on a complex inquiry into the scale of the loss if it is not obvious from the evidence before it. Compensation orders should only be made in a 'simple [and] straightforward case where the amount of compensation can be readily and easily ascertained'.[38] If the loss is difficult to ascertain, consideration should nonetheless be given to making a compensation order for an amount representing the agreed or likely

---

30 Sentencing Guidelines para 9 p155.
31 PCC(S)A 2000 s130(12).
32 PCC(S)A 2000 s131(1); Sentencing Guidelines para 2 p155.
33 For example, the suggested award for a bruise is £100 while for a fractured arm it is £1,500.
34 [1983] 1 WLR 40, QBD.
35 Sentencing Guidelines para 8 p155.
36 *R v Horsham Justices ex p Richards* [1985] 1 WLR 986, CA.
37 Sentencing Guidelines para 8 p155.
38 *R v Donovan* (1981) 3 Cr App R (S) 192, CA.

loss.[39] In most cases, however, the civil court is likely to be far better placed to award a realistic and substantial sum for the inconvenience suffered, especially as the means of the offender will be irrelevant and the civil court has the power to award exemplary and aggravated damages.

9.34   Regardless of whether the prosecutor is an occupier, the police or a local authority,[40] compensation may still be claimed on behalf of the injured party.[41]

9.35   If compensation is awarded, it does not bar the victim from taking civil proceedings, but any amount recovered pursuant to an award by a criminal court will be deducted from any damages subsequently awarded in civil proceedings. Any compensation awarded by the criminal court that is not recovered by the victim will, however, not be deducted.[42]

39 Sentencing Guidelines para 7 p155.
40 It is important for authorities bringing prosecutions to consult the victim about compensation and to remember that his or her role in the process is not merely as a witness.
41 In addition, a magistrates' court may, of its own volition and after considering any evidence and representations made to it, make any order it considers appropriate: PCC(S)A 2000 s130(1) and (4).
42 PCC(S)A 2000 s134(2).

APPENDICES

Examples of damages awarded

A.1 The following cases illustrate the amount of general, aggravated and exemplary damages which the courts have awarded. It is important to stress that they are only illustrations, not in any sense 'precedents', because the facts will always vary from case to case.

A.2 Cases which solely concern the amount of statutory damages under HA 1988 s28 are not recorded as they turn on the principles set out in paras 1.168–1.195 and expert evidence, so that the actual amount awarded in one case is irrelevant to another.

Court of Appeal

Devonshire and Smith v Jenkins (1978) 28 April, unreported, CA

A.3 The claimant tenants were subjected to severe harassment by their landlord. The harassment included excessive and deliberate noise (from a record player left on until 3am), forcible entry, pressure to leave, abusive language and physical assault. The landlord breached an undertaking to the court to stop the harassment. In the magistrates' court, the landlord was convicted of 16 counts of harassment under the Protection from Eviction Act (PEA) 1977. He was fined £1,200. In the county court, the landlord was ordered to pay the first claimant: a) £1,000 aggravated damages; and b) £500 exemplary damages. He was also ordered to pay the second claimant: a) £750 aggravated damages; and b) £1,500 exemplary damages.

The landlord appealed to the Court of Appeal. The court held that this was a case in which exemplary damages could be awarded. Ormrod LJ observed that for five months the landlord had made the tenants' lives 'hell'. Nevertheless, the court held that when the fine was taken into account, the total amount which the landlord was required to pay was excessive. The court increased the awards of aggravated damages to £1,250 for the first claimant and £1,000 for the second claimant, but made no award for exemplary damages.

Guppys (Bridport) Ltd v Brookling (1983) 14 HLR 1, CA

A.4   The defendants were tenants of bedsitting-rooms in a house. They were elderly men who had lived in the house since the early 1970s. The claimant company bought the house knowing that it was occupied by approximately 16 people. The company intended to convert it into seven self-contained flats, which the present occupiers could not afford. The company served notices to quit. All except three of the occupiers left. Possession proceedings were commenced against the defendants. During this period, building operations and works of reconstruction were started in the premises. The works caused serious disruption to the tenants. They brought proceedings which resulted in the company undertaking not to disconnect or discontinue the supply of electricity and water or the sanitary and washing facilities to the premises. Nonetheless, the sanitary and washing facilities were removed or discontinued by preventing access to them and the electricity supply was disconnected. For a period of six months, the company showed some restraint. Before the hearing of the action, however, while its undertaking to the court was still in force, it executed works in contravention of the undertaking. In view of the conditions in the property, in October 1981 the occupiers were forced out and were found alternative accommodation by the local authority, following which demolition work on their rooms was begun. In November 1981, the occupiers sought and obtained orders preventing further works on the building until after the action was heard. They also added counterclaims to their defences, including a claim for exemplary damages.

At the county court, the judge awarded general damages of £1,000, to include exemplary damages, in addition to agreed special damages. The company appealed. The Court of Appeal held that the award of £1,000 was not excessive given that the company's obvious motive was to make profit and its breach of undertaking.

McMillan v Singh (1985) 17 HLR 120, CA

A.5   From 1979, the claimant was the tenant of a bedsitting-room. The rent for the room was £16 per week. The defendant landlord realised that he could re-let the room at £26 per week. He put the tenant's belongings out of the room. When the tenant returned to his room, he found that all his belongings had disappeared. He bought a camp bed and stayed in the room overnight. The next day, when he met the landlord, the landlord threatened him and threw the camp bed out of the house. At the trial of the action, the county court judge found that the landlord had taken advantage of the tenant's absence to obtain an increase of £10 per week rent. He was invited to make an award of exemplary damages, but declined to do so on the ground that the tenant had been in arrears from time to time, and it would be inequitable to award them.

The Court of Appeal allowed an appeal, holding that the arrears were irrelevant to an award of exemplary damages. The correct approach to the assessment of damages was to quantify (where appropriate) damage to property or person, any aggravated damages for damage to feelings, and only then exemplary damages. The Court of Appeal assessed damages: a) £250 aggravated damages; and b) £250 exemplary damages.

Millington v Duffy (1985) 17 HLR 232, CA

A.6 The claimant was the tenant of a bedsitting-room which he had rented for 15 years. In 1982, his rent was increased from £6.25 per week to £7.75 per week. At that time he was 66 years old. His landlord accused him of soiling the communal lavatory and demanded that he clean it. The tenant denied responsibility and was told to leave. The landlord spat at the tenant and entered the room and removed all his belongings. The landlord re-let the room at £17.20 per week. The tenant had nowhere to take his belongings. For a few weeks he slept with a friend, after which he slept rough until accommodation was found for him by the local authority.

At trial, the tenant was awarded: a) £119.50 special damages for lost possessions; and b) £150 general damages for distress and inconvenience. The tenant appealed against the amount of general damages and against the refusal of an order for costs. The Court of Appeal held that the award of £150 for distress and inconvenience was so low as to be plainly wrong, and a sum of £500 was substituted.

Ramdath v Daly (1993) 25 HLR 273, CA

A.7 The claimant was the tenant of the first defendant. The second defendant (the landlord's son) managed the premises. The son demanded a rent increase from £40 per week to £100 per week. The claimant refused to pay. On 14 August 1991, he returned home to find that the locks had been changed and that some of his possessions had been removed. Further incidents occurred during August with the son orally abusing the claimant. On 19 September, the claimant felt safe to return but found that many of his belongings had gone missing.

At trial, the judge awarded against the landlord: a) £2,000 general damages; b) £510 special damages; and c) £1,000 exemplary damages. The judge awarded against the son: a) £1,250 general damages (including a sum of aggravated damages); b) £2,674 special damages; and c) £2,500 exemplary damages.

On appeal, the award of exemplary damages was upheld against the landlord, but not against his son as there was insufficient evidence that the son was closely concerning himself with his father's interests and he had not sought to make any money out of his wrongdoing. The court refused to hold that the award should stand in the alternative as aggravated damages, as these had already been included in the award of general damages. The Court of Appeal found that neither award of general damages was excessive.

Francis v Brown (1997) 30 HLR 143, CA

A.8   The claimant was a tenant. The first defendant was her landlord and the second defendant was the landlord's daughter. The defendants unlawfully evicted the claimant, who brought proceedings for damages against them. The first defendant wanted vacant possession to sell it to the daughter. The judge awarded £40,000 damages against the second defendant under Housing Act (HA) 1988 s28. He also awarded £40,000 against the first defendant, expressed to be for aggravated damages. The judge indicated that if he had not awarded HA 1988 s28 damages against the second defendant, he would have awarded the same sum against her in aggravated damages. The judge also awarded £1,500 special damages and £1,000 expressed to be for exemplary damages against both defendants. The second defendant appealed to the Court of Appeal.

At the hearing, it was conceded that the judge had confused aggravated damages with exemplary damages, and that the award for aggravated damages should be treated as for exemplary damages and vice versa. The award for HA 1988 s28 damages against the second defendant was set aside because she had no rights in the property. Nor, as the second defendant had no intention to profit from the eviction, could an award for exemplary damages be made against her. As an award for exemplary damages against joint tortfeasors should be the lowest for which any of the defendants could be liable, nor could any award be made for exemplary damages against the first defendant. In any event, even if an award of exemplary damages had been appropriate, £40,000 was clearly excessive.

King v Jackson (1997) 30 HLR 541, CA

A.9 The claimant was the assured shorthold tenant of a flat let to her by the defendant landlord. The tenant gave the landlord four weeks' notice to quit and promised to move out. The landlord arranged for another tenant to move in and unlawfully evicted the tenant six days before the day on which she had promised to leave. The tenant was awarded £11,000 under HA 1988 s28. The judge held that if statutory damages were not appropriate, he would have made an award of £1,500 general damages. The landlord appealed to the Court of Appeal.

The appeal was allowed. The claimant was not entitled to significant statutory damages as she had only had a very limited right to remain in the property at the date of the eviction, with only six days of her tenancy remaining. An award for £1,500 general damages was substituted.

High Court

Islam v Yap and others [2009] EWHC 3606 (QB)

A.10 The claimant was the non-secure tenant of Redbridge LBC. Redbridge let the property from a company who let the property from the defendant freeholder. Redbridge served the tenant with a notice to quit, but did not issue a claim for possession. The defendant decided to sell the property. His agent found a willing buyer and a sale price was agreed on condition that the property was obtained with vacant possession. The defendant's agent asked the tenant to leave the property. She agreed to leave provided she could find alternative accommodation. During the next few weeks, however, the tenant was unable to do so. The defendant's agent telephoned the tenant to tell her that the locks would be changed the following day, to forget about calling the police and that he would squat in the property until she left. His tone was threatening. The defendant's agent then contacted the defendant to tell him that he was going to change the locks. The defendant did not discourage him. The following day, the agent attended the property and changed the locks. He sat in the property for a few hours before the tenant agreed to leave. The tenant had nowhere else to go and was forced to leave her possessions in the property.

The tenant was awarded: a) £36 per day general damages from the date of her eviction to the order of the court, assessed as being the rental rate that was chargeable during that time from the defendant;

b) £3,000 aggravated damages from the defendant's agent; and c) £5,000 exemplary damages against the defendant.

Lee v Lasrado [2013] EWHC 2616 (QB)

A.11   The claimant was the assured shorthold tenant of a room in a house. She claimed that she had been harassed by the defendant landlord for a number of weeks, which had eventually led to the defendant changing the locks and evicting her. The defendant subsequently failed to comply with an injunction requiring her re-entry and he was committed for contempt of court. The claimant was homeless for 84 days before she obtained accommodation in a hostel.

The High Court, on an appeal by the defendant, upheld the county court award for damages comprising: a) general damages of £200 per day for the 84 days spent away from the premises; b) general damages of £1,000 for harassment; c) aggravated damages of £1,500; and d) exemplary damages of £1,500.

Choudhury v Garcia [2013] EWHC 3283 (QB)

A.12   The defendant let a room in a house to the claimant. The defendant lived in the same house. Neighbours began to place rubbish in the garden and against the window, which the defendant did not prevent. The defendant obtained a possession order. The claimant appealed against the order and obtained a stay on execution of the order but the defendant evicted him during the stay.

The High Court, on appeals by both parties, upheld the county court award for damages comprising: a) general damages of £7,000 for the unlawful eviction; b) exemplary damages of £5,000; and c) general damages of £1,800 for harassment.

Unlawful eviction and harassment county court cases[1] since 2007[2]

Diallo v Brosnan January 2007 Legal Action 21, Willesden County Court, DJ Morris

A.13   The claimant was an assured shorthold tenant of a room. His landlord was the assured shorthold tenant of the defendant. The

---

1   The court and the judge are identified where known.
2   See previous editions for earlier cases.

defendant attended the property and discovered that the tenant's landlord was no longer living at the property. The tenant and the defendant entered into a new oral tenancy agreement. The tenant paid rent to the defendant for several months, but ceased paying rent after the defendant refused to provide him with a written tenancy agreement which meant that he was unable to obtain housing benefit. Three weeks after the tenant stopped paying rent, he returned to the property to find that the locks had been changed. He broke back in. The following morning, the defendant attended the property with another man and threatened the tenant with a knife before forcibly evicting him. The tenant spent three nights at his partner's flat and one night sleeping in a car. The tenant was subsequently re-admitted to the property after an injunction was obtained.

The tenant was awarded: a) £1,000 general damages; and b) £1,000 'exemplary' (aggravated) damages for the use of a knife during the eviction.

Daramy v Streeks June 2007 *Legal Action* 37, Lambeth County Court, HHJ Crawford Lindsay

A.14   The claimant was an assured shorthold tenant. He lost his job and was unable to pay his rent. After he had accrued two months of arrears, the defendant landlord began to harass him for the rent and assaulted his wife. The defendant obtained a possession order, but evicted the tenant without a warrant and sold his belongings to recover the rent he was owed.

The tenant was awarded: a) £1,500 general damages for the harassment; b) £2,500 general damages for the eviction and the time spent out of the property; and c) £1,250 aggravated damages.

Naveed v Raja July 2007 *Legal Action* 32, Willesden County Court, HHJ Copley

A.15   The claimant was an assured shorthold tenant. After he was injured in a car accident, he was unable to work and therefore had no means of paying his rent. The tenant asked the defendant landlord for a written tenancy argument so that he could apply for housing benefit. The defendant refused and served him with a HA 1988 s21 notice. On the day the notice expired, the defendant's father attended the property with three other men, assaulted the tenant and forcibly evicted him. They then took all of his property. The tenant was forced to spend three nights in a car before he was re-admitted to the property after he had obtained an injunction. His belongings were never returned. Three weeks later, three men, one of whom had attended on the day of the eviction, came to the property and assaulted the tenant again, this time with wooden sticks. The tenant suffered injuries to his head, body and legs. His injuries required him to remain in hospital overnight. After being released from hospital, the tenant was too scared to return to the property.

The tenant was awarded: a) £10,000 general damages for the assaults and time spent out of the property; b) £2,000 special damages for his lost possessions; and c) £15,000 aggravated and exemplary damages.

Evans v Copping January 2008 *Legal Action* 30, Ashford County Court, DDJ Cagney

A.16 The claimant was an assured shorthold tenant of a flat. One day she returned home to find that the locks had been changed. She applied for an injunction to require the defendant landlord to re-admit her, but was unsuccessful after the defendant lied and told the court that he had already re-let the flat. The tenant was forced to stay with friends for the three months between the eviction and the date of trial.

The tenant was awarded: a) £2,500 general damages for the time spent away from the flat; b) £500 aggravated damages; and c) £1,500 exemplary damages.

Arabhalvaei v Rezaeipoor January 2008 *Legal Action* 36, Central London County Court, DJ Taylor

A.17 The defendant was the assured shorthold tenant of a one-bedroom flat. He lived at the flat with his wife. The flat suffered from disrepair. The claimant landlord harassed the tenant for a period of nearly eight years, despite being warned by a tenancy relations officer about his conduct. The harassment comprised verbal abuse, disconnecting the water supply, nuisance telephone calls, locks to the property being filled with glue and the smashing of a window. The tenant felt uncomfortable leaving his wife alone in the property and took time off work which meant he lost his job. In 2004, the claimant brought a claim for possession on the basis of rent arrears. The tenant counterclaimed for, among other things, harassment.

The tenant was awarded in respect of the harassment: a) £46,500 general damages assessed at £6,000 per annum; b) £67,500 for losing his job; c) £5,000 aggravated damages; and d) £5,000 exemplary damages.

Addison v Croft June 2008 *Legal Action* 31, HHJ Appleton

A.18 The claimant was an assured shorthold tenant. The defendant land-lord decided to sell property. One day, he entered the property without warning and demanded that the tenant leave. Two weeks later, the defendant returned, this time with other men. They forcibly evicted the tenant. The tenant spent 20 nights sleeping in his van and staying with friends before he was re-admitted to the property following an injunction.

The tenant was awarded: a) £3,000 general damage for the eviction; b) £1,000 aggravated damages; and c) £1,000 exemplary damages.

Evans v Ozkan and Hussein April 2009 *Legal Action* 20, Bromley County Court, HHJ Hallan

A.19 The claimant was the assured shorthold tenant of a room. Before entering into his tenancy agreement, he told his landlord, the first defendant, that his rent would be paid by housing benefit. The tenant fell into arrears after delays in the processing of his application for the benefit. A month into the tenancy, the first defendant attended the property and demanded that the tenant pay £1,000. The tenant told the first defendant that he did not have £1,000 to give him and the defendant left. At a later date, the tenant returned home to find the first defendant and two other men throwing his belongings on the pavement. The first defendant verbally abused the tenant. The police attended, but it was the tenant who was arrested. On his release that evening, the tenant found some of his belongings lying on the pavement; they had been crushed or smashed and some smelt of urine. The lilo he had been using as a mattress was full of holes and deflated. Some of his other belongings were missing. The tenant spent the night in his car away from the property, but returned the following day when he found that the locks had been changed. Both defendants, who had been waiting at the property, followed the tenant to the local pub where they threatened him with baseball bats and demanded £1,000. The tenant applied to his local authority as homeless and was eventually re-housed. He did, however, spend 63 nights in total without a home, which caused his health to deteriorate and he had suicidal thoughts.

The tenant was awarded: a) £15,750 general damages assessed at £250 per day for the period that he was homeless; b) £5,000 special damages for his lost possessions; c) £1,000 aggravated damages; and d) £2,000 exemplary damages.

Khan v Iqbal May 2009 *Legal Action* 25, Bury County Court, HHJ Tetlow

A.20   The claimant was the assured shorthold tenant of a property in which she lived with two children aged 15 and 12. After she accrued arrears of rent, the defendant landlord attended the property and demanded that she pay. He verbally abused the tenant, disconnected the central heating and electricity supply and also cut the telephone line to the property. At a later date, one of the defendant's sons entered the property without permission and began removing the tenant's belongings. The police were called; they provided the tenant with the telephone number of a women's refuge and said she should return to collect her belongings later. Instead she applied to the local authority for homeless assistance and they provided her and her children with bed and breakfast accommodation immediately. The tenant subsequently returned to the property to find that the locks had been changed and that most of her belongings were either missing or damaged.

The tenant was awarded: a) £10,200 general damages for 102 nights spent in bed and breakfast accommodation assessed at £100 per night; b) £2,000 in respect of the harassment prior to the eviction; c) £2,338.32 special damages; d) £2,000 aggravated damages; and e) £3,000 exemplary damages.

Abbas v Iqbal June 2009 *Housing Law Casebook* (7th edn, LAG, 2017) Bow County Court, HHJ Redgrave

A.21   The claimant was the assured shorthold tenant of a room. He had shared access to a kitchen and bathroom. He was an elderly man in poor health. In April 2008, the defendant served written notice (which did not comply with HA 1988 s21) on the tenant that he was required to leave the property within two weeks as he required vacant possession to convert the property into separate flats. The tenant did not leave. In May 2008, contractors started work at the property and disconnected the gas and water supply. The tenant was unable to cook his own meals, wash or take his medication. The tenant obtained an injunction ordering the defendant to reinstate the gas and water supply, but this order was not complied with and within a week the property was uninhabitable. The tenant was forced to leave and slept in his friend's business premises for three nights before the local authority accommodated him. The tenant's belongings and his furniture were subsequently disposed of by the defendant.

The tenant was awarded, in respect of the unlawful eviction: a) £750 general damages assessed at £250 per day for the three nights he had to spend in his friend's business premises; b) £1,950 general damages assessed at £150 per day for the 13 days in which he had to endure the buildings works and been without gas or water; c) £1,000 general damages as compensation for being forced to leave the property before the end of his tenancy agreement; d) £10,000 aggravated damages; e) £7,500 exemplary damages; and f) £5,494 special damages for his lost possessions.

Salah v Munro July 2009 *Legal Action* 31, Willesden County Court, HHJ Copley

A.22   The claimant was the assured shorthold tenant of a room. The defendant landlord discovered that the tenant was in receipt of housing benefit and told the tenant that he did not accept tenants who claimed housing benefit and that, if she did not leave, he would forcibly evict her from her room. One day shortly afterwards, the tenant returned home to find that the locks had been changed and her belongings left in black bags on the driveway. Some of her belongings were missing. She was forced to spend one night in hospital (following an asthma attack), two nights in bed and breakfast accommodation and eight nights on the sofa of a friend before she was re-admitted to the property after she obtained an injunction. She subsequently found out that some of her furniture had been removed and the defendant continued to harass her, which harassment included alleging that she was a prostitute. When the fixed term expired, the defendant disabled the electricity and gas supply. The tenant was forced to stay with a friend for a further 32 nights until, under the threat of a committal application, the defendant restored the electricity and gas supply.

The tenant was awarded: a) £8,600 general damages for the 43 nights she was away from the property assessed at £200 per night on the basis that the usual range was between £100 to £300 per night; b) £1,000 special damages; c) £2,000 aggravated damages; and d) £2,000 exemplary damages.

Ogle v Bundhoo September 2009 *Legal Action* 33, Mayor's and City of London County Court, HHJ Birtles

A.23   The claimant was the assured shorthold tenant of a room. He fell into arrears and the defendant landlord wrote to him stating that his tenancy had ceased. The tenant telephoned the defendant and said that he would clear the arrears. The defendant said that he wanted him to leave the property. That day, the tenant left the premises to attend the job centre. On his return home, he found that the lock to his room had been changed. The tenant contacted the defendant and asked to be re-admitted. The defendant refused. The tenant sought the advice of the Citizens Advice Bureau, who contacted the defendant but he refused to speak to them. The tenant then spent seven nights sleeping rough on the streets and 13 nights in bed and breakfast accommodation before he was re-admitted to the premises after he obtained an interim injunction.

The tenant was awarded: a) £2,171 general damages for the 13 nights spent in bed and breakfast accommodation assessed at £167 per night; b) £2,338 general damages for the seven nights that he was street homeless assessed at £334 per night; c) £1,054 special damages (which included the cost of the bed and breakfast accommodation); d) £2,300 aggravated damages; and e) £1,400 exemplary damages.

Anslow v Hayes October 2009 *Housing Law Casebook* (5th edn, LAG) Manchester County Court, Recorder Yip

A.24   The claimant was the assured shorthold tenant of a room. He failed to pay the rent and, a couple of months after the tenancy had started, the defendant threatened to evict him. One day, the tenant returned home to find that he could not gain access to the property. He contacted the defendant and asked to be admitted. This request was refused. A local authority tenancy relations officer contacted the defendant on the tenant's behalf and asked for the tenant to be re-admitted. This request was also refused, although the defendant said that the tenant could attend the property to collect his belongings. When the tenant arrived at the property, he found some of his belongings already packed up, and only his girlfriend was given access to the property to collect them. He later discovered that some of his belongings had been disposed of. The tenant was forced to spend 73 days in cramped conditions with his girlfriend before he found accommodation of his own.

The tenant was awarded: a) £7,000 general damages for the 73 days he had spent in cramped accommodation; b) £2,000 aggravated damages; and c) £1,000 exemplary damages (being the sum the defendant may have incurred had he evicted the tenant lawfully).

Aricioglu v Kaan October 2009 *Housing Law Casebook* (5th edn, LAG) Clerkenwell and Shoreditch County Court, HHJ Mitchell

A.25 The claimant was the assured shorthold tenant of a room. Shortly after moving in, he lost his job and told the defendant landlord that he was unable to pay the rent. The defendant told the tenant he would not accept housing benefit and gave him a week to find work. The defendant was subsequently warned by a tenancy relations officer not to evict the tenant without a court order. Despite this, the tenant was harassed on a daily basis for the next eight days before he was forcibly evicted. During the eviction, he was kicked and pushed down the stairs. He suffered a bruise to the head and a cut on his shoulder. His belongings were then packed and brought down to him. The police declined to intervene because the tenant did not have a tenancy agreement. The tenant was provided with bed and breakfast accommodation by a councillor over the weekend and slept on a sofa on the Monday night. A friend then agreed to accommodate him for a short period. The tenant applied for an injunction granting him re-entry to the room, but decided to withdraw the application after the defendant and a friend threatened him following a court hearing. Twenty-three days after his eviction, the tenant secured alternative accommodation.

The tenant was awarded: a) £2,875 general damages for 23 days before he found alternative accommodation, assessed at £125 per night; b) £1,000 general damages for the harassment before the eviction; c) £1,000 general damages for the assault, and trespass to goods and land; d) £2,500 aggravated damages; and e) £2,000 exemplary damages.

Hunt v Hussain October 2009 *Legal Action* 25, Epsom County Court, HHJ Reid QC

A.26 The claimant was the assured shorthold tenant of a room. He lost his job three months after the tenancy began. When he applied for housing benefit, the defendant landlord told him that he had to leave. An officer of the local authority wrote to the defendant and warned her that she could not evict the tenant without a court order. Despite this warning, the defendant changed the locks while the tenant was away from the property. The tenant was street homeless for 76 days before he was able to find alternative accommodation. During that period, he occasionally stayed with friends but mostly slept in either a broken down car or on the street in his sleeping bag. Both his physical and mental health deteriorated. Four years after the eviction, a psychiatrist gave evidence that the tenant suffered from severe depression, agoraphobia and paranoid ideation, all of which had been exacerbated by the time he had spent living on the streets. The defendant was prosecuted by the local authority, fined £300 and ordered to pay costs of £250.

In the county court proceedings, the tenant was awarded: a) £8,125 general damages assessed at £125 per day for a period of 65 days (rather than 76 days as the defendant could lawfully have determined the tenancy after 65 days); b) £100 special damages; and c) £45,000 general damages for the psychiatric harm.

Ordera v Iqbal January 2010 *Legal Action* 33, Luton County Court, HHJ Kay QC

A.27   The claimant was the assured shorthold tenant of a room in a property with shared facilities. She lived there with her 11-year-old daughter. Throughout the duration of the tenancy, the defendant landlord would often enter the property unannounced and without warning. In January 2008, the defendant served her with an invalid notice of seeking possession. The tenant sought and obtained alternative accommodation. In February 2008, the tenant packed away her belongings and told the defendant that she was leaving to collect her keys for her new accommodation. She was not, however, provided with the keys because she was unable to give her new landlord all of the deposit. The tenant returned to the room. Later that night, the defendant and another man attended the property, removed the tenant's belongings and dragged both the tenant and her daughter from the property. The tenant was forced to spend the night in emergency accommodation and then spent three nights with her sister before she moved into her new accommodation. When the tenant returned to collect her belongings, she found that they had been left in the back garden and they had been damaged by rain.

At trial the court accepted that the tenant had not surrendered her tenancy and that she had been unlawfully evicted. She was awarded: a) £500 general damages for breach of quiet enjoyment and trespass for the two weeks prior to eviction; b) £1,000 for the assault and method of eviction; c) £1,500 aggravated damages; and d) £1,000 exemplary damages.

Cashmere v Walsh, Downing and Veale January 2010 *Legal Action* 33, Central London County Court, HHJ Cowell

A.28   The claimant was the assured tenant of a flat. In 2000, the second defendant bought the reversionary interest in the flat, which he held on a bare trust for the first defendant. The third defendant was the first defendant's mother. On 2 December 2007, the first and third defendants asked the claimant to move out of the property while works to remedy items of disrepair were completed. The works were completed within a week. Part of the works included the fitting of a new door, which had a new lock. The claimant asked the defendants for a key but was told that he would not be given one because he was in rent arrears. The claimant instructed solicitors who wrote pre-action letters to each of the defendants demanding that he be allowed to return and that his belongings be restored to him. The second defendant told the claimant that the flat had been re-let.

At trial, the claimant was awarded damages under HA 1988 s28. He was additionally awarded: a) general damages of £8,000 against the first and third defendant for their part in the deception and the refusal to hand over keys; b) special damages in respect of the claimant's lost belongings; and c) aggravated damages of £10,000 against all three defendants.

Fakhari v Newman June 2010 *Legal Action* 35, Woolwich County Court, DJ Lee

A.29   The claimant landlord granted the defendant tenant an assured shorthold tenancy for a fixed term of one year. Seven months into the tenancy, the claimant repeatedly told the tenant, in the form of telephone calls and continuous text messages, that he did not want him to remain as a tenant. The claimant also threatened the tenant and told him that it was no longer safe for him to remain in the property and on occasions attended the property without appointment. The claimant told the police, untruthfully, that the tenant intended to blow up the property. The claimant issued a claim for possession on the basis of rent arrears. The tenant counterclaimed.

The tenant was awarded, in respect of the harassment: a) £2,000 general damages; and b) £2,000 exemplary damages.

Keddey v Hughes June 2010 *Legal Action* 36, Sheffield County Court, Recorder Khan

A.30   The claimant was an assured shorthold tenant. In October 2008, the defendant landlord decided to let the property to other tenants. He did not, however, determine the tenancy and the tenant refused to leave. The defendant physically assaulted the tenant before returning later in the day with three other men. The tenant was assaulted again and forcibly removed from the property. The locks, however, were not changed and the tenant returned to the property later that day. The local authority warned the defendant not to evict the tenant without a court order. Later that month, the tenant returned home to find the defendant in the property packing the tenant's belongings into bin liners. Some of his possessions were damaged. At this point the tenant opted to leave the property. He applied to the local authority for homeless assistance and was provided with bed and breakfast accommodation for four weeks before he was granted a non-secure tenancy under HA 1996.

The tenant was awarded: a) £4,620 general damages assessed at a rate of £165 per night for the 28 days he spent in bed and breakfast accommodation; b) £1,500 general damages for the assault, harassment and trespass to his property; c) £1,000 aggravated damages; and d) £2,000 exemplary damages.

Walsh v Shuangyan June 2010 *Legal Action* 35, Manchester County Court, DJ Richmond

A.31   The claimant was the assured shorthold tenant of a room in a house of multiple occupation. He shared the house with six other tenants. The defendant landlord disconnected the boiler and electricity supply, which caused the other tenants to leave the property. After the tenant declined to leave, the defendant subjected him to harassment and threats. On one occasion, he was physically assaulted by the defendant's father and on another he was forced to barricade his room after the defendant and her father stayed the night at the property. Eventually, the tenant returned home one evening to find that the locks had been changed. Some of his possessions had been put in bin bags outside the property but the majority remained inside his room. A tenancy relations officer contacted the defendant and told her that she must re-admit the tenant; she refused to do so. The tenant subsequently obtained an injunction requiring the defendant to re-admit him to the property, but the defendant still refused to do so, which resulted in her being committed to prison for 28 days. The tenant was forced to stay with various friends and families for 30 days (sleeping on their sofas) until he obtained alternative accommodation. During this period, he developed a bad back and was forced to miss work on occasions.

The tenant was awarded: a) £6,000 general damages assessed at £200 per night for the 30 days spent sleeping on sofas; b) £2,000 for the harassment before the eviction; c) £5,570 special damages; d) £4,000 aggravated damages; and e) £1,500 exemplary damages.

Schuchard v Fu June 2010 *Legal Action* 36, Brentford County Court, DJ Plaskow

A.32   The claimant was the assured shorthold tenant of a room in a house of multiple occupation. The defendant landlord wrote to each tenant of the property and asked that they give up possession as she intended to re-develop the property. She did not serve a HA 1988 s21 notice on the tenant. When the tenant did not leave, the defendant sent him a letter which demanded that he leave the next day because he owed arrears of rent. The following day, when the tenant was away from the property, the defendant changed the locks to the front door. That evening, the tenant returned and was unable to gain access. All of his belongings remained in his room. The day after, a tenancy relations officer contacted the defendant and asked that she re-admit the tenant, but she refused to do so. The tenant then instructed solicitors who wrote to the defendant and demanded that she re-admit the tenant to the property which she again refused to do. The local authority initially refused to accommodate the tenant and he was street homeless for 120 days. He was subsequently accommodated by the local authority for 77 days before they decided that they did not owe him a duty under National Assistance Act 1948 s21. The tenant was forced to spend the next 35 days, until trial, sleeping on a friend's floor.

The tenant was awarded: a) £24,000 general and aggravated damages assessed at £200 per night for the 120 days when the tenant was street homeless; b) £2,000 general damages for the remaining 77 days he was accommodated by the local authority; c) £4,375 general damages and aggravated damages for the period he slept on his friend's floor assessed at £125 per night; and d) £1,750 exemplary damages.

Naughton v Whittle and Chief Constable of Greater Manchester Police July 2010 *Legal Action* 29, Manchester County Court, HHJ Morgan

A.33   The claimant was an assured shorthold tenant. The first defendant was the tenant's landlord. He told the tenant that he wanted him to leave the property. When the tenant refused to do so, the first defendant's brother threatened the tenant and the first defendant assaulted the tenant's girlfriend. The first defendant then changed the locks. The police were called but arrested the tenant for breach of the peace. The tenant was away from the property for 28 days.

The second defendant agreed, in an out of court settlement, to pay the tenant £2,500 for the wrongful arrest and trespass to land. At trial, the first defendant was ordered to pay the tenant: a) £7,700 general damages assessed at £275 per day; and b) £1,500 aggravated damages.

Shyngle v Simmons July 2010 *Legal Action* 29, Slough County Court

A.34   The claimant was an assured shorthold tenant. The tenant withheld rent from the defendant landlord because of a dispute over payment of the utility bills. One day, he returned home to find that the locks had been tampered with and that he was unable to gain access. He obtained an injunction which required the defendant to re-admit him to the property. The injunction, however, could not be enforced because the defendant's mortgage lender had taken possession of the property in the interim.

The tenant was awarded: a) £5,075 general damages for 29 nights assessed at £175 per night; and b) £1,000 aggravated damages.

Boyle v Musso March 2011 *Legal Action* 27, Bristol County Court, DJ Watson

A.35   The claimant was an assured shorthold tenant. The tenant withheld rent following a flood to the property. The defendant landlord and another man attended the property and assaulted the tenant. The tenant was punched and stamped on when he fell to the floor. The tenant was forced to leave the property without his belongings. He spent 22 nights with friends, in bed and breakfast accommodation and hostels before he found alternative accommodation. The defendant was subsequently convicted of assault occasioning actual bodily harm.

The tenant was awarded: a) £4,000 general damages for the 22 nights in below standard accommodation; b) £15,000 general damages for the assault; c) £750 special damages for the loss of his belongings; and d) £2,000 exemplary damages.

Deelah v Rehman March 2011 *Housing Law Casebook* (7th edn, 2017, LAG) Clerkenwell & Shoreditch County Court, DJ Millard

A.36 The claimant was the assured shorthold tenant of a room and had shared access to a kitchen and bathroom. He lived in the room with his wife and two sons aged nine and 16. In June 2010, the defendant landlord, accompanied by a friend, asked the tenant to leave and threatened to change the locks if his family did not do so. The tenant refused to leave and, during the row, the defendant twisted his arm. A month later, the tenant's wife returned home to find that the locks had been changed. The defendant threatened to kill the tenant's son with a crowbar after he had climbed over a fence to try and gain access. As the family were ineligible for assistance under HA 1996 Part 7, they were forced to sleep in a friend's living room for four nights until the tenant obtained an injunction and secured re-entry to the property. During that period the children missed school. The defendant continued to harass the tenant and his family after they were re-admitted.

The tenant was awarded: a) £1,000 general damages for the four days he spent away from the property assessed at £250 per night; b) £1,500 general damages for the harassment before and after the eviction; c) £1,500 aggravated damages; and d) £2,500 exemplary damages.

Dada v Adeyeye March 2012 *Legal Action* 23, Central London County Court, HHJ Gerald

A.37 The claimant was an assured shorthold tenant of a room in a shared house. The defendant landlord began to harass him when he fell behind with his rent after losing his job. The defendant's adult son and an unknown man threatened to kill the tenant. The tenant's solicitors warned the defendant not to harass or unlawfully evict the tenant, despite which the defendant changed the locks. The tenant was street homeless for 13 nights and spent 53 weeks in temporary accommodation provided by the local authority. He became depressed.

The tenant was awarded: a) £1,500 general damages for the harassment and trespass; b) £2,600 for the 13 nights he was street homeless; c) £10,000 for the period spent in temporary accommodation; d) £2,000 exemplary damages; and e) £570 special damages.

Aiyedogbon v Best Move Estate Agent Ltd June 2012 Legal Action 35, Clerkenwell and Shoreditch County Court, DJ Cooper

A.38   The claimant was the assured shorthold tenant of a flat. The defendant landlords alleged that the tenant was in arrears of rent and threatened to change the locks. The tenant warned them not to do so and said that he would be away for a short period of time. In his absence, the defendants did change the locks. The tenant obtained an injunction and was readmitted. He discovered that some of his property was damaged and missing, his front door had been broken and could not be locked and he had to stay in a hotel for 20 nights until he could get it repaired.

The tenant was awarded: a) £3,800 general damages for the 20 nights spent in hotel accommodation assessed at £190 per night; b) £1,340 general damages for the distress caused by the unlawful eviction; c) £1,800 aggravated damages; d) £1,500 exemplary damages; and e) £1,603 special damages for the cost of the hotel accommodation and his lost belongings.

Henson v Blackwood and Blackwood August 2012 Legal Action 26, Mayor's and City of London Court, HHJ Birtles

A.39   The claimant was the assured shorthold tenant of a flat. The defendant landlords served her with a HA 1988 s21 notice. The day before the notice expired, one of the defendants (Mr Blackwood) attended the flat. He told the tenant that she had to leave the following day, and became aggressive. The following day, the tenant returned to the flat to find that the supply of gas, electricity and water had been disconnected. Some of her possessions were also missing. She decided to spend the night at a friend's flat. The following day, she found that the locks to her flat had been changed and went back to her friend's flat. Two days later, the tenant's solicitors wrote to the defendants and warned them that they had unlawfully evicted her. The defendants did not reply and the tenant issued a claim for an injunction to re-admit her to the flat and for the utilities to be re-connected. The injunction was granted. The defendants initially refused to re-admit the tenant to the flat as they contended that the flat had been re-let. They had not, however, re-let the flat and, four days after she had been evicted, the tenant was re-admitted. On returning, she found that her property had been put in bin bags in the communal hallway and her food had been disposed of. She also received a telephone call from Mr Blackwood who told her that as she had involved other people he would be sending 'more people' round. Accordingly, the tenant decided to stay with her mother for a week. On returning to the flat, she continued to receive nuisance telephone calls and was forced to change her telephone number. One evening, Mr Blackwood's brother let himself into the property and attempted to assault the tenant while she was in her underclothes; on another occasion, she found her lock had been glued. She eventually chose to leave the flat voluntarily.

The tenant was awarded: a) £2,000 general damages for the harassment prior to the eviction; b) £1,000 general damages for the eviction and three nights spent with her friend; c) £2,000 general damages for the harassment after the eviction; d) £2,000 aggravated damages; and e) £2,000 exemplary damages.

Hussain v Mir September 2012 *Legal Action* 20, Clerkenwell and Shoreditch County Court, DJ Stary

A.40 The claimant was the assured shorthold tenant of a room. He shared the house with six other tenants. The defendant landlord told the claimant and the other tenants that they had to move out immediately because his letting agent had failed to give him the rent they had paid. Some of the tenants left the following day. The claimant remained in occupation with two of the other tenants. Subsequently, the defendant, accompanied by his letting agent, changed the locks. When the claimant tried to regain access, the defendant pushed him away. Although the claimant called the police three times, the letting agent pushed him to the floor and kicked him in the back and chest. The claimant suffered soft tissue injuries to his neck and back and a grazed elbow. He was taken to hospital. After leaving hospital, the claimant spent one night staying with one of the other tenants in the house and 29 nights on a friend's floor. He was subsequently provided with hostel accommodation where he remained for five months. Six weeks after the eviction, the defendant marketed the property for a tenancy of the whole building.

The tenant was awarded: a) £1,000 general damages for the assault; b) £11,360 general damages assessed at £300 per night for the 29 days spent on a friend's floor and £190 per night restricted to 14 nights he spent in the hostel, because he was under an obligation to mitigate his losses; c) £2,000 aggravated damages; and d) £1,800 exemplary damages.

Oyzen v Bell-Gam September 2012 *Legal Action* 21, Croydon County Court, DJ Major

A.41   The claimant was the assured shorthold tenant of a flat. He could not access the part of the building where the payment meters for gas and electricity were and, accordingly, was without both for the first two days of his letting. The defendant then put money into the meters but, after the tenant connected his washing machine, it sparked and the fire brigade disconnected the electricity supply the next day. The following day, on discovering this, the defendant shouted at the tenant, accused him of wrecking the flat and told him to leave immediately. The tenant was subsequently street homeless for seven weeks and spent three weeks staying in a hostel.

The tenant was awarded: a) £14,000 general damages assessed at a daily rate of £200 for 70 days; b) £2,000 aggravated damages; and c) £1,500 exemplary damages.

Pyne v Aryeetey November 2013 *Legal Action* 31, Wandsworth County Court, DJ Jones

A.42   The defendant was the assured shorthold tenant of a flat which she rented from the claimant landlord. She lived at the property with her two young children. The claimant served the defendant with notice to quit and at the same time sent men to threaten the defendant to try to make her vacate the property. The claimant later disconnected water, gas and electricity, removed the toilet and washbasin, and left a notice telling the defendant that if she found her there the next time she visited she would change the locks. The defendant remained at the premises without water, lighting or heating for another 23 days, during which time she was forced to take the children to use the toilet at a local restaurant. The defendant subsequently found alternative accommodation in a single room. Later, the claimant threatened the defendant at her church, demanding unpaid rent, until the police were called to restrain her. The claimant sued the defendant for unpaid rent; the defendant counterclaimed for unlawful eviction.

At trial, the defendant was awarded: a) general damages of £1,000 for the pre-eviction threats; b) £300 per day for the time she was living in the flat without a toilet or utilities; c) £100 per day for a further 40 days during which the defendant was living in the single room; d) general damages of £2,000 for the harassment in front of the church congregation; and e) exemplary damages of £2,000.

Lopes and Alves v Singh and Singh November 2013 *Legal Action* 31, Bristol County Court, DDJ Close

A.43 The claimants were the assured shorthold tenants of a house which they rented from the first defendant. The second defendant was the landlord's brother-in-law. On 28 August 2012, after the claimants accrued arrears of rent, the defendants changed the locks at the property and, notwithstanding that it was a breach of an injunction obtained by the claimants three days later and that the first claimant was 18 weeks pregnant, refused to re-admit the claimants. The claimants spent one night in a hotel, the next nine nights with friends and then three nights in their car. Following the three nights spent in the car, the first claimant received hospital treatment for a bladder infection. On 31 August 2012, Ms Lopes and Mr Alves obtained an injunction ordering their immediate reinstatement. On 6 September 2012, the claimants surrendered their tenancy and went to stay at another friend's house.

At trial, the claimants were awarded: a) £3,000 at £300 per day for the ten days until the surrender; b) £2,100 at £25 per day for the 84 days spent staying with friends following the surrender until the six-month assured tenancy would have expired; c) aggravated damages of £2,000 for the first claimant and aggravated damages of £1,750 for the second claimant; d) exemplary damages of £1,500; and e) £122.75 for the costs associated with staying at the hotel.

Waliezada v Dickson March 2014 *Legal Action* 22, Manchester County Court, Recorder Smith

A.44 The defendant landlord obtained a possession order against the claimant tenant. The claimant sought to set aside the order. Before that application was heard, and in the absence of a warrant for possession being issued, the defendant changed the locks to the property and left some of the claimant's belongings outside. The claimant and his family spent six nights in temporary accommodation before they were re-housed by the local authority. The defendant gave an undertaking to return all of the claimant's remaining belongings, but only some of it was returned.

At trial, the claimant was awarded: a) general damages of £6,050 for the unlawful eviction; b) aggravated damages of £2,200; and c) exemplary damages of £1,650.

Premier Property Management v Adia April 2014 *Legal Action* 25, Bromley County Court, DJ Wilkinson

A.45   The defendant was the assured shorthold tenant of the claimant land-lord. The claimant changed the locks to the property. The defendant went to the claimant's agents to ask for a key. The agents verbally abused and assaulted the defendant. The defendant spent that night in cheap hotel accommodation. The following day, he instructed solicitors, who spoke to the claimant's agents. They did not agree to reinstate him. The defendant could not afford to pay for a hotel for a second night and wandered the streets until he went to work at 2am. On the third day, the agents agreed to give him the key, but when he went to the office, he was told to sign a document saying that he was in breach of his tenancy agreement. He refused to do so. After his solicitor had telephoned the agents, the defendant was told he could collect the key at 7pm. When he collected the key and tried to open his door, he discovered that it was the wrong key. He stayed the night with a friend. On the fourth day, the agents again agreed that he could collect a key, but when he did so, he was told to wait. After about two hours, he was still not given a key but was threatened by the manager gesturing towards him, with his hands in the shape of a gun, saying 'I'll kill you'. He was very frightened and reported it to the police. Eventually, after his solicitors had intervened again, the agents agreed to deliver the new key to the solicitors' office. When the defendant was able to get back into his flat, he discovered that £1,400 cash and two laptops had been removed. The claimant subsequently brought a claim for rent arrears and the defendant counterclaimed.

At trial, the defendant was awarded: a) general damages of £1,500 for the assault and threat to kill; b) general damages of £200 for the first night in a hotel and £300 for the second and third nights; c) aggravated damages of £2,500; d) exemplary damages at £2,000; and e) special damages in respect of the cash and two laptops.

Hahn v McLeary May 2014 *Legal Action* 21, Bristol County Court

A.46   The claimant was the assured shorthold tenant of a single room. On 2 February 2012, the defendant landlord gave him a note giving him a date on which to vacate the property. On 9 February 2012, the defendant sent the claimant a text message saying that he would start taking steps to 'clear' the flat within ten minutes. The claimant returned to the property to find that the locks had been changed and his possessions had been placed outside of the property. The defendant was advised subsequently by the local authority that he should allow the claimant to re-enter the property, but he refused. After the eviction, the claimant spent eight days sleeping on the streets and a further four days sofa-surfing with friends. He then spent 111 days in a hostel, during which time he caught scabies owing to the condition of the hostel.

After judgment was entered in default in respect of liability, the claimant was awarded: a) £250 per night for the time spent on the street; b) £166 per night for the time sofa-surfing; c) £100 per night for the time spent in hostel accommodation; d) £2,000 aggravated damages; and e) £1,600 exemplary damages.

Webb v Singh and Liberty Estate Agents Ltd October 2014 *Legal Action* 48, Birmingham County Court, DJ Mian

A.47 The claimant was an assured shorthold tenant. The first defendant was her landlord. The claimant lived at the property with her four-year-old son. She was away for three weeks visiting relatives, during which time the landlord changed the locks. She spent four-and-a-half months staying with friends before obtaining permanent accommodation. During this time, her son lost his place at school. She was told that she could not reclaim her possessions unless she paid a fee to the agent.

At trial, the claimant was awarded: a) general damages of £16,875; and b) aggravated and exemplary damages of £4,000.

Whittingham v Uddin October 2014 *Legal Action* 48, Clerkenwell and Shoreditch County Court, DJ Sterlini

A.48 The claimant was the tenant of the defendant. The claimant, after complaining to the defendant about disrepair, was subjected to harassment by the defendant. Over a period of three years, in addition to not carrying out the repairs, the defendant made threats of violence, sent abusive emails, disconnected the supply of gas and electricity to the property, let himself into the property (often with other people) and changed the lock to the front of the premises (albeit neighbouring tenants gave the claimant a key so he was never actually evicted).

At trial, the claimant was awarded: a) general damages of £10,000 for the harassment; b) aggravated damages of £3,000; and c) exemplary damages of £3,000.

Alabbas v Uppelle December 2014/January 2015 *Legal Action* 32, Leicester County Court, Recorder McNeill QC

A.49   The claimant was the assured shorthold tenant of the defendant landlord. In April 2009, the claimant complained to the defendant that water was leaking through to the kitchen from the bathroom. After no action was taken and the ceiling collapsed, the claimant complained to the local authority. In response, the defendant served the claimant with a notice requiring him to leave the property. The claimant did not leave and was then subjected to harassment and threats of violence by the defendant. In September 2009, the claimant was evicted by four men acting as the defendant's agents. One of the men had a knife. They shouted racist abuse, punched and beat the claimant and threatened to kill him. The claimant spent the night in hospital before sleeping on the streets for the next 16 days and in a hostel for a further 160 nights. The claimant received treatment for post-traumatic stress disorder for two months after the eviction.

At trial, the claimant was awarded: a) £1,000 general damages for the pre-eviction harassment; b) £330 per night for the time he was street homeless; c) £110 per night for the period spent in the hostel; d) £3,000 for the injuries occasioned by the assault; e) £3,000 aggravated damages and f) £2,500 exemplary damages.

Bitan v Holme December 2014/January 2015 *Legal Action* 33, Stockport County Court, DDJ Buckley

A.50   The defendant was the tenant of the claimant landlord. The defendant complained to the claimant about disrepair at the property. In response, the claimant became difficult and abusive, regularly telephoning and knocking on the door. On several occasions, large men attended the property and made clear that she and her children would be evicted and made homeless. The defendant withheld rent and the claimant sought possession from the defendant tenant. The defendant counterclaimed for, amongst other things, harassment arising from a breach of PHA 1997 s1.

At trial, the defendant was awarded general damages of £2,592.94 for the harassment.

Barrett v Two Angels Limited February 2015 *Legal Action* 40, Bow County Court, DJ Rollason

A.51   The claimant tenant was 25 years old. He suffered from post-traumatic stress disorder, depression and anxiety. He was granted an assured shorthold tenancy by the defendant landlord. The defendant was an organisation that provided accommodation and supported living to young vulnerable adults. Relations between the claimant and defendant deteriorated, which resulted in the claimant being asked to enter into agreement with the defendant requiring him to abide by the terms of his tenancy or face eviction. Relations did not improve and, on 7 May 2013, the defendant gave the claimant notice to leave his accommodation immediately. The claimant spent three nights sleeping in the waiting room at Whipps Cross hospital, before his brother found him a room, without furniture, carpets or heating, to stay in. On 29 May 2013, the claimant found alternative suitable accommodation.

At trial the claimant was awarded: a) £285 per night for the three nights spent at Whipps Cross hospital; b) £250 per night for the 19 nights in the room; and c) £3,200 in aggravated damages.

Sokoli v Zahid February 2015 *Legal Action* 41, Brentford County Court, DJ Willans

A.52 The claimant was the assured shorthold tenant of the defendant. The defendant landlord brought a claim for possession but it was dismissed, in the absence of the claimant, because the defendant was found not to have protected the deposit. The defendant subsequently forged a possession order and attached it to the front of the door. The defendant called the police and, with their assistance, evicted the claimant. The claimant spent the next 64 nights sleeping in his mother's room. The defendant subsequently refused to comply with an injunction that required that the claimant be re-admitted to the property.

At trial, the claimant was awarded: a) general damages of £8,640 for the eviction and time spent away from the property; b) exemplary damages of £2,000; and c) aggravated damages of £1,500.

Croft v Moon July/August 2015 *Legal Action* 48, Hastings County Court, DJ Wright

A.53 The claimants were the joint assured shorthold tenants of a three-bedroom chalet bungalow. The defendant was their landlord. Following complaints of disrepair, the landlord repeatedly entered the property without notice to the tenants. He swore at them and was gratuitously offensive. He served a HA 1988 s21 notice and, when they failed to move out, threatened to remove the roof. He dumped bricks in the garden and excluded the claimants from the property. At trial, it was found that the landlord had unlawfully attempted to recover possession to enable him to redevelop the property.

The claimants were awarded: a) general damages of £1,500 for the harassment; b) £100 per day for the period until the claimants were re-housed; c) £1,000 aggravated damages; and d) £3,000 exemplary damages.

Kazadi v Martin Brooks Lettings Estates Agents Limited and Faparusi September 2015 *Legal Action* 51, County Court at Edmonton, DJ Silverman

A.54   The claimant was the assured shorthold tenant of the second defendant landlord. The first defendant was the landlord's agent. On 8 January 2014, an employee of the agent tried to force his way into the property, was abusive and told the claimant that he would be evicted. On 11 January 2014, the landlord came to the property accompanied by a group of eight men. The claimant's visitors were thrown out of the property and the claimant was held down by the group of men. Following a struggle, a bladed article was held close to one of the claimant's eyes. He was told that if he continued to struggle, he would lose his eye. The claimant was held in the flat until the police arrived. The police escorted the claimant out of the property after giving him a few minutes to collect some belongings. Later that evening, the claimant returned to the property to find that some of his other belongings had been thrown onto the street and some were missing. The claimant was forced to sofa-surf with friends for 277 days until securing alternative accommodation.

After both defendants were debarred from defending the claim, the court awarded the claimant: a) £1,000 for the assault; b) £300 for the false imprisonment; c) £175 per day for six months, being the time it would have taken the landlord to recover possession lawfully; d) £3,000 aggravated damages; and e) £2,000 exemplary damages.

Autunes v Smith and Right Move Lettings & Property Management Ltd October 2015 *Legal Action* 40, County Court at Croydon, DJ Bishop

A.55   The claimant was the assured shorthold tenancy of the first defendant. The second defendant was the landlord's agent. An employee of the agent and three other men attempted to gain access to the property on at least seven occasions over a period of one month. After a possession order was obtained fraudulently (the claim form having incorrectly stated that a deposit had not been paid), the police and bailiffs evicted the claimant from the property. The claimant was forced to stay in a hotel for 11 days until he was re-admitted to the property pursuant to a court order.

After judgment was entered in default, the claimant was awarded: a) general damages of £2,000 for the pre-eviction harassment; b) £300 per day for the time spent away from the property; c) £257 special damages for the hotel costs; d) £2,000 aggravated damages; and e) £2,000 exemplary damages.

Akrigg v Pidgeon May 2016 *Legal Action* 40, County Court at Chippenham and Trowbridge, DDJ Horsey

A.56   The claimant tenant was a care leaver. In December 2013, the defendant landlord granted him an assured shorthold tenancy. In November 2014, the defendant gave the claimant one month's written notice to leave the property. The local authority advised the defendant that the notice was invalid. On 6 January 2015, the defendant served a second notice. The defendant, after having been told by the authority that the second notice was invalid, told the authority that he was going to evict the claimant and change the locks. He was told that this would constitute an illegal eviction. The defendant subsequently notified the authority's housing benefit department that the claimant was intending to leave the premises so that his housing benefit would be cancelled. On 2 April 2015, the claimant went to stay for the weekend at his partner's parent's house. On his return, four days later, he discovered that the locks had been changed and he was unable to gain access. On 9 April 2015, the defendant, pursuant to a court order, provided the claimant with a key to the premises.

After judgment in default had been entered against the defendant in respect of liability, the court awarded the claimant: a) £500 for general harassment arising from the defendant entering the premises, serving the spurious notices, lying about the condition of the premises and attempting to cancel housing benefit; b) £170 per night for the time away from the premises; c) aggravated damages of £1,500; and d) £1,000 exemplary damages.

Tyto v Narang July/August 2016 *Legal Action* 47, County Court at Brentford, DDJ McConnell

A.57   The claimant was the assured shorthold tenant of the defendant landlord. The claimant's family (her husband and three daughters) subsequently moved in to live with her. The defendant alleged that this breached her tenancy agreement and the claimant was asked to leave. After the claimant did not do so, the defendant evicted her by changing the locks. The local authority provided emergency accommodation comprising a single room with a shared bathroom and kitchen. The claimant obtained an injunction requiring the defendant to re-admit her. The defendant, however, refused to re-admit the whole family as the order only required him to re-admit the claimant. The claimant and her family returned to emergency accommodation after being verbally abused by the defendant's agent.

At trial, the claimant was awarded: a) £140 per night for the nights spent in the local authority accommodation up until a date one month after the expiry of the fixed term, being the notional date by which the defendant could lawfully have gained possession; b) £1,500 aggravated damages; and c) £1,500 in exemplary damages.

Sypniewski v Wakelin July/August 2016 *Legal Action* 47, County Court at Bournemouth, DJ Willis

A.58   The claimant was the assured shorthold tenant of the defendant landlord. On 13 September 2015, after the fixed-term expired, the defendant disconnected the utilities. On 10 October 2015, the defendant evicted the claimant by changing the locks. On 14 October 2015, the claimant was re-admitted and the utilities reconnected pursuant to an injunction. That prompted the defendant to install CCTV cameras to spy on the claimant and to smash the windscreen and windows of the claimant's truck and two cars. On 18 November 2015, the defendant disconnected the utilities again and, on 19 December 2015, evicted the claimant for a second time.

At trial, the district judge described the defendant's actions as 'amongst the worst he had seen' and awarded the claimant damages of: a) general damages of £17,720; b) aggravated damages of £2,000; and c) exemplary damage of £5,750.

Begache v Noreen July/August 2016 *Legal Action* 48, County Court at Birmingham, DJ Kelly

A.59   The claimant was the tenant of the defendant landlord. The defendant, while the claimant was on holiday for a week, moved into the property. The defendant did not move out when the claimant returned from holiday. The claimant was required to stay elsewhere for 16 nights before being re-admitted to the property.

The court awarded the claimant: a) £200 per night for the 16 nights that the tenant had to stay elsewhere; b) £300 for the week that the claimant was on holiday; c) £1,500 in aggravated damages; and d) £1,000 in exemplary damages.

Statutes: extracts[1]

HOUSING AND PLANNING ACT 2016

Chapter 2: Banning Orders

Banning orders: key definitions

14 'Banning order' and 'banning order offence'

(1) In this Part 'banning order' means an order, made by the First-tier Tribunal, banning a person from–

    (a) letting housing in England,

    (b) engaging in English letting agency work,

    (c) engaging in English property management work, or

    (d) doing two or more of those things.

(2) See also section 18 (which enables a banning order to include a ban on involvement in certain bodies corporate).

(3) In this Part 'banning order offence' means an offence of a description specified in regulations made by the Secretary of State.

(4) Regulations under subsection (3) may, in particular, describe an offence by reference to–

    (a) the nature of the offence,

    (b) the characteristics of the offender,

    (c) the place where the offence is committed,

    (d) the circumstances in which it is committed,

    (e) the court sentencing a person for the offence, or

    (f) the sentence imposed.

...

Consequences of Banning Order, Including Consequences of Breach

21 Offence of breach of banning order

(1) A person who breaches a banning order commits an offence.

(2) A person guilty of an offence under subsection (1) is liable on summary conviction to imprisonment for a period not exceeding 51 weeks or to a fine or to both.

(3) If a financial penalty under section 23 has been imposed in respect of the breach, the person may not be convicted of an offence under this section.

(4) Where a person is convicted under subsection (1) of breaching a banning order and the breach continues after conviction, the person commits a further offence and is liable on summary conviction to a fine not exceeding one-tenth of level 2 on the standard scale for each day or part of a day on which the breach continues.

(5) In proceedings for an offence under subsection (4) it is a defence to show that the person had a reasonable excuse for the continued breach.

(6) In relation to an offence committed before section 281(5) of the Criminal Justice Act 2003 comes into force, the reference in subsection (2) to 51 weeks is to be read as a reference to 6 months.

22 Offences by bodies corporate

(1) Where an offence under section 21 committed by a body corporate is proved to have been committed with the consent or connivance of, or to be attributable to any neglect on the part of, an officer of a body corporate, the officer as

well as the body corporate commits the offence and is liable to be proceeded against and punished accordingly.

(2) Where the affairs of a body corporate are managed by its members, subsection (1) applies in relation to the acts and defaults of a member in connection with the member's functions of management as if the member were an officer of the body corporate.

23 Financial penalty for breach of banning order

(1) The responsible local housing authority may impose a financial penalty on a person if satisfied, beyond reasonable doubt, that the person's conduct amounts to an offence under section 21(1).

(2) In this section 'responsible local housing authority' means the local housing authority for the area in which the housing to which the conduct relates is situated.

(3) Only one financial penalty under this section may be imposed in respect of the same conduct unless subsection (4) allows another penalty to be imposed.

(4) If a breach continues for more than 6 months, a financial penalty may be imposed for each additional 6 month period for the whole or part of which the breach continues.

(5) The amount of a financial penalty imposed under this section is to be determined by the authority imposing it, but must not be more than £30,000.

(6) The responsible local housing authority may not impose a financial penalty in respect of any conduct amounting to an offence under section 21(1) if–
   (a) the person has been convicted of an offence under that section in respect of the conduct, or
   (b) criminal proceedings for the offence have been instituted against the person in respect of the conduct and the proceedings have not been concluded.

(7) Schedule 1 deals with–
   (a) the procedure for imposing financial penalties,
   (b) appeals against financial penalties, and
   (c) enforcement of financial penalties.

(8) The Secretary of State may by regulations make provision about how local housing authorities are to deal with financial penalties recovered.

(9) The Secretary of State may by regulations amend the amount specified in subsection (5) to reflect changes in the value of money.

(10) A local housing authority must have regard to any guidance given by the Secretary of State about the exercise of its functions under this section or Schedule 1.

24 Saving for illegal contracts

A breach of a banning order does not affect the validity or enforceability of any provision of a tenancy or other contract entered into by a person despite any rule of law relating to the validity or enforceability of contracts in circumstances involving illegality.

...

Chapter 4: Rent Repayment Orders

Rent repayment orders: introduction

40 Introduction and key definitions

(1) This Chapter confers power on the First-tier Tribunal to make a rent repayment order where a landlord has committed an offence to which this Chapter applies.

(2) A rent repayment order is an order requiring the landlord under a tenancy of housing in England to–

    (a) repay an amount of rent paid by a tenant, or

    (b) pay a local housing authority an amount in respect of a relevant award of universal credit paid (to any person) in respect of rent under the tenancy.

(3) A reference to 'an offence to which this Chapter applies' is to an offence, of a description specified in the table, that is committed by a landlord in relation to housing in England let by that landlord.

	Act	*section*	*general description of offence*
1	Criminal Law Act 1977	section 6(1)	violence for securing entry
2	Protection from Eviction Act 1977	section 1(2), (3) or (3A)	eviction or harassment of occupiers
3	Housing Act 2004	section 30(1)	failure to comply with improvement notice
4		section 32(1)	failure to comply with prohibition order etc
5		section 72(1)	control or management of unlicensed HMO
6		section 95(1)	control or management of unlicensed house
7	This Act	section 21	breach of banning order

(4) For the purposes of subsection (3), an offence under section 30(1) or 32(1) of the Housing Act 2004 is committed in relation to housing in England let by a landlord only if the improvement notice or prohibition order mentioned in that section was given in respect of a hazard on the premises let by the landlord (as opposed, for example, to common parts).

Application for rent repayment order

41 Application for rent repayment order

(1) A tenant or a local housing authority may apply to the First-tier Tribunal for a rent repayment order against a person who has committed an offence to which this Chapter applies.

(2) A tenant may apply for a rent repayment order only if–

    (a) the offence relates to housing that, at the time of the offence, was let to the tenant, and

    (b) the offence was committed in the period of 12 months ending with the day on which the application is made.

(3) A local housing authority may apply for a rent repayment order only if—
  (a) the offence relates to housing in the authority's area, and
  (b) the authority has complied with section 42.
(4) In deciding whether to apply for a rent repayment order a local housing authority must have regard to any guidance given by the Secretary of State.

42 Notice of intended proceedings

(1) Before applying for a rent repayment order a local housing authority must give the landlord a notice of intended proceedings.
(2) A notice of intended proceedings must—
  (a) inform the landlord that the authority is proposing to apply for a rent repayment order and explain why,
  (b) state the amount that the authority seeks to recover, and
  (c) invite the landlord to make representations within a period specified in the notice of not less than 28 days ('the notice period').
(3) The authority must consider any representations made during the notice period.
(4) The authority must wait until the notice period has ended before applying for a rent repayment order.
(5) A notice of intended proceedings may not be given after the end of the period of 12 months beginning with the day on which the landlord committed the offence to which it relates.

Making of rent repayment order

43 Making of rent repayment order

(1) The First-tier Tribunal may make a rent repayment order if satisfied, beyond reasonable doubt, that a landlord has committed an offence to which this Chapter applies (whether or not the landlord has been convicted).
(2) A rent repayment order under this section may be made only on an application under section 41.
(3) The amount of a rent repayment order under this section is to be determined in accordance with—
  (a) section 44 (where the application is made by a tenant);
  (b) section 45 (where the application is made by a local housing authority);
  (c) section 46 (in certain cases where the landlord has been convicted etc).

44 Amount of order: tenants

(1) Where the First-tier Tribunal decides to make a rent repayment order under section 43 in favour of a tenant, the amount is to be determined in accordance with this section.
(2) The amount must relate to rent paid during the period mentioned in the table.

If the order is made on the ground that the landlord has committed	*the amount must relate to rent paid by the tenant in respect of*
an offence mentioned in row 1 or 2 of the table in section 40(3)	the period of 12 months ending with the date of the offence
an offence mentioned in row 3, 4, 5, 6 or 7 of the table in section 40(3)	a period, not exceeding 12 months, during which the landlord was committing the offence

(3) The amount that the landlord may be required to repay in respect of a period must not exceed–
  (a) the rent paid in respect of that period, less
  (b) any relevant award of universal credit paid (to any person) in respect of rent under the tenancy during that period.

(4) In determining the amount the tribunal must, in particular, take into account–
  (a) the conduct of the landlord and the tenant,
  (b) the financial circumstances of the landlord, and
  (c) whether the landlord has at any time been convicted of an offence to which this Chapter applies.

45 Amount of order: local housing authorities

(1) Where the First-tier Tribunal decides to make a rent repayment order under section 43 in favour of a local housing authority, the amount is to be determined in accordance with this section.

(2) The amount must relate to universal credit paid during the period mentioned in the table.

In the order is made on the ground that the landlord has committed	the amount must relate to universal credit paid in respect of
an offence mentioned in row 1 or 2 of the table in section 40(3)	the period of 12 months ending with the date of the offence
an offence mentioned in row 3, 4, 5, 6 or 7 of the table in section 40(3)	a period, not exceeding 12 months, during which the landlord was committing the offence

(3) The amount that the landlord may be required to repay in respect of a period must not exceed the amount of universal credit that the landlord received (directly or indirectly) in respect of rent under the tenancy for that period.

(4) In determining the amount the tribunal must, in particular, take into account–
  (a) the conduct of the landlord,
  (b) the financial circumstances of the landlord, and
  (c) whether the landlord has at any time been convicted of an offence to which this Chapter applies.

46 Amount of order following conviction

(1) Where the First-tier Tribunal decides to make a rent repayment order under section 43 and both of the following conditions are met, the amount is to be the maximum that the tribunal has power to order in accordance with section 44 or 45 (but disregarding subsection (4) of those sections).

(2) Condition 1 is that the order–
  (a) is made against a landlord who has been convicted of the offence, or
  (b) is made against a landlord who has received a financial penalty in respect of the offence and is made at a time when there is no prospect of appeal against that penalty.

(3) Condition 2 is that the order is made–
  (a) in favour of a tenant on the ground that the landlord has committed an offence mentioned in row 1, 2, 3, 4 or 7 of the table in section 40(3), or
  (b) in favour of a local housing authority.

(4) For the purposes of subsection (2)(b) there is 'no prospect of appeal', in relation to a penalty, when the period for appealing the penalty has expired and any appeal has been finally determined or withdrawn.

(5) Nothing in this section requires the payment of any amount that, by reason of exceptional circumstances, the tribunal considers it would be unreasonable to require the landlord to pay.

Enforcement of rent repayment order

47 Enforcement of rent repayment orders

(1) An amount payable to a tenant or local housing authority under a rent repayment order is recoverable as a debt.

(2) An amount payable to a local housing authority under a rent repayment order does not, when recovered by the authority, constitute an amount of universal credit recovered by the authority.

(3) The Secretary of State may by regulations make provision about how local housing authorities are to deal with amounts recovered under rent repayment orders.

Local housing authority functions

48 Duty to consider applying for rent repayment orders

If a local housing authority becomes aware that a person has been convicted of an offence to which this Chapter applies in relation to housing in its area, the authority must consider applying for a rent repayment order.

49 Helping tenants apply for rent repayment orders

(1) A local housing authority in England may help a tenant to apply for a rent repayment order.

(2) A local housing authority may, for example, help the tenant to apply by conducting proceedings or by giving advice to the tenant.

Amendments etc and interpretation

50 Rent repayment orders: consequential amendments

(1) The Housing Act 2004 is amended as follows.

(2) In section 73 (other consequences of operating unlicensed HMOs: rent repayment orders)–

    (a) in subsection (4), after 'section 74' insert '(in the case of an HMO in Wales) or in accordance with Chapter 4 of Part 2 of the Housing and Planning Act 2016 (in the case of an HMO in England)';

    (b) in subsection (5)(a), after 'HMO' insert 'in Wales'.

(3) In section 96 (other consequences of operating unlicensed houses: rent repayment orders)–

    (a) in subsection (4), after 'section 97' insert '(in the case of a house in Wales) or in accordance with Chapter 4 of Part 2 of the Housing and Planning Act 2016 (in the case of a house in England)';

    (b) in subsection (5)(a), after 'house' insert 'in Wales'.

51 Housing benefit: inclusion pending abolition

(1) In this Chapter a reference to universal credit or a relevant award of universal credit includes housing benefit under Part 7 of the Social Security Contributions and Benefits Act 1992.

(2) Where a local authority applies for a rent repayment order in relation to housing benefit, a reference in this Chapter to 'rent' includes any payment in respect of which housing benefit may be paid.

52 Interpretation of Chapter

(1) In this Chapter–
'offence to which this Chapter applies' has the meaning given by section 40;
'relevant award of universal credit' means an award of universal credit the calculation of which included an amount under section 11 of the Welfare Reform Act 2012;
'rent' includes any payment in respect of which an amount under section 11 of the Welfare Reform Act 2012 may be included in the calculation of an award of universal credit;
'rent repayment order' has the meaning given by section 40.
(2) For the purposes of this Chapter an amount that a tenant does not pay as rent but which is offset against rent is to be treated as having been paid as rent.

Chapter 6: Interpretation of Part 2

54 Meaning of 'letting agent' and related expressions

(1) In this Part 'letting agent' means a person who engages in letting agency work (whether or not that person engages in other work).
(2) But a person is not a letting agent for the purposes of this Part if the person engages in letting agency work in the course of that person's employment under a contract of employment.
(3) In this Part 'letting agency work' means things done by a person in the course of a business in response to instructions received from–
   (a) a person ('a prospective landlord') seeking to find another person to whom to let housing, or
   (b) a person ('a prospective tenant') seeking to find housing to rent.
(4) But 'letting agency work' does not include any of the following things when done by a person who does nothing else within subsection (3)–
   (a) publishing advertisements or disseminating information;
   (b) providing a means by which a prospective landlord or a prospective tenant can, in response to an advertisement or dissemination of information, make direct contact with a prospective tenant or a prospective landlord;
   (c) providing a means by which a prospective landlord and a prospective tenant can communicate directly with each other.
(5) In this Part 'English letting agency work' means letting agency work that relates to housing in England.

55 Meaning of 'property manager' and related expressions

(1) In this Part 'property manager' means a person who engages in English property management work.
(2) But a person is not a property manager for the purposes of this Part if the person engages in English property management work in the course of that person's employment under a contract of employment.
(3) In this Part 'English property management work' means things done by a person in the course of a business in response to instructions received from another person ('the client') where–

(a) the client wishes the person to arrange services, repairs, maintenance, improvements or insurance in respect of, or to deal with any other aspect of the management of, premises on the client's behalf, and

(b) the premises consist of housing in England let under a tenancy.

56 General interpretation of Part

In this Part–

'banning order' has the meaning given by section 14;

'banning order offence' has the meaning given by section 14;

'body corporate' includes a body incorporated outside England and Wales;

'database' means the database of rogue landlords and letting agents established under section 28;

'English letting agency work' has the meaning given by section 54;

'English property management work' has the meaning given by section 55;

'financial penalty' means a penalty that–

(a) is imposed in respect of conduct that amounts to an offence, but

(b) is imposed otherwise than following the person's conviction for the offence;

'housing' means a building, or part of a building, occupied or intended to be occupied as a dwelling or as more than one dwelling;

'letting'–

(a) includes the grant of a licence, but

(b) except in Chapter 4, does not include the grant of a tenancy or licence for a term of more than 21 years,

and 'let' is to be read accordingly;

'letting agency work' has the meaning given by section 54;

'letting agent' has the meaning given by section 54;

'local housing authority' has the meaning given by section 1 of the Housing Act 1985;

'officer', in relation to a body corporate, means–

(a) any director, secretary or other similar officer of the body corporate, or

(b) any person who was purporting to act in any such capacity;

'property agent' means a letting agent or property manager;

'property manager' has the meaning given by section 55;

'residential landlord' means a landlord of housing;

'tenancy'–

(a) includes a licence, but

(b) except in Chapter 4, does not include a tenancy or licence for a term of more than 21 years.

DEREGULATION ACT 2015

33 Preventing retaliatory eviction

(1) Where a relevant notice is served in relation to a dwelling-house in England, a section 21 notice may not be given in relation to an assured shorthold tenancy of the dwelling-house–

    (a) within six months beginning with the day of service of the relevant notice, or

    (b) where the operation of the relevant notice has been suspended, within six months beginning with the day on which the suspension ends.

(2) A section 21 notice given in relation to an assured shorthold tenancy of a dwelling-house in England is invalid where–

    (a) before the section 21 notice was given, the tenant made a complaint in writing to the landlord regarding the condition of the dwelling-house at the time of the complaint,

    (b) the landlord–

        (i) did not provide a response to the complaint within 14 days beginning with the day on which the complaint was given,

        (ii) provided a response to the complaint that was not an adequate response, or

        (iii) gave a section 21 notice in relation to the dwelling-house following the complaint,

    (c) the tenant then made a complaint to the relevant local housing authority about the same, or substantially the same, subject matter as the complaint to the landlord,

    (d) the relevant local housing authority served a relevant notice in relation to the dwelling-house in response to the complaint, and

    (e) if the section 21 notice was not given before the tenant's complaint to the local housing authority, it was given before the service of the relevant notice.

(3) The reference in subsection (2) to an adequate response by the landlord is to a response in writing which–

    (a) provides a description of the action that the landlord proposes to take to address the complaint, and

    (b) sets out a reasonable timescale within which that action will be taken.

(4) Subsection (2) applies despite the requirement in paragraph (a) for a complaint to be in writing not having been met where the tenant does not know the landlord's postal or e-mail address.

(5) Subsection (2) applies despite the requirements in paragraphs (a) and (b) not having been met where the tenant made reasonable efforts to contact the landlord to complain about the condition of the dwelling-house but was unable to do so.

(6) The court must strike out proceedings for an order for possession under section 21 of the Housing Act 1988 in relation to a dwelling-house in England if, before the order is made, the section 21 notice that would otherwise require the court to make an order for possession in relation to the dwelling-house has become invalid under subsection (2).

(7) An order for possession of a dwelling-house in England made under section 21 of the Housing Act 1988 must not be set aside on the ground that a rel-

evant notice was served in relation to the dwelling-house after the order for possession was made.

(8) Subsection (1) does not apply where the section 21 notice is given after–

   (a) the relevant notice has been wholly revoked under section 16 of the Housing Act 2004 as a result of the notice having been served in error,

   (b) the relevant notice has been quashed under paragraph 15 of Schedule 1 to that Act,

   (c) a decision of the relevant local housing authority to refuse to revoke the relevant notice has been reversed under paragraph 18 of Schedule 1 to that Act, or

   (d) a decision of the relevant local housing authority to take the action to which the relevant notice relates has been reversed under section 45 of that Act.

(9) Subsection (2) does not apply where the operation of the relevant notice has been suspended.

(10) References in this section and section 34 to a relevant notice served, or complaint made, in relation to a dwelling-house include a relevant notice served, or complaint made, in relation to any common parts of the building of which the dwelling-house forms a part.

(11) But subsection (10) applies only if–

   (a) the landlord has a controlling interest in the common parts in question, and

   (b) the condition of those common parts is such as to affect the tenant's enjoyment of the dwelling-house or of any common parts which the tenant is entitled to use.

(12) In this section and section 34 a reference to a complaint to a landlord includes a complaint made to a person acting on behalf of the landlord in relation to the tenancy.

(13) In this section and section 34–

'assured shorthold tenancy' means a tenancy within section 19A or 20 of the Housing Act 1988;

'common parts', in relation to a building, includes–

   (a) the structure and exterior of the building, and

   (b) common facilities provided (whether or not in the building) for persons who include one or more of the occupiers of the building;

'controlling interest' means an interest which is such as to entitle the landlord to decide whether action is taken in relation to a complaint within this section or a relevant notice;

'dwelling-house' has the meaning given by section 45 of the Housing Act 1988;

'relevant local housing authority', in relation to a dwelling-house, means the local housing authority as defined in section 261(2) and (3) of the Housing Act 2004 within whose area the dwelling-house is located;

'relevant notice' means–

   (a) a notice served under section 11 of the Housing Act 2004 (improvement notices relating to category 1 hazards),

   (b) a notice served under section 12 of that Act (improvement notices relating to category 2 hazards), or

(c) a notice served under section 40(7) of that Act (emergency remedial action);

'section 21 notice' means a notice given under section 21(1)(b) or (4)(a) of the Housing Act 1988 (recovery of possession on termination of shorthold tenancy).

34 Further exemptions to section 33

(1) Subsections (1) and (2) of section 33 do not apply where the condition of the dwelling-house or common parts that gave rise to the service of the relevant notice is due to a breach by the tenant of—
   (a) the duty to use the dwelling-house in a tenant-like manner, or
   (b) an express term of the tenancy to the same effect.

(2) Subsections (1) and (2) of section 33 do not apply where at the time the section 21 notice is given the dwelling-house is genuinely on the market for sale.

(3) For the purposes of subsection (2), a dwelling-house is not genuinely on the market for sale if, in particular, the landlord intends to sell the landlord's interest in the dwelling-house to—
   (a) a person associated with the landlord,
   (b) a business partner of the landlord,
   (c) a person associated with a business partner of the landlord, or
   (d) a business partner of a person associated with the landlord.

(4) In subsection (3), references to a person who is associated with another person are to be read in accordance with section 178 of the Housing Act 1996.

(5) For the purposes of subsection (3), a business partner of a person ('P') is a person who is—
   (a) a director, secretary or other officer of a company of which P is also a director, secretary or other officer,
   (b) a director, secretary or other officer of a company in which P has a shareholding or other financial interest,
   (c) a person who has a shareholding or other financial interest in a company of which P is a director, secretary or other officer,
   (d) an employee of P,
   (e) a person by whom P is employed, or
   (f) a partner of a partnership of which P is also a partner.

(6) Subsections (1) and (2) of section 33 do not apply where the landlord is a private registered provider of social housing.

(7) Subsections (1) and (2) of section 33 do not apply where—
   (a) the dwelling-house is subject to a mortgage granted before the beginning of the tenancy,
   (b) the mortgagee is entitled to exercise a power of sale conferred on the mortgagee by the mortgage or by section 101 of the Law of Property Act 1925, and
   (c) at the time the section 21 notice is given the mortgagee requires possession of the dwelling-house for the purpose of disposing of it with vacant possession in exercise of that power.

(8) In subsection (7)—
   (a) 'mortgage' includes a charge, and
   (b) 'mortgagee' includes a receiver appointed by the mortgagee under the terms of the mortgage or in accordance with the Law of Property Act 1925.

HOUSING (WALES) ACT 2014

Part 1: Regulation of private rented housing

Prohibition of letting and management without registration and licence

4 Requirement for a landlord to be registered

(1) The landlord of a dwelling subject to, or marketed or offered for let under, a domestic tenancy must be registered under this Part in respect of the dwelling (see sections 14 to 17), unless an exception in section 5 applies.

(2) A landlord who contravenes subsection (1) commits an offence and is liable on summary conviction to a fine not exceeding level 3 on the standard scale.

(3) In proceedings against a landlord for an offence under subsection (2) it is a defence that the landlord has a reasonable excuse for not being registered.

5 Exceptions to the requirement for a landlord to be registered

The requirement in section 4(1) does not apply–

(a) if the landlord has applied to the licensing authority to be registered in relation to that dwelling and the application has not been determined;

(b) for a period of 28 days beginning with the date the landlord's interest in the dwelling is assigned to the landlord;

(c) if the landlord takes steps to recover possession of the dwelling within a period of 28 days beginning with the date the landlord's interest in the dwelling is assigned to the landlord, for so long as the landlord continues to diligently pursue the recovery of possession;

(d) to a landlord who is a registered social landlord;

(e) to a landlord who is a fully mutual housing association;

(f) to a person of a description specified for the purposes of this section in an order made by the Welsh Ministers.

6 Requirement for landlords to be licensed to carry out lettings activities

(1) The landlord of a dwelling marketed or offered for let under a domestic tenancy must not do any of the things described in subsection (2) in respect of the dwelling unless–

(a) the landlord is licensed to do so under this Part for the area in which the dwelling is located,

(b) the thing done is arranging for an authorised agent to do something on the landlord's behalf, or

(c) an exception in section 8 applies.

(2) The things are–

(a) arranging or conducting viewings with prospective tenants;

(b) gathering evidence for the purpose of establishing the suitability of prospective tenants (for example, by confirming character references, undertaking credit checks or interviewing a prospective tenant);

(c) preparing, or arranging the preparation, of a tenancy agreement;

(d) preparing, or arranging the preparation, of an inventory for the dwelling or schedule of condition for the dwelling.

(3) The Welsh Ministers may by order–

(a) amend or omit the descriptions of things in subsection (2) (including things added under paragraph (b));

(b) add further descriptions of things to subsection (2).

(4) A landlord who contravenes subsection (1) commits an offence and is liable on summary conviction to a fine.

(5) In proceedings against a landlord for an offence under subsection (4) it is a defence that the landlord has a reasonable excuse for not being licensed.

(6) In subsection (1) 'authorised agent' means–

(a) a person licensed to carry out lettings work and property management work under this Part for the area in which the dwelling is located,

(b) a local housing authority (whether or not in exercise of its functions as a local housing authority), or

(c) in relation to preparing, or arranging the preparation of a tenancy agreement only, a qualified solicitor (within the meaning of Part 1 of the Solicitors Act 1974), a person acting on behalf of such a solicitor or any person of a description specified in an order made by the Welsh Ministers.

7 Requirement for landlords to be licensed to carry out property management activities

(1) The landlord of a dwelling subject to a domestic tenancy must not do any of the things described in subsection (2) in respect of the dwelling unless–

(a) the landlord is licensed to do so under this Part for the area in which the dwelling is located,

(b) the thing done is arranging for an authorised agent to do something on the landlord's behalf, or

(c) an exception in section 8 applies.

(2) The things are–

(a) collecting rent;

(b) being the principal point of contact for the tenant in relation to matters arising under the tenancy;

(c) making arrangements with a person to carry out repairs or maintenance;

(d) making arrangements with a tenant or occupier of the dwelling to secure access to the dwelling for any purpose;

(e) checking the contents or condition of the dwelling, or arranging for them to be checked;

(f) serving notice to terminate a tenancy.

(3) The landlord of a dwelling that was subject to a domestic tenancy, but is no longer subject to that domestic tenancy, must not check the contents or condition of the dwelling, or arrange for them to be checked, for any purpose connected with that tenancy unless–

(a) the landlord is licensed to do so under this Part for the area in which the dwelling is located,

(b) the thing done is arranging for an authorised agent to do it on the landlord's behalf, or

(c) an exception in section 8 applies.

(4) The Welsh Ministers may by order–

(a) amend or omit the descriptions of things in subsection (2) or (3) (including things added under paragraph (b)) that a landlord must not do unless any of paragraphs (a) to (c) of subsection (1) or (3) applies (as the case may be);

(b) add further descriptions of things for the purposes of this section (including by way of amendment to this Part).

(5) A landlord who contravenes subsection (1) or (3) commits an offence and is liable on summary conviction to a fine.

(6) In proceedings against a landlord for an offence under subsection (5) it is a defence that the landlord has a reasonable excuse for not being licensed.

(7) In subsection (1) 'authorised agent' means–

(a) a person licensed to carry out lettings work and property management work under this Part for the area in which the dwelling is located,

(b) a local housing authority (whether or not in exercise of its functions as a local housing authority), or

(c) in relation to serving notice to terminate a tenancy only, a qualified solicitor (within the meaning of Part 1 of the Solicitors Act 1974), a person acting on behalf of such a solicitor or any person of a description specified in an order made by the Welsh Ministers.

8 Exceptions to requirements for landlords to be licensed

The requirements in sections 6(1), 7(1) and 7(3) do not apply–

(a) if the landlord has applied to the licensing authority to be licensed, for the period from the date of the application until it is determined by the authority or (if the authority refuses the application) until all means of appealing against a decision to refuse an application have been exhausted and the decision is upheld;

(b) for a period of 28 days beginning with the date the landlord's interest in the dwelling is assigned to the landlord;

(c) if the landlord takes steps to recover possession of the dwelling within a period of 28 days beginning with the date the landlord's interest in the dwelling is assigned to the landlord, for so long as the landlord continues to diligently pursue the recovery of possession;

(d) to a landlord who is a registered social landlord;

(e) to a landlord who is a fully mutual housing association;

(f) in cases specified for the purposes of this section in an order made by the Welsh Ministers.

9 Requirement for agents to be licensed to carry out lettings work

(1) A person acting on behalf of the landlord of a dwelling marketed or offered for let under a domestic tenancy must not carry out lettings work in respect of the dwelling unless the person is licensed to do so under this Part for the area in which the dwelling is located.

(2) A person who contravenes this section commits an offence and is liable on summary conviction to a fine.

(3) In proceedings against a person for an offence committed under subsection (2) it is a defence that the person has a reasonable excuse for not being licensed.

10 Meaning of lettings work

(1) In this Part 'lettings work' means things done by any person in response to instructions received from–

(a) a person seeking to find another person wishing to rent a dwelling under a domestic tenancy and, having found such a person, to grant such a tenancy ('a prospective landlord');

(b) a person seeking to find a dwelling to rent under a domestic tenancy and, having found such a dwelling, to obtain such a tenancy of it ('a prospective tenant'); subject to the following subsections.

(2) 'Lettings work' does not include anything in the following paragraphs (a) or (b)–

(a) publishing advertisements or disseminating information;

(b) providing a means by which–

    (i) a prospective landlord (or the prospective landlord's agent) or a prospective tenant can, in response to an advertisement or dissemination of information, make direct contact with a prospective tenant or (as the case may be) prospective landlord (or the prospective landlord's agent);

    (ii) a prospective landlord (or the prospective landlord's agent) and a prospective tenant can continue to communicate directly with each other;

when done by a person who–

(c) does no other thing within subsection (1), and

(d) does no property management work in respect of the property.

(3) 'Lettings work' does not include doing any one of the things in the following paragraphs (a) to (c)–

(a) arranging and conducting viewings with prospective tenants;

(b) preparing, or arranging the preparation of, the tenancy agreement;

(c) preparing, or arranging the preparation of, any inventory or schedule of condition; when done by a person who–

(d) does no other thing in those paragraphs or anything else within subsection (1), and

(e) does nothing within section 12(1) in respect of the property.

(4) 'Lettings work' also does not include–

(a) doing things under a contract of service or apprenticeship with a landlord;

(b) doing things under a contract of service or apprenticeship, or a contract for services, with a person who is–

    (i) instructed to carry out the work by a landlord, and

    (ii) licensed to do so under this Part;

(c) anything done by a local housing authority (whether or not in exercise of its functions as a local housing authority);

(d) things of a description, or things done by a person of a description, specified for the purposes of this section in an order made by the Welsh Ministers.

11 Requirement for agents to be licensed to carry out property management work

(1) A person acting on behalf of the landlord of a dwelling subject to a domestic tenancy must not carry out property management work in respect of the dwelling unless the person is licensed to do so under this Part for the area in which the dwelling is located.

(2) Where a dwelling was subject to a domestic tenancy, but is no longer subject to that domestic tenancy, a person acting on behalf of the landlord of the dwelling must not check the contents or condition of the dwelling, or arrange for them to be checked, for any purpose connected with that tenancy unless–

(a) the person is licensed to do so under this Part for the area in which the dwelling is located,

(b) the person does no other thing in respect of the dwelling falling within–
- (i) section 10(1), except preparing, or arranging the preparation of, any inventory or schedule of condition, or
- (ii) section 12(1), or

(c) the activity would not, by virtue of section 12(3), be property management work.

(3) A person who contravenes subsection (1) or (2) commits an offence and is liable on summary conviction to a fine.

(4) In proceedings against a person for an offence committed under subsection (3) it is a defence that the person has a reasonable excuse for not being licensed.

12 Meaning of property management work

(1) In this Part, 'property management work' means doing any of the following things–

(a) collecting rent;

(b) being the principal point of contact for the tenant in relation to matters arising under the tenancy;

(c) making arrangements with a person to carry out repairs or maintenance;

(d) making arrangements with a tenant or occupier of the dwelling to secure access to the dwelling for any purpose;

(e) checking the contents or condition of the dwelling, or arranging for them to be checked;

(f) serving notice to terminate a tenancy.

(2) But 'property management work' does not include doing any one of the things in paragraphs (b) to (f) of subsection (1) when done by a person who–

(a) does no other thing within subsection (1), and

(b) does nothing within section 10(1) in respect of the dwelling.

(3) 'Property management work' also does not include–

(a) doing things under a contract of service or apprenticeship with a landlord;

(b) doing things under a contract of service or apprenticeship, or a contract for services, with a person who is–
- (i) instructed to carry out the work by a landlord, and
- (ii) licensed to do so under this Part;

(c) anything done by a local housing authority (whether or not in exercise of its functions as a local housing authority);

(d) things of a description, or things done by a person of a description, specified for the purposes of this section in an order made by the Welsh Ministers.

13 Offence of appointing an unlicensed agent

(1) The landlord of a dwelling marketed or offered for let under a domestic tenancy must not appoint or continue to allow a person to undertake lettings work on behalf of the landlord in relation to that dwelling, if–

  (a) the person does not hold a licence to do so under this Part for the area in which the dwelling is located, and

  (b) the landlord knows or should know that the person does not hold such a licence.

(2) The landlord of a dwelling subject to a domestic tenancy must not appoint or continue to allow a person to undertake property management work on behalf of the landlord in relation to that dwelling, if–

  (a) the person does not hold a licence to do so under this Part for the area in which the dwelling is located, and

  (b) the landlord knows or should know that the person does not hold such a licence.

(3) A landlord who contravenes subsection (1) or (2) commits an offence and is liable on summary conviction to a fine not exceeding level 4 on the standard scale.

  ...

28 Prosecution by a licensing authority or a local housing authority

(1) A licensing authority may bring criminal proceedings in respect of an offence under –

  (a) section 4(2), 6(4), 7(5), 9(2), 11(3) or 13(3) if the alleged offence arises in respect of a dwelling in the area for which it is the licensing authority;

  (b) section 16(3) or 23(3), in respect of information to be provided to the licensing authority;

  (c) subsection (1) or (4) of section 38, in respect of anything required by a notice given by a person authorised by the authority;

  (d) subsection (1) or (2) of section 39, in respect of information supplied to the authority.

(2) A local housing authority that is not the licensing authority for its area may, with the consent of the licensing authority for the area, bring criminal proceedings in respect of an offence under section 4(2), 6(4), 7(5), 9(2), 11(3) or 13(3), if the alleged offence arises in respect of a dwelling in its area.

(3) A licensing authority may give its consent under subsection (2) generally or in specific cases.

(4) This section does not affect–

  (a) any other power of the person designated under section 3 to bring legal proceedings;

  (b) section 222 of the Local Government Act 1972 (power of local authorities to prosecute or defend legal proceedings).

29 Fixed penalty notices

(1) Where on any occasion a person authorised in writing for the purpose of this section by a licensing authority has reason to believe that a person has committed an offence under this Part (other than an offence under section 13(3) or section 38(4)), the authorised person may, by notice, offer the person the opportunity of discharging any liability to conviction for that offence by payment of a fixed penalty to the authority.

(2) Where a person is given a notice under this section in respect of an offence–

    (a) no proceedings may be issued for that offence before the expiration of the period of 21 days following the date of the notice;

    (b) the person may not be convicted of the offence if the person pays the fixed penalty before the end of that period.

(3) A notice under this section must–

    (a) give such particulars of the circumstances alleged to constitute the offence as are necessary for giving reasonable information of the offence,

    (b) state the period during which proceedings will not be taken for the offence,

    (c) state the amount of the fixed penalty, and

    (d) state the person to whom and the address at which the fixed penalty may be paid.

(4) The fixed penalty payable to a licensing authority under this section is £150 unless the offence is an offence attracting an unlimited fine; in which case, the fixed penalty payable is £250.

(5) The Welsh Ministers may amend subsection (4) by order.

(6) Payment of a fixed penalty may be made by pre-paying and posting a letter containing the amount of the penalty (in cash or otherwise) to the person mentioned in subsection (3)(d) at the address so mentioned; but this does not prevent payment by another method.

(7) Where a letter is posted in accordance with subsection (6) payment is to be regarded as having been made at the time at which the letter would be delivered in the ordinary course of post.

(8) In any proceedings a certificate–

    (a) which purports to be signed on behalf of a person authorised for this purpose by the licensing authority, and

    (b) states that payment of a fixed penalty was or was not received by a date specified in the certificate,

is evidence of the facts stated.

(9) A licensing authority may use its fixed penalty receipts only for the purposes of its functions relating to the enforcement of this Part.

(10) In this section, 'licensing authority' means–

    (a) in the case of an offence under section 4(2), 6(4), 7(5), 9(2) or 11(3), the licensing authority for the area in which the dwelling to which the offence relates is located;

    (b) in the case of an offence under section 16(3) or 23(3), the licensing authority to which the information to which the offence relates was provided;

    (c) in the case of an offence under section 38(1), the licensing authority which authorised the person who gave the relevant notice;

    (d) in the case of an offence under section 39(1) or (2), the licensing authority to which the information was supplied.

(11) A local housing authority that is not the licensing authority for its area may, with the consent of the licensing authority for the area, exercise the functions of the licensing authority under this section concurrently with the licensing authority; but only in respect of the offences mentioned in subsection (10)(a).

(12) And where a local housing authority exercises functions under this section

by virtue of subsection (11), the references in subsections (1), (4), (8), (9) and (10)(a) to 'licensing authority' are to be read as if they were references to the local housing authority.

30 Rent stopping orders

(1) A residential property tribunal may, in accordance with this section, make an order (a 'rent stopping order') in relation to a dwelling subject to a domestic tenancy on an application made to it by–
   (a) the licensing authority for the area in which the dwelling is located, or
   (b) the local housing authority for the area in which the dwelling is located.
(2) But a local housing authority may not make an application under subsection (1) without the consent of the licensing authority mentioned in paragraph (a) of that subsection (unless it is the licensing authority); and consent for that purpose may be given generally or in respect of a particular application.
(3) Where the tribunal makes a rent stopping order–
   (a) periodical payments payable in connection with a domestic tenancy of the dwelling which relate to a period, or part of a period, falling between a date specified in the order (the 'stopping date') and a date specified by the tribunal when the order is revoked (see section 31(4)) are stopped,
   (b) an obligation under a domestic tenancy to pay an amount stopped by the order is treated as being met,
   (c) all other rights and obligations under such a tenancy continue unaffected,
   (d) any periodical payments stopped by the order but made by a tenant of the dwelling (whether before or after the stopping date) must be repaid by the landlord, and
   (e) the authority which made the application for the order must give a copy of it to–
       (i) the landlord of the dwelling to which the order relates;
       (ii) the tenant of the dwelling.
(4) The tribunal may make a rent stopping order only if it is satisfied of the matters mentioned in subsections (5) and (6).
(5) The tribunal must be satisfied that an offence is being committed under section 7(5) or 13(3) in relation to the dwelling (whether or not a person has been convicted or charged for the offence).
(6) The tribunal must be satisfied that–
   (a) the authority making the application for the order has given the landlord and the tenant of the dwelling a notice (a 'notice of intended proceedings')–
       (i) explaining that the authority is proposing to apply for a rent stopping order,
       (ii) setting out the reasons why it proposes to do so,
       (iii) explaining the effect of a rent stopping order,
       (iv) explaining how a rent stopping order may be revoked, and
       (v) in the case of a notice given to a landlord, inviting the landlord to make representations to the authority within a period of not less than 28 days specified in the notice,
   (b) the period for making representations has expired, and

(c) the authority considered any representations made to it within that period by the landlord.

(7) The tribunal may not specify a stopping date for the purpose of subsection (3)(a) which precedes the date on which the rent stopping order is made.

(8) An amount payable by virtue of subsection (3)(d) which is not repaid is recoverable by the tenant as a debt due to the tenant from the landlord.

(9) In subsection (5), the reference to an offence committed under section 13(3) does not include an offence committed in consequence of a contravention of subsection (1) of that section.

31 Revocation of rent stopping orders

(1) A residential property tribunal may, in accordance with this section, revoke a rent stopping order made in respect of a dwelling under section 30.

(2) The tribunal may revoke an order only–
   (a) on an application by–
      (i) the licensing authority for the area in which the dwelling is located,
      (ii) the local housing authority for the area in which the dwelling is located, or
      (iii) the landlord of the dwelling, and
   (b) if it is satisfied that an offence under section 7(5) or 13(3) is no longer being committed in relation to the dwelling.

(3) But a local housing authority may not make an application under subsection (2) without the consent of the licensing authority mentioned in paragraph (a)(i) of that subsection (unless it is the licensing authority); and consent for that purpose may be given generally or in respect of a particular application.

(4) Where the tribunal revokes a rent stopping order, periodical payments in connection with a domestic tenancy of the dwelling become payable from a date specified by the tribunal (which may, if the tribunal considers it appropriate, be a date earlier than the date on which the order is revoked).

(5) But revocation of a rent stopping order does not make a person liable to pay any periodical payments which, by virtue of the order, were stopped in respect of the period beginning with the stopping date (see section 30(3)(a)) and ending with the date specified by the tribunal when revoking the order.

(6) If a rent stopping order is revoked following an application made under subsection (2)(a)(i) or (ii), the authority which made the application must notify the following persons that the order is revoked and of the effect of the revocation–
   (a) any tenant or occupier of the dwelling, and
   (b) the landlord of the dwelling.

(7) Where revocation occurs following an application made by a landlord, the licensing authority for the area in which the dwelling is located must ensure that any tenant or occupier of the dwelling is notified that the order is revoked and of the effect of the revocation.

(8) In subsection (2)(b)–
   (a) the reference to an offence section 7(5) does not include an offence committed in consequence of a contravention of subsection (3) of that section, and
   (b) the reference to an offence committed under 13(3) does not include an

offence committed in consequence of a contravention of subsection (1) of that section.

32 Rent repayment orders

(1) A residential property tribunal may, in accordance with this section and section 33, make an order (a 'rent repayment order') in relation to a dwelling on an application made to it by–
(a) the licensing authority for the area in which the dwelling is located,
(b) the local housing authority for the area in which the dwelling is located, or
(c) a tenant of the dwelling.

(2) But a local housing authority may not make an application under subsection (1) without the consent of the licensing authority mentioned in paragraph (a) of that subsection (unless it is the licensing authority); and consent for that purpose may be given generally or in respect of a particular application.

(3) A 'rent repayment order' is an order made in relation to a dwelling which requires the appropriate person (see subsection (9)) to pay to the applicant such amount in respect of the relevant award or awards of universal credit or the housing benefit paid as mentioned in subsection (5)(b), or (as the case may be) the periodical payments paid as mentioned in subsection (7)(b), as is specified in the order.

(4) The tribunal may make a rent repayment order only if it is satisfied–
(a) where the applicant is the licensing authority or a local housing authority (as the case may be), of the matters mentioned in subsection (5);
(b) where the applicant is a tenant, of the matters mentioned in subsection (7).

(5) The tribunal must be satisfied–
(a) that at any time within the period of 12 months ending with the date of the notice of intended proceedings required by subsection (6) an offence under section 7(5) or 13(3) has been committed in relation to the dwelling (whether or not a person has been charged or convicted for the offence);
(b) that–
(i) one or more relevant awards of universal credit have been paid (to any person),or
(ii) housing benefit has been paid (to any person) in respect of periodical payments payable in connection with a domestic tenancy of the dwelling,
during any period during which it appears to the tribunal that such an offence was being committed, and
(c) the requirements of subsection (6) have been complied with in relation to the application.

(6) Those requirements are–
(a) that the authority making the application must have given the appropriate person a notice (a 'notice of intended proceedings')–
(i) informing the person that the authority is proposing to make an application for a rent repayment order,
(ii) setting out the reasons why it proposes to do so,
(iii) stating the amount that it will seek to recover under that subsection and how that amount is calculated, and

(iv) inviting the person to make representations to the authority within a period of not less than 28 days specified in the notice;

(b) that period must have expired, and

(c) that the authority must have considered any representations made to it within that period by the appropriate person.

(7) The tribunal must be satisfied that—

(a) a person has been convicted of an offence under section 7(5) or 13(3) in relation to the dwelling, or that a rent repayment order has required a person to make a payment in respect of—

(i) one or more relevant awards of universal credit, or

(ii) housing benefit paid in connection with a tenancy of the dwelling;

(b) the tenant paid to the appropriate person (whether directly or otherwise) periodical payments in respect of the tenancy of the dwelling during any period during which it appears to the tribunal that such an offence was being committed in relation to the dwelling, and

(c) the application is made within the period of 12 months beginning with—

(i) the date of the conviction or order, or

(ii) if such a conviction was followed by such an order (or vice versa), the date of the later of them.

(8) In this section—

(a) references to an offence under section 7(5) do not include an offence committed in consequence of a contravention of subsection (3) of that section, and

(b) references to an offence committed under section 13(3) do not include an offence committed in consequence of a contravention of subsection (1) of that section.

(9) In this section—

'appropriate person' (' person priodol '), in relation to any payment of universal credit or housing benefit or periodical payment in connection with a domestic tenancy of a dwelling, means the person who at the time of the payment was entitled to receive, on that person's own account, periodical payments in connection with the tenancy;

'housing benefit' (' budd-dal tai ') means housing benefit provided by virtue of a scheme under section 123 of the Social Security Contributions and Benefits Act 1992;

'relevant award of universal credit' (' dyfarniad perthnasol o gredyd cynhwysol ') means an award of universal credit the calculation of which included an amount under section 11 of the Welfare Reform Act 2012, calculated in accordance with Schedule 4 to the Universal Credit Regulations 2013 (housing costs element for renters) (SI 2013/376) or any corresponding provision replacing that Schedule, in respect of periodical payments in connection with a domestic tenancy of the dwelling;

'tenant' (' tenant '), in relation to any periodical payment, means a person who was a tenant at the time of the payment (and 'tenancy' has a corresponding meaning).

(10) For the purposes of this section an amount which—

(a) is not actually paid by a tenant but is used to discharge the whole or part of the tenant's liability in respect of a periodical payment (for example, by offsetting the amount against any such liability), and

(b) is not an amount of universal credit or housing benefit, is to be regarded as an amount paid by the tenant in respect of that periodical payment.

33 Rent repayment orders: further provision

(1) Where, on an application by the licensing authority or a local housing authority (as the case may be) for a rent repayment order, the tribunal is satisfied—
   (a) that a person has been convicted of an offence under section 7(5) or 13(3) in relation to the dwelling to which the application relates, and
   (b) that—
      (i) one or more relevant awards of universal credit were paid (whether or not to the appropriate person), or
      (ii) housing benefit was paid (whether or not to the appropriate person) in respect of periodical payments payable in connection with a domestic tenancy of the dwelling during any period during which it appears to the tribunal that such an offence was being committed in relation to the dwelling in question,
   the tribunal must make a rent repayment order requiring the appropriate person to pay to the authority which made the application the amount mentioned in subsection (2); but this is subject to subsections (3), (4) and (8).

(2) The amount is—
   (a) an amount equal to—
      (i) where one relevant award of universal credit was paid as mentioned in subsection (1)(b)(i), the amount included in the calculation of that award under section 11 of the Welfare Reform Act 2012, calculated in accordance with Schedule 4 to the Universal Credit Regulations 2013 (housing costs element for renters) (SI 2013/376) or any corresponding provision replacing that Schedule, or the amount of the award if less, or
      (ii) if more than one such award was paid as mentioned in subsection (1)(b)(i), the sum of the amounts included in the calculation of those awards as referred to in sub-paragraph (i), or the sum of the amounts of those awards if less, or
   (b) an amount equal to the total amount of housing benefit paid as mentioned in subsection (1)(b)(ii) (as the case may be).

(3) If the total of the amounts received by the appropriate person in respect of periodical payments payable as mentioned in paragraph (b) of subsection (1) ('the rent total') is less than the amount mentioned in subsection (2), the amount required to be paid by virtue of a rent repayment order made in accordance with subsection (1) is limited to the rent total.

(4) A rent repayment order made in accordance with subsection (1) may not require the payment of any amount which the tribunal is satisfied that, by reason of any exceptional circumstances, it would be unreasonable for that person to be required to pay.

(5) In a case where subsection (1) does not apply, the amount required to be paid by virtue of a rent repayment order is to be such amount as the tribunal considers reasonable in the circumstances; but this is subject to subsections (6) to (8).

(6) In such a case, the tribunal must take into account the following matters—
   (a) the total amount of relevant payments paid in connection with a tenancy

of the dwelling during any period during which it appears to the tribunal that an offence was being committed in relation to the dwelling under section 7(5) or 13(3);

(b) the extent to which that total amount–

    (i) consisted of, or derived from, payments of relevant awards of universal credit or

housing benefit, and

    (ii) was actually received by the appropriate person;

(c) whether the appropriate person has at any time been convicted of an offence under section 7(5) or 13(3);

(d) the conduct and financial circumstances of the appropriate person; and

(e) where the application is made by a tenant, the conduct of the tenant.

(7) In subsection (6) 'relevant payments' means–

(a) in relation to an application by the licensing authority or a local housing authority (as the case may be), payments of relevant awards of universal credit, housing benefit or periodical payments payable by tenants;

(b) in relation to an application by a tenant, periodical payments payable by the tenant, less–

    (i) where one or more relevant awards of universal credit were payable during the period in question, the amount mentioned in subsection (2)(a) in respect of the award or awards that related to the tenancy during that period, or

    (ii) any amount of housing benefit payable in respect of the tenancy of the dwelling during the period in question.

(8) A rent repayment order may not require the payment of any amount which–

(a) where the application is made by the licensing authority or a local housing authority (as the case may be), is in respect of any time falling outside the period of 12 months ending with the date of the notice of intended proceedings given under section 32(6), or

(b) where the application is made by a tenant, is in respect of any time falling outside the period of 12 months ending with the date of the tenant's application under section 32(1);

and the period to be taken into account under subsection (6)(a) is restricted accordingly.

(9) Any amount payable by virtue of a rent repayment order is recoverable as a debt due to the licensing authority, local housing authority or tenant (as the case may be) from the appropriate person.

(10) And an amount payable to the licensing authority or a local housing authority by virtue of such an order does not, when recovered by it, constitute an amount of universal credit or housing benefit (as the case may be) recovered by the authority.

(11) Subsections (8), (9) and (10) of section 32 apply for the purposes of this section as they apply for the purposes of section 32.

34 Power for Welsh Ministers to make regulations in relation to sections 32 and 33

(1) The Welsh Ministers may by regulations make such provision as they consider appropriate for supplementing the provisions of sections 32 and 33.

(2) Regulations made under subsection (1) may, for example, make provision–
   (a) for securing that persons are not unfairly prejudiced by rent repayment orders (whether in cases where there have been over-payments of universal credit or housing benefit or otherwise);
   (b) requiring or authorising amounts received by the licensing authority or local housing authorities by virtue of rent repayment orders to be dealt with in such manner as is specified in the regulations.
   ...

43 Activity in contravention of this Part: effect on tenancy agreements

(1) No rule of law relating to the validity or enforceability of contracts in circumstances involving illegality is to affect the validity or enforceability of any provision of a domestic tenancy of a dwelling in respect of which a contravention of this Part has occurred.
(2) But periodical payments–
   (a) payable in connection with such a tenancy may be stopped in accordance with section 30 (rent stopping orders), and
   (b) paid in connection with such a tenancy may be recovered in accordance with sections 32 and 33 (rent repayment orders).

44 Restriction on terminating tenancies

(1) A section 21 notice may not be given in relation to a dwelling subject to a domestic tenancy which is an assured shorthold tenancy if–
   (a) the landlord is not registered in respect of the dwelling, or
   (b) the landlord is not licensed under this Part for the area in which the dwelling is located and the landlord has not appointed a person who is licensed under this Part to carry out all property management work in respect of the dwelling on the landlord's behalf.
(2) But subsection (1) does not apply for the period of 28 days beginning with the day on which the landlord's interest in the dwelling is assigned to the landlord.
(3) In this section, a 'section 21 notice' means a notice under section 21(1)(b) or (4)(a) of the Housing Act 1988.

MOBILE HOMES (WALES) ACT 2013

Part 3: Protection from eviction

40 Application of Part

This Part applies in relation to any licence or contract (whenever made) under which a person is entitled–

(a) to station a mobile home on a protected site and occupy it as the person's residence, or

(b) if the mobile home is stationed on the protected site by another, to occupy it as the person's residence.

41 Minimum length of notice

In any case where a residential contract is determinable by notice given by either party to the other, a notice is of no effect unless it is given not less than 4 weeks before the date on which it is to take effect.

42 Protection of occupiers against eviction and harassment, false information etc.

(1) A person to whom any of subsections (2) to (6) applies commits an offence.

(2) This subsection applies to a person if, during the subsistence of a residential contract, the person unlawfully deprives the occupier of the mobile home of occupation on the protected site of any mobile home which the occupier is entitled by the contract to station and occupy, or to occupy, as the occupier's residence on the protected site.

(3) This subsection applies to a person if, after the expiry or determination of a residential contract, the person enforces, otherwise than by proceedings in the court, any right to exclude the occupier of the mobile home from the protected site or from any such mobile home, or to remove or exclude any such mobile home from the protected site.

(4) This subsection applies to a person if (whether during the subsistence, or after the expiry or determination, of a residential contract) with intent to cause the occupier of the mobile home–

(a) to abandon the occupation of the mobile home or remove it from the site, or

(b) to refrain from exercising any right or pursuing any remedy in respect of that,

the person does acts likely to interfere with the peace or comfort of the occupier or persons residing with the occupier, or withdraws or withholds services or facilities reasonably required for the occupation of the mobile home as a residence on the site.

(5) This subsection applies to a person if the person is, or is the agent of, the owner of the protected site and (whether during the subsistence or after the expiration or determination of a residential contract)–

(a) the person does acts likely to interfere with the peace or comfort of the occupier of the mobile home or persons residing with the occupier, or

(b) withdraws or withholds services or facilities reasonably required for the occupation of the mobile home as a residence on the site,

and (in either case) the person knows, or has reasonable cause to believe, that

that conduct is likely to cause the occupier to do any of the things mentioned in subsection (4)(a) or (b).

(6) This subsection applies to a person if the person is, or is the agent of, the owner of a protected site and, during the subsistence of a residential contract, the person–

(a) knowingly or recklessly provides information or makes a representation which is false or misleading in a material respect to any person, and

(b) knows, or has reasonable cause to believe, that doing so is likely to cause–

(i) the occupier to do any of the things mentioned in subsection (4)(a) or (b), or

(ii) a person who is considering whether to purchase or occupy the mobile home to

which the residential contract relates to decide not to do so.

(7) In subsections (5) and (6) references to the owner of a protected site include references to a person with an estate or interest in the site which is superior to that of the owner.

(8) In this section references to the occupier of the mobile home include references to the person who was the occupier of the mobile home under a residential contract which has expired or been determined and, in the case of the death of the occupier (whether during the subsistence or after the expiry or determination of the contract), to any person then residing with the occupier.

(9) Nothing in this section applies to the exercise by the owner of a mobile home of a right to take possession of the mobile home, other than a right conferred by or arising on the expiry or determination of a residential contract, or to anything done pursuant to the order of any court.

43 Offences under section 42: supplementary

(1) In proceedings for an offence of contravening section 42(2) or (3) it is a defence to prove that the accused believed, and had reasonable cause to believe, that the occupier of the mobile home had ceased to reside on the site.

(2) In proceedings for an offence of contravening section 42(5) it is a defence to prove that the accused had reasonable grounds for doing the acts or withdrawing or withholding the services or facilities in question.

(3) A person guilty of an offence under section 42 is liable–

(a) on summary conviction, to a fine or to imprisonment for a term not exceeding 12 months, or to both, or

(b) on conviction on indictment, to a fine or to imprisonment for a term not exceeding 2 years, or to both.

...

45 Supplementary

(1) The power of the court under section 44 to suspend the enforcement of an order extends to any order made but not executed before the commencement of this Part.

(2) Nothing in this Part affects the operation of section 13 of the Compulsory Purchase Act 1965.

(3) The Protection from Eviction Act 1977 does not apply to any premises consisting of a mobile home stationed on a protected site.

46 Offences

Proceedings for an offence under this Part may be instituted by any local authority.

47 Interpretation

(1) In this Part–

'occupier' ('meddiannydd') in relation to a mobile home and a protected site, means the person entitled as mentioned in section 40 in relation to a mobile home and the protected site;

'residential contract' ('contract preswyl') means a licence or contract within that section.

(2) In this Part 'the court' means the county court.

LEGAL AID, SENTENCING AND PUNISHMENT OF OFFENDERS ACT 2012

144 Offence of squatting in a residential building

(1) A person commits an offence if–

    (a) the person is in a residential building as a trespasser having entered it as a trespasser,

    (b) the person knows or ought to know that he or she is a trespasser, and

    (c) the person is living in the building or intends to live there for any period.

(2) The offence is not committed by a person holding over after the end of a lease or licence (even if the person leaves and re-enters the building).

(3) For the purposes of this section–

    (a) 'building' includes any structure or part of a structure (including a temporary or moveable structure), and

    (b) a building is 'residential' if it is designed or adapted, before the time of entry, for use as a place to live.

(4) For the purposes of this section the fact that a person derives title from a trespasser, or has the permission of a trespasser, does not prevent the person from being a trespasser.

(5) A person convicted of an offence under this section is liable on summary conviction to imprisonment for a term not exceeding 51 weeks or a fine not exceeding level 5 on the standard scale (or both).

(6) In relation to an offence committed before the commencement of section 281(5) of the Criminal Justice Act 2003, the reference in subsection (5) to 51 weeks is to be read as a reference to 6 months.

(7) For the purposes of subsection (1)(a) it is irrelevant whether the person entered the building as a trespasser before or after the commencement of this section.

(8) In section 17 of the Police and Criminal Evidence Act 1984 (entry for purpose of arrest etc)–

    (a) in subsection (1)(c), after sub-paragraph (v) insert–

        '(vi) section 144 of the Legal Aid, Sentencing and Punishment of Offenders Act 2012 (squatting in a residential building);';

    (b) in subsection (3), for 'or (iv)' substitute ', (iv) or (vi)'.

(9) In Schedule 10 to the Criminal Justice and Public Order Act 1994 (consequential amendments), omit paragraph 53(b).

HOUSING ACT 2004

Enforcement

72 Offences in relation to licensing of HMOs

(1) A person commits an offence if he is a person having control of or managing an HMO which is required to be licensed under this Part (see section 61(1)) but is not so licensed.

(2) A person commits an offence if—

(a) he is a person having control of or managing an HMO which is licensed under this Part,

(b) he knowingly permits another person to occupy the house, and

(c) the other person's occupation results in the house being occupied by more households or persons than is authorised by the licence.

(3) A person commits an offence if—

(a) he is a licence holder or a person on whom restrictions or obligations under a licence are imposed in accordance with section 67(5), and

(b) he fails to comply with any condition of the licence.

(4) In proceedings against a person for an offence under subsection (1) it is a defence that, at the material time—

(a) a notification had been duly given in respect of the house under section 62(1), or

(b) an application for a licence had been duly made in respect of the house under section 63,

and that notification or application was still effective (see subsection (8)).

(5) In proceedings against a person for an offence under subsection (1), (2) or (3) it is a defence that he had a reasonable excuse—

(a) for having control of or managing the house in the circumstances mentioned in subsection (1), or

(b) for permitting the person to occupy the house, or

(c) for failing to comply with the condition,

as the case may be.

(6) A person who commits an offence under subsection (1) or (2) is liable on summary conviction to a fine.

(7) A person who commits an offence under subsection (3) is liable on summary conviction to a fine not exceeding level 5 on the standard scale.

(7A) See also section 249A (financial penalties as alternative to prosecution for certain housing offences in England).

(7B) If a local housing authority has imposed a financial penalty on a person under section 249A in respect of conduct amounting to an offence under this section the person may not be convicted of an offence under this section in respect of the conduct.

(8) For the purposes of subsection (4) a notification or application is 'effective' at a particular time if at that time it has not been withdrawn, and either—

(a) the authority have not decided whether to serve a temporary exemption notice, or (as the case may be) grant a licence, in pursuance of the notification or application, or

(b) if they have decided not to do so, one of the conditions set out in subsection (9) is met.

(9) The conditions are—
- (a) that the period for appealing against the decision of the authority not to serve or grant such a notice or licence (or against any relevant decision of the appropriate tribunal) has not expired, or
- (b) that an appeal has been brought against the authority's decision (or against any relevant decision of such a tribunal) and the appeal has not been determined or withdrawn.

(10) In subsection (9) 'relevant decision' means a decision which is given on an appeal to the tribunal and confirms the authority's decision (with or without variation).

73 Other consequences of operating unlicensed HMOs: rent repayment orders

(1) For the purposes of this section an HMO is an 'unlicensed HMO' if—
- (a) it is required to be licensed under this Part but is not so licensed, and
- (b) neither of the conditions in subsection (2) is satisfied.

(2) The conditions are—
- (a) that a notification has been duly given in respect of the HMO under section 62(1) and that notification is still effective (as defined by section 72(8));
- (b) that an application for a licence has been duly made in respect of the HMO under section 63 and that application is still effective (as so defined).

(3) No rule of law relating to the validity or enforceability of contracts in circumstances involving illegality is to affect the validity or enforceability of—
- (a) any provision requiring the payment of rent or the making of any other periodical payment in connection with any tenancy or licence of a part of an unlicensed HMO, or
- (b) any other provision of such a tenancy or licence.

(4) But amounts paid in respect of rent or other periodical payments payable in connection with such a tenancy or licence may be recovered in accordance with subsection (5) and section 74 (in the case of an HMO in Wales) or in accordance with Chapter 4 of Part 2 of the Housing and Planning Act 2016 (in the case of an HMO in England).

(5) If—
- (a) an application in respect of an HMO in Wales is made to the appropriate tribunal by the local housing authority or an occupier of a part of the HMO, and
- (b) the tribunal is satisfied as to the matters mentioned in subsection (6) or (8),

the tribunal may make an order (a 'rent repayment order') requiring the appropriate person to pay to the applicant such amount in respect of the relevant award or awards of universal credit or the housing benefit paid as mentioned in subsection (6)(b), or (as the case may be) the periodical payments paid as mentioned in subsection (8)(b), as is specified in the order (see section 74(2) to (8)).

(6) If the application is made by the local housing authority, the tribunal must be satisfied as to the following matters—
- (a) that, at any time within the period of 12 months ending with the date of the notice of intended proceedings required by subsection (7), the

appropriate person has committed an offence under section 72(1) in relation to the HMO (whether or not he has been charged or convicted),

(b) that–
   (i)   one or more relevant awards of universal credit have been paid (to any person); or
   (ii) housing benefit has been paid (to any person) in respect of periodical payments payable in connection with the occupation of a part or parts of the HMO,

   during any period during which it appears to the tribunal that such an offence was being committed, and

(c) that the requirements of subsection (7) have been complied with in relation to the application.

(6A) In subsection (6)(b)(i), 'relevant award of universal credit' means an award of universal credit the calculation of which included an amount under section 11 of the Welfare Reform Act 2012, calculated in accordance with Schedule 4 to the Universal Credit Regulations 2013 (housing costs element for renters) (SI 2013/376) or any corresponding provision replacing that Schedule, in respect of periodical payments payable in connection with the occupation of a part or parts of the HMO.

(7) Those requirements are as follows–
   (a) the authority must have served on the appropriate person a notice (a 'notice of intended proceedings')–
      (i)   informing him that the authority are proposing to make an application under subsection (5),
      (ii)   setting out the reasons why they propose to do so,
      (iii) stating the amount that they will seek to recover under that subsection and how that amount is calculated, and
      (iv)   inviting him to make representations to them within a period specified in the notice of not less than 28 days;
   (b) that period must have expired; and
   (c) the authority must have considered any representations made to them within that period by the appropriate person.

(8) If the application is made by an occupier of a part of the HMO, the tribunal must be satisfied as to the following matters–
   (a) that the appropriate person has been convicted of an offence under section 72(1) in relation to the HMO, or has been required by a rent repayment order to make a payment in respect of–
      (i)   one or more relevant awards of universal credit, or
      (ii)   housing benefit paid in connection with occupation of a part or parts of the HMO,
   (b) that the occupier paid, to a person having control of or managing the HMO, periodical payments in respect of occupation of part of the HMO during any period during which it appears to the tribunal that such an offence was being committed in relation to the HMO, and
   (c) that the application is made within the period of 12 months beginning with–
      (i)   the date of the conviction or order, or
      (ii)   if such a conviction was followed by such an order (or vice versa), the date of the later of them.

(9) Where a local housing authority serve a notice of intended proceedings on any person under this section, they must ensure–

(a) that a copy of the notice is received by the department of the authority responsible for administering the housing benefit to which the proceedings would relate; and

(b) that that department is subsequently kept informed of any matters relating to the proceedings that are likely to be of interest to it in connection with the administration of housing benefit.

(10) In this section–

'the appropriate person', in relation to any payment of universal credit or housing benefit or periodical payment payable in connection with occupation of a part of an HMO, means the person who at the time of the payment was entitled to receive on his own account periodical payments payable in connection with such occupation;

'housing benefit' means housing benefit provided by virtue of a scheme under section 123 of the Social Security Contributions and Benefits Act 1992 (c 4);

'occupier', in relation to any periodical payment, means a person who was an occupier at the time of the payment, whether under a tenancy or licence or otherwise (and 'occupation' has a corresponding meaning);

'periodical payments' means–

(a) payments in respect of which an amount under section 11 of the Welfare Reform Act 2012 may be included in the calculation of an award of universal credit, as referred to in paragraph 3 of Schedule 4 to the Universal Credit Regulations 2013 ('relevant payments') (SI 2013/376) or any corresponding provision replacing that paragraph; and

(b) periodical payments in respect of which housing benefit may be paid by virtue of regulation 12 of the Housing Benefit Regulations 2006 or any corresponding provision replacing that regulation.

(11) For the purposes of this section an amount which–

(a) is not actually paid by an occupier but is used by him to discharge the whole or part of his liability in respect of a periodical payment (for example, by offsetting the amount against any such liability), and

(b) is not an amount of universal credit or housing benefit,

is to be regarded as an amount paid by the occupier in respect of that periodical payment.

74 Further provisions about rent repayment orders

(1) This section applies in relation to rent repayment orders made by residential property tribunals under section 73(5).

(2) Where, on an application by the local housing authority, the tribunal is satisfied–

(a) that a person has been convicted of an offence under section 72(1) in relation to the HMO, and

(b) that–

(i) one or more relevant awards of universal credit (as defined in section 73(6A)) were paid (whether or not to the appropriate person), or

(ii) housing benefit was paid (whether or not to the appropriate person) in respect of periodical payments payable in connection with occupation of a part or parts of the HMO,

during any period during which it appears to the tribunal that such an offence was being committed in relation to the HMO in question,

the tribunal must make a rent repayment order requiring the appropriate person to pay to the authority the amount mentioned in subsection (2A). This is subject to subsections (3), (4) and (8).

(2A) The amount referred to in subsection (2) is—

    (a) an amount equal to—

        (i) where one relevant award of universal credit was paid as mentioned in subsection (2)(b)(i), the amount included in the calculation of that award under section 11 of the Welfare Reform Act 2012, calculated in accordance with Schedule 4 to the Universal Credit Regulations 2013 (housing costs element for renters) (SI 2013/376) or any corresponding provision replacing that Schedule, or the amount of the award if less; or

        (ii) if more than one such award was paid as mentioned in subsection (2)(b)(i), the sum of the amounts included in the calculation of those awards as referred to in sub-paragraph (i), or the sum of the amounts of those awards if less, or

    (b) an amount equal to the total amount of housing benefit paid as mentioned in subsection (2)(b)(ii), (as the case may be).

(3) If the total of the amounts received by the appropriate person in respect of periodical payments payable as mentioned in paragraph (b) of subsection (2) ('the rent total') is less than the amount mentioned in subsection (2A), the amount required to be paid by virtue of a rent repayment order made in accordance with that subsection is limited to the rent total.

(4) A rent repayment order made in accordance with subsection (2) may not require the payment of any amount which the tribunal is satisfied that, by reason of any exceptional circumstances, it would be unreasonable for that person to be required to pay.

(5) In a case where subsection (2) does not apply, the amount required to be paid by virtue of a rent repayment order under section 73(5) is to be such amount as the tribunal considers reasonable in the circumstances.

This is subject to subsections (6) to (8).

(6) In such a case the tribunal must, in particular, take into account the following matters—

    (a) the total amount of relevant payments paid in connection with occupation of the HMO during any period during which it appears to the tribunal that an offence was being committed by the appropriate person in relation to the HMO under section 72(1);

    (b) the extent to which that total amount—

        (i) consisted of, or derived from, payments of relevant awards of universal credit or housing benefit, and

        (ii) was actually received by the appropriate person;

    (c) whether the appropriate person has at any time been convicted of an offence under section 72(1) in relation to the HMO;

    (d) the conduct and financial circumstances of the appropriate person; and

(e) where the application is made by an occupier, the conduct of the occupier.

(7) In subsection (6) 'relevant payments' means—

(a) in relation to an application by a local housing authority, payments of relevant awards of universal credit, housing benefit or periodical payments payable by occupiers;

(b) in relation to an application by an occupier, periodical payments payable by the occupier, less—

(i) where one or more relevant awards of universal credit were payable during the period in question, the amount mentioned in subsection (2A)(a) in respect of the award or awards that related to the occupation of the part of the HMO occupied by him during that period; or

(ii) any amount of housing benefit payable in respect of the occupation of the part of the HMO occupied by him during the period in question.

(8) A rent repayment order may not require the payment of any amount which—

(a) (where the application is made by a local housing authority) is in respect of any time falling outside the period of 12 months mentioned in section 73(6)(a); or

(b) (where the application is made by an occupier) is in respect of any time falling outside the period of 12 months ending with the date of the occupier's application under section 73(5);

and the period to be taken into account under subsection (6)(a) above is restricted accordingly.

(9) Any amount payable to a local housing authority under a rent repayment order—

(a) does not, when recovered by the authority, constitute an amount of universal credit or housing benefit recovered by them, and

(b) until recovered by them, is a legal charge on the HMO which is a local land charge.

(10) For the purpose of enforcing that charge the authority have the same powers and remedies under the Law of Property Act 1925 (c 20) and otherwise as if they were mortgagees by deed having powers of sale and lease, and of accepting surrenders of leases and of appointing a receiver.

(11) The power of appointing a receiver is exercisable at any time after the end of the period of one month beginning with the date on which the charge takes effect.

(12) If the authority subsequently grant a licence under this Part or Part 3 in respect of the HMO to the appropriate person or any person acting on his behalf, the conditions contained in the licence may include a condition requiring the licence holder—

(a) to pay to the authority any amount payable to them under the rent repayment order and not so far recovered by them; and

(b) to do so in such instalments as are specified in the licence.

(13) If the authority subsequently make a management order under Chapter 1 of Part 4 in respect of the HMO, the order may contain such provisions as the authority consider appropriate for the recovery of any amount payable to them under the rent repayment order and not so far recovered by them.

(14) Any amount payable to an occupier by virtue of a rent repayment order

is recoverable by the occupier as a debt due to him from the appropriate person.

(15) The appropriate national authority may by regulations make such provision as it considers appropriate for supplementing the provisions of this section and section 73, and in particular–

(a) for securing that persons are not unfairly prejudiced by rent repayment orders (whether in cases where there have been over-payments of universal credit or housing benefit or otherwise);

(b) for requiring or authorising amounts received by local housing authorities by virtue of rent repayment orders to be dealt with in such manner as is specified in the regulations.

(16) Section 73(10) and (11) apply for the purposes of this section as they apply for the purposes of section 73.

75 Other consequences of operating unlicensed HMOs: restriction on terminating tenancies

(1) No section 21 notice may be given in relation to a shorthold tenancy of a part of an unlicensed HMO so long as it remains such an HMO.

(2) In this section–

a 'section 21 notice' means a notice under section 21(1)(b) or (4)(a) of the Housing Act 1988 (c 50) (recovery of possession on termination of shorthold tenancy);

a 'shorthold tenancy' means an assured shorthold tenancy within the meaning of Chapter 2 of Part 1 of that Act;

'unlicensed HMO' has the same meaning as in section 73 of this Act.

...

96 Other consequences of operating unlicensed houses: rent repayment orders

(1) For the purposes of this section a house is an 'unlicensed house' if–

(a) it is required to be licensed under this Part but is not so licensed, and

(b) neither of the conditions in subsection (2) is satisfied.

(2) The conditions are–

(a) that a notification has been duly given in respect of the house under section 62(1) or 86(1) and that notification is still effective (as defined by section 95(7));

(b) that an application for a licence has been duly made in respect of the house under section 87 and that application is still effective (as so defined).

(3) No rule of law relating to the validity or enforceability of contracts in circumstances involving illegality is to affect the validity or enforceability of–

(a) any provision requiring the payment of rent or the making of any other periodical payment in connection with any tenancy or licence of the whole or a part of an unlicensed house, or

(b) any other provision of such a tenancy or licence.

(4) But amounts paid in respect of rent or other periodical payments payable in connection with such a tenancy or licence may be recovered in accordance with subsection (5) and section 97 (in the case of a house in Wales) or in accordance with Chapter 4 of Part 2 of the Housing and Planning Act 2016 (in the case of a house in England).

(5) If–
    (a) an application in respect of a house in Wales is made to the appropriate tribunal by the local housing authority or an occupier of the whole or part of the house, and
    (b) the tribunal is satisfied as to the matters mentioned in subsection (6) or (8),

the tribunal may make an order (a 'rent repayment order') requiring the appropriate person to pay to the applicant such amount in respect of the relevant award or awards of universal credit or the housing benefit paid as mentioned in subsection (6)(b), or (as the case may be) the periodical payments paid as mentioned in subsection (8)(b), as is specified in the order (see section 97(2) to (8)).

(6) If the application is made by the local housing authority, the tribunal must be satisfied as to the following matters–
    (a) that, at any time within the per iod of 12 months ending with the date of the notice of intended proceedings required by subsection (7), the appropriate person has committed an offence under section 95(1) in relation to the house (whether or not he has been charged or convicted),
    (b) that–
        (i) one or more relevant awards of universal credit have been paid (to any person); or
        (ii) housing benefit has been paid (to any person) in respect of periodical payments payable in connection with the occupation of the whole or any part or parts of the house,

during any period during which it appears to the tribunal that such an offence was being committed, and
    (c) that the requirements of subsection (7) have been complied with in relation to the application.

(6A) In subsection (6)(b)(i), 'relevant award of universal credit' means an award of universal credit the calculation of which included an amount under section 11 of the Welfare Reform Act 2012, calculated in accordance with Schedule 4 to the Universal Credit Regulations 2013 (housing costs element for renters) (SI 2013/376) or any corresponding provision replacing that Schedule, in respect of periodical payments payable in connection with the occupation of the whole or any part or parts of the house.

(7) Those requirements are as follows–
    (a) the authority must have served on the appropriate person a notice (a 'notice of intended proceedings')–
        (i) informing him that the authority are proposing to make an application under subsection (5),
        (ii) setting out the reasons why they propose to do so,
        (iii) stating the amount that they will seek to recover under that subsection and how that amount is calculated, and
        (iv) inviting him to make representations to them within a period specified in the notice of not less than 28 days;
    (b) that period must have expired; and
    (c) the authority must have considered any representations made to them within that period by the appropriate person.

(8) If the application is made by an occupier of the whole or part of the house, the tribunal must be satisfied as to the following matters–

    (a) that the appropriate person has been convicted of an offence under section 95(1) in relation to the house, or has been required by a rent repayment order to make a payment in respect of–

        (i) one or more relevant awards of universal credit, or

        (ii) housing benefit paid in connection with occupation of the whole or any part or parts of the house,

    (b) that the occupier paid, to a person having control of or managing the house, periodical payments in respect of occupation of the whole or part of the house during any period during which it appears to the tribunal that such an offence was being committed in relation to the house, and

    (c) that the application is made within the period of 12 months beginning with–

        (i) the date of the conviction or order, or

        (ii) if such a conviction was followed by such an order (or vice versa), the date of the later of them.

(9) Where a local housing authority serve a notice of intended proceedings on any person under this section, they must ensure–

    (a) that a copy of the notice is received by the department of the authority responsible for administering the housing benefit to which the proceedings would relate; and

    (b) that that department is subsequently kept informed of any matters relating to the proceedings that are likely to be of interest to it in connection with the administration of housing benefit.

(10) In this section–

'the appropriate person', in relation to any payment of universal credit or housing benefit or periodical payment payable in connection with occupation of the whole or a part of a house, means the person who at the time of the payment was entitled to receive on his own account periodical payments payable in connection with such occupation;

'housing benefit' means housing benefit provided by virtue of a scheme under section 123 of the Social Security Contributions and Benefits Act 1992 (c 4);

'occupier', in relation to any periodical payment, means a person who was an occupier at the time of the payment, whether under a tenancy or licence (and 'occupation' has a corresponding meaning);

'periodical payments' means–

    (a) payments in respect of which an amount under section 11 of the Welfare Reform Act 2012 may be included in the calculation of an award of universal credit, as referred to in paragraph 3 of Schedule 4 to the Universal Credit Regulations 2013 ('relevant payments') (SI 2013/376) or any corresponding provision replacing that paragraph; and

    (b) periodical payments in respect of which housing benefit may be paid by virtue of regulation 12 of the Housing Benefit Regulations 2006 or any corresponding provision replacing that regulation.

(11) For the purposes of this section an amount which–

    (a) is not actually paid by an occupier but is used by him to discharge the whole or part of his liability in respect of a periodical payment (for example, by offsetting the amount against any such liability), and

(b) is not an amount of universal credit or housing benefit,

is to be regarded as an amount paid by the occupier in respect of that periodical payment.

97 Further provisions about rent repayment orders

(1) This section applies in relation to orders made by residential property tribunals under section 96(5).

(2) Where, on an application by the local housing authority, the tribunal is satisfied—

(a) that a person has been convicted of an offence under section 95(1) in relation to the house, and

(b) that—

    (i) one or more relevant awards of universal credit (as defined in section 96(6A)) were paid (whether or not to the appropriate person), or

    (ii) housing benefit was paid (whether or not to the appropriate person) in respect of periodical payments payable in connection with occupation of the whole or any part or parts of the house,

during any period during which it appears to the tribunal that such an offence was being committed in relation to the house,

the tribunal must make a rent repayment order requiring the appropriate person to pay to the authority the amount mentioned in subsection (2A).

This is subject to subsections (3), (4) and (8).

(2A) The amount referred to in subsection (2) is—

(a) an amount equal to—

    (i) where one relevant award of universal credit was paid as mentioned in subsection (2)(b)(i), the amount included in the calculation of that award under section 11 of the Welfare Reform Act 2012, calculated in accordance with Schedule 4 to the Universal Credit Regulations 2013 (housing costs element for renters) (SI 2013/376) or any corresponding provision replacing that Schedule, or the amount of the award if less; or

    (ii) if more than one such award was paid as mentioned in subsection (2)(b)(i), the sum of the amounts included in the calculation of those awards as referred to in sub-paragraph (i), or the sum of the amounts of those awards if less, or

(b) an amount equal to the total amount of housing benefit paid as mentioned in subsection (2)(b)(ii), (as the case may be).

(3) If the total of the amounts received by the appropriate person in respect of periodical payments payable as mentioned in paragraph (b) of subsection (2) ('the rent total') is less than the amount mentioned in subsection (2A), the amount required to be paid by virtue of a rent repayment order made in accordance with that subsection is limited to the rent total.

(4) A rent repayment order made in accordance with subsection (2) may not require the payment of any amount which the tribunal is satisfied that, by reason of any exceptional circumstances, it would be unreasonable for that person to be required to pay.

(5) In a case where subsection (2) does not apply, the amount required to be paid

by virtue of a rent repayment order under section 96(5) is to be such amount as the tribunal considers reasonable in the circumstances.

This is subject to subsections (6) to (8).

(6) In such a case the tribunal must, in particular, take into account the following matters–

  (a) the total amount of relevant payments paid in connection with occupation of the house during any period during which it appears to the tribunal that an offence was being committed by the appropriate person in relation to the house under section 95(1);

  (b) the extent to which that total amount–

    (i) consisted of, or derived from, payments of relevant awards of universal credit or housing benefit, and

    (ii) was actually received by the appropriate person;

  (c) whether the appropriate person has at any time been convicted of an offence under section 95(1) in relation to the house;

  (d) the conduct and financial circumstances of the appropriate person; and

  (e) where the application is made by an occupier, the conduct of the occupier.

(7) In subsection (6) 'relevant payments' means–

  (a) in relation to an application by a local housing authority, payments of relevant awards of universal credit, housing benefit or periodical payments payable by occupiers;

  (b) in relation to an application by an occupier, periodical payments payable by the occupier, less–

    (i) where one or more relevant awards of relevant universal credit were payable during the period in question, the amount mentioned in subsection (2A)(a) in respect of the award or awards that related to the occupation of the part of the HMO occupied by him during that period; or

    (ii) any amount of housing benefit payable in respect of the occupation of the part of the HMO occupied by him during the period in question.

(8) A rent repayment order may not require the payment of an amount which–

  (a) (where the application is made by a local housing authority) is in respect of any time falling outside the period of 12 months mentioned in section 96(6)(a); or

  (b) (where the application is made by an occupier) is in respect of any time falling outside the period of 12 months ending with the date of the occupier's application under section 96(5);

and the period to be taken into account under subsection (6)(a) above is restricted accordingly.

(9) Any amount payable to a local housing authority under a rent repayment order–

  (a) does not, when recovered by the authority, constitute an amount of universal credit or housing benefit recovered by them, and

  (b) is, until recovered by them, a legal charge on the house which is a local land charge.

(10) For the purpose of enforcing that charge the authority have the same powers and remedies under the Law of Property Act 1925 (c 20) and otherwise

as if they were mortgagees by deed having powers of sale and lease, and of accepting surrenders of leases and of appointing a receiver.

(11) The power of appointing a receiver is exercisable at any time after the end of the period of one month beginning with the date on which the charge takes effect.

(12) If the authority subsequently grant a licence under Part 2 or this Part in respect of the house to the appropriate person or any person acting on his behalf, the conditions contained in the licence may include a condition requiring the licence holder–

(a) to pay to the authority any amount payable to them under the rent repayment order and not so far recovered by them; and

(b) to do so in such instalments as are specified in the licence.

(13) If the authority subsequently make a management order under Chapter 1 of Part 4 in respect of the house, the order may contain such provisions as the authority consider appropriate for the recovery of any amount payable to them under the rent repayment order and not so far recovered by them.

(14) Any amount payable to an occupier by virtue of a rent repayment order is recoverable by the occupier as a debt due to him from the appropriate person.

(15) The appropriate national authority may by regulations make such provision as it considers appropriate for supplementing the provisions of this section and section 96, and in particular–

(a) for securing that persons are not unfairly prejudiced by rent repayment orders (whether in cases where there have been over-payments of universal credit or housing benefit or otherwise);

(b) for requiring or authorising amounts received by local housing authorities by virtue of rent repayment orders to be dealt with in such manner as is specified in the regulations.

(16) Section 96(10) and (11) apply for the purposes of this section as they apply for the purposes of section 96.

98 Other consequences of operating unlicensed houses: restriction on terminating tenancies

(1) No section 21 notice may be given in relation to a shorthold tenancy of the whole or part of an unlicensed house so long as it remains such a house.

(2) In this section–

a 'section 21 notice' means a notice under section 21(1)(b) or (4)(a) of the Housing Act 1988 (c 50) (recovery of possession on termination of shorthold tenancy);

a 'shorthold tenancy' means an assured shorthold tenancy within the meaning of Chapter 2 of Part 1 of that Act;

'unlicensed house' has the same meaning as in section 96 of this Act.

...

Chapter 4: Tenancy Deposit Schemes

212 Tenancy deposit schemes

(1) The appropriate national authority must make arrangements for securing that one or more tenancy deposit schemes are available for the purpose of safeguarding tenancy deposits paid in connection with shorthold tenancies.

(2) For the purposes of this Chapter a 'tenancy deposit scheme' is a scheme which–

  (a) is made for the purpose of safeguarding tenancy deposits paid in connection with shorthold tenancies and facilitating the resolution of disputes arising in connection with such deposits, and

  (b) complies with the requirements of Schedule 10.

(3) Arrangements under subsection (1) must be arrangements made with any body or person under which the body or person ('the scheme administrator') undertakes to establish and maintain a tenancy deposit scheme of a description specified in the arrangements.

(4) The appropriate national authority may–

  (a) give financial assistance to the scheme administrator;

  (b) make payments to the scheme administrator (otherwise than as financial assistance) in pursuance of arrangements under subsection (1).

(5) The appropriate national authority may, in such manner and on such terms as it thinks fit, guarantee the discharge of any financial obligation incurred by the scheme administrator in connection with arrangements under subsection (1).

(6) Arrangements under subsection (1) must require the scheme administrator to give the appropriate national authority, in such manner and at such times as it may specify, such information and facilities for obtaining information as it may specify.

(6A) For further provision about what must be included in the arrangements, see section 212A.

(7) The appropriate national authority may make regulations conferring or imposing–

  (a) on scheme administrators, or

  (b) on scheme administrators of any description specified in the regulations,

such powers or duties in connection with arrangements under subsection (1) as are so specified.

(8) In this Chapter–

'authorised', in relation to a tenancy deposit scheme, means that the scheme is in force in accordance with arrangements under subsection (1);

'custodial scheme' and 'insurance scheme' have the meaning given by paragraph 1(2) and (3) of Schedule 10);

'money' means money in the form of cash or otherwise;

'shorthold tenancy' means an assured shorthold tenancy within the meaning of Chapter 2 of Part 1 of the Housing Act 1988 (c 50);

'tenancy deposit', in relation to a shorthold tenancy, means any money intended to be held (by the landlord or otherwise) as security for–

  (a) the performance of any obligations of the tenant, or

  (b) the discharge of any liability of his,

arising under or in connection with the tenancy.

(9) In this Chapter–

  (a) references to a landlord or landlords in relation to any shorthold tenancy or tenancies include references to a person or persons acting on his or their behalf in relation to the tenancy or tenancies, and

  (b) references to a tenancy deposit being held in accordance with a scheme include, in the case of a custodial scheme, references to an amount representing the deposit being held in accordance with the scheme.

212A Provision of information to local authorities

(1) Arrangements under section 212(1) made by the Secretary of State must require the scheme administrator—
   (a) to give a local housing authority in England any specified information that they request, or
   (b) to provide facilities for the sharing of specified information with a local housing authority in England.

(2) In subsection (1) 'specified information' means information, of a description specified in the arrangements, that relates to a tenancy of premises in the local housing authority's area.

(3) Arrangements made by virtue of this section may make the requirement to provide information or facilities to a local housing authority conditional on the payment of a fee.

(4) Arrangements made by virtue of this section may include supplementary provision, for example about—
   (a) the form or manner in which any information is to be provided,
   (b) the time or times at which it is to be provided, and
   (c) the notification of anyone to whom the information relates.

(5) Information obtained by a local housing authority by virtue of this section may be used only—
   (a) for a purpose connected with the exercise of the authority's functions under any of Parts 1 to 4 in relation to any premises, or
   (b) for the purpose of investigating whether an offence has been committed under any of those Parts in relation to any premises.

(6) Information obtained by a local housing authority by virtue of this section may be supplied to a person providing services to the authority for a purpose listed in subsection (5).

(7) The Secretary of State may by regulations amend the list of purposes in subsection (5).

213 Requirements relating to tenancy deposits

(1) Any tenancy deposit paid to a person in connection with a shorthold tenancy must, as from the time when it is received, be dealt with in accordance with an authorised scheme.

(2) No person may require the payment of a tenancy deposit in connection with a shorthold tenancy which is not to be subject to the requirement in subsection (1).

(3) Where a landlord receives a tenancy deposit in connection with a shorthold tenancy, the initial requirements of an authorised scheme must be complied with by the landlord in relation to the deposit within the period of 30 days beginning with the date on which it is received.

(4) For the purposes of this section 'the initial requirements' of an authorised scheme are such requirements imposed by the scheme as fall to be complied with by a landlord on receiving such a tenancy deposit.

(5) A landlord who has received such a tenancy deposit must give the tenant and any relevant person such information relating to—

    (a) the authorised scheme applying to the deposit,

    (b) compliance by the landlord with the initial requirements of the scheme in relation to the deposit, and

    (c) the operation of provisions of this Chapter in relation to the deposit,

  as may be prescribed.

(6) The information required by subsection (5) must be given to the tenant and any relevant person–

    (a) in the prescribed form or in a form substantially to the same effect, and

    (b) within the period of 30 days beginning with the date on which the deposit is received by the landlord.

(7) No person may, in connection with a shorthold tenancy, require a deposit which consists of property other than money.

(8) In subsection (7) 'deposit' means a transfer of property intended to be held (by the landlord or otherwise) as security for–

    (a) the performance of any obligations of the tenant, or

    (b) the discharge of any liability of his,

  arising under or in connection with the tenancy.

(9) The provisions of this section apply despite any agreement to the contrary.

(10) In this section–

    'prescribed' means prescribed by an order made by the appropriate national authority;

    'property' means moveable property;

    'relevant person' means any person who, in accordance with arrangements made with the tenant, paid the deposit on behalf of the tenant.

214 Proceedings relating to tenancy deposits

(1) Where a tenancy deposit has been paid in connection with a shorthold tenancy on or after 6 April 2007, the tenant or any relevant person (as defined by section 213(10)) may make an application to the county court on the grounds–

    (a) that section 213(3) or (6) has not been complied with in relation to the deposit, or

    (b) that he has been notified by the landlord that a particular authorised scheme applies to the deposit but has been unable to obtain confirmation from the scheme administrator that the deposit is being held in accordance with the scheme.

(1A) Subsection (1) also applies in a case where the tenancy has ended, and in such a case the reference in subsection (1) to the tenant is to a person who was a tenant under the tenancy.

(2) Subsections (3) and (4) apply in the case of an application under subsection (1) if the tenancy has not ended and the court–

    (a) is satisfied that section 213(3) or (6) has not been complied with in relation to the deposit, or

    (b) is not satisfied that the deposit is being held in accordance with an authorised scheme,

  as the case may be.

(2A) Subsections (3A) and (4) apply in the case of an application under subsection (1) if the tenancy has ended (whether before or after the making of the application) and the court–

   (a) is satisfied that section 213(3) or (6) has not been complied with in rela-
      tion to the deposit, or
   (b) is not satisfied that the deposit is being held in accordance with an author-
      ised scheme,
  as the case may be.
  (3) The court must, as it thinks fit, either–
   (a) order the person who appears to the court to be holding the deposit to
      repay it to the applicant, or
   (b) order that person to pay the deposit into the designated account held by
      the scheme administrator under an authorised custodial scheme,
  within the period of 14 days beginning with the date of the making of the
  order.
(3A) The court may order the person who appears to the court to be holding the
  deposit to repay all or part of it to the applicant within the period of 14 days
  beginning with the date of the making of the order.
  (4) The court must ... order the landlord to pay to the applicant a sum of money
  not less than the amount of the deposit and not more than three times the
  amount of the deposit within the period of 14 days beginning with the date of
  the making of the order.
  (5) Where any deposit given in connection with a shorthold tenancy could not
  be lawfully required as a result of section 213(7), the property in question is
  recoverable from the person holding it by the person by whom it was given as
  a deposit.
  (6) In subsection (5) 'deposit' has the meaning given by section 213(8).

215 Sanctions for non-compliance

  (1) Subject to subsection (2A), if (whether before, on or after 6 April 2007) a
  tenancy deposit has been paid in connection with a shorthold tenancy, no
  section 21 notice may be given in relation to the tenancy at a time when the
  deposit is not being held in accordance with an authorised scheme.
(1A) Subject to subsection (2A), if a tenancy deposit has been paid in connection
  with a shorthold tenancy on or after 6 April 2007, no section 21 notice may
  be given in relation to the tenancy at a time when section 213(3) has not been
  complied with in relation to the deposit.
  (2) Subject to subsection (2A), if section 213(6) is not complied with in relation to
  a deposit given in connection with a shorthold tenancy, no section 21 notice
  may be given in relation to the tenancy until such time as section 213(6)(a) is
  complied with.
(2A) Subsections (1), (1A) and (2) do not apply in a case where–
   (a) the deposit has been returned to the tenant in full or with such deduc-
      tions as are agreed between the landlord and tenant, or
   (b) an application to the county court has been made under section 214(1)
      and has been determined by the court, withdrawn or settled by agreement
      between the parties.
  (3) If any deposit given in connection with a shorthold tenancy could not be
  lawfully required as a result of section 213(7), no section 21 notice may be
  given in relation to the tenancy until such time as the property in question is
  returned to the person by whom it was given as a deposit.
  (4) In subsection (3) 'deposit' has the meaning given by section 213(8).

(5) In this section a 'section 21 notice' means a notice under section 21(1)(b) or (4)(a) of the Housing Act 1988 (recovery of possession on termination of shorthold tenancy).

215A Statutory periodic tenancies: deposit received before 6 April 2007

(1) This section applies where–
   (a) before 6 April 2007, a tenancy deposit has been received by a landlord in connection with a fixed term shorthold tenancy,
   (b) on or after that date, a periodic shorthold tenancy is deemed to arise under section 5 of the Housing Act 1988 on the coming to an end of the fixed term tenancy,
   (c) on the coming to an end of the fixed term tenancy, all or part of the deposit paid in connection with the fixed term tenancy is held in connection with the periodic tenancy, and
   (d) the requirements of section 213(3), (5) and (6) have not been complied with by the landlord in relation to the deposit held in connection with the periodic tenancy.
(2) If, on the commencement date–
   (a) the periodic tenancy is in existence, and
   (b) all or part of the deposit paid in connection with the fixed term tenancy continues to be held in connection with the periodic tenancy,
   section 213 applies in respect of the deposit that continues to be held in connection with the periodic tenancy, and any additional deposit held in connection with that tenancy, with the modifications set out in subsection (3).
(3) The modifications are that, instead of the things referred to in section 213(3) and (5) being required to be done within the time periods set out in section 213(3) and (6)(b), those things are required to be done–
   (a) before the end of the period of 90 days beginning with the commencement date, or
   (b) (if earlier) before the first day after the commencement date on which a court does any of the following in respect of the periodic tenancy–
      (i) determines an application under section 214 or decides an appeal against a determination under that section;
      (ii) makes a determination as to whether to make an order for possession in proceedings under section 21 of the Housing Act 1988 or decides an appeal against such a determination.
(4) If, on the commencement date–
   (a) the periodic tenancy is no longer in existence, or
   (b) no deposit continues to be held in connection with the periodic tenancy,
   the requirements of section 213(3), (5) and (6) are treated as if they had been complied with by the landlord in relation to any deposit that was held in connection with the periodic tenancy.
(5) In this section 'the commencement date' means the date on which the Deregulation Act 2015 is passed.

215B Shorthold tenancies: deposit received on or after 6 April 2007

(1) This section applies where–
   (a) on or after 6 April 2007, a tenancy deposit has been received by a landlord in connection with a shorthold tenancy ('the original tenancy'),

(b) the initial requirements of an authorised scheme have been complied with by the landlord in relation to the deposit (ignoring any requirement to take particular steps within any specified period),

(c) the requirements of section 213(5) and (6)(a) have been complied with by the landlord in relation to the deposit when it is held in connection with the original tenancy (ignoring any deemed compliance under section 215A(4)),

(d) a new shorthold tenancy comes into being on the coming to an end of the original tenancy or a tenancy that replaces the original tenancy (directly or indirectly),

(e) the new tenancy replaces the original tenancy (directly or indirectly), and

(f) when the new tenancy comes into being, the deposit continues to be held in connection with the new tenancy, in accordance with the same authorised scheme as when the requirements of section 213(5) and (6)(a) were last complied with by the landlord in relation to the deposit.

(2) In their application to the new tenancy, the requirements of section 213(3), (5) and (6) are treated as if they had been complied with by the landlord in relation to the deposit.

(3) The condition in subsection (1)(a) may be met in respect of a tenancy even if the tenancy deposit was first received in connection with an earlier tenancy (including where it was first received before 6 April 2007).

(4) For the purposes of this section, a tenancy replaces an earlier tenancy if—

(a) the landlord and tenant immediately before the coming to an end of the earlier tenancy are the same as the landlord and tenant at the start of the new tenancy, and

(b) the premises let under both tenancies are the same or substantially the same.

215C Sections 215A and 215B: transitional provisions

(1) Sections 215A and 215B are treated as having had effect since 6 April 2007, subject to the following provisions of this section.

(2) Sections 215A and 215B do not have effect in relation to—

(a) a claim under section 214 of this Act or section 21 of the Housing Act 1988 in respect of a tenancy which is settled before the commencement date (whether or not proceedings in relation to the claim have been instituted), or

(b) proceedings under either of those sections in respect of a tenancy which have been finally determined before the commencement date.

(3) Subsection (5) applies in respect of a tenancy if—

(a) proceedings under section 214 in respect of the tenancy have been instituted before the commencement date but have not been settled or finally determined before that date, and

(b) because of section 215A(4) or 215B(2), the court decides—

(i) not to make an order under section 214(4) in respect of the tenancy, or

(ii) to allow an appeal by the landlord against such an order.

(4) Subsection (5) also applies in respect of a tenancy if—

(a) proceedings for possession under section 21 of the Housing Act 1988 in

respect of the tenancy have been instituted before the commencement date but have not been settled or finally determined before that date, and
  (b) because of section 215A(4) or 215B(2), the court decides–
      (i) to make an order for possession under that section in respect of the tenancy, or
      (ii) to allow an appeal by the landlord against a refusal to make such an order.
(5) Where this subsection applies, the court must not order the tenant or any relevant person (as defined by section 213(10)) to pay the landlord's costs, to the extent that the court reasonably considers those costs are attributable to the proceedings under section 214 of this Act or (as the case may be) section 21 of the Housing Act 1988.
(6) Proceedings have been 'finally determined' for the purposes of this section if –
  (a) they have been determined by a court, and
  (b) there is no further right to appeal against the determination.
(7) There is no further right to appeal against a court determination if there is no right to appeal against the determination, or there is such a right but–
  (a) the time limit for making an appeal has expired without an appeal being brought, or
  (b) an appeal brought within that time limit has been withdrawn.
(8) In this section 'the commencement date' means the date on which the Deregulation Act 2015 is passed.

CRIMINAL JUSTICE AND POLICE ACT 2001

42A Offence of harassment etc of a person in his home

(1) A person commits an offence if–

  (a) that person is present outside or in the vicinity of any premises that are used by any individual ('the resident') as his dwelling;

  (b) that person is present there for the purpose (by his presence or otherwise) of representing to the resident or another individual (whether or not one who uses the premises as his dwelling), or of persuading the resident or such another individual–

   (i) that he should not do something that he is entitled or required to do; or

   (ii) that he should do something that he is not under any obligation to do;

  (c) that person–

   (i) intends his presence to amount to the harassment of, or to cause alarm or distress to, the resident; or

   (ii) knows or ought to know that his presence is likely to result in the harassment of, or to cause alarm or distress to, the resident; and

  (d) the presence of that person–

   (i) amounts to the harassment of, or causes alarm or distress to, any person falling within subsection (2); or

   (ii) is likely to result in the harassment of, or to cause alarm or distress to, any such person.

(2) A person falls within this subsection if he is–

  (a) the resident,

  (b) a person in the resident's dwelling, or

  (c) a person in another dwelling in the vicinity of the resident's dwelling.

(3) The references in subsection (1)(c) and (d) to a person's presence are references to his presence either alone or together with that of any other persons who are also present.

(4) For the purposes of this section a person (A) ought to know that his presence is likely to result in the harassment of, or to cause alarm or distress to, a resident if a reasonable person in possession of the same information would think that A's presence was likely to have that effect.

(5) A person guilty of an offence under this section shall be liable, on summary conviction, to imprisonment for a term not exceeding 51 weeks or to a fine not exceeding level 4 on the standard scale, or to both.

(6) In relation to an offence committed before the commencement of section 281(5) of the Criminal Justice Act 2003 (alteration of penalties for summary offences), the reference in subsection (5) to 51 weeks is to be read as a reference to 6 months.

(7) In this section 'dwelling' has the same meaning as in Part 1 of the Public Order Act 1986.

CRIME AND DISORDER ACT 1998

32 Racially or religiously aggravated harassment etc

(1) A person is guilty of an offence under this section if he commits–

  (a) an offence under section 2 or 2A of the Protection from Harassment Act 1997 (offences of harassment and stalking); or

  (b) an offence under section 4 or 4A of that Act (putting people in fear of violence and stalking involving fear of violence or serious alarm or distress),

  which is racially or religiously aggravated for the purposes of this section.

(2) ...

(3) A person guilty of an offence falling within subsection (1)(a) above shall be liable–

  (a) on summary conviction, to imprisonment for a term not exceeding six months or to a fine not exceeding the statutory maximum, or to both;

  (b) on conviction on indictment, to imprisonment for a term not exceeding two years or to a fine, or to both.

(4) A person guilty of an offence falling within subsection (1)(b) above shall be liable–

  (a) on summary conviction, to imprisonment for a term not exceeding six months or to a fine not exceeding the statutory maximum, or to both;

  (b) on conviction on indictment, to imprisonment for a term not exceeding 14 years or to a fine, or to both.

(5) If, on the trial on indictment of a person charged with an offence falling within subsection (1)(a) above, the jury find him not guilty of the offence charged, they may find him guilty of either basic offence mentioned in that provision.

(6) If, on the trial on indictment of a person charged with an offence falling within subsection (1)(b) above, the jury find him not guilty of the offence charged, they may find him guilty of an offence falling within subsection (1)(a) above.

(7) ...

PROTECTION FROM HARASSMENT ACT 1997

England and Wales

1 Prohibition of harassment

(1) A person must not pursue a course of conduct–
  (a) which amounts to harassment of another, and
  (b) which he knows or ought to know amounts to harassment of the other.
(1A) A person must not pursue a course of conduct–
  (a) which involves harassment of two or more persons, and
  (b) which he knows or ought to know involves harassment of those persons, and
  (c) by which he intends to persuade any person (whether or not one of those mentioned above)–
    (i) not to do something that he is entitled or required to do, or
    (ii) to do something that he is not under any obligation to do.
(2) For the purposes of this section or section 2A(2)(c), the person whose course of conduct is in question ought to know that it amounts to or involves harassment of another if a reasonable person in possession of the same information would think the course of conduct amounted to or involved harassment of the other.
(3) Subsection (1) or (1A) does not apply to a course of conduct if the person who pursued it shows–
  (a) that it was pursued for the purpose of preventing or detecting crime,
  (b) that it was pursued under any enactment or rule of law or to comply with any condition or requirement imposed by any person under any enactment, or
  (c) that in the particular circumstances the pursuit of the course of conduct was reasonable.

2 Offence of harassment

(1) A person who pursues a course of conduct in breach of section 1(1) or (1A) is guilty of an offence.
(2) A person guilty of an offence under this section is liable on summary conviction to imprisonment for a term not exceeding six months, or a fine not exceeding level 5 on the standard scale, or both.
(3) ...

2A Offence of stalking

(1) A person is guilty of an offence if–
  (a) the person pursues a course of conduct in breach of section 1(1), and
  (b) the course of conduct amounts to stalking.
(2) For the purposes of subsection (1)(b) (and section 4A(1)(a)) a person's course of conduct amounts to stalking of another person if–
  (a) it amounts to harassment of that person,
  (b) the acts or omissions involved are ones associated with stalking, and
  (c) the person whose course of conduct it is knows or ought to know that the course of conduct amounts to harassment of the other person.
(3) The following are examples of acts or omissions which, in particular circumstances, are ones associated with stalking–

(a) following a person,
(b) contacting, or attempting to contact, a person by any means,
(c) publishing any statement or other material–
    (i) relating or purporting to relate to a person, or
    (ii) purporting to originate from a person,
(d) monitoring the use by a person of the internet, email or any other form of electronic communication,
(e) loitering in any place (whether public or private),
(f) interfering with any property in the possession of a person,
(g) watching or spying on a person.

(4) A person guilty of an offence under this section is liable on summary conviction to imprisonment for a term not exceeding 51 weeks, or a fine not exceeding level 5 on the standard scale, or both.

(5) In relation to an offence committed before the commencement of section 281(5) of the Criminal Justice Act 2003, the reference in subsection (4) to 51 weeks is to be read as a reference to six months.

(6) This section is without prejudice to the generality of section 2.

2B Power of entry in relation to offence of stalking

(1) A justice of the peace may, on an application by a constable, issue a warrant authorising a constable to enter and search premises if the justice of the peace is satisfied that there are reasonable grounds for believing that–
(a) an offence under section 2A has been, or is being, committed,
(b) there is material on the premises which is likely to be of substantial value (whether by itself or together with other material) to the investigation of the offence,
(c) the material–
    (i) is likely to be admissible in evidence at a trial for the offence, and
    (ii) does not consist of, or include, items subject to legal privilege, excluded material or special procedure material (within the meanings given by sections 10, 11 and 14 of the Police and Criminal Evidence Act 1984), and
(d) either–
    (i) entry to the premises will not be granted unless a warrant is produced, or
    (ii) the purpose of a search may be frustrated or seriously prejudiced unless a constable arriving at the premises can secure immediate entry to them.

(2) A constable may seize and retain anything for which a search has been authorised under subsection (1).

(3) A constable may use reasonable force, if necessary, in the exercise of any power conferred by virtue of this section.

(4) In this section 'premises' has the same meaning as in section 23 of the Police and Criminal Evidence Act 1984.

3 Civil remedy

(1) An actual or apprehended breach of section 1(1) may be the subject of a claim in civil proceedings by the person who is or may be the victim of the course of conduct in question.

(2) On such a claim, damages may be awarded for (among other things) any anxiety caused by the harassment and any financial loss resulting from the harassment.

(3) Where–
   (a) in such proceedings the High Court or the county court grants an injunction for the purpose of restraining the defendant from pursuing any conduct which amounts to harassment, and
   (b) the plaintiff considers that the defendant has done anything which he is prohibited from doing by the injunction,
   the plaintiff may apply for the issue of a warrant for the arrest of the defendant.

(4) An application under subsection (3) may be made–
   (a) where the injunction was granted by the High Court, to a judge of that court, and
   (b) where the injunction was granted by the county court, to a judge of that court.

(5) The judge ... to whom an application under subsection (3) is made may only issue a warrant if–
   (a) the application is substantiated on oath, and
   (b) the judge ... has reasonable grounds for believing that the defendant has done anything which he is prohibited from doing by the injunction.

(6) Where–
   (a) the High Court or the county court grants an injunction for the purpose mentioned in subsection (3)(a), and
   (b) without reasonable excuse the defendant does anything which he is prohibited from doing by the injunction,
   he is guilty of an offence.

(7) Where a person is convicted of an offence under subsection (6) in respect of any conduct, that conduct is not punishable as a contempt of court.

(8) A person cannot be convicted of an offence under subsection (6) in respect of any conduct which has been punished as a contempt of court.

(9) A person guilty of an offence under subsection (6) is liable–
   (a) on conviction on indictment, to imprisonment for a term not exceeding five years, or a fine, or both, or
   (b) on summary conviction, to imprisonment for a term not exceeding six months, or a fine not exceeding the statutory maximum, or both.

3A Injunctions to protect persons from harassment within section 1(1A)

(1) This section applies where there is an actual or apprehended breach of section 1(1A) by any person ('the relevant person').

(2) In such a case–
   (a) any person who is or may be a victim of the course of conduct in question, or
   (b) any person who is or may be a person falling within section 1(1A)(c),
   may apply to the High Court or the county court for an injunction restraining the relevant person from pursuing any conduct which amounts to harassment in relation to any person or persons mentioned or described in the injunction.

(3) Section 3(3) to (9) apply in relation to an injunction granted under subsection

(2) above as they apply in relation to an injunction granted as mentioned in section 3(3)(a).

4 Putting people in fear of violence

(1) A person whose course of conduct causes another to fear, on at least two occasions, that violence will be used against him is guilty of an offence if he knows or ought to know that his course of conduct will cause the other so to fear on each of those occasions.

(2) For the purposes of this section, the person whose course of conduct is in question ought to know that it will cause another to fear that violence will be used against him on any occasion if a reasonable person in possession of the same information would think the course of conduct would cause the other so to fear on that occasion.

(3) It is a defence for a person charged with an offence under this section to show that–
   (a) his course of conduct was pursued for the purpose of preventing or detecting crime,
   (b) his course of conduct was pursued under any enactment or rule of law or to comply with any condition or requirement imposed by any person under any enactment, or
   (c) the pursuit of his course of conduct was reasonable for the protection of himself or another or for the protection of his or another's property.

(4) A person guilty of an offence under this section is liable–
   (a) on conviction on indictment, to imprisonment for a term not exceeding ten years, or a fine, or both, or
   (b) on summary conviction, to imprisonment for a term not exceeding six months, or a fine not exceeding the statutory maximum, or both.

(5) If on the trial on indictment of a person charged with an offence under this section the jury find him not guilty of the offence charged, they may find him guilty of an offence under section 2 or 2A.

(6) The Crown Court has the same powers and duties in relation to a person who is by virtue of subsection (5) convicted before it of an offence under section 2 or 2A as a magistrates' court would have on convicting him of the offence.

4A Stalking involving fear of violence or serious alarm or distress

(1) A person ('A') whose course of conduct–
   (a) amounts to stalking, and
   (b) either–
      (i) causes another ('B') to fear, on at least two occasions, that violence will be used against B, or
      (ii) causes B serious alarm or distress which has a substantial adverse effect on B's usual day-to-day activities,
   is guilty of an offence if A knows or ought to know that A's course of conduct will cause B so to fear on each of those occasions or (as the case may be) will cause such alarm or distress.

(2) For the purposes of this section A ought to know that A's course of conduct will cause B to fear that violence will be used against B on any occasion if a reasonable person in possession of the same information would think the course of conduct would cause B so to fear on that occasion.

(3) For the purposes of this section A ought to know that A's course of conduct will cause B serious alarm or distress which has a substantial adverse effect on B's usual day-to-day activities if a reasonable person in possession of the same information would think the course of conduct would cause B such alarm or distress.

(4) It is a defence for A to show that–
  (a) A's course of conduct was pursued for the purpose of preventing or detecting crime,
  (b) A's course of conduct was pursued under any enactment or rule of law or to comply with any condition or requirement imposed by any person under any enactment, or
  (c) the pursuit of A's course of conduct was reasonable for the protection of A or another or for the protection of A's or another's property.

(5) A person guilty of an offence under this section is liable–
  (a) on conviction on indictment, to imprisonment for a term not exceeding ten years, or a fine, or both, or
  (b) on summary conviction, to imprisonment for a term not exceeding twelve months, or a fine not exceeding the statutory maximum, or both.

(6) In relation to an offence committed before the commencement of section 154(1) of the Criminal Justice Act 2003, the reference in subsection (5)(b) to twelve months is to be read as a reference to six months.

(7) If on the trial on indictment of a person charged with an offence under this section the jury find the person not guilty of the offence charged, they may find the person guilty of an offence under section 2 or 2A.

(8) The Crown Court has the same powers and duties in relation to a person who is by virtue of subsection (7) convicted before it of an offence under section 2 or 2A as a magistrates' court would have on convicting the person of the offence.

(9) This section is without prejudice to the generality of section 4.

5 Restraining orders on conviction

(1) A court sentencing or otherwise dealing with a person ('the defendant') convicted of an offence ... may (as well as sentencing him or dealing with him in any other way) make an order under this section.

(2) The order may, for the purpose of protecting the victim or victims of the offence, or any other person mentioned in the order, from ... conduct which–
  (a) amounts to harassment, or
  (b) will cause a fear of violence,
  prohibit the defendant from doing anything described in the order.

(3) The order may have effect for a specified period or until further order.

(3A) In proceedings under this section both the prosecution and the defence may lead, as further evidence, any evidence that would be admissible in proceedings for an injunction under section 3.

(4) The prosecutor, the defendant or any other person mentioned in the order may apply to the court which made the order for it to be varied or discharged by a further order.

(4A) Any person mentioned in the order is entitled to be heard on the hearing of an application under subsection (4).

(5) If without reasonable excuse the defendant does anything which he is prohibited from doing by an order under this section, he is guilty of an offence.

(6) A person guilty of an offence under this section is liable–

    (a) on conviction on indictment, to imprisonment for a term not exceeding five years, or a fine, or both, or

    (b) on summary conviction, to imprisonment for a term not exceeding six months, or a fine not exceeding the statutory maximum, or both.

(7) A court dealing with a person for an offence under this section may vary or discharge the order in question by a further order.

5A Restraining orders on acquittal

(1) A court before which a person ('the defendant') is acquitted of an offence may, if it considers it necessary to do so to protect a person from harassment by the defendant, make an order prohibiting the defendant from doing anything described in the order.

(2) Subsections (3) to (7) of section 5 apply to an order under this section as they apply to an order under that one.

(3) Where the Court of Appeal allow an appeal against conviction they may remit the case to the Crown Court to consider whether to proceed under this section.

(4) Where–

    (a) the Crown Court allows an appeal against conviction, or

    (b) a case is remitted to the Crown Court under subsection (3),

the reference in subsection (1) to a court before which a person is acquitted of an offence is to be read as referring to that court.

(5) A person made subject to an order under this section has the same right of appeal against the order as if–

    (a) he had been convicted of the offence in question before the court which made the order, and

    (b) the order had been made under section 5.

6 Limitation

In section 11 of the Limitation Act 1980 (special time limit for actions in respect of personal injuries), after subsection (1) there is inserted–

    '(1A) This section does not apply to any action brought for damages under section 3 of the Protection from Harassment Act 1997.'

7 Interpretation of this group of sections

(1) This section applies for the interpretation of sections 1 to 5A.

(2) References to harassing a person include alarming the person or causing the person distress.

(3) A 'course of conduct' must involve–

    (a) in the case of conduct in relation to a single person (see section 1(1)), conduct on at least two occasions in relation to that person, or

    (b) in the case of conduct in relation to two or more persons (see section 1(1A)), conduct on at least one occasion in relation to each of those persons.

(3A) A person's conduct on any occasion shall be taken, if aided, abetted, counselled or procured by another–

(a) to be conduct on that occasion of the other (as well as conduct of the person whose conduct it is); and
(b) to be conduct in relation to which the other's knowledge and purpose, and what he ought to have known, are the same as they were in relation to what was contemplated or reasonably foreseeable at the time of the aiding, abetting, counselling or procuring.
(4) 'Conduct' includes speech.
(5) References to a person, in the context of the harassment of a person, are references to a person who is an individual.

...

General

12 National security, etc

(1) If the Secretary of State certifies that in his opinion anything done by a specified person on a specified occasion related to–
(a) national security,
(b) the economic well-being of the United Kingdom, or
(c) the prevention or detection of serious crime,
and was done on behalf of the Crown, the certificate is conclusive evidence that this Act does not apply to any conduct of that person on that occasion.
(2) In subsection (1), 'specified' means specified in the certificate in question.
(3) A document purporting to be a certificate under subsection (1) is to be received in evidence and, unless the contrary is proved, be treated as being such a certificate.

HOUSING ACT 1988

Chapter IV: Protection from Eviction

27 Damages for unlawful eviction

(1) This section applies if, at any time after 9th June 1988, a landlord (in this section referred to as 'the landlord in default') or any person acting on behalf of the landlord in default unlawfully deprives the residential occupier of any premises of his occupation of the whole or part of the premises.

(2) This section also applies if, at any time after 9th June 1988, a landlord (in this section referred to as 'the landlord in default') or any person acting on behalf of the landlord in default—

    (a) attempts unlawfully to deprive the residential occupier of any premises of his occupation of the whole or part of the premises, or

    (b) knowing or having reasonable cause to believe that the conduct is likely to cause the residential occupier of any premises—

        (i) to give up his occupation of the premises or any part thereof, or

        (ii) to refrain from exercising any right or pursuing any remedy in respect of the premises or any part thereof,

    does acts likely to interfere with the peace or comfort of the residential occupier or members of his household, or persistently withdraws or withholds services reasonably required for the occupation of the premises as a residence,

and, as a result, the residential occupier gives up his occupation of the premises as a residence.

(3) Subject to the following provisions of this section, where this section applies, the landlord in default shall, by virtue of this section, be liable to pay to the former residential occupier, in respect of his loss of the right to occupy the premises in question as his residence, damages assessed on the basis set out in section 28 below.

(4) Any liability arising by virtue of subsection (3) above—

    (a) shall be in the nature of a liability in tort; and

    (b) subject to subsection (5) below, shall be in addition to any liability arising apart from this section (whether in tort, contract or otherwise).

(5) Nothing in this section affects the right of a residential occupier to enforce any liability which arises apart from this section in respect of his loss of the right to occupy premises as his residence; but damages shall not be awarded both in respect of such a liability and in respect of a liability arising by virtue of this section on account of the same loss.

(6) No liability shall arise by virtue of subsection (3) above if—

    (a) before the date on which proceedings to enforce the liability are finally disposed of, the former residential occupier is reinstated in the premises in question in such circumstances that he becomes again the residential occupier of them; or

    (b) at the request of the former residential occupier, a court makes an order (whether in the nature of an injunction or otherwise) as a result of which he is reinstated as mentioned in paragraph (a) above;

and, for the purposes of paragraph (a) above, proceedings to enforce a liability are finally disposed of on the earliest date by which the proceedings (including any proceedings on or in consequence of an appeal) have been determined and any time for appealing or further appealing has expired, except that if any appeal is abandoned, the proceedings shall be taken to be disposed of on the date of the abandonment.

(7) If, in proceedings to enforce a liability arising by virtue of subsection (3) above, it appears to the court–

(a) that, prior to the event which gave rise to the liability, the conduct of the former residential occupier or any person living with him in the premises concerned was such that it is reasonable to mitigate the damages for which the landlord in default would otherwise be liable, or

(b) that, before the proceedings were begun, the landlord in default offered to reinstate the former residential occupier in the premises in question and either it was unreasonable of the former residential occupier to refuse that offer or, if he had obtained alternative accommodation before the offer was made, it would have been unreasonable of him to refuse that offer if he had not obtained that accommodation,

the court may reduce the amount of damages which would otherwise be payable to such amount as it thinks appropriate.

(8) In proceedings to enforce a liability arising by virtue of subsection (3) above, it shall be a defence for the defendant to prove that he believed, and had reasonable cause to believe–

(a) that the residential occupier had ceased to reside in the premises in question at the time when he was deprived of occupation as mentioned in subsection (1) above or, as the case may be, when the attempt was made or the acts were done as a result of which he gave up his occupation of those premises; or

(b) that, where the liability would otherwise arise by virtue only of the doing of acts or the withdrawal or withholding of services, he had reasonable grounds for doing the acts or withdrawing or withholding the services in question.

(9) In this section–

(a) 'residential occupier', in relation to any premises, has the same meaning as in section 1 of the 1977 Act;

(b) 'the right to occupy', in relation to a residential occupier, includes any restriction on the right of another person to recover possession of the premises in question;

(c) 'landlord', in relation to a residential occupier, means the person who, but for the occupier's right to occupy, would be entitled to occupation of the premises and any superior landlord under whom that person derives title;

(d) 'former residential occupier', in relation to any premises, means the person who was the residential occupier until he was deprived of or gave up his occupation as mentioned in subsection (1) or subsection (2) above (and, in relation to a former residential occupier, 'the right to occupy' and 'landlord' shall be construed accordingly).

28 The measure of damages

(1) The basis for the assessment of damages referred to in section 27(3) above is the difference in value, determined as at the time immediately before the

residential occupier ceased to occupy the premises in question as his residence, between–

(a) the value of the interest of the landlord in default determined on the assumption that the residential occupier continues to have the same right to occupy the premises as before that time; and

(b) the value of that interest determined on the assumption that the residential occupier has ceased to have that right.

(2) In relation to any premises, any reference in this section to the interest of the landlord in default is a reference to his interest in the building in which the premises in question are comprised (whether or not that building contains any other premises) together with its curtilage.

(3) For the purposes of the valuations referred to in subsection (1) above, it shall be assumed–

(a) that the landlord in default is selling his interest on the open market to a willing buyer;

(b) that neither the residential occupier nor any member of his family wishes to buy; and

(c) that it is unlawful to carry out any substantial development of any of the land in which the landlord's interest subsists or to demolish the whole or part of any building on that land.

(4) In this section 'the landlord in default' has the same meaning as in section 27 above and subsection (9) of that section applies in relation to this section as it applies in relation to that.

(5) Section 113 of the Housing Act 1985 (meaning of 'members of a person's family') applies for the purposes of subsection (3)(b) above.

(6) The reference in subsection (3)(c) above to substantial development of any of the land in which the landlord's interest subsists is a reference to any development other than–

(a) development for which planning permission is granted by a general development order for the time being in force and which is carried out so as to comply with any condition or limitation subject to which planning permission is so granted; or

(b) a change of use resulting in the building referred to in subsection (2) above or any part of it being used as, or as part of, one or more dwelling-houses;

and in this subsection 'general development order' has the meaning given in section 56(6) of the Town and Country Planning Act 1990 and other expressions have the same meaning as in that Act.

CRIMINAL LAW ACT 1977

Part II: Offences relating to Entering and Remaining on Property

6 Violence for securing entry

(1) Subject to the following provisions of this section, any person who, without lawful authority, uses or threatens violence for the purpose of securing entry into any premises for himself or for any other person is guilty of an offence, provided that–

    (a) there is someone present on those premises at the time who is opposed to the entry which the violence is intended to secure; and

    (b) the person using or threatening the violence knows that that is the case.

(1A) Subsection (1) above does not apply to a person who is a displaced residential occupier or a protected intending occupier of the premises in question or who is acting on behalf of such an occupier; and if the accused adduces sufficient evidence that he was, or was acting on behalf of, such an occupier he shall be presumed to be, or to be acting on behalf of, such an occupier unless the contrary is proved by the prosecution.

(2) Subject to subsection (1A) above, the fact that a person has any interest in or right to possession or occupation of any premises shall not for the purposes of subsection (1) above constitute lawful authority for the use or threat of violence by him or anyone else for the purpose of securing his entry into those premises.

(3) ...

(4) It is immaterial for the purposes of this section–

    (a) whether the violence in question is directed against the person or against property; and

    (b) whether the entry which the violence is intended to secure is for the purpose of acquiring possession of the premises in question or for any other purpose.

(5) A person guilty of an offence under this section shall be liable on summary conviction to imprisonment for a term not exceeding six months or to a fine not exceeding level 5 on the standard scale or to both.

(6) ...

(7) Section 12 below contains provisions which apply for determining when any person is to be regarded for the purposes of this Part of this Act as a displaced residential occupier of any premises or of any access to any premises and section 12A below contains provisions which apply for determining when any person is to be regarded for the purposes of this Part of this Act as a protected intending occupier of any premises or of any access to any premises.

7 Adverse occupation of residential premises

(1) Subject to the following provisions of this section and to section 12A(9) below, any person who is on any premises as a trespasser after having entered as such is guilty of an offence if he fails to leave those premises on being required to do so by or on behalf of–

    (a) a displaced residential occupier of the premises; or

    (b) an individual who is a protected intending occupier of the premises.

(2) In any proceedings for an offence under this section it shall be a defence for the accused to prove that he believed that the person requiring him to leave

the premises was not a displaced residential occupier or protected intending occupier of the premises or a person acting on behalf of a displaced residential occupier or protected intending occupier.

(3) In any proceedings for an offence under this section it shall be a defence for the accused to prove–

    (a) that the premises in question are or form part of premises used mainly for non-residential purposes; and

    (b) that he was not on any part of the premises used wholly or mainly for residential purposes.

(4) Any reference in the preceding provisions of this section to any premises includes a reference to any access to them, whether or not any such access itself constitutes premises, within the meaning of this Part of this Act.

(5) A person guilty of an offence under this section shall be liable on summary conviction to imprisonment for a term not exceeding six months or to a fine not exceeding level 5 on the standard scale or to both.

(6) ...

(7) Section 12 below contains provisions which apply for determining when any person is to be regarded for the purposes of this Part of this Act as a displaced residential occupier of any premises or of any access to any premises and section 12A below contains provisions which apply for determining when any person is to be regarded for the purposes of this Part of this Act as a protected intending occupier of any premises or of any access to any premises.

12 Supplementary provisions

(1) In this Part of this Act–

    (a) 'premises' means any building, any part of a building under separate occupation, any land ancillary to a building, the site comprising any building or buildings together with any land ancillary thereto, and (for the purposes only of sections 10 and 11 above) any other place; and

    (b) 'access' means, in relation to any premises, any part of any site or building within which those premises are situated which constitutes an ordinary means of access to those premises (whether or not that is its sole or primary use).

(2) References in this section to a building shall apply also to any structure other than a movable one, and to any movable structure, vehicle or vessel designed or adapted for use for residential purposes; and for the purposes of subsection (1) above–

    (a) part of a building is under separate occupation if anyone is in occupation or entitled to occupation of that part as distinct from the whole; and

    (b) land is ancillary to a building if it is adjacent to it and used (or intended for use) in connection with the occupation of that building or any part of it.

(3) Subject to subsection (4) below, any person who was occupying any premises as a residence immediately before being excluded from occupation by anyone who entered those premises, or any access to those premises, as a trespasser is a displaced residential occupier of the premises for the purposes of this Part of this Act so long as he continues to be excluded from occupation of the premises by the original trespasser or by any subsequent trespasser.

(4) A person who was himself occupying the premises in question as a trespasser

immediately before being excluded from occupation shall not by virtue of subsection (3) above be a displaced residential occupier of the premises for the purposes of this Part of this Act.

(5) A person who by virtue of subsection (3) above is a displaced residential occupier of any premises shall be regarded for the purposes of this Part of this Act as a displaced residential occupier also of any access to those premises.

(6) Anyone who enters or is on or in occupation of any premises by virtue of–
   (a) any title derived from a trespasser; or
   (b) any licence or consent given by a trespasser or by a person deriving title from a trespasser,
shall himself be treated as a trespasser for the purposes of this Part of this Act (without prejudice to whether or not he would be a trespasser apart from this provision); and references in this Part of this Act to a person's entering or being on or occupying any premises as a trespasser shall be construed accordingly.

(7) Anyone who is on any premises as a trespasser shall not cease to be a trespasser for the purposes of this Part of this Act by virtue of being allowed time to leave the premises, nor shall anyone cease to be a displaced residential occupier of any premises by virtue of any such allowance of time to a trespasser.

(8) No rule of law ousting the jurisdiction of magistrates' courts to try offences where a dispute of title to property is involved shall preclude magistrates' courts from trying offences under this Part of this Act.

12A Protected intending occupiers: supplementary provisions

(1) For the purposes of this Part of this Act an individual is a protected intending occupier of any premises at any time if at that time he falls within subsection (2), (4) or (6) below.

(2) An individual is a protected intending occupier of any premises if–
   (a) he has in those premises a freehold interest or a leasehold interest with not less than two years still to run;
   (b) he requires the premises for his own occupation as a residence;
   (c) he is excluded from occupation of the premises by a person who entered them, or any access to them, as a trespasser; and
   (d) he or a person acting on his behalf holds a written statement–
      (i) which specifies his interest in the premises;
      (ii) which states that he requires the premises for occupation as a residence for himself; and
      (iii) with respect to which the requirements in subsection (3) below are fulfilled.

(3) The requirements referred to in subsection (2)(d)(iii) above are–
   (a) that the statement is signed by the person whose interest is specified in it in the presence of a justice of the peace or commissioner for oaths; and
   (b) that the justice of the peace or commissioner for oaths has subscribed his name as a witness to the signature.

(4) An individual is also a protected intending occupier of any premises if–
   (a) he has a tenancy of those premises (other than a tenancy falling within subsection (2)(a) above or (6)(a) below) or a licence to occupy those

premises granted by a person with a freehold interest or a leasehold interest with not less than two years still to run in the premises;

(b) he requires the premises for his own occupation as a residence;

(c) he is excluded from occupation of the premises by a person who entered them, or any access to them, as a trespasser; and

(d) he or a person acting on his behalf holds a written statement–

    (i) which states that he has been granted a tenancy of those premises or a licence to occupy those premises;

    (ii) which specifies the interest in the premises of the person who granted that tenancy or licence to occupy ('the landlord');

    (iii) which states that he requires the premises for occupation as a residence for himself; and

    (iv) with respect to which the requirements in subsection (5) below are fulfilled.

(5) The requirements referred to in subsection (4)(d)(iv) above are–

(a) that the statement is signed by the landlord and by the tenant or licensee in the presence of a justice of the peace or commissioner for oaths;

(b) that the justice of the peace or commissioner for oaths has subscribed his name as a witness to the signatures.

(6) An individual is also a protected intending occupier of any premises if–

(a) he has a tenancy of those premises (other than a tenancy falling within subsection (2)(a) or (4)(a) above) or a licence to occupy those premises granted by an authority to which this subsection applies;

(b) he requires the premises for his own occupation as a residence;

(c) he is excluded from occupation of the premises by a person who entered the premises, or any access to them, as a trespasser; and

(d) there has been issued to him by or on behalf of the authority referred to in paragraph (a) above a certificate stating that–

    (i) he has been granted a tenancy of those premises or a licence to occupy those premises as a residence by the authority; and

    (ii) the authority which granted that tenancy or licence to occupy is one to which this subsection applies, being of a description specified in the certificate.

(7) Subsection (6) above applies to the following authorities–

(a) any body mentioned in section 14 of the Rent Act 1977 (landlord's interest belonging to local authority etc);

(b) the Regulator of Social Housing;

(ba) a non-profit registered provider of social housing;

(bb) a profit-making registered provider of social housing, but only in relation to premises which are social housing within the meaning of Part 2 of the Housing and Regeneration Act 2008;

(c) ... and

(d) a registered social landlord within the meaning of the Housing Act 1985 (see section 5(4) and (5) of that Act).

(7A) Subsection (6) also applies to the Secretary of State if the tenancy or licence is granted by him under Part III of the Housing Associations Act 1985.

(8) A person is guilty of an offence if he makes a statement for the purposes of subsection (2)(d) or (4)(d) above which he knows to be false in a material

particular or if he recklessly makes such a statement which is false in a material particular.

(9) In any proceedings for an offence under section 7 of this Act where the accused was requested to leave the premises by a person claiming to be or to act on behalf of a protected intending occupier of the premises–

    (a) it shall be a defence for the accused to prove that, although asked to do so by the accused at the time the accused was requested to leave, that person failed at that time to produce to the accused such a statement as is referred to in subsection (2)(d) or (4)(d) above or such a certificate as is referred to in subsection (6)(d) above; and

    (b) any document purporting to be a certificate under subsection (6)(d) above shall be received in evidence and, unless the contrary is proved, shall be deemed to have been issued by or on behalf of the authority stated in the certificate.

(10) A person guilty of an offence under subsection (8) above shall be liable on summary conviction to imprisonment for a term not exceeding six months or to a fine not exceeding level 5 on the standard scale or to both.

(11) A person who is a protected intending occupier of any premises shall be regarded for the purposes of this Part of this Act as a protected intending occupier also of any access to those premises.

PROTECTION FROM EVICTION ACT 1977

Part I: Unlawful Eviction and Harassment

1 Unlawful eviction and harassment of occupier

(1) In this section 'residential occupier', in relation to any premises, means a person occupying the premises as a residence, whether under a contract or by virtue of any enactment or rule of law giving him the right to remain in occupation or restricting the right of any other person to recover possession of the premises.

(2) If any person unlawfully deprives the residential occupier of any premises of his occupation of the premises or any part thereof, or attempts to do so, he shall be guilty of an offence unless he proves that he believed, and had reasonable cause to believe, that the residential occupier had ceased to reside in the premises.

(3) If any person with intent to cause the residential occupier of any premises–
  (a) to give up the occupation of the premises or any part thereof; or
  (b) to refrain from exercising any right or pursuing any remedy in respect of the premises or part thereof;

does acts likely to interfere with the peace or comfort of the residential occupier or members of his household, or persistently withdraws or withholds services reasonably required for the occupation of the premises as a residence, he shall be guilty of an offence.

(3A) Subject to subsection (3B) below, the landlord of a residential occupier or an agent of the landlord shall be guilty of an offence if–
  (a) he does acts likely to interfere with the peace or comfort of the residential occupier or members of his household, or
  (b) he persistently withdraws or withholds services reasonably required for the occupation of the premises in question as a residence,

and (in either case) he knows, or has reasonable cause to believe, that that conduct is likely to cause the residential occupier to give up the occupation of the whole or part of the premises or to refrain from exercising any right or pursuing any remedy in respect of the whole or part of the premises.

(3B) A person shall not be guilty of an offence under subsection (3A) above if he proves that he had reasonable grounds for doing the acts or withdrawing or withholding the services in question.

(3C) In subsection (3A) above 'landlord', in relation to a residential occupier of any premises, means the person who, but for–
  (a) the residential occupier's right to remain in occupation of the premises, or
  (b) a restriction on the person's right to recover possession of the premises,
would be entitled to occupation of the premises and any superior landlord under whom that person derives title.

(4) A person guilty of an offence under this section shall be liable–
  (a) on summary conviction, to a fine not exceeding the prescribed sum or to imprisonment for a term not exceeding 6 months or to both;
  (b) on conviction on indictment, to a fine or to imprisonment for a term not exceeding 2 years or to both.

(5) Nothing in this section shall be taken to prejudice any liability or remedy

to which a person guilty of an offence thereunder may be subject in civil proceedings.

(6) Where an offence under this section committed by a body corporate is proved to have been committed with the consent or connivance of, or to be attributable to any neglect on the part of, any director, manager or secretary or other similar officer of the body corporate or any person who was purporting to act in any such capacity, he as well as the body corporate shall be guilty of that offence and shall be liable to be proceeded against and punished accordingly.

2   Restriction on re-entry without due process of law
Where any premises are let as a dwelling on a lease which is subject to a right of re-entry or forfeiture it shall not be lawful to enforce that right otherwise than by proceedings in the court while any person is lawfully residing in the premises or part of them.

3   Prohibition of eviction without due process of law
(1) Where any premises have been let as a dwelling under a tenancy which is neither a statutorily protected tenancy nor an excluded tenancy and—
   (a) the tenancy (in this section referred to as the former tenancy) has come to an end, but
   (b) the occupier continues to reside in the premises or part of them,
   it shall not be lawful for the owner to enforce against the occupier, otherwise than by proceedings in the court, his right to recover possession of the premises.
(2) In this section 'the occupier', in relation to any premises, means any person lawfully residing in the premises or part of them at the termination of the former tenancy.
(2A) Subsections (1) and (2) above apply in relation to any restricted contract (within the meaning of the Rent Act 1977) which—
   (a) creates a licence; and
   (b) is entered into after the commencement of section 69 of the Housing Act 1980;
   as they apply in relation to a restricted contract which creates a tenancy.
(2B) Subsections (1) and (2) above apply in relation to any premises occupied as a dwelling under a licence, other than an excluded licence, as they apply in relation to premises let as a dwelling under a tenancy, and in those subsections the expressions 'let' and 'tenancy' shall be construed accordingly.
(2C) References in the preceding provisions of this section and section 4(2A) below to an excluded tenancy do not apply to—
   (a) a tenancy entered into before the date on which the Housing Act 1988 came into force, or
   (b) a tenancy entered into on or after that date but pursuant to a contract made before that date,
   but, subject to that, 'excluded tenancy' and 'excluded licence' shall be construed in accordance with section 3A below.
(3) This section shall, with the necessary modifications, apply where the owner's right to recover possession arises on the death of the tenant under a statutory tenancy within the meaning of the Rent Act 1977 or the Rent (Agriculture) Act 1976.

3A Excluded tenancies and licences

(1) Any reference in this Act to an excluded tenancy or an excluded licence is a reference to a tenancy or licence which is excluded by virtue of any of the following provisions of this section.

(2) A tenancy or licence is excluded if—
  (a) under its terms the occupier shares any accommodation with the landlord or licensor; and
  (b) immediately before the tenancy or licence was granted and also at the time it comes to an end, the landlord or licensor occupied as his only or principal home premises of which the whole or part of the shared accommodation formed part.

(3) A tenancy or licence is also excluded if—
  (a) under its terms the occupier shares any accommodation with a member of the family of the landlord or licensor;
  (b) immediately before the tenancy or licence was granted and also at the time it comes to an end, the member of the family of the landlord or licensor occupied as his only or principal home premises of which the whole or part of the shared accommodation formed part; and
  (c) immediately before the tenancy or licence was granted and also at the time it comes to an end, the landlord or licensor occupied as his only or principal home premises in the same building as the shared accommodation and that building is not a purpose-built block of flats.

(4) For the purposes of subsections (2) and (3) above, an occupier shares accommodation with another person if he has the use of it in common with that person (whether or not also in common with others) and any reference in those subsections to shared accommodation shall be construed accordingly, and if, in relation to any tenancy or licence, there is at any time more than one person who is the landlord or licensor, any reference in those subsections to the landlord or licensor shall be construed as a reference to any one of those persons.

(5) In subsections (2) to (4) above—
  (a) 'accommodation' includes neither an area used for storage nor a staircase, passage, corridor or other means of access;
  (b) 'occupier' means, in relation to a tenancy, the tenant and, in relation to a licence, the licensee; and
  (c) 'purpose-built block of flats' has the same meaning as in Part III of Schedule 1 to the Housing Act 1988;
  and section 113 of the Housing Act 1985 shall apply to determine whether a person is for the purposes of subsection (3) above a member of another's family as it applies for the purposes of Part IV of that Act.

(6) A tenancy or licence is excluded if it was granted as a temporary expedient to a person who entered the premises in question or any other premises as a trespasser (whether or not, before the beginning of that tenancy or licence, another tenancy or licence to occupy the premises or any other premises had been granted to him).

(7) A tenancy or licence is excluded if—
  (a) it confers on the tenant or licensee the right to occupy the premises for a holiday only; or
  (b) it is granted otherwise than for money or money's worth.

(7A) A tenancy or licence is excluded if it is granted in order to provide accommodation under *section 4 or²* Part VI of the Immigration and Asylum Act 1999.

[(7B) Section 32 of the Nationality, Immigration and Asylum Act 2002 (accommodation centre: tenure) provides for a resident's licence to occupy an accommodation centre to be an excluded licence.]³

(7C) A tenancy or licence is excluded if it is granted in order to provide accommodation under the Displaced Persons (Temporary Protection) Regulations 2005.

(7D) A tenancy or licence is excluded if–

    (a) it is a residential tenancy agreement within the meaning of Chapter 1 of Part 3 of the Immigration Act 2014, and

    (b) the condition in section 33D(2) of that Act is met in relation to that agreement.

(8) A licence is excluded if it confers rights of occupation in a hostel, within the meaning of the Housing Act 1985, which is provided by–

    (a) the council of a county, county borough, district or London Borough, the Common Council of the City of London, the Council of the Isle of Scilly, the Inner London Education Authority, [a fire and rescue authority created by an order under section 4A of the Fire and Rescue Services Act 2004,]⁴ [the London Fire and Emergency Planning Authority,] [the London Fire Commissioner,]⁵ a joint authority within the meaning of the Local Government Act 1985 or a residuary body within the meaning of that Act;

    (aa) an economic prosperity board established under section 88 of the Local Democracy, Economic Development and Construction Act 2009;

    (ab) a combined authority established under section 103 of that Act;

    (b) a development corporation within the meaning of the New Towns Act 1981;

    (c) the new towns residuary body;

    (d) an urban development corporation established by an order under section 135 of the Local Government, Planning and Land Act 1980;

    (da) a Mayoral development corporation;

    (e) a housing action trust established under Part III of the Housing Act 1988;

    (f) ...

    (g) the Regulator of Social Housing ...;

    (ga) the Secretary of State under section 89 of the Housing Associations Act 1985;

    (h) a housing trust (within the meaning of the Housing Associations Act 1985) which is a charity, a private registered provider of social housing

---

2   Words 'section 4 or' in italics repealed by the Immigration Act 2016 s66 Sch 11 Pt 1 para 2(b)(i). Not yet in force.

3   Inserted by the Nationality, Immigration and Asylum Act 2002 s32(5). Not yet in force.

4   Inserted by the Policing and Crime Act 2017 s6, Sch 1, Pt 2, para 39. Not yet in force.

5   Words in italics repealed and subsequent words in square brackets substituted by the Policing and Crime Act 2017 s9(3)(c), Sch 2, Pt 2, para 55.

or a registered social landlord (within the meaning of the Housing Act 1985); or

(i) any other person who is, or who belongs to a class of person which is, specified in an order made by the Secretary of State.

(8A) In subsection (8)(c) above 'new towns residuary body' means–

(a) in relation to England, the Homes and Communities Agency so far as exercising functions in relation to anything transferred (or to be transferred) to it as mentioned in section 52(1)(a) to (d) of the Housing and Regeneration Act 2008 [or the Greater London Authority so far as exercising its new towns and urban development functions]; and

(b) in relation to Wales, means the Welsh Ministers so far as exercising functions in relation to anything transferred (or to be transferred) to them as mentioned in section 36(1)(a)(i) to (iii) of the New Towns Act 1981.

(9) The power to make an order under subsection (8)(i) above shall be exercisable by statutory instrument which shall be subject to annulment in pursuance of a resolution of either House of Parliament.

4 Special provisions for agricultural employees

(1) This section shall apply where the tenant under the former tenancy (within the meaning of section 3 of this Act) occupied the premises under the terms of his employment as a person employed in agriculture, as defined in section 1 of the Rent (Agriculture) Act 1976, but is not a statutory tenant as defined in that Act.

(2) In this section 'the occupier', in relation to any premises, means–

(a) the tenant under the former tenancy; or

(b) the [surviving spouse or surviving civil partner] of the tenant under the former tenancy residing with him at his death or, if the former tenant leaves no such [surviving spouse or surviving civil partner], any member of his family residing with him at his death.

(2A) In accordance with section 3(2B) above, any reference in subsections (1) and (2) above to the tenant under the former tenancy includes a reference to the licensee under a licence (other than an excluded licence) which has come to an end (being a licence to occupy premises as a dwelling); and in the following provisions of this section the expressions 'tenancy' and 'rent' and any other expressions referable to a tenancy shall be construed accordingly.

(3) Without prejudice to any power of the court apart from this section to postpone the operation or suspend the execution of an order for possession, if in proceedings by the owner against the occupier the court makes an order for the possession of the premises the court may suspend the execution of the order on such terms and conditions, including conditions as to the payment by the occupier of arrears of rent, mesne profits and otherwise as the court thinks reasonable.

(4) Where the order for possession is made within the period of 6 months beginning with the date when the former tenancy came to an end, then, without prejudice to any powers of the court under the preceding provisions of this section or apart from this section to postpone the operation or suspend the execution of the order for a longer period, the court shall suspend the execution of the order for the remainder of the said period of 6 months unless the court–

(a) is satisfied either–
  (i) that other suitable accommodation is, or will within that period be made, available to the occupier; or
  (ii) that the efficient management of any agricultural land or the efficient carrying on of any agricultural operations would be seriously prejudiced unless the premises are available for occupation by a person employed or to be employed by the owner; or
  (iii) that greater hardship (being hardship in respect of matters other than the carrying on of such a business as aforesaid) would be caused by the suspension of the order until the end of that period than by its execution within that period; or
  (iv) that the occupier, or any person residing or lodging with the occupier, has been causing damage to the premises or has been guilty of conduct which is a nuisance or annoyance to persons occupying other premises; and
(b) considers that it would be reasonable not to suspend the execution of the order for the remainder of that period.

(5) Where the court suspends the execution of an order for possession under subsection (4) above it shall do so on such terms and conditions, including conditions as to the payment by the occupier of arrears of rent, mesne profits and otherwise as the court thinks reasonable.

(6) A decision of the court not to suspend the execution of the order under subsection (4) above shall not prejudice any other power of the court to postpone the operation or suspend the execution of the order for the whole or part of the period of 6 months mentioned in that subsection.

(7) Where the court has, under the preceding provisions of this section, suspended the execution of an order for possession, it may from time to time vary the period of suspension or terminate it and may vary any terms or conditions imposed by virtue of this section.

(8) In considering whether or how to exercise its powers under subsection (3) above, the court shall have regard to all the circumstances and, in particular, to–
  (a) whether other suitable accommodation is or can be made available to the occupier;
  (b) whether the efficient management of any agricultural land or the efficient carrying on of any agricultural operations would be seriously prejudiced unless the premises were available for occupation by a person employed or to be employed by the owner; and
  (c) whether greater hardship would be caused by the suspension of the execution of the order than by its execution without suspension or further suspension.

(9) Where in proceedings for the recovery of possession of the premises the court makes an order for possession but suspends the execution of the order under this section, it shall make no order for costs, unless it appears to the court, having regard to the conduct of the owner or of the occupier, that there are special reasons for making such an order.

(10) Where, in the case of an order for possession of the premises to which subsection (4) above applies, the execution of the order is not suspended under that subsection or, the execution of the order having been so suspended, the

suspension is terminated, then, if it is subsequently made to appear to the court that the failure to suspend the execution of the order or, as the case may be, the termination of the suspension was–

(a) attributable to the provisions of paragraph (a)(ii) of subsection (4), and

(b) due to misrepresentation or concealment of material facts by the owner of the premises,

the court may order the owner to pay to the occupier such sum as appears sufficient as compensation for damage or loss sustained by the occupier as a result of that failure or termination.

Part II: Notice to Quit

5 Validity of notices to quit

(1) Subject to subsection (1B) below no notice by a landlord or a tenant to quit any premises let (whether before or after the commencement of this Act) as a dwelling shall be valid unless–

(a) it is in writing and contains such information as may be prescribed, and

(b) it is given not less than 4 weeks before the date on which it is to take effect.

(1A) Subject to subsection (1B) below, no notice by a licensor or licensee to determine a periodic licence to occupy premises as a dwelling (whether the licence was granted before or after the passing of this Act) shall be valid unless–

(a) it is in writing and contains such information as may be prescribed, and

(b) it is given not less than 4 weeks before the date on which it is to take effect.

(1B) Nothing in subsection (1) or subsection (1A) above applies to–

(a) premises let on an excluded tenancy which is entered into on or after the date on which the Housing Act 1988 came into force unless it is entered into pursuant to a contract made before that date; or

(b) premises occupied under an excluded licence.

(2) In this section 'prescribed' means prescribed by regulations made by the Secretary of State by statutory instrument, and a statutory instrument containing any such regulations shall be subject to annulment in pursuance of a resolution of either House of Parliament.

(3) Regulations under this section may make different provision in relation to different descriptions of lettings and different circumstances.

Part III: Supplemental Provisions

6 Prosecution of offences

Proceedings for an offence under this Act may be instituted by any of the following authorities–

(a) councils of districts and London boroughs;

(aa) councils of Welsh counties and county boroughs;

(b) the Common Council of the City of London;

(c) the Council of the Isles of Scilly.

7 Service of notices

(1) If for the purpose of any proceedings (whether civil or criminal) brought or intended to be brought under this Act, any person serves upon–

(a) any agent of the landlord named as such in the rent book or other similar document, or

(b) the person who receives the rent of the dwelling,

a notice in writing requiring the agent or other person to disclose to him the full name and place of abode or place of business of the landlord, that agent or other person shall forthwith comply with the notice.

(2) If any such agent or other person as is referred to in subsection (1) above fails or refuses forthwith to comply with a notice served on him under that subsection, he shall be liable on summary conviction to a fine not exceeding [level 4 on the standard scale] unless he shows to the satisfaction of the court that he did not know, and could not with reasonable diligence have ascertained, such of the facts required by the notice to be disclosed as were not disclosed by him.

(3) In this section 'landlord' includes–

(a) any person from time to time deriving title under the original landlord,

(b) in relation to any dwelling-house, any person other than the tenant who is or, but for Part VII of the Rent Act 1977 would be, entitled to possession of the dwelling-house, and

(c) any person who, ... grants to another the right to occupy the dwelling in question as a residence and any person directly or indirectly deriving title from the grantor.

8 Interpretation

(1) In this Act 'statutorily protected tenancy' means–

(a) a protected tenancy within the meaning of the Rent Act 1977 or a tenancy to which Part I of the Landlord and Tenant Act 1954 applies;

(b) a protected occupancy or statutory tenancy as defined in the Rent (Agriculture) Act 1976;

(c) a tenancy to which Part II of the Landlord and Tenant Act 1954 applies;

(d) a tenancy of an agricultural holding within the meaning of the Agricultural Holdings Act 1986 which is a tenancy in relation to which that Act applies;

(e) an assured tenancy or assured agricultural occupancy under Part I of the Housing Act 1988;

(f) a tenancy to which Schedule 10 to the Local Government and Housing Act 1989 applies.

(g) a farm business tenancy within the meaning of the Agricultural Tenancies Act 1995.

(2) For the purposes of Part I of this Act a person who, under the terms of his employment, had exclusive possession of any premises other than as a tenant shall be deemed to have been a tenant and the expressions 'let' and 'tenancy' shall be construed accordingly.

(3) In Part I of this Act 'the owner', in relation to any premises, means the person who, as against the occupier, is entitled to possession thereof.

(4) In this Act 'excluded tenancy' and 'excluded licence' have the meaning assigned by section 3A of this Act.

(5) If, on or after the date on which the Housing Act 1988 came into force, the terms of an excluded tenancy or excluded licence entered into before that date are varied, then–

(a) if the variation affects the amount of the rent which is payable under the tenancy or licence, the tenancy or licence shall be treated for the purposes of sections 3(2C) and 5(1B) above as a new tenancy or licence entered into at the time of the variation; and

(b) if the variation does not affect the amount of the rent which is so payable, nothing in this Act shall affect the determination of the question whether the variation is such as to give rise to a new tenancy or licence.

(6) Any reference in subsection (5) above to a variation affecting the amount of the rent which is payable under a tenancy or licence does not include a reference to–

(a) a reduction or increase effected under Part III or Part VI of the Rent Act 1977 (rents under regulated tenancies and housing association tenancies), section 78 of that Act (power of ... tribunal in relation to restricted contracts) or sections 11 to 14 of the Rent (Agriculture) Act 1976; or

(b) a variation which is made by the parties and has the effect of making the rent expressed to be payable under the tenancy or licence the same as a rent for the dwelling which is entered in the register under Part IV or section 79 of the Rent Act 1977.

9 The court for purposes of Part I

(1) The court for the purposes of Part I of this Act shall, subject to this section, be–

(a) the county court, in relation to premises with respect to which the county court has for the time being jurisdiction in actions for the recovery of land; and

(b) the High Court, in relation to other premises.

(2) ...

(3) Nothing in this Act shall affect the jurisdiction of the High Court in proceedings to enforce a lessor's right of re-entry or forfeiture or to enforce a mortgagee's right of possession in a case where the former tenancy was not binding on the mortgagee.

(4) Nothing in this Act shall affect the operation of–

(a) section 59 of the Pluralities Act 1838;

(b) section 19 of the Defence Act 1842;

(c) section 6 of the Lecturers and Parish Clerks Act 1844;

(d) paragraph 3 of Schedule 1 to the Sexual Offences Act 1956; or

(e) section 13 of the Compulsory Purchase Act 1965.

10 Application to Crown

In so far as this Act requires the taking of proceedings in the court for the recovery of possession or confers any powers on the court it shall (except in the case of section 4(10)) be binding on the Crown.

11 Application to Isles of Scilly

(1) In its application to the Isles of Scilly, this Act (except in the case of section 5) shall have effect subject to such exceptions, adaptations and modifications as the Secretary of State may by order direct.

(2) The power to make an order under this section shall be exercisable by statutory instrument which shall be subject to annulment, in pursuance of a resolution of either House of Parliament.

(3) An order under this section may be varied or revoked by a subsequent order.

13 Short title, etc

(1) This Act may be cited as the Protection from Eviction Act 1977.

(2) This Act shall come into force on the expiry of the period of one month beginning with the date on which it is passed.

(3) This Act does not extend to Scotland or Northern Ireland.

(4) References in this Act to any enactment are references to that enactment as amended, and include references thereto as applied by any other enactment including, except where the context otherwise requires, this Act.

CARAVAN SITES ACT 1968

Part I: Provisions for Protection of Residential Occupiers

1 Application of Part I

(1) This Part of this Act applies in relation to any licence or contract (whether made before or after the passing of this Act) under which a person is entitled to station a caravan on a protected site (as defined by subsection (2) below) and occupy it as his residence, or to occupy as his residence a caravan stationed on any such site; and any such licence or contract is in this Part referred to as a residential contract, and the person so entitled as the occupier.

(2) For the purposes of this Part of this Act a protected site is any land in England in respect of which a site licence is required under Part I of the Caravan Sites and Control of Development Act 1960 or would be so required if paragraph 11of Schedule 1 to that Act (exemption of local authority sites) were omitted, not being land in respect of which the relevant planning permission or site licence–

(a) is expressed to be granted for holiday use only; or

(b) is otherwise so expressed or subject to such conditions that there are times of the year when no caravan may be stationed on the land for human habitation.

(3) References in this Part of this Act to the owner of a protected site are references to the person who is or would apart from any residential contract be entitled to possession of the land.

2 Minimum length of notice

In any case where a residential contract is determinable by notice given by either party to the other, a notice so given shall be of no effect unless it is given not less than four weeks before the date on which it is to take effect.

3 Protection of occupiers against eviction and harassment, false information etc

(1) Subject to the provisions of this section, a person shall be guilty of an offence under this section–

(a) if, during the subsistence of a residential contract, he unlawfully deprives the occupier of his occupation on the protected site of any caravan which the occupier is entitled by the contract to station and occupy, or to occupy, as his residence thereon;

(b) if, after the expiration or determination of a residential contract, he enforces, otherwise than by proceedings in the court, any right to exclude the occupier from the protected site or from any such caravan, or to remove or exclude any such caravan from the site;

(c) if, whether during the subsistence or after the expiration or determination of a residential contract, the person–

(i) does anything likely to interfere with the peace or comfort of the occupier or persons residing with the occupier; or

(ii) persistently withdraws or withholds services or facilities reasonably required for the occupation of the caravan as a residence on the site,

and (in either case) knows, or has reasonable cause to believe, that that conduct is likely to cause the occupier to abandon the occupation of the caravan or remove it from the site or to refrain from exercising any right or pursuing any remedy in relation to the caravan.

(1AA) The owner of a protected site ... or the owner's agent is guilty of an offence under this section if, during the subsistence of a residential contract, the owner or (as the case may be) agent—

(a) knowingly or recklessly provides information or makes a representation which is false or misleading in a material respect to any person, and

(b) knows, or has reasonable cause to believe, that doing so is likely to cause—

   (i) the occupier to do any of the things mentioned in subsection (1)(c)(i) or (ii), or

   (ii) a person who is considering whether to purchase or occupy the caravan to which the residential contract relates to decide not to do so.

(2) References in this section to the occupier include references to the person who was the occupier under a residential contract which has expired or been determined and, in the case of the death of the occupier (whether during the subsistence or after the expiration or determination of the contract), to any person then residing with the occupier being—

(a) the widow, widower or surviving civil partner of the occupier; or

(b) in default of a widow, widower or surviving civil partner so residing, any member of the occupier's family.

(3) A person guilty of an offence under this section shall, without prejudice to any liability or remedy to which he may be subject in civil proceedings, be liable on summary conviction—

(a) in the case of a first offence, to a fine not exceeding the statutory maximum;

(b) in the case of a second or subsequent offence, to a fine not exceeding the statutory maximum or to imprisonment for a term not exceeding 6 months, or to both.

(4) In proceedings for an offence under paragraph (a) or (b) of subsection (1) of this section it shall be a defence to prove that the accused believed, and had reasonable cause to believe, that the occupier of the caravan had ceased to reside on the site.

(4A) In proceedings for an offence under subsection (1)(c) of this section it shall be a defence to prove that the accused had reasonable grounds for doing the acts or withdrawing or withholding the services or facilities in question.

(5) Nothing in this section applies to the exercise by any person of a right to take possession of a caravan of which he is the owner, other than a right conferred by or arising on the expiration or determination of a residential contract, or to anything done pursuant to the order of any court.

5 Supplementary

(1) In this Part of this Act 'the court' means the county court.

(2) The power of the court under section 4 of this Act to suspend the enforcement of an order shall extend to any order made but not executed before the commencement of this Part of this Act.

(3) Nothing in this Part of this Act shall affect the operation of section 13 of the Compulsory Purchase Act 1965.

(4) Subsection (1) of section 12 of the Caravan Sites and Control of Development

Act 1960 (power of site occupier to take possession and terminate a licence or tenancy in cases of contravention of section 1 of that Act) shall have effect subject to the foregoing provisions of this Part of this Act.

(5) The Protection from Eviction Act 1977 (protection against harassment and eviction without due process of law) shall not apply to any premises being a caravan stationed on a protected site.

Statutory instruments: extracts[1]

SMOKE AND CARBON MONOXIDE ALARM (ENGLAND) REGULATIONS 2015 SI NO 1693

Part 1: Introduction

1 Citation, commencement and application

(1) These Regulations may be cited as the Smoke and Carbon Monoxide Alarm (England) Regulations 2015 and come into force on 1st October 2015.

(2) These Regulations apply to England only.

2 Interpretation

(1) In these Regulations—

'authorised person' means a person authorised in writing by the local housing authority for the purpose of taking remedial action under regulation 7;

'building' includes part of a building;

'penalty charge' means a monetary penalty imposed under regulation 8;

'premises' does not include vehicles or vessels or—

(a) an HMO (as defined in section 77 of the Housing Act 2004) in respect of which a licence is required under Part 2 of that Act, or

(b) a house (as defined in section 99 of that Act) in respect of which a licence is required under Part 3 of that Act;

'prescribed alarm' means an alarm which is required to be equipped at residential premises under regulation 4(1)(a);

'remedial action' means action—

(a) to install a prescribed alarm;

(b) to repair a prescribed alarm; or

(c) to check a prescribed alarm is in proper working order;

'remedial notice' means a notice requiring the landlord on whom it is served to take such remedial action as is specified in the notice in accordance with regulation 5(2)(c);

'rent' includes any sum paid in the nature of rent;

'residential premises' means premises (as defined above) all or part of which comprise a dwelling; and

'specified tenancy' means a tenancy of residential premises in England which—

(a) grants one or more persons the right to occupy all or part of the premises as their only or main residence;

(b) provides for payment of rent (whether or not a market rent); and

(c) is not a tenancy of a description specified in the Schedule to these Regulations.

Part 2: Prescribed Alarms

3 Meaning of 'relevant landlord'

(1) For the purposes of these Regulations, a landlord is a 'relevant landlord' if the landlord—

(a) is the immediate landlord in respect of a specified tenancy; and

(b) is not a registered provider of social housing (as to which see section 80(2) of the Housing and Regeneration Act 2008).

(2) In paragraph (1) 'immediate landlord'–
  (a) where the premises are occupied under a specified tenancy which is not a licence means the person for the time being entitled to the reversion expectant on that tenancy; and
  (b) where the premises are occupied under a specified tenancy which is a licence means the licensor, except that where the licensor himself or herself occupies the premises under a specified tenancy which is not a licence, it means the person for the time being entitled to the reversion expectant on that tenancy.

4 Duties of relevant landlord in relation to prescribed alarms
(1) A relevant landlord in respect of a specified tenancy must ensure that–
  (a) during any period beginning on or after 1st October 2015 when the premises are occupied under the tenancy–
      (i) a smoke alarm is equipped on each storey of the premises on which there is a room used wholly or partly as living accommodation;
      (ii) a carbon monoxide alarm is equipped in any room of the premises which is used wholly or partly as living accommodation and contains a solid fuel burning combustion appliance; and
  (b) checks are made by or on behalf of the landlord to ensure that each pre-scribed alarm is in proper working order on the day the tenancy begins if it is a new tenancy.
(2) For the purposes of paragraph (1)(a), a bathroom or lavatory is to be treated as a room used as living accommodation.
(3) For the purposes of paragraph (1)(b), a tenancy begins on the day on which, under the terms of the tenancy, the tenant is entitled to possession under that tenancy.
(4) In this regulation–
  'new tenancy' means a tenancy granted on or after 1st October 2015, but does not include–
    (a) a tenancy granted in pursuance of an agreement entered into before that date;
    (b) a periodic shorthold tenancy which arises under section 5 of the Housing Act 1988 on the coming to an end of a fixed term shorthold tenancy;
    (c) a tenancy which comes into being on the coming to an end of an earlier tenancy, under which, on its coming into being–
        (i) the landlord and tenant are the same as under the earlier tenancy as at its coming to an end; and
        (ii) the premises let are the same or substantially the same as those let under the earlier tenancy as at that time;
  'room' includes a hall or landing; and
  'shorthold tenancy' means an assured shorthold tenancy within the meaning of Chapter 2 of Part 1 of the Housing Act 1988.

Part 3: Remedial Action

5 Duty of local housing authority to serve a remedial notice
(1) Where a local housing authority has reasonable grounds to believe that, in relation to premises situated within its area, a relevant landlord is in breach

of one or more of the duties under regulation 4(1), the authority must serve a remedial notice on the landlord.

(2) A remedial notice must–
   (a) specify the premises to which the notice relates;
   (b) specify the duty or duties that the local housing authority considers the landlord is failing or has failed to comply with;
   (c) specify the remedial action the local housing authority considers should be taken;
   (d) require the landlord to take that action within 28 days beginning with the day on which the notice is served;
   (e) explain that the landlord is entitled to make written representations against the notice within 28 days beginning with the day on which the notice is served;
   (f) specify the person to whom, and the address (including if appropriate any email address) at which, any representations may be sent; and
   (g) explain the effect of regulations 6, 7 and 8, including the maximum penalty charge which a local housing authority may impose.

(3) The local housing authority must serve a remedial notice within 21 days beginning with the day on which the authority decides it has reasonable grounds under paragraph (1).

6 Duty of relevant landlord to comply with a remedial notice

(1) Where a remedial notice is served on a landlord who is in breach of one or more of the duties under regulation 4(1), the landlord must take the remedial action specified in the notice within the period specified in regulation 5(2)(d).

(2) A landlord is not to be taken to be in breach of the duty under paragraph (1) if the landlord can show he, she or it has taken all reasonable steps, other than legal proceedings, to comply with the duty.

7 Duty of local housing authority to arrange remedial action

(1) Where a local housing authority is satisfied, on the balance of probabilities, that a landlord on whom it has served a remedial notice is in breach of the duty under regulation 6(1), the authority must, if the necessary consent is given, arrange for an authorised person to take the remedial action specified in the remedial notice.

(2) The local housing authority must ensure the authorised person takes the remedial action within 28 days beginning with the day on which the authority is first satisfied under paragraph (1).

(3) An authorised person must–
   (a) give not less than 48 hours' notice of the remedial action to the occupier of the premises on which it is to be taken; and
   (b) if required to do so by or on behalf of the landlord or occupier, produce evidence of identity and authority.

(4) In paragraph (1) 'the necessary consent' means the consent of the occupier of the premises on which the remedial action is to be taken.

(5) A local housing authority is not to be taken to be in breach of a duty under this regulation where the authority can show it has taken all reasonable steps, other than legal proceedings, to comply with the duty.

Part 4: Penalty Charges

8 Penalty for breach of the duty under regulation 6(1)

(1) Where a local housing authority is satisfied, on the balance of probabilities, that a landlord on whom it has served a remedial notice is in breach of the duty under regulation 6(1), the authority may require the landlord to pay a penalty charge of such amount as the authority may determine.

(2) The amount of the penalty charge must not exceed £5,000.

(3) Where a local housing authority decides to impose a penalty charge, the authority must serve notice of that fact on the landlord ('a penalty charge notice') within six weeks beginning with the day on which the authority is first satisfied under paragraph (1).

9 Content of penalty charge notice

(1) A penalty charge notice must state–
   (a) the reasons for imposing the penalty charge;
   (b) the premises to which the penalty charge relates;
   (c) the number and type of prescribed alarms (if any) which an authorised person has installed at the premises;
   (d) the amount of the penalty charge;
   (e) that the landlord is required, within a period specified in the notice–
      (i) to pay the penalty charge, or
      (ii) to give written notice to the local housing authority that the landlord wishes the authority to review the penalty charge notice;
   (f) how payment of the penalty charge must be made; and
   (g) the person to whom, and the address (including if appropriate any email address) at which, a notice requesting a review may be sent and to which any representations relating to the review may be addressed.

(2) A penalty charge notice may specify that if the landlord complies with the requirement in paragraph (1)(e)(i) or (ii) within 14 days beginning with the day on which the penalty charge notice is served, the penalty charge will be reduced by an amount specified in the notice.

(3) The period specified under paragraph (1)(e) must not be less than 28 days beginning with the day on which the penalty charge notice is served.

10 Review of penalty charge notice

(1) Paragraph (2) applies if, within the period specified under regulation 9(1)(e), the landlord serves a notice on the local housing authority requesting a review.

(2) The local housing authority must–
   (a) consider any representations made by the landlord;
   (b) decide whether to confirm, vary or withdraw the penalty charge notice; and
   (c) serve notice of its decision to the landlord.

(3) A notice under paragraph (2)(c) confirming or varying the penalty charge notice must also state the effect of regulation 11.

11 Appeals

(1) A landlord who is served with a notice under regulation 10(2)(c) confirming or varying a penalty charge notice may appeal to the First-tier Tribunal against the local housing authority's decision.

(2) The grounds for appeal are that–
  (a) the decision to confirm or vary the penalty charge notice was based on an error of fact;
  (b) the decision was wrong in law;
  (c) the amount of the penalty charge is unreasonable;
  (d) the decision was unreasonable for any other reason.
(3) Where a landlord appeals to the First-tier Tribunal, the operation of the penalty charge notice is suspended until the appeal is finally determined or withdrawn.
(4) The Tribunal may quash, confirm or vary the penalty charge notice, but may not increase the amount of the penalty charge.

12 Recovery of penalty charge

(1) The local housing authority may recover the penalty charge on the order of a court, as if payable under a court order.
(2) Proceedings for the recovery of the penalty charge may not be started before the end of the period specified under regulation 9(1)(e).
(3) Paragraph (4) applies if, within that period, the landlord gives notice to the local housing authority that the landlord wishes the authority to review the penalty charge notice.
(4) Proceedings for the recovery of the penalty charge may not be started–
  (a) before the end of the period within which the landlord may appeal to the First-tier Tribunal against the local housing authority's decision on review; and
  (b) where the landlord so appeals, before the end of the period of 28 days beginning with the day on which the appeal is finally determined or withdrawn.
(5) In proceedings for the recovery of the penalty charge a certificate which is–
  (a) signed by the local housing authority's chief finance officer (within the meaning of section 5 of the Local Government and Housing Act 1989), and
  (b) states that the penalty charge has not been received by a date specified in that certificate,
  is conclusive evidence of that fact, and a certificate to that effect and purporting to be signed is to be treated as being signed, unless the contrary is proved.
(6) Sums received by a local housing authority under a penalty charge may be used by the authority for any of its functions.

13 Information to be published by local housing authority

(1) A local housing authority must prepare and publish a statement of principles which it proposes to follow in determining the amount of a penalty charge.
(2) A local housing authority may revise its statement of principles and, where it does so, it must publish the revised statement.
(3) In determining the amount of a penalty charge, a local housing authority must have regard to the statement of principles which was most recently prepared and published at the time when the breach in question occurred.

Part 5: Notices

14 Service of notices

(1) Any notice served on a landlord under these Regulations must be in writing and may be amended, suspended or revoked in writing at any time.

(2) A notice is to be taken to be served on a landlord on–
  (a) the day it is given to the landlord in person;
  (b) the second business day after it is sent by first class post to the landlord's last known address;
  (c) the day it is delivered by hand to the landlord's last known address; or
  (d) where the landlord has provided the local housing authority with an email address at which the landlord is content to accept service, the day it is sent by email to that address.

(3) The reference in paragraph (2)(b) and (c) to the landlord's last known address includes a reference to the address last provided by the landlord in accordance with section 48 of the Landlord and Tenant Act 1987 to a tenant of the landlord.

(4) If the name or address of any landlord on whom a notice is to be served under these Regulations cannot, after reasonable inquiry, be ascertained, the notice may be taken to be served on the day it is conspicuously affixed to a building or object on the premises to which the notice relates.

(5) In paragraph (2)(b) 'business day' means any day other than a Saturday, Sunday, Christmas Day, Good Friday, or a day which is a bank holiday in England under the Banking and Financial Dealings Act 1971.

Part 6: Licences under Parts 2 and 3 of the Housing Act 2004

15 Amendments to Schedule 4 to the Housing Act 2004

(1) In paragraph 1 of Schedule 4 to the Housing Act 2004 (licences under parts 2 and 3: mandatory conditions)–
  (a) in sub-paragraph (4)–
    (i) before paragraph (a) insert–
      '(za) where the house is in England–
        (i) to ensure that a smoke alarm is installed on each storey of the house on which there is a room used wholly or partly as living accommodation, and
        (ii) to keep each such alarm in proper working order;';
    (ii) in paragraph (a), at the beginning insert 'where the house is in Wales,'
    (iii) in paragraph (b), at the beginning insert 'in either case,';
  (b) after sub-paragraph (4) insert–
    '(4A) Where the house is in England, conditions requiring the licence holder–
      (a) to ensure that a carbon monoxide alarm is installed in any room in the house which is used wholly or partly as living accommodation and contains a solid fuel burning combustion appliance;
      (b) to keep any such alarm in proper working order; and
      (c) to supply the authority, on demand, with a declaration by him as to the condition and positioning of any such alarm.'; and
  (c) after sub-paragraph (5) insert–

'(6) In sub-paragraph (4A) 'room' includes a hall or landing.

(7) For the purposes of sub-paragraphs (4) and (4A), a bathroom or lavatory is to be treated as a room used as living accommodation.'

(2) The amendments made by paragraph (1) apply only to licences granted or renewed on or after 1st October 2015.

SCHEDULE: Excluded Tenancies

Regulation 2

Shared accommodation with landlord or landlord's family

1(1) A tenancy under the terms of which the occupier shares any accommodation with the landlord or a member of the landlord's family.

(2) For the purposes of this paragraph—

    (a) an occupier shares accommodation with another person if the occupier has the use of an amenity in common with that person (whether or not also in common with others);

    (b) 'amenity' includes a toilet, personal washing facilities, a kitchen or a living room but excludes any area used for storage, a staircase, corridor or other means of access;

    (c) a person is a member of the same family as another person if—

        (i) those persons live as a couple;

        (ii) one of them is the relative of the other; or

        (iii) one of them is, or is a relative of, one member of a couple and the other is a relative of the other member of the couple;

    (d) 'couple' means two people who are married to, or civil partners of, each other or who live together as if they are a married couple or civil partners;

    (e) 'relative' means parent, grandparent, child, grandchild, brother, sister, aunt, nephew, niece or cousin;

    (f) a relationship of the half-blood is to be treated as a relationship of the whole blood; and

    (g) a stepchild of a person is to be treated as that person's child.

Long leases

2(1) A tenancy that—

    (a) is a long lease; or

    (b) grants a right of occupation for a term of 7 years or more.

(2) In this paragraph 'long lease' means a lease which is a long lease for the purposes of Chapter 1 of Part 1 of the Leasehold Reform, Housing and Urban Development Act 1993 or which, in the case of a shared ownership lease (within the meaning given by section 7(7) of that Act), would be such a lease if the tenant's total share (within the meaning given by that section) were 100 per cent.

(3) A tenancy does not grant a right of occupation for a term of 7 years or more if the agreement can be terminated at the option of a party before the end of 7 years from the commencement of the term.

Student halls of residence

3(1) A tenancy that grants a right of occupation in a building which—

    (a) is used wholly or mainly for the accommodation of students, and

(b) is a hall of residence.

(2) In this paragraph 'student' has the same meaning as in paragraph 4 of Schedule 1 to the Local Government Finance Act 1992.

Hostels and refuges

4(1) A tenancy that grants a right of occupation of accommodation in a hostel or refuge.

(2) In this paragraph 'hostel' means a building which satisfies the following two conditions.

(3) The first condition is that the building is used for providing to persons generally, or to a class of persons–
   (a) residential accommodation otherwise than in separate and self-contained premises; and
   (b) board or facilities for the preparation of food adequate to the needs of those persons (or both).

(4) The second condition is that either of the following applies in relation to the building–
   (a) it is managed by a private registered provider of social housing;
   (b) it is not operated on a commercial basis and its costs of operation are provided wholly or in part by a government department or agency, or by a local authority;
   (c) it is managed by a voluntary organisation or charity.

(5) In this paragraph 'refuge' means a building which satisfies the second condition in sub-paragraph (4) and is used wholly or mainly for providing accommodation to persons who have been subject to any incident, or pattern of incidents, of–
   (a) controlling, coercive or threatening behaviour;
   (b) physical violence;
   (c) abuse of any other description (whether physical or mental in nature); or
   (d) threats of any such violence or abuse.

(6) In this paragraph 'government department' includes any body or authority exercising statutory functions on behalf of the Crown.

(7) In this paragraph 'voluntary organisation' means a body, other than a public or local authority, whose activities are not carried on for profit.

Care homes

5(1) A tenancy that grants a right of occupation in a care home.

(2) In this paragraph 'care home' has the meaning given in section 3 of the Care Standards Act 2000.

Hospitals and hospices

6(1) A tenancy that grants a right of occupation of accommodation in a hospital or hospice.

(2) In this paragraph 'hospital' has the meaning given in section 275 of the National Health Service Act 2006.

(3) In this paragraph 'hospice' means an establishment other than a hospital whose primary function is the provision of palliative care to persons resident there who are suffering from a progressive disease in its final stages.

Other accommodation relating to healthcare provision

7(1) A tenancy–
   (a) under which accommodation is provided to a person as a result of a duty imposed on a relevant NHS body by an enactment; and
   (b) which is not excluded by another provision of this Schedule.
 (2) In this paragraph 'relevant NHS body' means–
   (a) a clinical commissioning group; or
   (b) the National Health Service Commissioning Board.
 (3) In this paragraph 'enactment' includes an enactment contained in subordinate legislation within the meaning of the Interpretation Act 1978.

ENERGY EFFICIENCY (PRIVATE RENTED PROPERTY) (ENGLAND AND WALES) REGULATIONS 2015 SI NO 962

Part 3: Minimum Level of Energy Efficiency

Chapter 1: Interpretation of Part 3

19 Domestic PR property

(1) For the purposes of this Part, 'domestic PR property' means a property which falls within section 42(1)(a) of the Act, subject to paragraph (2).

(2) A property is not a domestic PR property if—

(a) it was not required, and is not part of a building which was required, to have an energy performance certificate by the Energy Performance of Buildings (Certificates and Inspections) (England and Wales) Regulations 2007, and

(b) it is not required, and is not part of a building which is required, to have an energy performance certificate by the Building Regulations 2010 or the EPB Regulations.

20 Non-domestic PR property

(1) For the purposes of this Part, 'non-domestic PR property' means a property which falls within section 42(1)(b) of the Act, subject to paragraphs (2) and (3).

(2) A property is not a non-domestic PR property if—

(a) it was not required, and is not part of a building which was required, to have an energy performance certificate by the Energy Performance of Buildings (Certificates and Inspections) (England and Wales) Regulations 2007, and

(b) it is not required, and is not part of a building which is required, to have an energy performance certificate by the Building Regulations 2010 or the EPB Regulations.

(3) A property is not a non-domestic PR property if it is let—

(a) on a tenancy granted for a term certain not exceeding six months, unless—

(i) the tenancy agreement contains provision for renewing the term or for extending it beyond six months from its beginning, or

(ii) at the time when the tenancy is granted, the tenant has been in occupation for a continuous period which exceeds 12 months, or

(b) on a tenancy granted for a term certain of 99 years or more.

21 Landlord and tenant

For the purposes of this Part—

(a) 'tenant' means a person to whom—

(i) a domestic PR property is let on a tenancy which falls within section 42(1)(a) of the Act, or

(ii) a non-domestic PR property is let,

(b) 'landlord' means a person who lets, or proposes to let—

(i) a domestic PR property on a tenancy which falls within section 42(1)(a) of the Act, or

(ii) a non-domestic PR property.

22 Sub-standard property

For the purposes of this Part–

(a) a domestic PR property, or a non-domestic PR property, is 'sub-standard' where the valid energy performance certificate expresses the energy performance indicator of the property as being below the minimum level of energy efficiency,

(b) 'minimum level of energy efficiency', in relation to a domestic PR property and a non-domestic PR property, means an energy performance indicator of band E,

(c) an energy performance certificate for a property is 'valid' where–

(i) it was entered on the register required to be maintained by regulation 27(1) of the EPB Regulations no more than 10 years before the date on which it is relied on for the purposes of these Regulations, and

(ii) no other energy performance certificate for the property has since been entered on that register.

Chapter 2: Domestic PR Property Falling Below the Minimum Level of Energy Efficiency

23 Prohibition on letting of sub-standard property

(1) A landlord of a sub-standard domestic PR property must not let the property unless regulation 25, or one or more of the exemptions in Chapter 4, applies.

(2) For the purposes of paragraph (1), 'let the property' means–

(a) on or after 1st April 2018, grant a new tenancy which falls within section 42(1)(a) of the Act, or let the property on such a tenancy as a result of an extension or renewal of an existing tenancy, or

(b) on after 1st April 2020, continue to let the property on such a tenancy.

24 Relevant energy efficiency improvements

(1) Subject to paragraph (2), for the purposes of paragraph (a) in the definition of 'relevant energy efficiency improvements' in section 43(4) of the Act, a relevant energy efficiency improvement is an energy efficiency improvement–

(a) which–

(i) falls within sub-paragraph (a) of the definition of 'energy efficiency improvement' in regulation 2(1) and is listed in the Schedule to the Green Deal (Qualifying Energy Improvements) Order 2012, and

(ii) is identified as a recommended improvement for that property in a green deal report, a recommendation report, or a report prepared by a surveyor, or

(b) which falls within sub-paragraph (b) of the definition of 'energy efficiency improvement' in regulation 2(1).

(2) An energy efficiency improvement which falls within any of paragraphs (d), (n) or (v) of the Schedule to the Green Deal (Qualifying Energy Improvements) Order 2012 is not a relevant energy efficiency improvement where the landlord has obtained a written opinion from–

(a) a relevant person, or

(b) an independent installer of the energy efficiency improvement in question who meets the relevant installer standards,

advising that it is not an appropriate improvement, due to its potential negative impact on the fabric or structure of the domestic PR property, or the building of which it forms part, and the landlord has registered information in accordance with regulation 36(2).

(3) For the purposes of paragraph (b)(iv) in the definition of 'relevant energy efficiency improvements' in section 43(4) of the Act, an energy efficiency improvement is a relevant energy efficiency improvement where the cost of purchasing and installing it–

(a) can be wholly financed, at no cost to the landlord, by means of funding provided by central government, a local authority, or any other person, or

(b) can be wholly financed by a combination of two or more of the financial arrangements in paragraph (a), and paragraph (b)(i) to (iii) in the definition of 'relevant energy efficiency improvements' in section 43(4) of the Act.

25 Relevant energy efficiency improvements undertaken

(1) Subject to paragraph (2), this regulation applies where–

(a) the landlord of a sub-standard domestic PR property has made all the relevant energy efficiency improvements for the property, or

(b) there are no relevant energy efficiency improvements that can be made to the property.

(2) This regulation applies for a period of five years starting with the date on which the landlord registers information in accordance with regulation 36(2).

26 Sub-standard property let in breach of these Regulations

In any case where a landlord lets, or continues to let, a domestic PR property in breach of regulation 23, that breach does not affect the validity or enforceability of any provision of the tenancy.

...

Chapter 4: Exemptions–Domestic and Non-Domestic PR Property

31 Consent exemption

(1) Subject to paragraph (2), regulations 23 and 27 do not apply at any time when the landlord has, within the preceding five years, been unable to increase the energy performance indicator for the property to not less than the minimum level of energy efficiency as a result of–

(a) the tenant refusing–

(i) consent to any relevant energy efficiency improvement being made, or

(ii) to give any confirmation which must be obtained from the tenant by virtue of regulation 36 of the Framework Regulations before any green deal plan with which the landlord proposed to fund the making of the relevant energy efficiency improvement could be entered into, or

(b) despite reasonable efforts by the landlord to obtain third party consent, that consent having been–

(i) refused, or

(ii) granted subject to a condition with which the landlord cannot reasonably comply.

(2) A landlord may rely on the exemption in paragraph (1) only where the landlord has registered information in accordance with regulation 36(2).

32 Devaluation exemption

(1) Subject to paragraph (3), regulations 23 and 27 do not apply at any time when, within the preceding five years, the landlord been unable to increase the energy performance indicator for the property to not less than the minimum level of energy efficiency because paragraph (2) applies.
(2) This paragraph applies where the landlord has not made a relevant energy efficiency improvement because the landlord has obtained a report prepared by an independent surveyor which states that making that relevant energy efficiency improvement would result in a reduction of more than 5% in the market value of the property, or of the building of which it forms part.
(3) A landlord may rely on the exemption in paragraph (1) only where the landlord has registered information in accordance with regulation 36(2).

33 Temporary exemption in certain circumstances

(1) Subject to paragraph (5), regulations 23 and 27 do not apply to a landlord until six months after whichever is the later of–
  (a) the date on which the landlord becomes, or continues to be, the landlord of that property by virtue of any of the circumstances set out in paragraph (2), or
  (b) the date on which an order falling within paragraph (2)(f) is made.
(2) The circumstances referred to in paragraph (1) are–
  (a) the grant of a lease pursuant to a contractual obligation,
  (b) a tenant's insolvency, by virtue of the landlord having been the tenant's guarantor,
  (c) the landlord having been a guarantor, or a former tenant, who has exercised the right to obtain an overriding lease of a property pursuant to section 19 of the Landlord and Tenant (Covenants) Act 1995,
  (d) the deemed creation of a new lease by operation of law,
  (e) the grant of a new lease pursuant to the provisions of Part 2 of the Landlord and Tenant Act 1954,
  (f) the grant of a lease by order of the court not falling within sub-paragraph (e).
(3) Subject to paragraph (5), regulation 23(2)(b) and regulation 27(2)(b) do not apply to a person until six months from the date on which the person becomes the landlord by virtue of the circumstances set out in paragraph (4).
(4) The circumstances referred to in paragraph (3) are–
  (a) the landlord became the landlord of the domestic PR property, or non-domestic PR property (as the case may be), on purchasing an interest in that property, and
  (b) on the date of the purchase, the property was let on an existing tenancy.
(5) A landlord may rely on a temporary exemption in paragraph (1) or paragraph (3) only where the landlord has registered information in accordance with regulation 36(2).

Chapter 5: Enforcement Authorities and Compliance—Domestic and Non-Domestic PR Property

34 Enforcement authorities

(1) In this Part 'enforcement authority'–
   (a) in relation to a domestic PR property means a local authority,
   (b) in relation to a non-domestic PR property means a local weights and measures authority.
(2) An enforcement authority must enforce compliance with the requirements of this Part in relation to properties in its area.
   ...

Chapter 6: Penalties—Domestic and Non-Domestic PR Property

38 Penalty notices

(1) An enforcement authority may, on or after 1st April 2018, serve a notice on L (a 'penalty notice') in any case where it is satisfied that L is, or has been at any time in the 18 months preceding the date of service of the penalty notice, in breach of one or more of the following–
   (a) regulation 23,
   (b) regulation 27,
   (c) regulation 37(4)(a),
   imposing a financial penalty, a publication penalty, or both a financial penalty and a publication penalty, in accordance with this Chapter.
(2) A penalty notice must–
   (a) specify the provision of these Regulations which the enforcement authority believes L has breached,
   (b) give such particulars as the enforcement authority considers necessary to identify the matters constituting the breach,
   (c) specify–
      (i) any action the enforcement authority requires L to take to remedy the breach,
      (ii) the period within which such action must be taken,
   (d) specify–
      (i) the amount of any financial penalty imposed and, where applicable, how it has been calculated,
      (ii) whether the publication penalty has been imposed,
   (e) require L to pay any financial penalty within a period specified in the notice,
   (f) specify the name and address of the person to whom any financial penalty must be paid and the method by which payment may be made,
   (g) state the effect of regulations 42 to 45, and
   (h) specify–
      (i) the name and address of the person to whom a notice requesting a review in accordance with regulation 42 may be sent (and to whom any representations relating to the review must be addressed), and
      (ii) the period within which such a notice may be sent.
(3) Each of the periods specified under paragraph (2)(c) and (e) must not be less than one month, beginning on the day on which the penalty notice is served.

(4) Where L fails to take the action required by a penalty notice within the period specified in that penalty notice in accordance with paragraph (2)(c), the enforcement authority may issue a further penalty notice.

39 Publication penalty

(1) In this Chapter, the 'publication penalty' means publication on the PRS Exemptions Register of such of the following information in relation to a penalty notice as the enforcement authority decides–
  (a) where L is not an individual, L's name,
  (b) details of the breach of these Regulations in respect of which the penalty notice has been issued,
  (c) the address of the property in relation to which the breach has occurred, and
  (d) the amount of any financial penalty imposed.
(2) The information in paragraph (1) must be published for a minimum period of 12 months, and may be published for such longer period as the enforcement authority may decide.
(3) A publication penalty does not take effect until–
  (a) the period specified for requesting a review under regulation 38(2)(h)(ii) has expired or, where a review has been requested, the enforcement authority has not served notice of its decision under regulation 42(2)(c), and
  (b) the period specified for any appeal against the penalty notice has expired or, where an appeal is made, until the appeal has been determined.

40 Breaches in relation to domestic PR property

(1) The penalties set out in this regulation apply where L is, or was, the landlord of a domestic PR property.
(2) Where L has breached regulation 23 and, at the time the penalty notice is served has, or had, been in breach for less than three months, the penalties are–
  (a) a financial penalty not exceeding £2,000, and
  (b) the publication penalty.
(3) Where L has breached regulation 23 and, at the time the penalty notice is served has, or had, been in breach for three months or more, the penalties are–
  (a) a financial penalty not exceeding £4,000, and
  (b) the publication penalty.
(4) Where L has registered false or misleading information under regulation 36(2), the penalties are–
  (a) a financial penalty not exceeding £1,000, and
  (b) the publication penalty.
(5) Where L has failed to comply with a compliance notice in breach of regulation 37(4)(a), the penalties are–
  (a) a financial penalty not exceeding £2,000, and
  (b) the publication penalty.
(6) Where an enforcement authority imposes financial penalties on L in relation to a breach of regulation 23 in respect of a domestic PR property–
  (a) under paragraph (2) or (3), and
  (b) under one or both of paragraphs (4) and (5),
  the total of the financial penalties imposed on L must be no more than £5,000.

ENERGY PERFORMANCE OF BUILDINGS (ENGLAND AND WALES) REGULATIONS 2012 SI NO 3118

Part 1: Introductory

3 Meaning of 'prospective buyer or tenant'

A person becomes a prospective buyer or tenant in relation to a building when he or she–

(a) requests any information about the building from the relevant person or the relevant person's agent for the purpose of deciding whether to buy or rent the building;

(b) makes a request to view the building for the purpose of deciding whether to buy or rent the building; or

(c) makes an offer, whether oral or written, to buy or rent the building.

...

5 Application of Part 2

(1) This Part does not apply to–

(a) buildings officially protected as part of a designated environment or because of their special architectural or historical merit, in so far as compliance with certain minimum energy performance requirements would unacceptably alter their character or appearance;

(b) buildings used as places of worship and for religious activities;

(c) temporary buildings with a time of use of two years or less;

(d) industrial sites, workshops and non-residential agricultural buildings with low energy demand;

(e) non-residential agricultural buildings which are in use by a sector covered by a national sectoral agreement on energy performance;

(f) residential buildings which are used or intended to be used–

(i) for less than four months of the year, or

(ii) for a limited annual time of use and with an expected energy consumption of less than 25% of what would be the result of all-year use; and

(g) stand-alone buildings with a total useful floor area of less than 50m .

(2) Nothing in this Part requires an energy performance certificate to be given or made available to a prospective buyer or tenant at any time before the construction of the building has been completed.

6 Energy performance certificates on sale and rent

(1) Subject to regulation 8, this regulation applies where a building is to be sold or rented out.

(2) The relevant person shall make available free of charge a valid energy performance certificate to any prospective buyer or tenant–

(a) at the earliest opportunity; and

(b) in any event no later than whichever is the earlier of–

(i) in the case of a person who requests information about the building, the time at which the relevant person first makes available any information in writing about the building to the person; or

(ii) in the case of a person who makes a request to view the building, the time at which the person views the building.

(3) Paragraph (2) does not apply if the relevant person believes on reasonable grounds that the prospective buyer or tenant–
    (a) is unlikely to have sufficient means to buy or rent the building;
    (b) is not genuinely interested in buying or renting a building of a general description which applies to the building; or
    (c) is not a person to whom the relevant person is likely to be prepared to sell or rent out the building.
(4) Nothing in paragraph (3) authorises the doing of anything which constitutes an unlawful act of discrimination.
(5) The relevant person must ensure that a valid energy performance certificate has been given free of charge to the person who ultimately becomes the buyer or tenant.

34 Enforcement authorities
(1) Every local weights and measures authority is an enforcement authority for the purpose of this Part.
(2) It is the duty of each enforcement authority to enforce in their area the duties under regulations 6(2), 6(5), 7(2), 7(3), 7(4), 7(5), 7A(2), 7A(3), 10(2),., 11(2), 14(3), 18(1), 20, 21 and 35(5).

34A Enforcement and local authority buildings
(1) This regulation applies in relation to all buildings in respect of which a local authority is subject to a duty under any of regulations 6(2), 6(5), 7(2), 7(3), 7(4), 7(5), 7A(2), 7A(3),10(2), 11(2), 14(3), 18(1), 20, 21 and 35(5) ('local authority buildings').
(2) The local weights and measures authority for an area ('Authority 1') must agree in writing with the local weights and measures authority for another area ('Authority 2') that Authority 2 will enforce regulations 6(2), 6(5), 7(2), 7(3), 7(4), 7(5), 7A(2), 7A(3), 10(2), 11(2), 14(3), 18(1), 20, 21 and 35(5) in respect of local authority buildings in the area of Authority 1.
(3) Once an agreement made under paragraph (2) comes into effect–
    (a) it is the duty of Authority 2 to enforce regulations 6(2), 6(5), 7(2), 7(3), 7(4), 7(5), 7A(2), 7A(3), 10(2), 11(2), 14(3), 18(1), 20, 21 and 35(5) in respect of local authority buildings in the area of Authority 1; and
    (b) Authority 1 must publish that fact.
(4) Authority 1 must notify an agreement made under paragraph (2) to the Secretary of State in writing.
(5) An agreement under paragraph (2) may relate to part only of the area of Authority 1, but in that case Authority 1 must make one or more other agreements under that paragraph to ensure that there are such agreements in place in respect of the whole of its area.
(6) Where more than one agreement under paragraph (2) is in place in respect of the area of Authority 1–
    (a) the references to Authority 2 in paragraph (3) apply to each authority with which Authority 1 has made such an agreement, but only within the part of the area of Authority 1 to which the agreement relates; and
    (b) Authority 1 must publish information in relation to every such agreement in accordance with paragraph (3)(b), and notify every such agreement to the Secretary of State in accordance with paragraph (4), stating in each case the part of its area to which the agreement relates.

(7) Every local weights and measures authority must have complied with paragraphs (2), (3)(b) and (4) by the end of the period of three months beginning on the day after these Regulations come into force, or, if it is not reasonably practicable to do so within that time, as soon as is reasonably practicable after that time.

34B Enforcement plans

(1) Every enforcement authority must ensure that it collects sufficient information concerning the buildings for which it has enforcement duties under regulations 34(2) and 34A(3) to enable it to plan effective enforcement action under this Part.

(2) Enforcement action under this Part must be planned in accordance with guidance issued by the Secretary of State.

34C Annual reports by enforcement authorities

(1) Every enforcement authority must make and keep a record of all action that it takes under this Part.

(2) Every enforcement authority must make in respect of every financial year of the authority a report ('the annual report') to the Secretary of State on the actions that it has taken under this Part during that year.

(3) The annual report must—
   (a) be made by the end of the period of two months beginning on the day after the end of the financial year concerned.
   (b) be in a form and contain information in accordance with guidance issued by the Secretary of State;
   (c) identify such agreements as the enforcement authority has entered into with any other enforcement authority under regulation 34A(2) to act as enforcement authority in relation to local authority buildings in the area of either; and
   (d) state any changes in the responsibility of enforcement authorities under such agreements.

(4) A report made under this paragraph may be published by the enforcement authority by which it is made or by the Secretary of State.

35 Power to require production of documents

(1) An authorised officer of an enforcement authority may require a person who appears to him to be or to have been subject to any of the duties under regulation 6, 7A, 14(3), 18(1) or 20 to produce for inspection a copy of—
   (a) a valid energy performance certificate;
   (b) a recommendation report; or
   (c) an inspection report.

(2) An authorised officer of an enforcement authority may require a person who appears to him to have been subject to the duty under regulation 7(3) to produce for inspection a copy of any request made in accordance with regulation 7(6)(d).

(3) The powers conferred by paragraphs (1) and (2) include power to take copies of any document produced for inspection.

(4) A requirement under this regulation may not be imposed more than six months after the last day on which the person concerned was subject to such a duty in relation to the building.

(5) It is the duty of a person subject to such a requirement to comply with it within the period of seven days beginning with the day after that on which it is imposed.
(6) A person is not required to comply with such a requirement if he has a reasonable excuse for not complying with the requirement.

36 Penalty charge notices

(1) An authorised officer of an enforcement authority may, if he believes that a person has committed a breach of any duty under regulation 6(2), 6(5), 7(2), 7(3), 7(4), 7(5), 7A(2), 7A(3), 10(2), 11(2), 14(3), 18(1), 20, 21, or 35(5) give a penalty charge notice to that person.
(2) A penalty charge notice may not be given after the end of the period of six months beginning with the day (or in the case of a continuing breach the last day) on which the breach of duty was committed.
(3) A penalty charge notice must–
    (a) state the officer's belief that the person has committed a breach of duty;
    (b) give such particulars of the circumstances as may be necessary to give reasonable notice of the breach of duty;
    (c) require that person, within a period specified in the notice–
       (i) to pay a penalty charge specified in the notice; or
       (ii) to give notice to the enforcement authority that he wishes the authority to review the notice;
    (d) state the effect of regulation 41;
    (e) specify the person to whom and the address at which the penalty charge may be paid and the method or methods by which payment may be made; and
    (f) specify the person to whom and the address at which a notice requesting a review may be sent (and to which any representations relating to the review may be addressed).
(4) The period specified under paragraph (3)(c) must not be less than 28 days beginning with the day after that on which the penalty charge notice was given.
(5) The enforcement authority may extend the period for complying in any particular case if they consider it appropriate to do so.
(6) The enforcement authority may, if they consider that the penalty charge notice ought not to have been given, give the recipient a notice withdrawing the penalty charge notice.
(7) The enforcement authority must withdraw a penalty charge notice where the recipient can demonstrate that–
    (a) he took all reasonable steps and exercised all due diligence to avoid breaching the duty; or
    (b) regulation 37 (defence) applies.

37 Defence when energy performance certificate unobtainable

(1) A relevant person shall not be liable to a penalty charge notice for a breach of the duty imposed by regulation 6 where he can demonstrate that–
    (a) he is not a person to whom the duty under regulation 7(2) previously applied and he made a request for an energy performance certificate as soon as possible after he became subject to the duty, and, despite all

reasonable efforts and enquiries by the relevant person, he did not have in his possession or control a valid energy performance certificate at the relevant time; or

   (b) in the case of a failure to make available an energy performance certificate to a prospective tenant–

   (i) the prospective tenant was seeking to rent the building due to an emergency which required the tenant's urgent relocation;

   (ii) at the relevant time the relevant person did not have in his possession or control a valid energy performance certificate;

   (iii) there was insufficient time in which the relevant person could reasonably have been expected to obtain a certificate before renting out the building to the prospective tenant; and

   (iv) the relevant person has given a valid energy performance certificate to the tenant as soon as reasonably practicable after renting out the building.

(2) A relevant person shall not be liable to a penalty charge notice for a breach of the duty imposed by regulation 6 where he can demonstrate that–

   (a) he is a person to whom the duty under regulation 7(2) applies;

   (b) he complied with that duty; and

   (c) despite all reasonable efforts and enquiries by the relevant person he did not have in his possession or control a valid energy performance certificate at the relevant time.

(3) In paragraph (1)(a) the reference to a request is to a request properly addressed to a person who usually provides or is likely to provide an energy performance certificate for the category of building in question and which includes such payment or an undertaking to make such payment as is usually necessary to obtain an energy performance certificate.

(4) In this regulation, 'relevant time' means the point in time by which the relevant person is required to have made an energy performance certificate available to a prospective buyer or tenant by virtue of regulation 6(2).

38 Penalty amount

(1) The penalty charge specified in the notice shall be–

   (a) in relation to a breach of a duty under regulation 6(2), 6(5), 7(2), 7(3), (4), 7(5), 7A(2) or 7A(3) –

   (i) where the building is a dwelling, £200;

   (ii) where the building is not a dwelling, calculated in accordance with the formula in paragraph (2);

   (b) in relation to a breach of a duty under regulation 14(3)(a), £1000;

   (c) in relation to a breach of a duty under [regulation 10(2) or 14(3)(b), £500;

   (d) in relation to a breach of a duty under regulation 18(1), 20(1), 20(2) or 21, £300; and

   (e) in relation to a breach of a duty under [regulation 11(2) or 35(5), £200.

(2) Subject to the minimum and maximum penalty charges prescribed by paragraph (3), the penalty charge for the purposes of paragraph (1)(a)(ii) shall be–

   (a) where the building constitutes a hereditament, 12.5% of the rateable value of the hereditament;

(b) where no other building (other than a building which is exempt from Part 2 by virtue of—
  (i) regulation 5(1)(a), (b), (d) or (e), or
  (ii) for a building which is not a dwelling, regulation 5(1)(c) or (g)), forms a part of the same hereditament, 12.5% of the rateable value of the hereditament of which the building forms a part;

(c) where the building comprises more than one hereditament, 12.5% of the sum of the rateable values of each hereditament that comprise the building; and

(d) where—
  (i) one or more buildings (other than a building which is exempt from Part 2 by virtue of—
    (aa) regulation 5(1)(a), (b),, (d) or (e), or
    (bb) for a building which is not a dwelling, regulation 5(1)(c) or (g)) form part of the same hereditament; or
  (ii) the building is not, or does not form part of, a hereditament which appears on a local non-domestic rating list at the relevant time, £750.

(3) The minimum and maximum penalty charges for the purposes of paragraph (2) are £500 and £5000 respectively.

...

(5) In this regulation the following definitions also apply—
  'hereditament' means a hereditament which, pursuant to section 42 of the Local Government Finance Act 1988, is shown on a local non-domestic rating list in force at the relevant time;
  'local non-domestic rating list' means a local non-domestic rating list maintained in
  accordance with section 41 of the Local Government Finance Act 1988;
  'rateable value' means the rateable value shown for a hereditament on a local non-domestic rating list at the relevant time; and
  'relevant time' means the time at which the penalty charge notice is given.

39 Reviews

(1) If, within the period specified under regulation 36(3)(c) (or that period as extended under regulation 36(5)), the recipient of the penalty charge notice gives notice to the enforcement authority requesting a review, the authority shall—
  (a) consider any representations made by the recipient and all other circumstances of the case;
  (b) decide whether to confirm or withdraw the notice; and
  (c) give notice of their decision to the recipient.

(2) A notice confirming the penalty charge notice must also state the effect of regulations 40 and 41.

(3) If the authority are not satisfied that—
  (a) the recipient committed the breach of duty specified in the notice;
  (b) the notice was given within the time allowed by regulation 36(2) and complies with the other requirements imposed by these Regulations; and
  (c) in the circumstances of the case it was appropriate for a penalty charge notice to be given to the recipient,
  they shall withdraw the penalty charge notice.

40 Appeal to the county court

(1) If, after a review, the penalty charge notice is confirmed by the enforcement authority, the recipient may, within the period of 28 days beginning with the day after that on which the notice under regulation 39(1)(c) is given, appeal to the county court against the penalty charge notice.

(2) The county court may extend the period for appealing against the notice.

(3) Such an appeal must be on one (or more) of the following grounds–

    (a) that the recipient did not commit the breach of duty specified in the penalty charge notice;

    (b) that the notice was not given within the time allowed by regulation 36(2) or does not comply with any other requirement imposed by these Regulations; or

    (c) that in the circumstances of the case it was inappropriate for the notice to be given to the recipient.

(4) An appeal against a penalty charge notice shall be by way of a rehearing; and the court shall either uphold the notice or quash it.

(5) If the penalty charge notice is withdrawn or quashed, the authority shall repay any amount previously paid as a penalty charge in pursuance of the notice.

41 Recovery of penalty charges

(1) The amount of the penalty charge is recoverable from the recipient of the penalty charge notice as a debt owed to the authority unless–

    (a) the notice has been withdrawn or quashed; or

    (b) the charge has been paid.

(2) Proceedings for the recovery of the penalty charge may not be commenced before the end of the period mentioned in regulation 39(1).

(3) If within that period the recipient of the penalty charge notice gives notice to the authority that he wishes the authority to review the penalty charge notice, such proceedings may not be commenced–

    (a) before the end of the period mentioned in regulation 40(1); and

    (b) where the recipient appeals against the penalty charge notice, before the end of the period of 28 days beginning with the day on which the appeal is withdrawn or determined.

(4) In proceedings for the recovery of the penalty charge, a certificate which–

    (a) purports to be signed by or on behalf of the person having responsibility for the financial affairs of the enforcement authority; and

    (b) states that payment of the penalty charge was or was not received by a date specified in the certificate, is evidence of the facts stated.

42 Service of documents

(1) A penalty charge notice and any other notice mentioned in this Part may be given by post.

(2) Any such notice may be given–

    (a) in the case of a body corporate, to the secretary or clerk of that body; and

    (b) in the case of a partnership, to any partner or to a person having control or management of the partnership business.

43 Offences relating to enforcement officers

(1) A person who obstructs an officer of an enforcement authority acting in pursuance of regulation 35 is guilty of an offence.

(2) A person who, not being an authorised officer of an enforcement authority, purports to act as such in pursuance of this Part is guilty of an offence.

(3) A person guilty of an offence under this regulation is liable on summary conviction to a fine not exceeding level 5 on the standard scale.

REGULATORY REFORM (FIRE SAFETY) ORDER 2005 SI NO 1541

Part 1: General

...

2 Interpretation
In this Order–
'alterations notice' has the meaning given by article 29;
'child' means a person who is not over compulsory school age, construed in accordance with section 8 of the Education Act 1996;
'the CLP Regulation' means Regulation (EC) No 1272/2008 of the European Parliament and of the Council of 16 December 2008 on classification, labelling and packaging of substances and mixtures, amending and repealing Directives 67/548/EEC and 1999/45/EC and amending Regulation (EC) No 1907/2006, of which Articles 6(5), 11(3), 12, 14, 18(3)(b), 23, 25 to 29, 35(2) second and third sub-paragraphs and Annexes I to VII are to be read as amended from time to time;
'dangerous substance' means–
  (a) a substance or mixture which meets the criteria for classification as hazardous within any physical hazard class laid down in the CLP Regulation, other than 'corrosive to metals' or 'gases under pressure', whether or not the substance or mixture is classified under that Regulation;
  (b) a substance or mixture which because of its physico-chemical or chemical properties and the way it is used or is present in or on premises creates a risk; and
  (c) any dust, whether in the form of solid particles or fibrous materials or otherwise, which can form an explosive mixture with air or an explosive atmosphere;
'domestic premises' means premises occupied as a private dwelling (including any garden, yard, garage, outhouse, or other appurtenance of such premises which is not used in common by the occupants of more than one such dwelling);
'employee' means a person who is or is treated as an employee for the purposes of the Health and Safety at Work etc Act 1974 and related expressions are to be construed accordingly;
'enforcement notice' has the meaning given by article 30;
'enforcing authority' has the meaning given by article 25;
'explosive atmosphere' means a mixture, under atmospheric conditions, of air and one or more dangerous substances in the form of gases, vapours, mists or dusts in which, after ignition has occurred, combustion spreads to the entire unburned mixture;
'fire and rescue authority' means a fire and rescue authority under the Fire and Rescue Services Act 2004;
'fire inspector'[, in relation to Wales,][2] means an inspector or assistant inspec-

---

2   Words ', in relation to Wales,' in square brackets inserted by the Policing and Crime Act 2017 s12(1), (2)(a). Not yet in force: see Policing and Crime Act 2017 s183(1).

tor appointed under *section 28* [section 28(1)][3] of the Fire and Rescue Services Act 2004;

'general fire precautions' has the meaning given by article 4;

'hazard', in relation to a dangerous substance, means the physico-chemical or chemical property of that substance which has the potential to give rise to fire affecting the safety of a person, and references in this Order to 'hazardous' are to be construed accordingly;

'inspector' means an inspector appointed under article 26 or a fire inspector;

'licensing authority' has the meaning given by article 42(3);

'normal ship-board activities' include the repair of a ship, save repair when carried out in dry dock;

'owner' means the person for the time being receiving the rackrent of the premises in connection with which the word is used, whether on his own account or as agent or trustee for another person, or who would so receive the rackrent if the premises were let at a rackrent;

'personal protective equipment' means all equipment which is intended to be worn or held by a person in or on premises and which protects that person against one or more risks to his safety, and any addition or accessory designed to meet that objective;

'place of safety' in relation to premises, means a safe area beyond the premises.

'premises' includes any place and, in particular, includes–

(a) any workplace;

(b) any vehicle, vessel, aircraft or hovercraft;

(c) any installation on land (including the foreshore and other land intermittently covered by water), and any other installation (whether floating, or resting on the seabed or the subsoil thereof, or resting on other land covered with water or the subsoil thereof); and

(d) any tent or movable structure;

'preparation' means a mixture or solution of two or more substances;

'preventive and protective measures' means the measures which have been identified by the responsible person in consequence of a risk assessment as the general fire precautions he needs to take to comply with the requirements and prohibitions imposed on him by or under this Order;

'prohibition notice' has the meaning given by article 31;

'public road' means a highway maintainable at public expense within the meaning of section 329 of the Highways Act 1980;

'rackrent' in relation to premises, means a rent that is not less than two-thirds of the rent at which the property might reasonably be expected to be let from year to year, free from all usual tenant's rates and taxes, and deducting from it the probable average cost of the repairs, insurance and other expenses (if any) necessary to maintain the property in a state to command such rent;

'the relevant local authority', in relation to premises, means–

(a) if the premises are in Greater London but are not in the City of Lon-

---

3 Words 'section 28' in italics revoked and subsequent words in square brackets substituted by the Policing and Crime Act 2017 s12(1), (2)(b). Not yet in force: see Policing and Crime Act 2017 s183(1).

don, the London Borough in the area of which the premises are situated;

(b) if the premises are in the City of London, the Common Council of the City of London;

(c) if the premises are in England in a metropolitan county, the district council in the area of which the premises are situated;

(d) if the premises are in England but are not in Greater London or a metropolitan county–

(i) the county council in the area of which the premises are situated; or

(ii) if there is no county council in the area of which the premises are situated, the district council in that area;

(e) if the premises are in Wales, the county council or county borough council in the area of which the premises are situated;

'relevant persons' means–

(a) any person (including the responsible person) who is or may be lawfully on the premises; and

(b) any person in the immediate vicinity of the premises who is at risk from a fire on the premises,

but does not include a fire-fighter who is carrying out his duties in relation to a function of a fire and rescue authority under section 7, 8 or 9 of the Fire and Rescue Services Act 2004 (fire-fighting, road traffic accidents and other emergencies), other than in relation to a function under section 7(2)(d), 8(2)(d) or 9(3)(d) of that Act;

'responsible person' has the meaning given by article 3;

'risk' means the risk to the safety of persons from fire;

'risk assessment' means the assessment required by article 9(1);

'safety' means the safety of persons in respect of harm caused by fire; and 'safe' shall be interpreted accordingly;

'safety data sheet' means a safety data sheet within the meaning of Regulation (EC) No 1907/2006 of the European Parliament and of the Council of 18 December 2006 concerning the Registration, Evaluation, Authorisation and Restriction of Chemicals (REACH), establishing a European Chemicals Agency, amending Directive 1999/45/EC and repealing Council Regulation (EEC) No 793/93 and Commission Regulation (EC) No 1488/94 as well as Council Directive 76/769/EEC and Commission Directives 91/155/EEC, 93/67/EEC, 93/105/EC and 2000/21/EC;

'ship' includes every description of vessel used in navigation;

'special, technical and organisational measures' include–

(a) technical means of supervision;

(b) connecting devices;

(c) control and protection systems;

(d) engineering controls and solutions;

(e) equipment;

(f) materials;

(g) protective systems; and

(h) warning and other communication systems;

'substance' means any natural or artificial substance whether in solid or liquid form or in the form of a gas or vapour;

'visiting force' means any such body, contingent, or detachment of the forces of any country as is a visiting force for the purposes of any of the provisions of the Visiting Forces Act 1952;

'workplace' means any premises or parts of premises, not being domestic premises, used for the purposes of an employer's undertaking and which are made available to an employee of the employer as a place of work and includes–

(a) any place within the premises to which such employee has access while at work; and

(b) any room, lobby, corridor, staircase, road, or other place–

(i) used as a means of access to or egress from that place of work; or

(ii) where facilities are provided for use in connection with that place of work,

other than a public road;

'young person' means any person who has not attained the age of 18.

3 Meaning of 'responsible person'

In this Order 'responsible person' means–

(a) in relation to a workplace, the employer, if the workplace is to any extent under his control;

(b) in relation to any premises not falling within paragraph (a)–

(i) the person who has control of the premises (as occupier or otherwise) in connection with the carrying on by him of a trade, business or other undertaking (for profit or not); or

(ii) the owner, where the person in control of the premises does not have control in connection with the carrying on by that person of a trade, business or other undertaking.

4 Meaning of 'general fire precautions'

(1) In this Order 'general fire precautions' in relation to premises means, subject to paragraph (2)–

(a) measures to reduce the risk of fire on the premises and the risk of the spread of fire on the premises;

(b) measures in relation to the means of escape from the premises;

(c) measures for securing that, at all material times, the means of escape can be safely and effectively used;

(d) measures in relation to the means for fighting fires on the premises;

(e) measures in relation to the means for detecting fire on the premises and giving warning in case of fire on the premises; and

(f) measures in relation to the arrangements for action to be taken in the event of fire on the premises, including–

(i) measures relating to the instruction and training of employees; and

(ii) measures to mitigate the effects of the fire.

(2) The precautions referred to in paragraph (1) do not include special, technical or organisational measures required to be taken or observed in any workplace in connection with the carrying on of any work process, where those measures–

(a) are designed to prevent or reduce the likelihood of fire arising from such a work process or reduce its intensity; and

(b) are required to be taken or observed to ensure any compliance with any requirement of–
    (i) the relevant statutory provisions within the meaning given in Part 1 of the Health and Safety at Work etc Act 1974;
    (ii) sections 1, 3 to 6, 22 and 24A of the Nuclear Installations Act 1965;
    (iii) the provisions of Part 3 of the Energy Act 2013;
    (iv) the provisions of nuclear regulations other than any provisions of such regulations identified in accordance with section 74(9) of the Energy Act 2013 as made for the nuclear safeguards purposes;
(3) In paragraph (2) 'work process' means all aspects of work involving, or in connection with–
    (a) the use of plant or machinery; or
    (b) the use or storage of any dangerous substance.

5 Duties under this Order

(1) Where the premises are a workplace, the responsible person must ensure that any duty imposed by articles 8 to 22 or by regulations made under article 24 is complied with in respect of those premises.
(2) Where the premises are not a workplace, the responsible person must ensure that any duty imposed by articles 8 to 22 or by regulations made under article 24 is complied with in respect of those premises, so far as the requirements relate to matters within his control.
(3) Any duty imposed by articles 8 to 22 or by regulations made under article 24 on the responsible person in respect of premises shall also be imposed on every person, other than the responsible person referred to in paragraphs (1) and (2), who has, to any extent, control of those premises so far as the requirements relate to matters within his control.
(4) Where a person has, by virtue of any contract or tenancy, an obligation of any extent in relation to–
    (a) the maintenance or repair of any premises, including anything in or on premises; or
    (b) the safety of any premises,
that person is to be treated, for the purposes of paragraph (3), as being a person who has control of the premises to the extent that his obligation so extends.
(5) Articles 8 to 22 and any regulations made under article 24 only require the taking or observance of general fire precautions in respect of relevant persons.

6 Application to premises

(1) This Order does not apply in relation to–
    (a) domestic premises, except to the extent mentioned in article 31(10);
    (b) an offshore installation within the meaning of regulation 3 of the Offshore Installation and Pipeline Works (Management and Administration) Regulations 1995;
    (c) a ship, in respect of the normal ship-board activities of a ship's crew which are carried out solely by the crew under the direction of the master;
    (d) fields, woods or other land forming part of an agricultural or forestry undertaking but which is not inside a building and is situated away from the undertaking's main buildings;

(e) an aircraft, locomotive or rolling stock, trailer or semi-trailer used as a means of transport or a vehicle for which a licence is in force under the Vehicle Excise and Registration Act 1994 or a vehicle exempted from duty under that Act;

(f) a mine within the meaning of section 180 of the Mines and Quarries Act 1954, other than any building on the surface at a mine;

(g) a borehole site to which the Borehole Sites and Operations Regulations 1995 apply.

(2) Subject to the preceding paragraph of this article, this Order applies in relation to any premises.

...

Part 2: Fire Safety Duties

8 Duty to take general fire precautions

(1) The responsible person must–

(a) take such general fire precautions as will ensure, so far as is reasonably practicable, the safety of any of his employees; and

(b) in relation to relevant persons who are not his employees, take such general fire precautions as may reasonably be required in the circumstances of the case to ensure that the premises are safe.

9 Risk assessment

(1) The responsible person must make a suitable and sufficient assessment of the risks to which relevant persons are exposed for the purpose of identifying the general fire precautions he needs to take to comply with the requirements and prohibitions imposed on him by or under this Order.

(2) Where a dangerous substance is or is liable to be present in or on the premises, the risk assessment must include consideration of the matters set out in Part 1 of Schedule 1.

(3) Any such assessment must be reviewed by the responsible person regularly so as to keep it up to date and particularly if–

(a) there is reason to suspect that it is no longer valid; or

(b) there has been a significant change in the matters to which it relates including when the premises, special, technical and organisational measures, or organisation of the work undergo significant changes, extensions, or conversions,

and where changes to an assessment are required as a result of any such review, the responsible person must make them.

(4) The responsible person must not employ a young person unless he has, in relation to risks to young persons, made or reviewed an assessment in accordance with paragraphs (1) and (5).

(5) In making or reviewing the assessment, the responsible person who employs or is to employ a young person must take particular account of the matters set out in Part 2 of Schedule 1.

(6) As soon as practicable after the assessment is made or reviewed, the responsible person must record the information prescribed by paragraph (7) where–

(a) he employs five or more employees;

(b) a licence under an enactment is in force in relation to the premises; or

(c) an alterations notice requiring this is in force in relation to the premises.
(7) The prescribed information is–
 (a) the significant findings of the assessment, including the measures which have been or will be taken by the responsible person pursuant to this Order; and
 (b) any group of persons identified by the assessment as being especially at risk.
(8) No new work activity involving a dangerous substance may commence unless–
 (a) the risk assessment has been made; and
 (b) the measures required by or under this Order have been implemented.
 ...

11 Fire safety arrangements

(1) The responsible person must make and give effect to such arrangements as are appropriate, having regard to the size of his undertaking and the nature of its activities, for the effective planning, organisation, control, monitoring and review of the preventive and protective measures.
(2) The responsible person must record the arrangements referred to in paragraph (1) where–
 (a) he employs five or more employees;
 (b) a licence under an enactment is in force in relation to the premises; or
 (c) an alterations notice requiring a record to be made of those arrangements is in force in relation to the premises.

12 Elimination or reduction of risks from dangerous substances

(1) Where a dangerous substance is present in or on the premises, the responsible person must ensure that risk to relevant persons related to the presence of the substance is either eliminated or reduced so far as is reasonably practicable.
(2) In complying with his duty under paragraph (1), the responsible person must, so far as is reasonably practicable, replace a dangerous substance, or the use of a dangerous substance, with a substance or process which either eliminates or reduces the risk to relevant persons.
(3) Where it is not reasonably practicable to eliminate risk pursuant to paragraphs (1) and (2), the responsible person must, so far as is reasonably practicable, apply measures consistent with the risk assessment and appropriate to the nature of the activity or operation, including the measures specified in Part 4 of Schedule 1 to this Order to–
 (a) control the risk, and
 (b) mitigate the detrimental effects of a fire.
(4) The responsible person must–
 (a) arrange for the safe handling, storage and transport of dangerous substances and waste containing dangerous substances; and
 (b) ensure that any conditions necessary pursuant to this Order for ensuring the elimination or reduction of risk are maintained.

13 Fire-fighting and fire detection

(1) Where necessary (whether due to the features of the premises, the activity carried on there, any hazard present or any other relevant circumstances)

in order to safeguard the safety of relevant persons, the responsible person must ensure that–

(a) the premises are, to the extent that it is appropriate, equipped with appropriate fire-fighting equipment and with fire detectors and alarms; and

(b) any non-automatic fire-fighting equipment so provided is easily accessible, simple to use and indicated by signs.

(2) For the purposes of paragraph (1) what is appropriate is to be determined having regard to the dimensions and use of the premises, the equipment contained on the premises, the physical and chemical properties of the substances likely to be present and the maximum number of persons who may be present at any one time.

(3) The responsible person must, where necessary–

(a) take measures for fire-fighting in the premises, adapted to the nature of the activities carried on there and the size of the undertaking and of the premises concerned;

(b) nominate competent persons to implement those measures and ensure that the number of such persons, their training and the equipment available to them are adequate, taking into account the size of, and the specific hazards involved in, the premises concerned; and

(c) arrange any necessary contacts with external emergency services, particularly as regards fire-fighting, rescue work, first-aid and emergency medical care.

(4) A person is to be regarded as competent for the purposes of paragraph (3)(b) where he has sufficient training and experience or knowledge and other qualities to enable him properly to implement the measures referred to in that paragraph.

14 Emergency routes and exits

(1) Where necessary in order to safeguard the safety of relevant persons, the responsible person must ensure that routes to emergency exits from premises and the exits themselves are kept clear at all times.

(2) The following requirements must be complied with in respect of premises where necessary (whether due to the features of the premises, the activity carried on there, any hazard present or any other relevant circumstances) in order to safeguard the safety of relevant persons–

(a) emergency routes and exits must lead as directly as possible to a place of safety;

(b) in the event of danger, it must be possible for persons to evacuate the premises as quickly and as safely as possible;

(c) the number, distribution and dimensions of emergency routes and exits must be adequate having regard to the use, equipment and dimensions of the premises and the maximum number of persons who may be present there at any one time;

(d) emergency doors must open in the direction of escape;

(e) sliding or revolving doors must not be used for exits specifically intended as emergency exits;

(f) emergency doors must not be so locked or fastened that they cannot be easily and immediately opened by any person who may require to use them in an emergency;

(g) emergency routes and exits must be indicated by signs; and

(h) emergency routes and exits requiring illumination must be provided with emergency lighting of adequate intensity in the case of failure of their normal lighting.

15 Procedures for serious and imminent danger and for danger areas

(1) The responsible person must–

(a) establish and, where necessary, give effect to appropriate procedures, including safety drills, to be followed in the event of serious and imminent danger to relevant persons;

(b) nominate a sufficient number of competent persons to implement those procedures in so far as they relate to the evacuation of relevant persons from the premises; and

(c) ensure that no relevant person has access to any area to which it is necessary to restrict access on grounds of safety, unless the person concerned has received adequate safety instruction.

(2) Without prejudice to the generality of paragraph (1)(a), the procedures referred to in that sub-paragraph must–

(a) so far as is practicable, require any relevant persons who are exposed to serious and imminent danger to be informed of the nature of the hazard and of the steps taken or to be taken to protect them from it;

(b) enable the persons concerned (if necessary by taking appropriate steps in the absence of guidance or instruction and in the light of their knowledge and the technical means at their disposal) to stop work and immediately proceed to a place of safety in the event of their being exposed to serious, imminent and unavoidable danger; and

(c) save in exceptional cases for reasons duly substantiated (which cases and reasons must be specified in those procedures), require the persons concerned to be prevented from resuming work in any situation where there is still a serious and imminent danger.

(3) A person is to be regarded as competent for the purposes of paragraph (1) where he has sufficient training and experience or knowledge and other qualities to enable him properly to implement the evacuation procedures referred to in that paragraph.

...

17 Maintenance

(1) Where necessary in order to safeguard the safety of relevant persons the responsible person must ensure that the premises and any facilities, equipment and devices provided in respect of the premises under this Order or, subject to paragraph (6), under any other enactment, including any enactment repealed or revoked by this Order, are subject to a suitable system of maintenance and are maintained in an efficient state, in efficient working order and in good repair.

(2) Where the premises form part of a building, the responsible person may make arrangements with the occupier of any other premises forming part of the building for the purpose of ensuring that the requirements of paragraph (1) are met.

(3) Paragraph (2) applies even if the other premises are not premises to which this Order applies.

(4) The occupier of the other premises must co-operate with the responsible person for the purposes of paragraph (2).

(5) Where the occupier of the other premises is not also the owner of those premises, the references to the occupier in paragraphs (2) and (4) are to be taken to be references to both the occupier and the owner.

(6) Paragraph (1) only applies to facilities, equipment and devices provided under other enactments where they are provided in connection with general fire precautions.

Part 4: Offences and Appeals

32 Offences

(1) It is an offence for any responsible person or any other person mentioned in article 5(3) to—

   (a) fail to comply with any requirement or prohibition imposed by articles 8 to 22 and 38 (fire safety duties) where that failure places one or more relevant persons at risk of death or serious injury in case of fire;

   (b) fail to comply with any requirement or prohibition imposed by regulations made, or having effect as if made, under article 24 where that failure places one or more relevant persons at risk of death or serious injury in case of fire;

   (c) fail to comply with any requirement imposed by article 29(3) or (4) (alterations notices);

   (d) fail to comply with any requirement imposed by an enforcement notice;

   (e) fail, without reasonable excuse, in relation to apparatus to which article 37 applies (luminous tube signs)—

      (i) to ensure that such apparatus which is installed in premises complies with article 37(3) and (4);

      (ii) to give a notice required by article 37(6) or (8), unless he establishes that some other person duly gave the notice in question;

      (iii) to comply with a notice served under article 37(9).

(2) It is an offence for any person to—

   (a) fail to comply with article 23 (general duties of employees at work) where that failure places one or more relevant persons at risk of death or serious injury in case of fire;

   (b) make in any register, book, notice or other document required to be kept, served or given by or under, this Order, an entry which he knows to be false in a material particular;

   (c) give any information which he knows to be false in a material particular or recklessly give any information which is so false, in purported compliance with any obligation to give information to which he is subject under or by virtue of this Order, or in response to any inquiry made by virtue of article 27(1)(b);

   (d) obstruct, intentionally, an inspector in the exercise or performance of his powers or duties under this Order;

   (e) fail, without reasonable excuse, to comply with any requirements imposed by an inspector under article 27(1)(c) or (d);

(f) pretend, with intent to deceive, to be an inspector;

(g) fail to comply with the prohibition imposed by article 40 (duty not to charge employees);

(h) fail to comply with any prohibition or restriction imposed by a prohibition notice.

(3) Any person guilty of an offence under paragraph (1)(a) to (d) and (2)(h) is liable–

(a) on summary conviction to a fine not exceeding the statutory maximum; or

(b) on conviction on indictment, to a fine, or to imprisonment for a term not exceeding two years, or to both.

(4) Any person guilty of an offence under paragraph (1)(e)(i) to (iii) is liable on summary conviction to a fine not exceeding level 3 on the standard scale.

(5) Any person guilty of an offence under paragraph (2)(a) is liable–

(a) on summary conviction to a fine not exceeding the statutory maximum; or

(b) on conviction on indictment, to a fine.

(6) Any person guilty of an offence under paragraph (2)(b), (c), (d) or (g) is liable on summary conviction to a fine not exceeding level 5 on the standard scale.

(7) Any person guilty of an offence under paragraph (2)(e) or (f) is liable on summary conviction to a fine not exceeding level 3 on the standard scale.

(8) Where an offence under this Order committed by a body corporate is proved to have been committed with the consent or connivance of, or to be attributable to any neglect on the part of, any director, manager, secretary or other similar officer of the body corporate, or any person purporting to act in any such capacity, he as well as the body corporate is guilty of that offence, and is liable to be proceeded against and punished accordingly.

(9) Where the affairs of a body corporate are managed by its members, paragraph (8) applies in relation to the acts and defaults of a member in connection with his functions of management as if he were a director of the body corporate.

(10) Where the commission by any person of an offence under this Order, is due to the act or default of some other person, that other person is guilty of the offence, and a person may be charged with and convicted of the offence by virtue of this paragraph whether or not proceedings are taken against the first-mentioned person.

(11) Nothing in this Order operates so as to afford an employer a defence in any criminal proceedings for a contravention of those provisions by reason of any act or default of–

(a) an employee of his; or

(b) a person nominated under articles 13(3)(b) or 15(1)(b) or appointed under 18(1).

33 Defence

Subject to article 32(11), in any proceedings for an offence under this Order, except for a failure to comply with articles 8(1)(a) or 12, it is a defence for the person charged to prove that he took all reasonable precautions and exercised all due diligence to avoid the commission of such an offence.

34 Onus of proving limits of what is practicable or reasonably practicable

In any proceedings for an offence under this Order consisting of a failure to comply with a duty or requirement so far as is practicable or so far as is reasonably practicable, it is for the accused to prove that it was not practicable or reasonably practicable to do more than was in fact done to satisfy the duty or requirement.

35 Appeals

(1) A person on whom an alterations notice, an enforcement notice, a prohibition notice or a notice given by the fire and rescue authority under article 37 (fire-fighters' switches for luminous tube signs) is served may, within 21 days from the day on which the notice is served, appeal to the court.

(2) On an appeal under this article the court may either cancel or affirm the notice, and if it affirms it,

GAS SAFETY (INSTALLATION AND USE) REGULATIONS 1998 SI NO 2451 reg 36

36 Duties of Landlords

(1) In this regulation–

'landlord' means–

    (a) in England and Wales–

        (i) where the relevant premises are occupied under a lease, the person for the time being entitled to the reversion expectant on that lease or who, apart from any statutory tenancy, would be entitled to possession of the premises; and

        (ii) where the relevant premises are occupied under a licence, the licensor, save that where the licensor is himself a tenant in respect of those premises, it means the person referred to in paragraph (i) above;

    (b) in Scotland, the person for the time being entitled to the landlord's interest under a lease;

'lease' means–

    (a) a lease for a term of less than 7 years; and

    (b) a tenancy for a periodic term; and

    (c) any statutory tenancy arising out of a lease or tenancy referred to in sub-paragraphs (a) or (b) above,

and in determining whether a lease is one which falls within sub-paragraph (a) above–

    (i)   in England and Wales, any part of the term which falls before the grant shall be left out of account and the lease shall be treated as a lease for a term commencing with the grant;

    (ii) a lease which is determinable at the option of the lessor before the expiration of 7 years from the commencement of the term shall be treated as a lease for a term of less than 7 years;

    (iii) a lease (other than a lease to which sub-paragraph (b) above applies) shall not be treated as a lease for a term of less than 7 years if it confers on the lessee an option for renewal for a term which, together with the original term, amounts to 7 years or more; and

    (iv) a 'lease' does not include a mortgage term;

'relevant gas fitting' means–

    (a) any gas appliance (other than an appliance which the tenant is entitled to remove from the relevant premises) or any installation pipework installed in any relevant premises; and

    (b) any gas appliance or installation pipework which, directly or indirectly, serves the relevant premises and which either–

        (i) is installed in any part of premises in which the landlord has an estate or interest; or

        (ii) is owned by the landlord or is under his control,

except that it shall not include any gas appliance or installation pipework exclusively used in a part of premises occupied for non-residential purposes;

'relevant premises' means premises or any part of premises occupied, whether exclusively or not, for residential purposes (such occupation being in consideration of money or money's worth) under–

(a) a lease; or

(b) a licence;

'statutory tenancy' means–

(a) in England and Wales, a statutory tenancy within the meaning of the Rent Act 1977 and the Rent (Agriculture) Act 1976; and

(b) in Scotland, a statutory tenancy within the meaning of the Rent (Scotland) Act 1984, a statutory assured tenancy within the meaning of the Housing (Scotland) Act 1988 or a secure tenancy within the meaning of the Housing (Scotland) Act 1987;

'tenant' means a person who occupies relevant premises being–

(a) in England and Wales–

(i) where the relevant premises are so occupied under a lease, the person for the time being entitled to the term of that lease; and

(ii) where the relevant premises are so occupied under a licence, the licensee;

(b) in Scotland, the person for the time being entitled to the tenant's interest under a lease.

(2) Every landlord shall ensure that there is maintained in a safe condition–

(a) any relevant gas fitting; and

(b) any flue which serves any relevant gas fitting,

so as to prevent the risk of injury to any person in lawful occupation or relevant premises.

(3) Without prejudice to the generality of paragraph (2) above, a landlord shall–

(a) ensure that each appliance and flue to which that duty extends is checked for safety within 12 months of being installed and at intervals of not more than 12 months since it was last checked for safety (whether such check was made pursuant to these Regulations or not);

(b) in the case of a lease commencing after the coming into force of these Regulations, ensure that each appliance and flue to which the duty extends has been checked for safety within a period of 12 months before the lease commences or has been or is so checked within 12 months after the appliance or flue has been installed, whichever is later; and

(c) ensure that a record in respect of any appliance or flue so checked is made and retained for a period of 2 years from the date of that check, which record shall include the following information–

(i)   the date on which the appliance or flue was checked;

(ii)   the address of the premises at which the appliance or flue is installed;

(iii) the name and address of the landlord of the premises (or, where appropriate, his agent) at which the appliance or flue is installed;

(iv) a description of and the location of each appliance or flue checked;

(v)   any defect identified;

(vi) any remedial action taken;

(vii) confirmation that the check undertaken complies with the requirements of paragraph (9) below;

(viii) the name and signature of the individual carrying out the check; and

(ix) the registration number with which that individual, or his employer, is registered with a body approved by the Executive for the purposes of regulation 3(3) of these Regulations.

(4) Every landlord shall ensure that any work in relation to a relevant gas fitting or any check of a gas appliance or flue carried out pursuant to paragraphs (2) or (3) above is carried out by, or by an employee of, a member of a class of persons approved for the time being by the Health and Safety Executive for the purposes of regulation 3(3) of these Regulations.

(5) The record referred to in paragraph (3)(c) above, or a copy thereof, shall be made available upon request and upon reasonable notice for the inspection of any person in lawful occupation of relevant premises who may be affected by the use or operation of any appliance to which the record relates.

(6) Notwithstanding paragraph (5) above, every landlord shall ensure that–

(a) a copy of the record made pursuant to the requirements of paragraph (3)(c) above is given to each existing tenant of premises to which the record relates within 28 days of the date of the check; and

(b) a copy of the last record made in respect of each appliance or flue is given to any new tenant of premises to which the record relates before that tenant occupies those premises save that, in respect of a tenant whose right to occupy those premises is for a period not exceeding 28 days, a copy of the record may instead be prominently displayed within those premises.

(7) Where there is no relevant gas appliance in any room occupied or to be occupied by the tenant in relevant premises, the landlord may, instead of ensuring that a copy of the record referred to in paragraph (6) above is given to the tenant, ensure that there is displayed in a prominent position in the premises (from such time as a copy would have been required to have been given to the tenant under that paragraph), a copy of the record with a statement endorsed on it that the tenant is entitled to have his own copy of the record on request to the landlord at an address specified in the statement; and on any such request being made, the landlord shall give to the tenant a copy of the record as soon as is practicable.

(8) A copy of the record given to a tenant pursuant to paragraph (6)(b) above need not contain a copy of the signature of the individual carrying out the check if the copy of the record contains a statement that another copy containing a copy of such signature is available for inspection by the tenant on request to the landlord at an address specified in the statement, and on any such request being made the landlord shall make such a copy available for inspection as soon as is practicable.

(9) A safety check carried out pursuant to paragraph (3) above shall include, but shall not be limited to, an examination of the matters referred to in sub-paragraphs (a) to (d) of regulation 26(9) of these Regulations.

(10) Nothing done or agreed to be done by a tenant of relevant premises or by any other person in lawful occupation of them in relation to the maintenance or checking of a relevant gas fitting or flue in the premises (other than one in part of premises occupied for non-residential purposes) shall be taken into account in determining whether a landlord has discharged his obligations under this regulation (except in so far as it relates to access to that gas fitting or flue for the purposes of such maintenance or checking).

(11) Every landlord shall ensure that in any room occupied or to be occupied as sleeping accommodation by a tenant in relevant premises there is not fitted a

relevant gas fitting of a type the installation of which would contravene regulation 30(2) or (3) of these Regulations.

(12) Paragraph (11) above shall not apply in relation to a room which since before the coming into force of these Regulations has been occupied or intended to be occupied as sleeping accommodation.

NOTICES TO QUIT ETC (PRESCRIBED INFORMATION) REGULATIONS 1988 SI NO 2201

1 These Regulations may be cited as the Notices to Quit etc (Prescribed Information) Regulations 1988 and shall come into force on 15th January 1989.

2 Where, on or after the date these Regulations come into force, a landlord gives a notice to quit any premises let as a dwelling, or a licensor gives a notice to determine a periodic licence to occupy premises as a dwelling (and the premises are not let or occupied as specified in section 5(1B) of the Protection from Eviction Act 1977), the information prescribed for the purposes of section 5 of the Protection from Eviction Act 1977 shall be that in the Schedule to these Regulations.

3 ...

SCHEDULE

PRESCRIBED INFORMATION

Regulation 2

1 If the tenant or licensee does not leave the dwelling, the landlord or licensor must get an order for possession from the court before the tenant or licensee can lawfully be evicted. The landlord or licensor cannot apply for such an order before the notice to quit or notice to determine has run out.

2 A tenant or licensee who does not know if he has any right to remain in possession after a notice to quit or a notice to determine runs out can obtain advice from a solicitor. Help with all or part of the cost of legal advice and assistance may be available under the Legal Aid Scheme. He should also be able to obtain information from a Citizens' Advice Bureau, a Housing Aid Centre or a rent officer.

Index